On the Constitutionality of Compiling a Civil Code of China

Zhu Wang

On the Constitutionality of Compiling a Civil Code of China

A Process Map for Legislation Born out of Pragmatism

中国政法大学出版社

 Springer

Zhu Wang
Law School
Sichuan University
Chengdu, China

Sponsored by Chinese Fund for the Humanities and Social Sciences (本书获中华社会科学基金资助)

ISBN 978-981-13-7902-4   ISBN 978-981-13-7900-0   (eBook)
https://doi.org/10.1007/978-981-13-7900-0

Jointly published with China University of Political Science and Law Press
The print edition is not for sale in China Mainland. Customers from China Mainland please order the print book from: China University of Political Science and Law Press.

This Springer imprint is published by the registered company Springer Nature Singapore Pte Ltd.
The registered company address is: 152 Beach Road, #21-01/04 Gateway East, Singapore 189721, Singapore

*Dedicated to my dear Jie, thoughtful
Minghan and smart Mingrui*

Foreword by Prof. LIANG Huixing

Born in 1980s, Dr. WANG Zhu is one of the top young scholars in China's civil law community. His publications frequently updated on the Web site of Law Information Research Center of China Law Society are the best evidence for his diligence and devotion to academic research. Every time I visited Law School of Sichuan University, Zhu would share with me his latest findings and the subjects he was studying. Discussing with him the academic and social issues of common concern, I was always touched by the vigor and historical responsibility displayed by him as a young generation of scholars.

The focus of his study is tort law, but it is just a part of his interest. He has a unique insight into the legislation of the Civil Code. He is well informed of countless domestic works on civil law study before the promulgation of The General Principles of the Civil Law and the translated works of the former Soviet Union and countries of East Europe that pursued public ownership system and has had many interviews with scholars of older generations on civil law study. Instead of choosing a law of a foreign country as the criteria for judgment, he intends to place the issues in question in a particular historic background. For example, his paper on the issue of apology, collected into the Civil and Commercial Law Review edited by me, starts from the Movement of Socialist Patriotic Convention in 1957, and moves all the way to all the drafts of the Criminal Law, the Civil Code, the General Principles of the Civil Law since then. It is based on such historic investigation and the current legal and practical background that he has produced his own particular understanding of this issue. His "Pragmatic Method" to compile the Civil Code also represents a kind of legislative model that merits the attention of the civil law community. "The Process Map for Compiling a Civil Code" attached to this book directly shows his legislative design. It is worth mentioning that he has successfully answered "how many existing valid laws are there in China?", the question that has been neglected for a long time but is of vital importance to the compilation of the Civil Code. His design to compile a Cross-Strait-Quad-Regions Model Civil Law and the plan to "Investigate Civil Customs Reflected in Judgment Documents" are both worth highly concerned by the academic community.

This book is an evidence for the rapid improvement of academic performance and even broader vision of research by the new generation of civil law scholars. I am convinced that with the joint efforts of generations of civil law scholars, the dream that has been obsessing the Chinese academic community for a century of making a civil code of our own will finally come true.

Beijing, China   Prof. LIANG Huixing
June 2015   Academician of Chinese Academy
                                                                   of Social Sciences

Foreword by Prof. HAN Dayuan

Professor WANG Zhu is a scholar of civil law born in the 1980s. In recent years, he has been showing a particular interest in the relationship between constitutional law and civil law, and especially the constitutional concerns that may occur in the process of compiling the Civil Code. He is good at detect constitutional issues from the legal practices of civil law and civil law issues from the constitutional practices. In the Chinese academic community which pursues a way that treats the constitutional law and civil law values separately, it is really rare for a civil law scholar to study constitutional issues and voice an "offbeat" idea based on objective stance. He represents a younger generation of scholars who are empowered with dreams and a sense of responsibility for academic pursuit, and at the same time, persist their interest in interdisciplinary academic topics. On the Constitutionality of Compiling a Civil Code of China is not only a record of his academic thought on the relationship between constitutional law and civil law, but also an important achievement that merits the attention of the academic community.

Historically, the relationship between the constitutional law and civil law has gone through three stages, namely "estrangement," "superior-subordinate," and "splitting-up."

From the end of the Qing Dynasty to the year 1949, the constitutional law and civil law were estranged from each other, and there was no research that studied the relationship between the two. During the process of modernization at that time, the Chinese legal system was severely influenced by the Roman Law that focused on the dichotomy between the public law and the private law, leaving the relationship between the constitutional law and civil law untouched by the academia. For example, Professor SHI Shangkuan during the reign of the Republic of China did not mention the Constitution when exploring the origin of civil law in his General Principles of Civil Law. In return, the work study on the constitutional law did not say anything about the relationship between the two.

From 1949 to 1980s, the relationship between constitutional law and civil law became superior-subordinate. During this period, the differentiation between public law and private law was practically denied. It had become a universal acceptance of the academia that the Constitution was the "mother law," or superior law, and the civil laws, the "son law," or subordinate law, and there was no strict borderline between the public and private laws.

Since 1990s, the constitutional law and civil law have been splitting up with each other. With the development of market economy, the academia has put a new emphasis on the protection of private rights, and therefore, the separation between the public and private laws has been put back on the table. After affirming the value of private rights, the civil law community began to seek the autonomous position of civil law and try to detach it from the Constitution. Their idea is that it would be better for civil law to keep a certain distance from the Constitution. Since 1990s, many theoretical propositions have been produced, represented by "superiority of private laws," "apposition of civil laws and the Constitution," "the building of civil society," etc. Although these theories have provided useful ideas or methods for the study of relationship between the Constitution and civil laws, from the perspective of constitutional law, they are still questionable in terms of their fundamental propositions. It cannot be denied that since civil law and constitutional law fall into different disciplines, they have a different scope of studies and social functions. In this sense, efforts should be made to implant the idea of constitution into the system of civil law, so as to make a constitution-friendly civil law that reflects the value of the Constitution. In 2005, the concern about unconstitutionality of Property Right Law (Draft) pushed the discussion on the relationship between the Constitution and civil law to a new high. Many scholars of both constitution and civil law proposed their own ideas on this issue, many of which have become new subjects for further studies.

As a scholar of civil law, Zhu has demonstrated his constitutional vision in choosing and arguing academic propositions. He attaches special importance to the constitutional way of thinking, constitutional ideas, and constitutional culture in the overall system of civil law. There are four parts in this book, each of which discusses different relationships between the Constitution and civil law, in particular, whether the compilation of civil code will breach the legal procedure provided by the Constitution. The book reflects Zhu's pursuit that in this time of disciplinary crossover and transformation, the adherence to basic principles of civil law and pursuit of constitutionalism will help to review, in terms of facts and value, the issues of civil law in the system of constitutional law, distinguish the different functions of the two in terms of norms, and give a priority to the Constitution in the system of values. Generally, the Constitution and other laws are different functionally, leading to the different logics of constitutional and other legal issues. The dominance of the Constitution over other laws is obvious when it comes to the ground of legislation and the process of implementation of these laws. In other words, all the laws, regulations, and regulatory documents shall not be in conflict with the Constitution. To seek the constitutional ground for legislating civil law, based on actual practices, Zhu gives reasonable explanations to the issues concerned. His attempt is to find a hermeneutical basis for civil law from the Constitution.

Hermeneutically, Zhu has introduced the concept of constitutionality in explaining the legislative process of civil code. He tries to analyze the legislation of civil law on the basis of constitutionality and the relationship between the value of civil law and that of the Constitution, which means we need to jump out of the civil law to discuss the constitutional basis for the legislation. In order to safeguard the constitutional value, he has staged the civil law in the macrovision of the legislature, with the purpose to promote the compilation of civil code in a more pragmatic manner. Such an innovative way of thinking and arguments will expand, to some extent, the traditional methodological system of civil law study. His contributions are as follows: first, as a kind of norm and ideological system, the interpretation and application of the concept of constitutionality will exert an important influence on the practice of civil law, act as a constitutionally guiding principle and provide reasonable methodology for the hermeneutics of civil law. Second, the actual application of the concept of constitutionality in the practice of civil law will help to further explore and interpret the rich resources of civil law. Third, introducing constitutional value into the practice of civil law will deepen people's understanding of the modern system of civil law and help to solve the newly emerging civil issues in the risk society.

Proceeding from the academic propositions, Zhu has actively answered the newly emerging issues in practice. While keeping his theoretical stance, he has produced many unique insights into these controversial issues. In discussing whether the clauses concerning private property prescribed in Property Right Law breaches the Constitution, Zhu's academic judgment is objective and rational. He is of the opinion that although to judge whether a law conforms to the Constitution depends on its legislative process, it is actually reflected in the process of its implementation. To judge whether a law "has a constitutional ground" is to see if its concepts, basic principles and specific contents conform to the norms, principles, and spirit of the Constitution. It means that the law has to be in agreement with the Constitution not only in substance but also in form. In practice, it is really necessary to distinguish substantial constitutionality from formal constitutionality. If the substantial constitutionality is the judgment criterion, people have to consider not only the interior meaning of structural significance of the Constitution but also its exterior value. This criterion means that people can only take the norms regulated by the Constitution as the standard to judgment, and they cannot arbitrarily expand the extension of that criterion. It is important that the civil code should have an overall constitutional ground. Although there exist some other non-constitutional judgment criteria, in order to guarantee the objectivity and actuality of the constitutional ground, the judgment of civil code should still be confined to the connotation regulated by the norms of the Constitution.

In terms of research methods, Zhu sets the relationship between the Constitution and civil law in the background of a specific social life. A systematic domain formed under such a comprehensive vision and framework helps to boost the persuasiveness of the argument and add the depth and breadth of the theories. In particular, the "The Process Map for Compiling a Civil Code" designed by him will have a positive influence on the future preparatory work of civil code.

In sum, by giving a highlight to sensitivity to academic issues and practical rationality, oriented by problems and concerns, this book is a good academic work of innovation and creativity. Its glow cannot be overshadowed by some minor failures, such as the problems of structures and validity of basic laws, the influence of value of constitutionality and legitimacy on civil law legislation, and the inner relationship between constitutional law and civil law interpretations, all of which needs further study and investigation. In addition, it would be more appropriate if Zhu, when studying constitutional ground of civil law, probed further into propositions such as how to maintain the expertise of research methodology and the comparative independence of knowledge system.

The publication of this book is of important significance in classifying the relationship between civil code compilation and constitutional value and between the constitutional law and civil law. I hope Zhu will continue his efforts in exploring the constitutional elements of civil law, expanding the scope of study of civil law, and making further contribution to the prosperity of civil law studies.

Beijing, China   Prof. HAN Dayuan
June 2015   Dean of Law School of Renmin
                                                   University of China, Chairman
                                                  of Chinese Research Association
                                                       of Constitutional Law

Contents

Part I
Political Analysis on the Compilation of *Civil Code*

Legislation is ultimately an issue relating to political choices rather than academic disputes. Setting aside the jurists' own academic pursuit and academic honor, the compilation of *Civil Code* is really an issue about opportunity, which to a great extent depends on political enlightened and constitutional progress. The compilation of *Civil Code* requires not only the national consensus on the rule of law, but also the firm determination of politicians. The consideration on the constitutionality of the compilation of *Civil Code* must start with political analysis.

Chapter 1 Necessity of Substantially Compiling the *Civil Code* as Soon as Possible.

Chapter 2 Awareness of Constitutionality in the Compilation of *Civil Code*.

Chapter 3 Pragmatic Thinking for the Compilation of *Civil Code*.

Chapter 1
Necessity of Substantially Compiling the *Civil Code* as Soon as Possible

1.1 Importance of the Decision to Compile the *Civil Code* in *Decision to Rule by Law* Should Be Evaluated Objectively

On October 23, 2014, *Decision of the Central Committee of the Communist Party of China on Some Major Issues Concerning Comprehensively Promoting the Efforts to Rule by Law* (hereinafter referred to as *Decision to Rule by Law*) was adopted by the 4th Plenary Session of the 18th Central Committee of Communist Party of China. This decision is composed of seven parts, namely "First, adhere to the path of socialist rule of law with Chinese characteristics, and build the socialist system of rule of law with Chinese characteristics"; "Second, perfect the socialist legal system with Chinese characteristics which takes the *Constitution* as core, and strengthen the implementation of the *Constitution*"; "Third, further promote the level of administration by law, and accelerate the construction of law-based government"; "Fourth, ensure the fair justice, and improve the judicial credibility"; "Fifth, enhance the national concept of rule of law, and keep pushing forward the construction of law-based society"; "Sixth, strengthen the team building for the construction of rule of law" and "Seventh, strengthen and improve the CPC's Leadership on Promotion of Rule by Law".

Under the title "Second, perfect the socialist legal system with Chinese characteristics which takes *Constitution* as core, and strengthen the implementation of *Constitution*", there are four subtitles, namely "(1) Perfect the constitutional implementation and supervision system", "(2) Improve the legislative system", "(3) Further promote the level of scientific legislation and democratic legislation" and "(4) Strengthen the legislation in key fields". Under the subtitle (4) "Strengthen the legislation in key fields", there are eight paragraphs. The first paragraph is the decision for legal protection for civil rights, the second paragraph is the decision for legal protection for socialist market economy, the third paragraph is the decision for legal protection for socialist democratic politics, the fourth paragraph is the decision

© China University of Political Science and Law Press 2020

Z. Wang, *On the Constitutionality of Compiling a Civil Code of China*,
https://doi.org/10.1007/978-981-13-7900-0_1

for legal protection for socialist advanced culture, the fifth paragraph is the decision for legal protection for livelihood and social governance, the sixth paragraph is the decision for legal protection for national security, the seventh paragraph is the decision for legal protection for ecosystem, and the eighth paragraph is the decision for the link of legislation and reform decision.

The second paragraph "decision for legal protection for socialist market economy" is divided into three parts. The first part serves as guiding principle: "In order to enable the market to play the decisive role in resource allocation and bring the role of government into full play, it is necessary to take protection for property rights, protection for contracts, uniform market, equal exchange, fair competition and effective regulation as basic orientation, and improve the legal systems for socialist market economy." Subsequently, the contents are divided into two aspects, namely perfecting the protection system for property rights and strengthening the construction of legal system for market economy. Perfecting the protection system for property rights involves: First, "perfect the protection system for property rights which takes fairness as core principle, strengthen the protection for property rights of economic organizations in various ownership systems and natural persons, and delete the unfair provisions in laws and regulations." Second, "innovate the protection system for property rights which is beneficial to various forms for realization of public ownership system, and strengthen the protection for the state and collective ownership right and management right as well as the property rights of various legal persons." Third, "The State protects the property rights of legal persons in order to carry out the self-management and self-financing, and an enterprise is entitled to refuse any illegal claim by any organization or individual." Fourth, "strengthen the legislation relating to social responsibilities of enterprises." Fifth, "perfect the innovation-driven property rights system, intellectual property rights system and the institutional mechanisms for promoting the conversion of scientific and technical achievements."

The specific decisions for strengthening the construction of legal system for market economy: first, "to compile the *Civil Code*"[1]; second, "to formulate and perfect the laws and regulations relating to development planning, investment management, land management, energy and mineral resources, agriculture, fiscal revenue and tax and finance, and promote the free movement, fair dealing and equal use of commodities and market elements"; third, "to legally strengthen and improve the macro-economic control and market regulation, oppose monopoly, promote the reasonable competition, and maintain the fair competition market order"; fourth, "to strengthen the protection for civil-military integration."

By patiently stating the structure of the *Decision to Rule by Law* and the relative position of the decision "to compile the *Civil Code*", the Writer wants to remind the civil law community to objectively evaluate the importance of the decision "to

---

[1] In the *Decision to Rule by Law*, after "to compile the *Civil Code*", comma but not period exists. However, in terms of expressed content, it may be distinguished from the contents of the same sentence thereafter. This is also evidences of the orientation of content of such decision from another angle.

compile the *Civil Code*" in the *Decision to Rule by Law*, and take such evaluation as the starting point for political choice for the compilation of *Civil Code*. The Writer believes that, under the *Decision to Rule by Law*, the decision "to compile the *Civil Code*" should be evaluated as follows, and such evaluation should be taken as the starting point for discussion on specific legislative route for such decision:

First, the *Decision to Rule by Law* clearly puts the compilation of *Civil Code* onto the legislative agenda. After Mr. WU Bangguo, former National People's Congress (hereinafter referred to as "NPC") Chairman, announced in 2011 that "the socialist legal system with Chinese characteristics has officially formed."[2] It confirms the Central Committee's efforts to perfect the socialist civil law system with Chinese characteristics, and point out the direction and road for civil legislative works in future in China.[3]

Second, as the first decision for "strengthening the construction of legal system for market economy", the decision "to compile the *Civil Code*" is subject to the part of "(4) Strengthen the legislation in key fields", indicating the relative importance of the decision "to compile the *Civil Code*".

Third, the future *Civil Code* should contain the contents relating to personal rights and property rights. However, the contents relating to personal rights are given in the part "protection for civil rights" located in the front, while the main contents of the property rights are included into "perfect the protection system for property rights", which is obviously inconsistent with the position of the decision "compile the *Civil Code*" in "strengthening the construction of legal system for market economy". This indicates that the decision "to compile the *Civil Code*" is not taken as an important system element of "(4) Strengthen the legislation in key fields", but regarded as a component of "legal protection for socialist market economy", which is different from the functional orientation of *Civil Code* by civil law scholars.

Fourth, as a part of "Second, perfect the socialist legal system with Chinese characteristics which takes the *Constitution* as core, and strengthen the implementation of *Constitution*", the decision "to compile the *Civil Code*" should pay more attention to the constitutionality of the compilation of *Civil Code*.

The 31st Meeting of the Standing Committee of the 9th NPC deliberated the *Civil Law of the People's Republic of China (draft)* (hereinafter referred to as *2002 Civil Law (draft)*) on December 23, 2002, and now 15 years have passed. It is really encouraging that the compilation of *Civil Code* is initiated by the decision "to compile the *Civil Code*", but the Writer is *cautiously optimistic towards* whether the legislature can "democratically" and "scientifically" complete the compilation of *Civil Code* within a relatively short period of time, namely the tenure of the 13th NPC. The Writer believes that, the next important work of civil law community is to urge the legislatures to convert this political choice of the Central Committee of CPC into the legislative activity for substantial compilation of *Civil Code* as soon as

---

[2]Wu (2011).
[3]Wang (2014).

possible through the legislative procedure which complies with the framework of the current the *Constitution* and the *Legislation Law*, so as to promote the legalization of the socialist market economy.

1.2 Substantial Codification Should Be Stuck To

1.2.1 Assembly of Civil Laws Is Different from the Compilation of Civil Code

2002 Civil Law (draft) was actually an assembled one.[4] The Writer is of the view that since assembly itself does not involve legislative techniques or legal experts, it actually does not substantially promote the development of law. Besides, the database for electronic legal documents has also further decreased the value of assembled legal documents. Moreover, differences between upper level and lower level laws, general and special norms, or the basic and general principles are not highlighted in the assembly, which will inevitably lead to a negative influence of de-systematicity.[5] The current civil law in China is a coexistence of numerous single laws and regulations governing civil affairs, which should be provided in the *Civil Code*. Therefore, it is urgent to systemize the civil laws. It should be pointed out that since, hierarchically, a complete *Civil Code* will help to lift the rank of single laws to basic laws, and to uniform the basic civil system, and to regulate the civil norms established in special laws.

1.2.2 Basic Civil Law as a Framework Under Which Basic Norms for Civil Affairs in Special Laws Can Be Regulated

Paragraph 3 of Article 62 of the *Constitution* states: "The National People's Congress exercises the following functions and powers: … (3) to enact and amend basic laws governing criminal offences, civil affairs, the state organs and other matters;…" Paragraph 2 of Article 7 of the *Legislation Law* states: "NPC enacts and amends basic laws governing criminal, civil, state organs and other affairs." Although the *Constitution* does not clarify the relationship between basic laws and non-basic laws, considering the solemnity of the legislative procedures, basic laws

---

[4]Liang (2003).
[5]Wang (2008).

should enjoy a certain degree of privilege,[6] serving as a framework for the non-basic laws. This is because of their role in the legal system. As the core of a civil law legal system, the *Civil Code* is subordinate only to the *Constitution*, and therefore, in the absence of the law that stipulates otherwise,[7] basic norms for civil affairs regulated by special laws shall not contradict the provisions of basic civil laws.[8]

1.2.3 Only Way to Upgrade Civil Single Laws to Basic Civil Laws Is Through Substantial Codification

It cannot be denied that since the *Tort Liability Law* was enacted by the Standing Committee of NPC, instead of NPC itself, it has to be deemed as non-basic civil law. According to this logic, the laws, even though enacted by NPC itself, should also be considered as non-basic laws as per the *Constitution*.[9] The laws on par with the *Tort Liability Law* are the *Marriage Law*, the *Succession Law*, the *Contract Law* and the *Real Rights Law*.

Paragraph 1 of Article 94 of the *Legislation Law* states: "if there is a difference between a new general provision and an old special provision in respect of the same matter among two laws, and the applicable provision can not be decided, a ruling shall be made by the Standing Committee of NPC." In this sense, if a law cannot be ascertained as a "basic law," the Standing Committee of NPC will be in a dilemma in ruling, since the law concerned cannot be accurately positioned in the legal hierarchy. A substantially codified *Civil Code* will raise the rank of single laws, which make up the civil legal system, making them civil basic laws in the real sense. This will help the Standing Committee of NPC in making a ruling as to

---

[6]Constitution law scholars conclude such "privilege" means that (1) "non-basic laws" enacted by NPC cannot contradict "basic laws", and (2) laws enacted by the Standing Committee of NPC cannot contradict basic laws. See Han (2003).

[7]"The law that stipulates otherwise" refers to the fact that there is a law that establishes clearly that the application rule of a certain law is an "absolute special law", e.g. Article 2 of *Law on the Protection of Consumer Rights and Interests* states: "The rights and interests of consumers in purchasing and using commodities or receiving services for daily consumption shall be under the protection of the present law, or under the protection of other relevant laws and regulations in absence of stipulations in this law." Article 3 states: "Business operators shall, in their supply of commodities produced and sold by them or services to consumers, abide by the present law, or abide by other relevant laws and regulations in absence of stipulations in the present law." As to the difference between "comparative special law" and "absolute special law", see Wang (2012).

[8]Wang (2008).

[9]As to the analysis on the constitutionality and deduction, see Wang (2010). This issue will be further elaborated in the following context.

which provisions are applicable, effectively eliminating the interference of group interests, and coordination problems between various government departments in the deciding of civil issues.[10]

1.3 Three Major Problems Will Arise if the *Civil Code* Cannot Be Compiled in a Timely Manner

The academic community has produced the following reasons for the codification of *Civil Code* as the best way to rebuild the civil legal system of China: (1) systematization (including consistency in the form and value, and the self-sufficiency of logic); (2) comprehensiveness; (3) authority; (4) stability; (5) unity.[11] Besides these generally accepted reasons that show the necessity of the compilation of *Civil Code*, the Writer is also of the view that three major problems will arise if the *Civil Code* is not compiled in a timely manner.

1.3.1 *"Socialist Legal System with Chinese Characteristics" Is Not Living Up to Its Name*

The "socialist legal system with Chinese characteristics" can be defined as: "a legal system that is rooted in the actual conditions and realities of China, that serves the needs of reform—such as the drive towards opening-up and socialist modernization, that collectively reflects the will of the CPC and the Chinese people, and that features a multi-level configuration composed of laws, administrative regulations, and local regulations centered on laws concerning the *Constitution*, along with civil and commercial laws."[12] In this statement, the "civil and commercial laws" belong to one of the two major legal branches explicitly stated, second only to "laws concerning the *Constitution*." The academic community understands that the statement has affirmed that the civil and commercial law system that directly serves the socialist market economy has already been formed.[13]

To further understand the concept of socialist legal system with Chinese characteristics, we need to study horizontally from the perspective of comparative laws and vertically from the angle of history the degree to which a socialist civil law system has been formed. From the perspective of comparative laws, there are five countries that proclaim to pursue a socialist path: Cuba, North Korea, Vietnam, Laos and China. Among them, Cuba, North Korea, and Vietnam promulgated their

---

[10]Wang (2008).
[11]Wang (2008).
[12]Wu (2011).
[13]Sun (2013).

Civil Codes respectively in 1987, 1990 and 1995. Laos enacted the *Property Law*, the *Contract Law*, the *Family Law* and the *Non-Contractual Obligation Law* in 1990,[14] and started to compile the *Civil Code* in 2012 and expect to finish it in 2015.[15] Historically, the former socialist countries, such as former Czechoslovakia (1950),[16] former Yugoslavia (1955), Hungary (1959), Poland (1964), and former German Democratic Republic (1975)[17] all enacted their own *Civil Codes*.[18] Since the collapse of the Soviet Union, its fifteen union republics enacted their own *Civil Codes* from 1993 to 2004.[19] *Civil Code* of Mongolia was also enacted in 1995.[20]

China is the leader of the socialist camp in today's world. The socialist legal system is incomplete without the *Civil Code*. The *Civil Code* itself is a legal guarantee for the consolidation and development of the socialist market economy, and an important sign of the great rejuvenation of the Chinese nation. If the phrase "Chinese characteristics" does not refer to the lack of *Civil Code*, it can only be understood as a temporary systematic defect in the current legal system. In this sense, compiling the *Civil Code* is an important step in the timely completion and improvement of the socialist legal system with Chinese characteristics.

1.3.2   Dilemma of Long Delay—Endless Efforts to Compile the Civil Code in a Stable Political Environment

Since its foundation, the People's Republic of China ("PRC") has witnessed three attempts to the enactment of *Civil Code* (1955–1958, 1963–1964, and 1980–1985). All of which, though they yielded a complete draft *Civil Code*, were aborted because of political turmoil or economy policy adjustment. In 2002, the draft of *Civil Code* of PRC, which was deliberated by NPC, was the only draft version that entered the legislative procedure in history.[21] Article 42 of the *Legislation Law* states that "for a bill which has been put on the agenda of the session of the Standing Committee, if deliberation on the bill has been postponed for two years due to major differences among the concerned constituents on major issues such as the necessity or feasibility of enacting such bill, or voting was postponed and the

---

[14]The English translated text of every volume of Lao Civil Law is available at http://www.ilp.gov.la/Lao_Law_Eng.asp, the latest access time: August 31, 2017. See Wang (2017).

[15]First Civil Code in Laos Being Drafted, available at http://www.aseanaffairs.com/laos_news/politics/first_civil_code_in_laos_being_drafted, the latest access time: August 31, 2017.

[16]*Civil Code of Czechoslovak Socialist Republic*, trans. by Zheng Min, Law Press, 1956.

[17]*Civil Code of German Democratic Republic*, trans. by Fei Zongyi, Law Press, 1982.

[18]Xu (2000).

[19]See Wei (2008).

[20]*Civil Code of Mongolia*, trans. by Hai Tang & Wu Zhengping, China Legal Publishing House, 2002.

[21]Xu (2003).

bill has not been put on the agenda of the session of the Standing Committee for two years, the Chairman's Committee shall make a report to the Standing Committee, whereupon deliberation on the bill shall terminate." Now 15 years has passed, this is a rare case in China's legislative history.[22] It also represents the flaws of the *Legislation Law* in regulating the deliberation obligations of legislatures.

According to Kato Masanobu, a Japanese scholar, whenever the need to develop the economy becomes urgent, the compilation of *Civil Code* will come back onto the legislative agenda; otherwise, it will be neglected or even suffer setbacks.[23] Currently, since the macro-policy of China attaches great importance to economic growth and the improvement of people's living standards, and there has been no political event severe enough to terminate the deliberation of the draft of *Civil Code*, it is necessary to put the compilation of *Civil Code* back onto the political agenda. How long will this unsolved issue continue? Not only the countries and regions in the rest of the world,[24] but also Taiwan, Hong Kong, and Macao are waiting. As long as the draft of *Civil Code* stays on the waiting list of the deliberation agenda, it will become a never-ending political burden for China.

1.3.3 Failing to Exercise the Right to Enact the Basic Civil Laws as Provided by the Constitution Causes the Continuous Risk

Paragraph 1 of Article 15 of the *Constitution* states: "The state practices socialist market economy." In this sense, *General Principles of the Civil Law* enacted in 1986 accordingly can only be regarded as transitional basic civil law. In the 30 years that followed, before the enactment of the *General Provisions of Civil Law*, Paragraph 3 of Article 62 of the *Constitution*, which states that the effort "to enact and amend basic laws governing…civil affairs…" has been de facto given up. This has resulted in the absence of a basic civil system in the form of laws provided by the *Legislation Law* and further inconsistent application of civil laws. To solve this problem, the Supreme People's Court has no other choice but to promulgate numerous judicial interpretations to clarify the legal applications and to fill in the gaps in the legislation. Therefore, the legal authority and judicial consistency are jeopardized.

More seriously, political stability and legal authority are at risk because, in the absence of a unified *Civil Code*, the retail style of legislative tactics employed to make single civil laws has already caused controversies over its constitutionality. Since the beginning of the 21st Century, the general public and the academic community have a growing awareness of constitution, but the Legislature has failed

---

[22]Liu (2012).

[23]Kato (2001).

[24]Su (2010).

to recognize and answer their concerns. In 2001, the Standing Committee of NPC modified 39 Articles in its *Decision on Amending Marriage Law*. T o be specific, 21 Articles were amended, 17 added, and 1 deleted. Considering the sheer numbers, 105% of the 37 original Articles of the 1980 *Marriage Law* were modified, an apparent violation of Paragraph 3 of Article 67 of the *Constitution*, which lays out the legislative right to "partially supplement and amend."[25] In 2005, the draft of *Real Rights Law* caused a nationwide controversy over its constitutionality, putting the legislative efforts in an extremely awkward situation.[26] In 2007, when the *Real Rights Law* was enacted, Articles 166 and 167 were also challenged for their conformity to the *Constitution*.[27] In 2009, the *Tort Liability Law*, passed by the Standing Committee of NPC instead of NPC, became again the target of criticism from the academic community for its legislative procedure.[28] The future *Personality Rights Law*, which involves many issues concerning human rights, may also be questioned about its conformity to the *Constitution*, unless due attention is paid to this particular issue.

Criminal law has been so far immune to similar challenges to its constitutionality. This is because the *Criminal Code* was made in 1979 and was then amended as a whole by NPC in 1997, thus eliminating the risk of continuous disconformity to the *Constitution*. By comparison, since the enactment of *General Principles of the Civil Law*, wholesale legislative tactics have been abandoned. Instead, retail tactics are the very reason behind the constant outbreak of controversies over the constitutionality of single laws. It is not hard to foresee that unless NPC compile the *Civil Code* as a whole, newly civil legislation will inevitably run the risk of violating the *Constitution*.

References

Han Dayuan, Liu Songshan, *"Empirical Analysis on 'Basic Laws' in Texts of Constitution"*, *Legal Science Monthly*, No. 4, 2003

Kato Masanobu, "A Study on Relationship Between Enactment of Civil Code and Politics", trans. by QU Tao, *Global Law Review*, Autumn issue, 2001.

Liang Huixing, "Civil Code Assembled in a Loose Manner Does not Suit For China's National Condition", *Tribune of Political Science and Law*, No. 1, 2003.

Lin Yan, "A Study on the Failure of the Right to Amend Basic Laws and its Reasons", *Legal Science Monthly*, No. 7, 2002.

Liu Jingwei, "Civil Code that is Drifting Far Away", *Journal of Comparative Law*, No. 1, 2012.

Su Yongqin, "System Design and Rule of Construction of Modern Civil Code—Suggestions for the Civil Code Project of Mainland China", *SJTU Law Review*, No. 1, 2010.

---

[25]See Lin (2002).

[26]As to this "controversy over constitutionality", relevant academic discussions and the ideas of the author, see Wang (2006).

[27]Yang (2008).

[28]As to discussion over its constitutionality, see Wang (2010).

Sun Xianzhong, "Avoid Fragmentary Legislative Practices and Promulgate Civil Code Promptly", *Journal of CUPL*, No. 1, 2013.

Wang Liming, "Characteristics of the Times and Compilation Steps of the Civil Code", *Tsinghua University Law Journal*, No. 6, 2014.

Wang Liming, "Pathway of Systemizing Legislative Efforts of Civil Law in China", *Chinese Journal of Law*, No. 6, 2008.

Wang Zhu, "Interpretation of Constitutionality of the Legislative Procedure of Tort Liability Law", *Legal Science Monthly*, No. 5, 2010.

Wang Zhu, "On Constitutionality of General Principles of Civil Law and *Real Rights Law* (Draft)", *Case Study*, No. 3, 2006.

Wang Zhu, "Study on Legislative Mode of 'General Rules of Obligations Law' in Pursuing Pragmatic Methods of Drafting Civil Code", *Journal of Sichuan University (Social Science Edition)*, No. 3, 2012

Wang Zhu, Liu Zhongxuan, "Brief Comment on Lao Tort Law", *Civil and Commercial Law Debate*, vol. 11, 2017

Wei Leijie, "Legal Transplant and Compilation of Civil Code in Post-Soviet Union Era", *Journal of Comparative Law*, No. 5, 2008.

Wu Bangguo, "Speech at the Colloquium of Forming Socialist Legal System with Chinese Characteristics", *People's Daily*, January 27, 2011, p. 2.

Xu Guodong, "Civil and Commercial Code and Legislative Practices of Union Republics After the Dissolution of the Soviet Union", *Collected Essays on Civil and Commercial Law*, ed. by LIANG Huixing, Vol. 14, Law Press, 2000.

Xu Guodong, "Seriously Re-Thinking of the Organizing Methods of the 4th Drafting of Civil Code of PRC", *Law Science*, No. 5, 2003.

Yang Lixin, Wang Zhu, "Article 166 and 167 of the *Real Rights Law* from the Perspective of Hermeneutics", *Journal of Henan Administrative Institute of Politics and Law*, No. 1, 2008.

Chapter 2
Awareness of Constitutionality in the Compilation of *Civil Code*

2.1 Compile the *Civil Code* "Democratically" and "Scientifically"

The first three drafting processes of *Civil Code* and the deliberation of every volume of fourth drafting of *Civil Code* reveal that, the civil law scholars of several generations have made unremitting efforts for scientifically compiling the *Civil Code*, but the Legislatures is seldom found in democratically drafting the *Civil Code*. Since the fourth drafting of *Civil Code*, every draft is the indoor draft independently prepared by the Civil Law Office of NPC Legislative Affairs Commission,[1] and it's not drafted scientifically and democratically. The public solicitation of opinions on the *Real Rights Law (draft)* would be a historic progress, but was involved in the event of violation of the *Constitution*. Thereafter, it is understandable that the public solicitation of opinions on the *Tort Liability Law (draft)* was slightly hasty. Today when the compilation of *Civil Code* is solemnly initiated, it is especially important to re-mention the flags of democracy and science held high by those wise men in the May Fourth Movement occurred one hundred years ago.

2.1.1 Procedural Guarantee: To Compile the Civil Code Democratically

The Writer hopes that, every deputy of NPC will carry out substantial deliberation rather than formal deliberation when deliberating the *Civil Code (draft)* in the future. Otherwise, the exercise of legislative right for basic laws will not comply

---

[1]For the "indoor draft", See Xu (2005).

© China University of Political Science and Law Press 2020
Z. Wang, *On the Constitutionality of Compiling a Civil Code of China*,
https://doi.org/10.1007/978-981-13-7900-0_2

with the substantial requirements on legal reservation as provided in the *Constitution* and the *Legislation Law*. The Writer hopes that, as the legislature with the most affinity to the people in the political life in China, NPC can carry out thorough discussion over the *Civil Code (draft)* which will affect the life of most people, and at least ensure that every deputy will read every article thereof. Of course, the *Civil Code* with relatively high academic level could also be generated by undemocratic means. For example, the *Civil Code of Ethiopia* drafted by Professor Rene David was formally promulgated after the words "the conquering lion of the Tribe of Judah, Haile Selassie I, the Ethiopian emperor selected by the God" were added into "Preface".[2] However, the said *Civil Code* is regarded as "a delight of comparative jurists and a nightmare of Africans", and just existed as "a tiger without teeth" for 40 years owing to the fact that it was not adapted to the national conditions of Ethiopia.[3] Compiling the *Civil Code* "democratically" is a procedural guarantee, which involves the substantial deliberation by the NPC deputies on the *Civil Code (draft)* and the public solicitation of opinions on the *Civil Code (draft)*.

2.1.1.1 Substantial Deliberation by NPC Deputies on the *Civil Code (Draft)*

As the most important democratic political system in China, the national people's congress system has gone through more than 60 years of ups and downs, and is still being continuously improved. Of course, there are many imperfections in legislation-related democratic political system in China, and with respect to the adoption of law, it is always difficult to avoid the denouncement that the legislature only acts as "rubber stamp". In the process of legislation, there is few confrontation or compromise but many arrangements and cooperation. During the compilation of *Civil Code*, maybe such a legislature has no strong motivation to interfere with the contents of legislation. This even meets the faint expectation of some civil law scholars in a sense, as if it can be guaranteed that the advices of scholars will become the final text of legislation to a greater extent. However, this is exactly not what the Writer pursues.

It is advised by the Writer that, under the current political system of China, high respect should be extended to our NPC deputies. The Writer sincerely hopes that, the more than 2,000 NPC deputies will have the opportunity to carefully deliberate every volume of the drafted *Civil Code*, and at least the *Civil Code* will be adopted only after every deputy has read every word of the *Civil Code*. It really doesn't seem that this is what every civil law scholar pursues or even most of civil law scholars pursue.

---

[2]*Civil Code of Ethiopia*, trans. by XUE Jun, Law Press, 2000, p. 17.
[3]Xu (2002).

2.1.1.2 Public Solicitation of Opinions on the *Civil Code (draft)*

As the legal department in legal system which has the most affinity to common people and is most linked with the life of common people, the democratic process of the compilation of *Civil Code* can't do without full participation. The relevant department of the Standing Committee of NPC should not only set up the special column on official website so as to continuously publish the draft of every volume of the *Civil Code*,[4] but also make public the written record of discussion as much as possible. The manner adopted for public solicitation of opinions on the *Civil Code* should also be more friendly for common people. In addition to the drafted text of law published, media should be encouraged and experts should be invited to explain the difference between articles of law and current provisions, so as to ensure that the common people will not only have the right to know, but also truly understand the meaning of legal provisions and bring forth their own comments and advices.

As for the opinions and advices given by citizens on every volume of the *Civil Code*, it is advised to make arrangement for specific working personnel to summarize the opinions after combining the same opinions as much as possible, make public the summarized opinions and the distribution of opinions, and highlight the articles of law which common people concern about most, rather than randomly summarize the legislative appeals of common people and thus formalize the public solicitation of opinions.

2.1.2 Content Control: To Compile the Civil Code "Scientifically"

Strictly speaking, the word "scientifically" is not suitable for describing the compilation of *Civil Code*,[5] but meets the habit of expression gradually formed in academic community in China since the May Fourth Movement. The Writer hopes that the research findings obtained by civil law scholars of several generations during dozens of years as well as the legislative needs arising from the economic development since the reform and opening up and the future social & economic advancement in China can be fully and properly reflected in the *Civil Code*, so as to

---

[4]The *General Provisions of the Civil Law* has shown such tendency in the legislation process. On the website of the Standing Committee of NPC, on July 5, 2016, the *General Provisions of Civil Law of the People's Republic of China (Draft) (draft for solicitation of opinion in first deliberation)* was published. On November 18, 2016, the *General Provisions of the Civil Law (draft for solicitation of opinion in second deliberation)* was published. On December 17, 2016, the *General Provisions of the Civil Law (draft for solicitation of opinion in third deliberation)* was published. The three drafts is made public during the whole process and it deserves commendations.

[5]The Writer translates "科学地 (scientifically)" into "substantially" to achieve the free translation purpose.

support the great rejuvenation of the Chinese *nation*. Scientifically compiling the *Civil Code* is a control on contents, involving two aspects, namely full participation by scholars into compilation of *Civil Code* and the legislation carried out by NPC Legislative Affairs Commission in an open manner.

2.1.2.1 Full Participation by Scholars into the Compilation of *Civil Code*

The drafting process of the *Contract Law* is a legislative activity which saw the highest participation degree of scholars so far during the drafting of *Civil Code* in China, but this mode is still insufficient for such a great legislative undertaking as the compilation of *Civil Code*. The compilation of *Civil Code* requires more time and more efforts from old, middle-aged and young civil law scholars. The scholars actually participating in drafting should have the courage to burn their bridge, and fully devote themselves to preparation of "scholar-proposed draft". With respect to the academic seminars held for the compilation of *Civil Code*, there should be the mechanisms for making meeting minutes, sorting out various opinions and publishing relevant information in time, so that the attending scholars can sort out their thoughts by reviewing the meeting materials, and the scholars which have not attended such seminars can understand the progress of compilation of *Civil Code* by reading the meeting materials. Special emphasis should be placed on participation by scholars nationwide, so as to avoid the regional limit on participation by scholars.

2.1.2.2 Legislation Carried Out by NPC Legislative Affairs Commission in an Open Manner

It is advised that, NPC Legislative Affairs Commission will, rather than adopt the mode whereby both "indoor draft" and "scholar-proposed draft" are respectively prepared, directly accept the "scholar-proposed draft" which is relatively mature after being discussed by academic community as "indoor draft" and realize the smooth transition, so as to reduce the costs for including the academic opinions into "indoor draft". It is advised to set up the Expert Committee for the Compilation of *Civil Code* with official background, make the experts full-time members of such committee by means of temporarily transfer, and provide the committee with sufficient funds. It is advised to select the young civil law scholars to set up the Secretariat, providing the Expert Committee for the Compilation of *Civil Code* with high-quality academic assistance. In addition to the help from academic community, it is also advised to listen to the opinions from all sides, especially the opinions from judicial practice circle as well as the expectation opinions from legal affair departments of transnational institutions and foreign law firms.

2.1.3 Concerted Route for Compiling the **Civil Code** Democratically and Scientifically

In a sense, there is certain tension between democratically and scientifically compiling the *Civil Code*. On one hand, the feature that the NPC deputies are not full-time deputies[6] leads to the situation that only a very few NPC deputies with legal background can meet the needs for democratically and scientifically compiling the *Civil Code*; on the other hand and more importantly, we have not yet explored into a concerted route for democratically and scientifically compiling the *Civil Code*. As for design of legislative route for the compilation of *Civil Code*, we should not only pursue the high-quality text of *Civil Code*, but also hold high the flags of democracy and science. What we pursue should not be purely drafting the text of the *Civil Code* in a scientific manner or formally adopting the *Civil Code* in a democratic manner, but compiling the *Civil Code* democratically and scientifically. As a result, we should, under the framework of the *Constitution* and the *Legislation Law*, in accordance with the *Rules of Procedure of National People's Congress* and the *Rules of Procedure of Standing Committee of National People's Congress* as well as the current meeting mechanism for NPC and its Standing Committee, and in light of the legislative needs, carefully design the legislative procedure, decompose the refined *Civil Code (draft)* into the text which meets the actual ability of the NPC deputies and the member of NPC Standing Committee to read and deliberate the text of *Civil Code*, get every part deliberated by the Standing Committee of NPC, and then submit the *Civil Code* to NPC for voting, so as to finally realize the centennial dream to democratically and scientifically compile the *Civil Code* during the tenure of the 13th NPC!

2.2 Strengthen the Awareness of Constitutionality in the Compilation of *Civil Code*

The drafting process of *Civil Code* volume by volume over recent 30 year reveals that, even against the background that the compilation of *Civil Code* has been clearly proposed by the *Decision to Rule by Law*, there is still a long way to go before the *Civil Code* is really compiled. In order to avoid the new unconstitutional risk in the future, we should draw lessons from the "unconstitutional event", and strengthen the constitutional awareness in the compilation of *Civil Code*. The Writer believes that, we should start with the following five respects.

---

[6]Article 40 of the *Organic Law of the National People's Congress* provides that "Deputies to the National People's Congress must observe the *Constitution* and the law in an exemplary way, keep state secrets and, in the course of production, other work and the public activities in which they take part, assist in the enforcement of the *Constitution* and the law".

2.2.1 Constitutionality of Legislative Basis—Directness and Indirectness

As the important practice in legislation in China, there is a chapter "General Provisions" in almost every law, and the legislative purpose and legislative basis are set forth in Article 1. The *Constitution* is the direct legislative basis for "basic laws", and as "basic laws", both the *Criminal Code* and *General Principles of the Civil Law* contain the words "this Law is hereby enacted on the basis of the *Constitution*" in the article of legislative purpose. For example, it is provided in Article 1 of the *Criminal Code* that: "With a view to punishing crimes and protecting the people, this Law is hereby enacted on the basis of the *Constitution* and in the light of the concrete experiences and actual circumstances in fight against crimes in China." It is provided in Article 1 of *General Principles of the Civil Law* that: "With a view to protecting the lawful civil rights and interests of citizens and legal persons, correctly adjusting the civil relationship and meeting the needs of realization of socialist modernization, this Law is hereby enacted on the basis of the *Constitution* and in light of the actual circumstances and practical experience in civil activities in China." It is provided in Article 1 of the *General Provisions of Civil Law* that: "With a view to protecting the lawful rights and interests of civil subjects, adjusting the civil relationship, maintaining the social and economic order, meeting the needs of development of socialism with the Chinese characteristics and carrying forward the core values of socialism, this Law is enacted on the basis of the *Constitution*."

Among all civil legislations which act as components of the *Specific Provisions Volumes of Civil Code*, only the *Succession Law* and the *Real Rights Law* contain the words "this Law is hereby enacted on the basis of the *Constitution*". It is provided in Article 1 of the *Succession Law* that: "With a view to protecting the succession right of private properties of citizens, this Law is hereby enacted on the basis of the provisions of the *Constitution of the People's Republic of China*." It is provided in Article 1 of the *Real Rights Law* that: "With a view to maintaining the basic economic system of China, maintaining the order of socialist market economy, clarifying the ownership of properties, bringing the role of properties into full play, and protecting the real rights of right holders, this Law is hereby enacted on the basis of the *Constitution*." In consideration of the fact that the *Succession Law* was enacted before *General Principles of the Civil Law* and the words "this Law is hereby enacted on the basis of the *Constitution*" were added in Article 1 in the fifth draft of *Real Rights Law* only after the "unconstitutional event" occurred, the Writer believes that, the direct basis for every volume of the *Civil Code* is *General Principles of the Civil Law* rather than the *Constitution*,[7] and actually it is

---

[7]Therefore, the Writer also approves of Director Wang Shengming's understanding (Wang Shengming deems that the *Tort Liability Law* is the detailing, supplement and improvement of the *General Principles of Civil Law* and other laws). As the transitional civil basic law, *General Principles of the Civil Law* should not act as the legislative basis of every volume of the future *Civil Code*. Therefore, every volume of the *Civil Code* does not have to regard the *General*

unnecessary to contain the words "this Law is hereby enacted on the basis of the *Constitution*" in the article of legislative purpose. Therefore, it is also unnecessary to contain the words "this Law is hereby enacted on the basis of the *Constitution*" in Article 1 of the *Personality Rights Law* and the *General Provisions of Obligation Law* which may be enacted in the future, but it is necessary to ensure the constitutionality of their contents. The *Civil Code* to be enacted in the future should contain the words "this Law is hereby enacted on the basis of the *Constitution*" in Article 1.

2.2.2   Constitutionality of Legislative Procedure—Integrity and Partiality

According to the allocation of legislative authorities between NPC and the Standing Committee of NPC as provided in the *Constitution* and the *Legislation Law*, as the components of the *Civil Code,* the *Personality Rights Law* and the *General Provisions of Obligation Law* which may be enacted in the future may be adopted by the Standing Committee of NPC. From the viewpoint of appropriateness, however, the *Personality Rights Law* is closely related to the basic rights in the *Constitution*. It will be more appropriate if the *Personality Rights Law* can be adopted by NPC. Since much coordination has to be carried out between the *General Provisions of Obligation Law* and the *Contract Law*, such coordination may be completed in the future when the *Civil Code* is enacted. It should be emphasized that, in the future, the *Civil Code* must be adopted by NPC as a whole. The current compilation of every volume of the *Civil Code* and the *2002 Civil Law (draft)* reveal that, there will be more than 1200 articles in the *Civil Code* in the future, about three times the articles in large laws previously adopted by NPC, such as the *1997 Criminal Code* and the *1999 Contract Law* each of which has more than 400 articles. The systematic contents involved in the "general provisions—specific provisions" structure of the *Civil Code* will increase the difficulty in deliberation of such law. If necessary, the duration of meeting of NPC may be extended, so as to ensure the quality of deliberation of the *Civil Code*.

2.2.3   Constitutionality of Legislative Spirit—Formality and Essentiality

Every component of the *Civil Code* must be consistent with the *Constitution* in the aspect of legislative spirit, and this is the constitutionality requirement for

---

Principles of the Civil Law as the legislative basis. This is the convention of civil legislation of China.

legislation under the mode whereby the *Civil Code* is enacted volume by volume. The criticism involved in "unconstitutional event" in 2005 that the *Real Rights Law* fails to provide "the public properties of socialism are sacred and inviolable" falls in this scope. As for the judgment on constitutionality of legislative spirit, under the compilation mode whereby the *Civil Code* is enacted volume by volume, it is necessary to consider the formal meaning and essential meaning of judgment object. It is well known that, there exist the formal civil law and the essential civil law. The former refers to the systematically-compiled civil legislation, namely the *Civil Code*; the latter collectively refers to the legal norms which adjust the property relationship and personal relationship among equal subjects. Accordingly, under the compilation mode whereby the *Civil Code* is enacted volume by volume, the components of the *Civil Code* also involve formality and essentiality. For example, the formal real rights law refers to the *Real Rights Law*, while the essential real rights law collectively refers to the legal norms which adjust the property right relationship among equal subjects, not only including the *Real Rights Law*, but also including the property-related legal norms in laws such as *General Principles of the Civil Law*, the *Guarantee Law*, the *Land Administration Law*, the *Urban Real Estate Administration Law* and the *Rural land Contract Law*. On the basis of this logic, the Writer has ever pointed out in the "unconstitutional event" that, since *General Principles of the Civil Law* has provided that "the state properties are sacred and inviolable", if the constitutionality of *General Principles of the Civil Law* is recognized, the constitutionality of essential real rights law should also be recognized. However, if the *Civil Code* is compiled by means of codification in the future, it is really necessary to carefully consider whether such statement must be remained in the "General Provisions Volume" or "Real Rights Volume".[8]

2.2.4   Constitutionality of Amendment of Laws—Comprehensiveness and Partialness

In the practice of civil legislation in China, the amendment of relevant parts of the *Civil Code* enacted by NPC, such as the *Decision on Amendment of the Adoption Law of the People's Republic of China* in 1998 and the *Decision on Amendment of the Marriage Law of the People's Republic of China* in 2001 were adopted by the Standing Committee of NPC. It is provided in Paragraph 3 of Article 67 of the *Constitution* that: "The Standing Committee of National People's Congress shall exercise the following powers and duties: …③ To partially supplement and amend the laws enacted by the National People's Congress during the period when the National People's Congress is not in session, provided that the basic principles of such laws may not be violated; …" It is provided in Paragraph 3 of Article 7 of the *Legislation Law* that: "The Standing Committee of National People's Congress

---

[8]See Wang (2006).

shall enact and amend all laws other than those which shall be enacted by the National People's Congress; and partially supplement and amend the laws enacted by the National People's Congress during the period when the National People's Congress is not in session, provided that the basic principles of such laws may not be violated." The above provisions of the *Constitution* and the *Legislation Law* reveal that, during the period when NPC is not in session, the laws enacted by NPC, no matter whether they are basic laws, can only be "partially" supplement and amend, and "the basic principles of such laws may not be violated". Therefore, during the compilation of *Civil Code* volume by volume, it is necessary to distinguish between partial and full supplementation and amendment.

The *Decision of the Standing Committee of National People's Congress on Amendment of Some Laws* issued on August 27, 2009 amends Article 7 of *General Principles of the Civil Law* into "All civil activities shall respect the social morals, may not damage social public interests, and may not disturb the social and economic orders", and deletes Item 6 of Paragraph 1of Article 58. This is the amendment carried out accordingly after the basic economic system has been amended in the *Constitution*. In fact, such decision involves dozens of laws, including many laws enacted by NPC, and the scale of amendment also meets the provisions of the *Constitution* and the *Legislation Law*. However, the amendment made by the NPC Standing Committee to the *Marriage Law* is comprehensive, and this is worth reflection. Some scholars have pointed out that, the *1980 Marriage Law* has 37 articles, the *2001 Amendment to the Marriage Law* amends 21 articles, adds 17 articles and deletes 1 article, respectively accounting for 56.76, 45.95 and 2.7% of original articles; a total of 39 articles are amended, accounting for 105.41% of original articles. Without doubt, the amendment in such a scale can't be described as "partial supplementation and amendment", and it is more appropriate to consider it as "re-enactment".[9] In the future, before the *Civil Code* is formally enacted, any amendment carried out by the NPC Standing Committee of any component of the *Civil Code* adopted by the National People's Congress should be limited to "partial supplementation and amendment". Especially in the process of codification, the articles of the *Guarantee Law* will be comprehensively deleted and adjusted. It is advised by the Writer that such legislative activity should be completed by NPC rather than the NPC Standing Committee.

2.2.5   Constitutionality of Legal Interpretation—Restrictiveness and Extensiveness

With respect to the application of legal interpretation, there is also the constitutionality issue. For example, it is provided in Article 166 of the *Real Rights Law* that: "When the dominant tenement as well as the right to the contracted

---

[9]See Lin (2002).

management of land, the right to use land for construction or the right to use house site thereon is partially transferred, and if the easement is involved in the transferred part, the transferee shall enjoy the easement at the same time." The careful analysis on structure of this article reveals that, the first part of this article actually describes two legal facts, namely the transfer of "dominant tenement" and the transfer of "land contractual management right and construction land use right on dominant tenement". It is provided in Paragraph 4 of Article 10 of the *Constitution* that: "Neither entity nor individual may misappropriate, buy, sell or otherwise illegally transfer any land. The use right of land may be transferred in accordance with the provisions of laws." It is thus clear that, there is apparent contradiction between the partial transfer of "dominant tenement" and the provisions of the *Constitution*. The provisions relating to transfer of "servient tenement" in Article 167 of the *Real Rights Law* also involve the same problem. From the review point of constitutionality interpretation, the Writer believes that, the so-called transfer of "dominant tenement/servient tenement" in Article 166 and Article 167 of the *Real Rights Law* does not include land and space, and should only be deemed as building by using the restrictive interpretation. In this way, the apparent contradiction between these two articles and the *Constitution* can be eliminated. However, from the viewpoint of legislative techniques, these two articles and even the whole usufructuary right part really involve the formulary thinking that "The real estate are land". In the future, in the course of amendment of the *Real Rights Law* or the codification of the *Civil Code*, the design of usufructuary right of building should be enhanced.[10]

As for the types of civil rights and interests enumerated in Paragraph 2 of Article 2 of the *Tort Liability Law*, the extensive interpretation should be applied. Such paragraph does not provide the personal dignity and personal freedom, while Article 37 and Article 38 of the *Constitution* respectively provide the personal dignity and personal freedom. Especially, it is provided in Item 3 of Paragraph 1 of Article 1 of the *Interpretation of Supreme People's Court on Several Issues in Determination of Civil Tort Moral Damage Compensation Liabilities* that: "In case a natural person bring an action with the people's court for compensation for moral damage because any of the following personality rights is illegally infringed upon, the people's court shall legally accept such request: …③ Personal dignity right and personal freedom right." Since *General Principles of the Civil Law* does not provide the personal freedom right, the basis of such judicial interpretation should be the *Constitution*. Thus, it should be concluded that, the "personal dignity" and "personal freedom" provided in the *Constitution* are contained in the "other personal and property rights and interests". On the basis of this consideration, Article 109 of the *General Provisions of Civil Law* actually provides the personality rights in the *Constitution* rather than the general personality rights: "The personal freedom and personal dignity of natural persons are protected by laws." In the compilation of

---

[10]See Yang and Wang (2008).

Personality Rights Law in the future, the legislature should refer to the advices given by scholars on full protection of personality rights as provided in the *Constitution*,[11] pay special attention to the enumeration of personality rights as provided in the *Constitution*, and avoid any omission.

References

Lin Yan, "On Anomie of the Authority to Amend Basic Laws and its Reason", *Law Science*, No. 7, 2002.

Wang Liming, *Scholar-proposed Draft and Legislation reasons of Chinese Civil Code: Personal Rights volume. Marrige and Family Volume. Succession Volume*, Law Press, 2005, pp. 189–192.

Wang Zhu, "On the Constitutionality of *General Provisions of the Civil Law* and the Draft of *Real rights law*—to Keep the Essential Real Rights Law as Core", *Renmin University Law Review*, No. 3, 2006.

Xu Guodong, "The Ethiopia Civil Code: A Result of Two Reforms Collision", *Law Science*, No, 2, 2002.

Xu Guodong, "Two Institutions of the Green Civil Code", *Journal of Fujian Normal University (Philosophy and Social Science Edition)*, No. 1, 2005.

Yang Lixin, *China Personal Right Law Legislation Report*, Intellectual Property Publishing House, 2005, pp. 501–504.

Yang Lixin, Wang Zhu, "Article 166 and 167 of *Real Rights Law* from the Perspective of Hermeneutics", *Journal of Henan Administrative Institute of Politics and Law*, No. 1, 2008.

---

[11]See Yang (2005) and Wang (2005).

Chapter 3
Pragmatic Thinking for the Compilation of *Civil Code*

3.1 Fourth Thinking for the Compilation of *Civil Code*—"Pragmatic Thinking"

3.1.1 Three Thinkings Pursued in the Fourth Drafting of Civil Code

After the adoption of the *Contract Law* in 1999, with the enactment of the *Real Rights Law,* the fourth compilation of *Civil Code* has been put on the agenda. At that time, with respect to the overall thinking for the fourth compilation of *Civil Code*, there were "loose and federal type" thinking, idealist thinking and realistic thinking in the academic circle. The so-called "loose and federal type" thinking means to form the *Civil Code* by gathering together *General Principles of the Civil Law,* the *Contract Law,* the *Guarantee Law,* the *Succession Law* and the *Marriage Law* which had been adopted as well as the *Real Rights Law* which were being enacted, of which the essence is the assembly of civil laws. The so-called idealist thinking means to refer to the Roman laws and adopt the "three-volume system". The so-called realistic thinking means to finally realize the codification in light of the actual situation of China and on the basis of the five-volume system of Germany and *General Principles of the Civil Law*.[1]

The compilation process of *Civil Code* over recent ten years reveals that, the idealist thinking is inconsistent with the actuality that China is influenced by the *Civil Code of German*,[2] so that it will not be adopted as the legislative mode for *Civil Code* in China, unless there is a major political selection. In addition, the legislature also did not show any intention to make choice between "loose and federal type" thinking and realistic thinking. It should be noted that, these two thinkings are not different from each other in the aspect of essential contents, and

---

[1]For the summary of three thoughts, see Liang (2003).
[2]Liu (2002).

© China University of Political Science and Law Press 2020
Z. Wang, *On the Constitutionality of Compiling a Civil Code of China*,
https://doi.org/10.1007/978-981-13-7900-0_3

are only different from each other in the aspect whether the codification will be finally carried out. The Writer believes that, in the last phase of the fourth compilation of *Civil Code*, the civil law community must find a new thinking to ensure that the compilation of *Civil Code* will be completed as early as possible.

3.1.2 Pragmatic Thinking for the Compilation of Civil Code

Some scholars proposed a thinking for the compilation of *Civil Code* at the beginning of 2002; whereby the current laws would not be amended greatly, and the *General Provisions of Civil Law* would not be established, instead *General Principles of the Civil Law* can be amended and taken as the first volume of *Civil Code*. They regarded such thinking as the most natural development of legislative process in China, and regarded such thinking as better compliant with the background of civil legislation in China.[3] This thinking in relatively strong pragmatic style seemed not so mainstream more than ten years ago when the compilation of *Civil Code* was carried out vigorously, but gradually obtained stronger reasonableness after the legislature declared that the socialist legal system with Chinese characteristics has been formed. The basic thinking for the compilation of *Civil Code* held by the Writer for long time is in line with such thinking. As a result, against the background that the decision for the compilation of *Civil Code* is made, the Writer named such thinking as "pragmatic thinking", and took it as the fourth thinking for the fourth compilation of *Civil Code*.

Since the *Tort Liability Law* was adopted by the NPC Standing Committee rather than NPC, it can be concluded that the *Tort Liability Law* is not a basic civil law within the meaning of the *Constitution*. This legislative mode indicates that, the legislature has selected the legislative mode whereby various volumes of *Civil Code* will be adopted in accordance with the legislative procedure for basic laws, and finally the *Civil Code* will be formed through the codification process. This imposes on the legislature the obligation to draft the *Civil Code*, and also vetoes the "loose and federal type" thinking. It is thus clear that, with respect to the final "codification" issue, the goal of "pragmatic thinking" is identical with that of "realistic thinking". The pragmatic characteristics of "pragmatic thinking" are mainly embodied in the following three aspects:

Firstly, the "pragmatic thinking" emphasizes the continuation of legislative traditional which can facilitate the application of laws, and also focus on the settlement of actual problems. In the current legal system of China, except for the *Succession Law*, most of the laws were adopted or amended after *General Principles of the Civil Law*. *General Principles of the Civil Law* is not only the legislative basis for current civil and commercial laws, but also the legislative basis for civil and commercial legal norms in departmental law. The judicial practice

---

[3]Liu (2002).

circle has also got used to the application of laws centering around the civil and commercial laws enacted after *General Principles of the Civil Law*. Therefore, in the compilation of *Civil Code*, the current laws and articles should be remained as much as possible, and the change of laws caused by the compilation of *Civil Code* should be minimized; in addition, the newly-added articles should focus on the settlement of actual problems. Frankly speaking, the aesthetics of legislation should give place to the practicability to a certain extent.

Secondly, the "pragmatic thinking" emphasizes the reduction of legislative costs and the coordination between the compilation of *Civil Code* and the current legal system. The *Civil Code* of China will be finally completed after the legislature has declared that "the socialist legal system with Chinese characteristics has been formed". This decides that the compilation of *Civil Code* will be oriented as further enriching and improving the socialist legal system with Chinese characteristics.[4] Maybe this orientation is lower than the expectation of civil law community to a certain extent. In order to ensure the smooth compilation of *Civil Code*, the civil law community should actively assist the legislature in reducing the legislative costs of compilation of *Civil Code* and maximize the coordination between the compilation of *Civil Code* and the current legal system. On the basis of the allocation of legislative authorities as provided in the *Constitution*, the future *Civil Code* must be adopted by NPC. From the viewpoint of possibility of deliberation, it is also necessary to minimize the difficulty of deliberation; otherwise the possibility of completion of codification will be affected, or the legislative procedure will become formalized and can't ensure the democracy and scientificalness of legislation.

Thirdly, the "pragmatic thinking" emphasizes the influence of legislative procedure on legislative mode of *Civil Code*, and focus on the possibility of legislative procedure. The legislative procedure of the *Tort Liability Law* indicates that, the selection of legislative procedure made by the legislature will greatly influence the legislative mode of *Civil Code*. It can be expected that, the *Personality Rights Law*, if being enacted in the future, will also be adopted by the NPC Standing Committee. With respect to the procedure, since the *2002 Civil Law (draft)* did not contain the Volume "*General Provisions of Obligation Law*", if the legislature decides to enact the *General Provisions of Obligation Law* in the future, the proposal of new law must be submitted to the NPC Standing Committee in accordance with Article 26 of the *Legislation Law*. With respect to the contents, if the *General Provisions of Obligation Law* is enacted separately, it is surely necessary to comprehensively amend the *Contract Law* and the *Tort Liability Law*, which will involved the systematic adjustment of several laws, and will be no different from the codification of *Civil Code*. It is difficult to imagine that, under the circumstance that the legislative tasks are very heavy, the legislature can carry out the essential codification-related legislative activities for *Civil Code* for two times. The Writer believes that, the mode which can be accepted by the civil law community and the legislature is as follows: after NPC adopts the *General Provisions of Civil Law*, the

---

[4]Wang (2012).

NPC Standing Committee will comprehensively amend and improve the components of future *Civil Code*, and then the *Civil Law of the People's Republic of China* will be adopted through the codification-related legislative activity by NPC. Frankly speaking, the systematicness of *Civil Code* should give place to procedure to a certain extent.

3.1.3 *Further Unfolding of "Pragmatic Thinking"* Against *the Background of* Decision to Rule by Law

These principles of pragmatic methods employed in the compilation of *Civil Code* will be elaborated below:

First, the existing research findings can only lead to the conclusion that what we need is simply a civil code in form, not in nature.[5] Within the socialist legal system with Chinese characteristics that has formed, other legal sectors are by no means perfect. Regardless of the ideal of perfection pursued by civil law scholars, there is no reason to insist that the civil law be better than other laws. At the very least, the civil law will not be the least perfect one. In drafting the *Marriage Law* and the *Succession Law* in the 1980s, the *Adoption Law*, the *Guarantee Law* or the *Contract Law* in the 1990s, and amending the *Marriage Law*, drafting the *Real Rights Law* and the *Tort Liability Law* in the past 10 years, legislators and scholars, out of a "complex for *Civil Code*,"[6] have technically left a "plug-in" for the prospective *Civil Code*. Therefore, civil single laws are coherent in spirit.

Second, it is unnecessary to continue the macro discussion on whether the "Three-Volume" structure in the style of the French *Civil Code*, or the "Five-Volume" structure like the German BGB should be adopted. Focus should be given to designing the *Civil Code* outline based on the civil single laws on hand. Some scholars think that the influence of the Pandekten System on China was the result of a joke of fate, an act not thoroughly thought through, as well as the Japanese's efforts to flatter the Western imperialist countries.[7] However, As Professor YANG Zhenshan points out, in the current campaign to compile the *Civil Code* in China it is hard to escape from the conceptual framework of the German BGB, since these concepts and ideas have long been absorbed by our legislative efforts and textbooks. The attempt to create a new conceptual system is nothing but a rearrangement of these concepts.[8] In this sense, we are really not very far away from having a civil code.

---

[5]Feng (2003).
[6]Su (2005).
[7]Monateri (2004).
[8]Yang (2003).

Third, the grand mission of "synthesizing the newly created systems of the 20th Century"[9] and the never-dying dream of making the "landmark of the 21st Century"[10] should be abandoned. It would be a huge achievement if we ultimately accomplish a civil code, though "imperfect" in form but conforming to the national situation of China.[11] Moreover, it is obvious from the judicial practices since the enactment of *General Principles of the Civil Law* that judicial interpretations issued by the Supreme People's Court have become a working method to regulate the ruling practices of people's courts at various levels.[12] Even a "perfect" *Civil Code* would not invalidate the existing judicial interpretations or prevent the Supreme People's Court from issuing new judicial interpretations or guiding cases. Therefore, it is more feasible to encourage a healthy interaction between the Legislature and the Supreme People's Court, so that a civil law in a substantial sense can be supplemented with judicial interpretations or guiding cases, with the reasonable elements of judicial interpretations being absorbed by means of amendments. This may be a new way to produce a civil code with Chinese characteristics.

Fourth, it is obvious that the Legislature will not give up the existing single laws and create a completely new one.[13] Considering the pattern of volume by volume in the past 30 years since the promulgation of *General Principles of the Civil Law*, and the deliberation capacity of the legislatures,[14] it is highly unlikely that the Legislature of China would enact the *Civil Code* from scratch, except at special times when major political decisions have to be made. The fact that *Decision to Rule by Law* chooses the term "compile" instead of "enact" may be deemed as a preference in choosing the drafting method for *Civil Code*.[15] In this sense, the urgent tasks at present should be to collect the existing resources necessary for the compilation of *Civil Code* and to study the major difficulties. In terms of legislative procedure, efforts should especially be made to see if there exists a legislative scheme under the framework of the *Constitution* that can be accepted by the Legislature subjectively and objectively. Only in this way can the work of compiling the *Civil Code* proceed in a substantial way.

---

[9]Ji (2003).

[10]Yi (2004).

[11]Xue and Liu (1999).

[12]Art. 8 of *Several Opinions on Regulating Relations Between Ruling Practices of Upper and Lower People's Courts by the Supreme People's Court* (61st Doc, 2010) states: The Supreme People's Court exercises guidance on ruling practices of local people's courts at all levels and special people's courts through accepting and judging cases, making judicial interpretations or normative documents, issuing guiding cases, convening meetings on ruling practices, and organizing trainings for judges.

[13]Liu (2012).

[14]See later analysis.

[15]When it comes to civil code, *Decision to Rule by Law* use the word "compile", while as to other laws, the word "enact" is used.

3.2 Design of the Structure of *Civil Code* Under Pragmatic Thinking

What may be easily ignored is that, the enumeration of civil rights and interests in Paragraph 2 of Article 2 of the *Tort Liability Law* has important reference value for the determination of the structure of future *Civil Code*. It is provided in such article that: "For the purpose of this law, civil rights or interests include personal or property rights or interests, such as right to life, right to health, right to name of natural person, right to reputation, right to honor, right to portrait, right to privacy, right to marital autonomy, right to guardianship, right to ownership, usufructuary rights, rights for security, copyrights, patent rights, exclusive trademark rights, right of discovery, stock right, right of succession." The comparison with the structure of the *2002 Civil Law (draft)* reveals that, the "right to life, right to health, right to name of natural person, right to reputation, right to honor, right to portrait, right to privacy" correspond to Volume 4 "*Personality Rights Law*", the "right to marital autonomy, right to guardianship" correspond to Volume 5 "*Marriage Law*" and Volume 6 "*Adoption Law*", "right to ownership, usufructuary rights, rights for security" correspond to Volume 2 "*Real Rights Law*", and the "right of succession" correspond to Volume 7 "*Succession Law*". According to the authentic interpretation given by the legislature, the plural "personal or property rights or interests" cover the issue about obligatory rights arising from third-party infringement,[16] and can be deemed as corresponding to Volume 3 "*Contract Law*".

Since the order of civil rights enumerated is different from that in the *2002 Civil Law (draft)*, Article 2 of the *Tort Liability Law* actually shows the new idea of the legislature on the structure of future *Civil Code*, which includes the following key points: The first is that, the *Civil Code* will adopt the structure "general provisions volume—specific provisions volumes—liability volume". This is different from the three-volume system adopted by the *Civil Code of France*[17] and the five-volume system adopted by the *Civil Code of Germany*, and is the civil code structure with Chinese characteristics. The second is that, with respect to the "specific provisions volumes", the *Personality Rights Law* may be formulated into a separate volume in parallel to other civil rights, and be taken as the logic for the unfolding of "specific provisions". According to the planning for various types of rights, it is necessary to give macro-provisions for "obligatory rights" which are parallel to "real rights" and "personality rights", but whether the *General Provisions of Obligation Law* will be enacted must be further considered. The third is that, with respect to the "liability volume", the *Tort Liability Law* is the protection law for all civil rights and interests, and this is the systematic value of the provision "[One who] infringes on

---

[16]See Wang (Wang 2010).

[17]The *Civil Code of France* was modified into the "five-volume system" in 2006. Volume 4 is Guarantee. Volume 5 "Regulations Applicable for Mayotte". Here, it is the traditional three-volume system structure of the *Civil Code of France*. See *Code Civil of France*, Translated by LUO Jiezhen, Peking University Press, 2010, p. 2.

the civil rights or interests [of another], shall bear tort liability according to this law." in Paragraph 1 of Article 2 of such law.

Articles 109–111 of Chapter 5 "Civil Rights" of the *General Provisions of Civil Law* give the provisions for personality rights and interests, Article 112 gives the provisions for identity right, Articles 113–117 give the provisions for real rights, Articles 118–122 give the provisions for obligatory rights, Article 123 gives the provisions for intellectual property rights, and Article 124 gives the provisions for succession right. The Writer believes that, the order of civil rights enumerated in the *General Provisions of Civil Law* carries forward the planning for structure of future *Civil Code* as given in the *Tort Liability Law*. From the "pragmatic thinking", this legislative idea of legislature should be respected. In light of the above-mentioned analysis and on the basis of the order of "personal" and "property" in "personal and property rights and interests", the correspondence between the structure of the future *Civil Code* and current laws will be as follows:

Volume 1 *General Provisions* (the 2017 *General Provisions of Civil Law*)
Volume 2 *Personality Rights* (draft for first deliberation in the fourth compilation of *2002 Civil Law draft*)[18]
Volume 3 *Marriage and Family* (the *Marriage Law* enacted in 1980 and amended in 2001 & the *Adoption Law* enacted in 1991 and amended in 1998)
Volume 4 *Succession* (the 1985 *Succession Law*)
Volume 5 *Real Rights* (the 2007 *Real Rights Law*)
Volume 6 *Contract* (the 1999 *Contract Law* & Chapter 2 "Guarantee" and Chapter 6 "Deposit" of the 1995 *Guarantee Law*)
Volume 7 *Tort Liability* (the 2009 *Tort Liability Law*).

References

Feng Lekun, "From Absolute Reason to Relative Reason—Method to Codify the Civil Law", *Modern Law Science*, No. 6, 2003.
Ji Weidong, "Abandoning Persistence and Embrace the Truth—An Outsider's View of Twists and Turns in the Pathway of Compiling Civil Code", *Book Town*, No. 2, 2003.
Liang Huixing, "Three Thoughts on the Current Codification of Chinese Civil Law", *Lawyer World*, No. 2, 2003.
Liu Jingwei, "Civil Code that is Drifting Far Away", *Journal of Comparative Law*, No. 1, 2012.
Liu Shiguo, "On the Organizing Structure of Chinese Civil Code", *Law and Social Development*, No. 3, 2002.
Monateri P.G., "Questions and Answers on the Compilation of Civil Code of China—Centered by the Framework and System of the Civil Code", *Peking University Law Journal*, Vol. 16, No. 6, 2004.
Su Yigong, "Highly Conceited, from Complex of Tang Code to that of Civil Code", *China Social Sciences*, No. 1, 2005.

---

[18]The dispute still exists on whether the *Personality* Rights Lawis independently enacted into a volume.

Wang Liming, "Codification of the Civil Code after the Formation of Legal System", *Social Science in Guangdong*, No. 1, 2012.

Wang Shengming, *The Interpretation of Tort Law of People's Republic of China*, China Legal Publishing House, 2010, P11.

Xue Feng, Liu fengjing, "On Conditions of Legislating Civil Code from the Perspective of Jurisprudence", *The Jurist*, No. 6, 1999.

Yang Zhenshan, "Several Major Issues in Drafting Civil Code", *Tribune of Political Science and Law*, No. 1, 2003.

Yi Jiming, "Immortality of Civil Code—Challenges of the Times Facing the Making of Civil Code", *China Legal Science*, No. 5, 2004.

Part II
Consideration of the Constitutionality in the Compilation of *Civil Code*

The writer believes that, in the compilation of *Civil Code*, it is necessary to further strengthen the constitution awareness. The positive demonstration for constitutionality should be carried out for any doubt on constitutionality brought forth in the course of the compilation of *Civil Code*. This can not only prevent the progress of the compilation of *Civil Code* from being affected by defect in constitutionality, but also improve the constitution awareness in the civil law community, and finally promote the rule-by-law strategy under the framework of the *Constitution*.

Chapter 4 Object of Constitutionality Judgment—Taking "Unconstitutional Event" in Drafting of the *Real Rights Law* as an Example.

Chapter 5 Constitutionality of Legal Interpretation—Taking Interpretation of Article 166 and 167 of the *Real Rights Law* as an Example.

Chapter 6 Constitutionality of Legislative Procedure—Taking Constitutionality Interpretation for Legislative Procedure of the *Tort Liability Law* as an Example.

Chapter 7 Constitutionality of Legal Application—Taking Determination and Legislative Prospect of Essential Tort Law as an Example.

Chapter 4
Object of Constitutionality Judgment—Taking "Unconstitutional Event" in Drafting of the *Real Rights Law* as an Example

4.1 Brief Review and Academic Evaluation of "Unconstitutional Event"

4.1.1 Brief Review of the Real Rights Law (Draft) *Against Background of "Unconstitutional Event"*

The *2005 Real Rights Law (draft)* issued for solicitation of public opinions aroused wide concerns from all walks of life. Most of the opinions believed that the *Real Rights Law (draft)* reflects the fundamental interests of the broad masses of the people, and also fully reflects the basic results of reform and opening-up. Represented by the Public Letter issued by Professor Gong Xiantian of Law School of Peking University,[1] a few opinions believe that the *Real Rights Law (draft)* is unconstitutional. This caused widespread controversy in theoretical circle and the public at that time, known as "Lang-Gu Dispute in Law community".[2] Some persons suspected whether something was secretly done under the cover of the *Real Rights Law (draft)*,[3] while some other persons sighed for the ups and downs in the enactment of the *Real Rights Law* in China.[4] This event also drew extensive attention from overseas media, and was regarded as the first ideological debate faced by the legislature in China about "capitalist or socialist legislation".[5] As times went by, the debate gradually expanded from oral, Internet and meeting discussion

---

[1] Gong Xiantian: "A Real Rights Law (draft) in Violation of the Constitution and against the Socialist Basic Principles". If no descriptions are made for the viewpoint of Professor Gong Xiantian in the following, the content is quoted from the "Public Letter".
[2] See Lv (2006).
[3] See Guo (2006).
[4] See He (2006).
[5] "NPC of PRC Pay Attention to the Debate of Socialism and Capitalism", *New York Times*, available at http://china.dayoo.com/gb/content/2006-03/13/content_2438341.htm, the latest access time: August 31, 2017.

© China University of Political Science and Law Press 2020
Z. Wang, *On the Constitutionality of Compiling a Civil Code of China*,
https://doi.org/10.1007/978-981-13-7900-0_4

into academic journals, and many famous scholars expressed the opinion on the issue whether the *Real Rights Law (draft)* is unconstitutional by wiring papers and carried out face-to-face academic battle, which was not found at the early phase of "unconstitutional event". In fact, the issue whether the *Real Rights Law (draft)* is unconstitutional is only a branch in the academic evaluation for the *Real Rights Law (draft)* and even the *Civil Law (draft)*. In consideration of the special interactive relationship between the draft recommended by scholars and the draft for deliberation prepared by NPC Legal Affairs Commission in China, the Writer will review every *Real Rights Law (draft)* issued around 2000 on the basis of the drafts issued by scholars and the officially-issued drafts respectively, and take the findings as background for discussion.

4.1.1.1   Review on Basis of Continuously Issued and Amended Scholar Drafts

After the *Contract Law* was promulgated in 1999, the focus of civil law community in China changed from contract law to real rights law. As the *Recommended Draft of Real Rights Law of China*[6] prepared by Professor Liang Huixing and the *Recommended Draft of Real Rights Law of China and Explanation Thereon* prepared by Professor Wang Liming[7] were published respectively in 2000 and 2001, there was the academic trend of "commentary on draft" in civil law community in China. The commentary in the circle firstly aimed at the scholar-recommended draft. Thereafter, the scope of commentary expanded from the *Real Rights Law (draft)* to the *Civil Law (draft)*, and the target also gradually expanded from publications to the indoor draft of the Civil Law Office of NPC Legal Affairs Commission and the "draft recommended by scholars" as issued by Law Institute of Chinese Academy of Social Sciences and the Civil and Commercial Law Science Research Institute of Renmin University of China. The drafts subsequently involved into the debate also included the *Recommended Draft of Real Rights Law of China* published by Professor Meng Qinguo[8] and the *Draft of Green Civil Code* prepared by Professor Xu Guodong.[9] Professor Liang Huixing[10] and Professor Wang Liming[11] in 2003 and 2004 respectively issued the formal draft containing legislative reasons. Thereafter, Through more than one year's preparation, two mainstream drafter of *Civil Code*, namely the Law Institute of Chinese Academy of Social Sciences[12] and the Civil and Commercial Law Science Research Institute of

---

[6]See Liang (2000).
[7]See Wang (2001).
[8]Meng (2002).
[9]See Xu (2004).
[10]See Liang (2003).
[11]See Wang (2004).
[12]See Liang (2004).

Renmin University of China[13] respectively published the detailed draft of *Civil Code* containing explanation, legislative reasons and references at the end of 2004 and in 2005, with the Volume of *Real Rights Law* separately published. Since at that time the legislature was inclined to "enact the *Real Rights Law* as soon as possible", after the beginning of 2004, the academic circle did not aim at the *Civil Law (draft)* any longer, but aimed at the *Real Rights Law (draft)*.

4.1.1.2 Review on Basis of the *Civil Law (draft)* and the *Real Rights Law (draft)* issued by NPC Legal Affairs Commission

On December 23, 2002, the *Civil Law (draft)* was fully deliberated at the 31st Meeting of Standing Committee of 9th NPC, and then was, as the "draft for solicitation of opinions", sent to local people's congresses, government departments, courts and law institutes for solicitation of opinions. However, the academic circle and judicial practice circle gave few positive opinions on such draft. Therefore, it was stated in the *Explanation on Amendment of the Real Rights Law (draft) of the People's Republic of China* attached to the *Draft for Deliberation at Chairman Meeting* formulated in January 2004 that: "Many standing committee members and concerned parties believe that, since the *Civil Law* involves large coverage and complicated contents, it will take relatively long time to complete the drafting and amendment of the *Civil Law*. As a result, it is appropriate to deliberate and adopt it volume by volume. At present, it is necessary to enact the *Real Rights Law* as soon as possible." Under this circumstance, the enactment of the *Real Rights Law* was separately listed into the legislative agenda. On June 26, 2005, the *Real Rights Law (draft)* was deliberated at the 16th Meeting of 10th NPC Standing Committee for the third time. On July 7, after going through three deliberations, the *Real Rights Law (draft)* was issued for soliciting opinions from the public throughout the country, and more than 10,000 pieces of comments and advices were received.[14] On October 22, 2005, the *Real Rights Law (draft)* was deliberated at the 18th Meeting of 10th NPC Standing Committee for the fourth time.

Between the third deliberation and fourth deliberation, on August 12, 2005, Professor Gong Xiantian published online a writing titled "*A Real Rights Law (draft) in Violation of the Constitution and against the Socialist Basic Principles—Public Letter Written for Abolishment of Article 12 of the Constitution and Article 73 of the 86 General Principles of the Civil Law*", which aroused great repercussions. On September 13, Hu Kangsheng, the deputy director of NPC Law Committee and the director of Legal Affairs Commission of the NPC Standing Committee, met with Professor Gong Xiantian. On September 26, Wu Bangguo,

---

[13]See Wang (2005).

[14]See "Advices on the Draft of *Real Rights Law* from the Masses" and " Advices on the Draft of *Real Rights Law* from the Masses (Continued)", *The People's Congress of China*, No. 15, 16, 2005.

the chairman of the NPC Standing Committee, gave three instructions for the further amendment of the *Real Rights Law (draft)*. On October 10, in the report on amendment of the *Real Rights Law of the People's Republic of China (draft)* given on behalf of the NPC Law Committee, the deputy director Hu Kangsheng embodied the instructions of the chairman Wu Bangguo into three principles: "The first is to adhere to the correct political direction; the second is to adhere to the situation and actuality of China; the third is to properly handle the relationship between the *Real Rights Law* and other relevant laws." Thereafter, the fifth deliberation for the *Real Rights Law (draft)* was not carried out as planned, and the *Real Rights Law (draft)* was not submitted to the 4th Meeting of 10th NPC for deliberation in 2006. After ten months' preparation, the *Real Rights Law (draft)* (draft for fifth deliberation) was submitted to the 23rd Meeting of 10th NPC Standing Committee for deliberation on August 22, 2006.

4.1.2 Evaluation on Impact of "Commentary on Draft" and Public Letter

With the formal publication of the *Several Issues about Enactment of Real Rights Law of China*[15] written by Professor Liang Huixing and the issuance of the first draft of *Real Rights Law (draft)*, the "commentary on draft" for *Real Rights Law* of China in the 21st century was formally kicked off. Thereafter, for the reason mentioned above, the debate focused on the *Real Rights Law (draft)*. According to the search by the Writer on www.cnki.net on October 10, 2006, there were more than 300 "papers for commentary on draft of *Real Rights Law*" only on mainstream law journals,[16] in addition to those theses on numerous monograph, newspaper, books and assembly of theses. There was even the situation that some papers were firstly published via Internet in order to ensure the timeliness. Coincidentally, taking the time when Professor Gong Xiantian published the Public Letter as the division line, by the beginning of October 2006, the above-mentioned 300 papers equally fell into two time periods, about 150 pieces for each period. Through a rough study on the titles of such papers and the contents of some papers, the Writer found that, the "commentary on draft" before August 2005 was purely technical. In addition to academic circle, the actual practice circle, such as China Land Science Society[17] and China Property Management

---

[15]Liang (2000).

[16]The "papers for commentary on draft of real rights law" of the Writer refer to the articles which are collected on www.cnki.net and whose title and subtitle explicitly mention "property rights law" and "draft" key words, excluding the analysis articles of specific institution of *Real Rights Law* and the articles which are for the draft of *Real Rights Law* but do not explicitly mention them in the title and subtitle. The range of retrieval time is 2000–2006.

[17]See Xu (2006).

Association,[18] also organized the symposiums, and brought forth the formal written comments.

Among the relevant papers after the publication of Public Letter, there are more than 30 papers of which the title and subtitle are directly related to unconstitutional issue, accounting for about 1/5. Among the remaining 4/5, there are few papers which totally avoid such issue. In Issue 3 of the *Journal of Henan Administrative Institute of Politics and Law* in 2006, under the title "*Real Rights Law* and Building of Harmonious Society in China", the papers submitted by six famous civil law scholars (namely Wang Liming, Yang Lixin, Guo Mingrui, Yin Tian, Zhao Wanyi And Liu Jingwei) to the Symposium on *Real Rights Law* and Building of Harmonious Socialist Society in China held in the Renmin University of China on February 25, 2006 was published, which represented the mainstream opinions of the civil law community. In Issue 3 of the *Legal Science* in 2006, under the title "Comments of Constitution Scholars for Debate on Constitutionality and Unconstitutionality of *Real Rights Law (draft)*", four scholars, namely Tong Zhiwei, Han Dayuan, Zhang Qianfan And Jiao Hongchang were invited to respectively write papers for discussion. In Issue 7 and Issue 8 of the *Legal Science* in 2006, the *On Constitutional Issue of Real Rights Law (draft) and Solution* written by Professor Tong Zhiwei and the *My Opinions on Unconstitutional Issue of Real Rights Law (draft)* written by Professor Hao Tiechuan were also published, so as to express the different comments in the constitution circle.

Therefore, though it is impossible and unnecessary to determine whether the deliberation of the *Real Rights Law (draft)* was interrupted by the Public Letter of Professor Gong Xiantian, it can be determined that, the Public Letter affected the theoretical direction of the whole circle, and to a certain extent disturbed the normal atmosphere for academic discussion over the draft of *Real Rights Law*. Fortunately, most scholars carefully treated the "unconstitutional event", and also continued to give careful and academic comments on the fourth and fifth drafts of the *Real Rights Law (draft)*. Among them, the relatively influential comments include the "Special Issue for *Real Rights Law*" in Issue 1 of the *Peking University Law Journal* in 2006 and the "Comparative Study on Anglo-American *Property Law* and Continental *Real Rights Law*" in Issue 1 of the *Global Law Review* in 2006, as well as the theoretical papers written by civil law scholars such as Liang Huixing, Wang Liming, Yang Lixin, Sun Xianzhong, Yin Tian, Meng Qinguo, Chen Huabing, Liu Baoyu, Yi Jiming And Wang Yi. After the "unconstitutional event" which lasted for more than one year, the discussion on the *Real Rights Law (draft)* in academic circle gradually returned to academic trail.

---

[18]See the 8 series papers in *Property Management* No. 8, 2005.

4.1.3 Different Opinions and Evaluation
on Constitutionality of the Real Rights Law (Draft)

With respect to the constitutionality issue of the *Real Rights Law (draft)*, the jurisprudence scholars, constitution law scholars and civil law scholars carried out the relatively large discussion, mainly involving the following opinions.

The first is the unconstitutional doctrine. After Professor Gong Xiantian firstly brought forth the "unconstitutional doctrine", Professor Tong Zhiwei also proposed that the original intention of the *Constitution* is to implement the differentiated protection on properties under different ownership systems,[19] giving further explanation on unconstitutional doctrine.

The second is the constitutional doctrine. Tit for tat, the civil law scholars represented by Professor Wang Liming believed that, the *Constitution* does not implement the principle of differentiated protection for properties under different ownership systems, so that the *Real Rights Law (draft)* is constitutional. Some constitution law scholars also believed that, the principle of equal protection on public properties (including state and collective properties) and private properties in the *Real Rights Law (draft)* is essentially different from the differentiated treatment on public properties and private properties in the *Constitution*, and the principle of equal protection in the *Real Rights Law (draft)* is not unconstitutional.[20]

The third is the constitution revision doctrine. Some scholars believe that, according to its focus and significance, this debate is an issue of the *Constitution* rather than an unconstitutional issue of the *Real Rights Law*.[21] On the excuse that the non-equal protection will give a handle to "those persons who don't recognize China as a state with market economy", some other scholars directly proposed that: "if some provisions of the *Constitution* are inconsistent with the principle of the *Real Rights Law* which is a private law and an important component of the *Constitution*, we should not blame the *Real Rights Law*, but amend the *Constitution*, because from the viewpoint of jurisprudence, the private laws are the foundation of the *Constitution*, and the *Constitution* is the distillation of the principles of private laws and should be consistent with the principles of private laws."[22]

The fourth is the compromise doctrine. As a compromise, some scholars believe that there is certain contradiction between "equal protections on real rights" and "the public properties are sacred and inviolable".[23] When explaining the draft for the fifth deliberation, the person in charge of NPC Legal Affairs Commission also said that: "Adhering to the basic economic system of China and providing equal

---

[19]Tong (2006).

[20]Jiao (2006).

[21]Gao (2017).

[22]Hao (2006).

[23]Ji (2006).

protection for state properties, collective properties and private properties constitute an unified organism. Without the former, the socialist nature will be changed; without the latter, the principle of market economy will be violated, which will, in turn, damage the basic economic system."[24]

With respect the above-mentioned four opinions on constitutionality of the *Real Rights Law (draft)*, the Writer believes that:

Firstly, according to the opinions of "unconstitutional doctrine" and "constitutional doctrine", with respect to the question whether the *Constitution* implements the differentiated protection for properties under different ownership systems, the constitution law scholars and the civil law scholars have the conclusions which are obviously different but based on repeated argument. However, this did not prevent some constitution law scholars from believing that the *Constitution* provides the "differentiated protection", and also believing that the "equal protection" implemented by the *Real Rights Law (draft)* is not unconstitutional.[25] Through demonstration on the basis of legal theory of constitution law, some scholars believed that, the judgment on "unconstitutionality" is not a simple judgment, requires considering comprehensive factors, and should be reasonably made in light of the enactment process, adoption procedure and implementation.[26] It is thus clear that, whether the provisions of the *Constitution* should be interpreted as "differentiated protection" will not directly affect the constitutionality of *Real Rights Law (draft)*, and the "constitutionality" only consider whether the spirits of them are consistent with each other.

Secondly, the so-called "constitution revision doctrine", is essentially the inevitable continuation of the discussion on revision of constitution in 2002. Since some proposals on revision of constitution in 2002 were not approved, they will surely conflict with the subsequent *Real Rights Law (draft)*. From the viewpoint of actuality, it is impossible for this opinion to be implemented, and the Writer will also not give any comment thereon. The "unconstitutional doctrine" and "constitutional doctrine" are analyzed respectively as follows.

Thirdly, in fact, the opinions of compromise doctrine have been embodied in the *Real Rights Law (draft)* (fifth draft), and the words "this Law is hereby enacted on the basis of the *Constitution*" have been added in Article 1. However, this opinion actually fails to settle the essential problem. It can be expected that, if some opinions of "unconstitutional doctrine" are only met literally, the "unconstitutional event" will not thus be terminated.

---

[24]Li (2017).
[25]Jiao (2006).
[26]Han (2006).

4.2 Several Comments on "Unconstitutional Event"

4.2.1 Positive Significance of "Unconstitutional Event"

Though the question about the constitutionality of the *Real Rights Law (draft)* is not related to the final conclusion, it is of much positive significance, mainly involving the following respects:

Firstly, the Mass Line which has been always implemented in legislative process in China is embodied. The attention and feedback drawn by the *Real Rights Law (draft)* from the public is almost unprecedented. How to properly integrate the professional legislation and public participation and how to properly integrate the independent exercise of judicial authority by judicial organ and the judicial democracy will become an important issue encountered by the development of legal system of China in the future.[27]

Secondly, the significance of cross-study by several disciplines is highlighted. As the discussion on the *Real Rights Law (draft)* was carried out, the scholars of Civil & Commercial law, Jurisprudence, constitution and administrative law carried out intensified cross-study; the whole academic circle, include the scholars of economy and politics also participated in the discussion. The *Real Rights Law* enacted in this way will better meet the actual of China and the requirement of times, and will not become a textbook-type real rights law.[28]

Thirdly, it is good to find some problems which may be ignored in the enactment of *Real Rights Law*. Some constitution law scholars believed that some civil law scholars have the trend to ignore the relevant provisions of the *Constitution* in the course of drafting of *Real Rights Law*,[29] and this kind reminding is favorable for preventing "work behind closed doors". The experience in drafting of *Civil Code* in various countries reveals that, the settlement of this problem requires the legislature to formulate a clear legislative program, including the guiding thoughts and important principle of legislation.

4.2.2 "It's Not Personal"—To Provide Academic Room for Exploration into Constitutionality

Since the "unconstitutional doctrine" is not limited to a few scholars of Jurisprudence such as Professor Gong Xiantian, though the starting point is different, some constitutional scholars have also joined into the "unconstitutional doctrine". Different from the constitution and civil law scholars who actively

---

[27]Zhu (2017).

[28]Ma (2017).

[29]Tong (2006).

participated in the discussion by publishing papers, the promoters of "unconstitutional doctrine" did not publish any academic paper for academic argument, but only expressed opinions via Internet[30] in the form of "Third Question for Some Drafters of *Real Rights Law*" and "Fourth Answer about *Real Rights Law* to Friends". They gradually faded out from the "unconstitutional event", and focused their discussion on academic issues such as interpretation of the *Constitution* and the judgment standard for constitutionality. The atmosphere of the discussion also gradually shifted to "concern oneself with facts and not with individuals", and the "unconstitutional" also shifted from "unconstitutional draft" to "unconstitutional details".[31] This is the precondition for properly exploring into the constitutionality of the *Real Rights Law (draft)*, and provides the academic room for exploration into constitutionality.

4.2.3 *"Overcorrecting"—Viewing Equal Protection by Jumping Out from "Unconstitutional Event"*

Jumping out of the "unconstitutional event", we cast our eyes on the papers about "evaluation on draft" issued before the Public Letter. In fact, with respect to the equal protection of public and private properties, there always exist the "monistic theory" and "trialistic theory" among the civil law scholars. The former believes that the ownership system should not be provided in the *Real Rights Law*, and the latter believes that three different ownership systems, namely state, collective and individual, should be confirmed. In the volume of *Real Rights* in the *2002 Civil Law (draft)*, there is the compromised treatment for "equal protection" which was regarded by "monistic theory" scholars as "half step forward": Since such deliberation draft does not provide "the public properties are sacred and inviolable" or "the state properties are sacred and inviolable", and does not adopt three systems used by traditional socialist civil law to specially protect the state properties, it is praised as "forward"; since it still retains the classification method in the theory of traditional socialist civil law, divides the ownership into "state ownership", "collective ownership" and "private ownership" (Chapters 5, 6 and 7) on the basis of different ownership systems, and fails to clearly reflect the spirit "equal protection for lawful properties", so that it can only be regarded as "half step forward".[32] If these two debates about "equal protection" are linked with each other, we will find that, maybe the discussion carried out at that time is the continuity of the controversy between "monistic theory" and "trialistic theory", and there is the sense of "overcorrecting". Maybe the "unconstitutional doctrine" scholars know nothing about the previous controversy between "monistic theory" and "trialistic theory";

---

[30]Mainly the website of Utopia, http://www.wyzxsx.com.

[31]See Tong (2006).

[32]See Liu (2005).

the "constitutional doctrine" scholars also have never thought that, the compromised "trialistic theory" is marked as "unconstitutional", so that it is understandable that their reaction is slightly strong.

4.2.4   "Civil Law and Socialism"—"Contradictory" or "Thought-Provoking" Combination

The "unconstitutional event" reminds the Writer of the *Civil Law and Socialism* written by Japanese scholar Okamura. Is the Civil Law and Socialism a "contradictory combination" or a "thought-provoking combination"?[33] The sense of "contradictory" and "thought-provoking" can only be felt by those civil law scholars who have experienced such two debates on "equal protection" and upheld the vivid Chinese characteristics[34] of the *Real Rights Law (draft)*. Mr. Jiao Yitang pointed out in 1930 that: "The *Civil Law* is the law used to protect the private rights, so as to maintain the social order. The socialists are those who study and try to eliminate the unequal phenomena in society, so as to improve the society. Their method is different, but their purpose is the same. Therefore, when studying the socialism, the *Civil Law* should be considered and taken as a tool for the improvement of society. In addition, the drafters of the *Civil Law* should carefully study the socialism, and take it as the basis for legislation. … If no practicable solution is obtained, the long-term peace and stability of society will not be realized!"[35] In order to ensure that the compilation of *Civil Code* is constitutional, it is very necessary to correctly understand the relationship between the specific articles of the *Civil Law (draft)* (especially the *Real Rights Law (draft)*) and the basic principles of socialism.

4.2.5   Core of "Unconstitutional Doctrine" and Constitutionality of General Principles of the Civil Law

The four most important reasons of "unconstitutional doctrine" are as follows: First, the abolishment of core articles of the *Constitution* and *General Principles of the Civil Law* by the *Real Rights Law (draft)* is unconstitutional; second, the "equal protection" principle conflicts with the provisions "The socialist public properties are sacred and inviolable" and thus is unconstitutional; third, the *Real Rights Law (draft)* goes against the socialist principles provided in the *Constitution* and the

---

[33]Ji (2003, p. 18).

[34]See Yang (2006).

[35]Ji (2003, p. 14).

1986 General Principles of the Civil Law and thus is unconstitutional; fourth, the *Real Rights Law (draft)* fails to provide "This Law is hereby enacted on the basis of the *Constitution*" and thus is unconstitutional. From the subtitle of the Public Letter —*Public Letter Written for Abolishment of Article 12 of the Constitution and Article 73 of 1986 General Principles of Civil Law*, we can easily find the common logical line of these four reasons: The *1986 General Principles of the Civil Law* provides "on the basis of the Constitution" and "the state properties are sacred and inviolable", so that they are constitutional; the *Real Rights Law (draft)* fails to provide "on the basis of the Constitution" and "The state properties are sacred and inviolable", so that it goes against the socialist principles provided in the *Constitution* and the *1986 General Principles of the Civil Law* and is unconstitutional. The other two reasons are unfolded from different branches of this main logical line.

Therefore, we can conclude that: *General Principles of the Civil Law* is constitutional. This can be said as the common view of all people over recent 20 years, and is also the few common view between "unconstitutional doctrine" scholars and "constitutional doctrine" scholars; otherwise, what is unconstitutional is not the *Real Rights Law*, but *General Principles of the Civil Law* and even the whole theory of civil law. Of course, this is intolerable for all persons who are willing to maintain the results of reform and opening-up. If this conclusion which seems innocuous can be established, hereinafter the constitutionality of *General Principles of the Civil Law* and the *Real Rights Law (draft)* will be demonstrated on the basis of the constitutionality of *General Principles of the Civil Law* and from the viewpoint of civil law, so as to ask for explanation from "unconstitutional doctrine".

4.3 Constitutionality of Essential Civil Law and Real Rights Law

4.3.1 *Constitutionality of Essential Civil Law*

4.3.1.1 Constitutionality of *General Principles of the Civil Law* Acceptable by Both Parties in "Unconstitutional Event"

It is provided in Article 1 of *General Principles of the Civil Law* that, "With a view to protecting the lawful civil rights and interests of citizens and legal persons, to correctly adjusting the civil relationship and meeting the needs of realization of socialist modernization, this Law is hereby enacted on the basis of the *Constitution* and in light of the actual circumstances and practical experience in civil activities in China." This indicates that, the basis of *General Principles of the Civil Law* is the *Constitution*. It is provided in Article 12 of the *Constitution* that: "socialist public properties are sacred and inviolable." It is also provided in Article 73 of *General*

Principles of the Civil Law that: "The state properties are owned by the whole people. The state properties are sacred and inviolable, and may not be misappropriated, looted, divided, intercepted or deducted by any entity or individual." This is the implementation of basic principle of the *Constitution* by *General Principles of the Civil Law* recognized by both parties in "unconstitutional event". Of course, some "constitutional doctrine" scholars believe that, the implementation of basic principle of the *Constitution* by *General Principles of the Civil Law* is far more from that, while the "unconstitutional doctrine" scholars also did not clearly expressed that this is all for constitutionality of *General Principles of the Civil Law*. However, it can be confirmed that, this is the basic common view which can be concluded by both parties.

4.3.1.2 Essential Civil Law and Formal Civil Law

It is well known that, there exist the formal civil law and the essential civil law. The former refers to the systematically-compiled civil legislation, namely the *Civil Code*; the latter collectively refers to the legal norms which adjust the property relationship and personal relationship among equal subjects, which not only include the *Civil Code*, but also include the civil legal norms in other laws, regulations and judicial interpretations. There is no official civil code in China, and the separate civil laws such as *General Principles of the Civil Law*, the *Real Rights Law*, the *Contract Law*, the *Guarantee Law*, the *Marriage Law*, the *Succession Law*, the *Adoption Law* and the *Tort Liability Law* constitute the subject of essential civil law. Therefore, in the current legal system of China, the implementation of basic principles of the *Constitution* by the Civil Law is also realized through the constitutionality of essential civil law.

4.3.2 Constitutionality of Essential Real Rights Law

4.3.2.1 Essential Real Rights Law

Just as formal civil law and essential civil law, there are also formal *Real Rights Law* and essential real rights law. The formal real rights law refers to the *Real Rights Law*, while the essential real rights law collectively refers to the legal norms which adjust the real right relationship among equal subjects, not only including the *Real Rights Law*, but also including the real rights related legal norms in laws such as *General Principles of the Civil Law*, the *Guarantee Law*, the *Land Administration Law*, the *Urban Real Estate Administration Law* and the *Rural land Contract Law*. Therefore, in the current legal system of China, the implementation of basic principles of the *Constitution* by the *Real Rights Law* is also realized through the constitutionality of essential real rights law.

4.3.2.2 Validity of Article 73 of *General Principles of the Civil Law* after the *Real Rights Law* is promulgated

According to the current legislative plan, during the compilation of the *Civil Code*, *General Principles of the Civil Law* will continue to play the role of "basic civil law" for long time. According to the normal practice in drafting of *Civil Law* in China, the *Real Rights Law* does not fully replace Section 1 of Chapter 5 of *General Principles of the Civil Law* as basic article for protection on properties, and legislature also has not declared such contents as invalid. Therefore, Article 73 of *General Principles of the Civil Law* will remain in force and effect, and will be applicable to the whole field of civil property right law.

4.3.2.3 Constitutionality of Essential Real Rights Law

The "unconstitutional doctrine" also notices the fact that *General Principles of the Civil Law* clearly provides 'The socialist public (state) properties are sacred and inviolable', but ignores the major and basic legal principles of *General Principles of the Civil Law* and the *Real Rights Law* as components of essential real rights law, and on this basis obtains the ridiculous conclusion that "The Draft abolishes such article, and thus is not consistent with the basic spirit and provisions of *General Principles of the Civil Law*, violates the continuity principle of legislation and is also unconstitutional". On the contrary, if every law must copy word for word all relevant articles in the *Constitution*, then among the current laws, administrative regulations and local regulations in China, how many are not unconstitutional? In the course of the enactment of *Real Rights Law*, owing to the special civil legislative arrangement made by the legislature, the basic principles and specific articles of the *Constitution* have been fully implemented only thanks to the long-term existence of *General Principles of the Civil Law*. It seems somewhat ridiculous and naïve to believe that the *Real Rights Law (draft)* is unconstitutional for the reason that it fails to mechanically repeat a certain article of the *Constitution* in defiance of the existence of *General Principles of the Civil Law* and the relationship between *General Principles of the Civil Law* and the *Real Rights Law*, and the fact that the *Real Rights Law (draft)* plans to implement the norms of the *Constitution* through detailed and strict rules.[36]

4.3.2.4 Other Arguments and Objections

It is provided in Article 1 of Chapter 1 "General Provisions" in Volume 1 "General Provisions" of the *2002 Civil Law (draft)* that: "With a view to protecting the lawful civil rights and interests of natural persons and legal persons, normalizing the civil

---

[36]Cui and Li (2017).

relationships, and promoting the development of socialist modernization, this Law is hereby enacted in accordance with the *Constitution*." However, Article 1 of Chapter 1 "General Provisions" in Volume 2 "*Real Rights Law*" provides "With a view to protecting the real rights of natural persons and legal persons, maintaining the social and economic order, and promoting the development of socialist modernization, this Law is hereby enacted" rather than "this Law is hereby enacted on the basis of the *Constitution*". The reason is very simple. Since the *Civil Code* rather than the *Real Rights Law* was submitted at that time, the whole *Civil Law (draft)* uses the words "This Law is enacted on the basis of the *Constitution*". It should be noted that, such draft of *Civil Code* also did not provide "The socialist public properties are sacred and inviolable", which is not opposed by "unconstitutional doctrine" scholars. Again, it is provided in Article 1 of Chapter 1 "General Provisions" of the *1995 Guarantee Law* that: "With a view to promoting the raising of funds and circulation of commodities, ensuring the realization of obligatory rights and developing the socialist market economy, this Law is hereby enacted." In fact, the above provisions also fail to copy word by word the relevant article of the *Constitution*, but have not been opposed during a period which is as long as more than 20 years. Then, in the essential real rights law composed of relevant articles of the *Real Rights Law*, *General Principles of the Civil Law* and the *Guarantee Law*, why only the *Real Rights Law (draft)* is subject to such a serious "unconstitutional event" owing to failing to copy word by word the above-mentioned article?

4.3.2.5 Brief Summary

Through the above-mentioned careful and comprehensive study of the contents of the *Real Rights Law (draft)* on the basis of the exploration into basic legal principles of essential real rights law as carried out by the Writer, we can easily draw the conclusion that: the *Real Rights Law* is enacted on the basis of the basic principles of the *Constitution* and is consistent with the basic principles of *General Principles of the Civil Law*, and there is no contradiction.[37] The essential *Real Rights Law* is constitutional.

4.3.3 Will the Words "This Law Is Hereby Enacted on the Basis of the Constitution" Be Written?

It is provided in Article 3 of the *Legislation Law* that: "Legislation shall be conducted under the fundamental principles laid down in the *Constitution*, focusing on economic development, and in adherence to the socialist path, the people's democratic dictatorship, the leadership of the Communist Party of China,

---

[37]Yang (2017).

Marxism-Leninism, Mao Zedong thoughts and Deng Xiaoping theory, and reform and opening up." According to the survey carried out by scholars, Article 1 of some laws does not clearly point out the *Constitution* as the basis of such laws. For example, the *Law on Organization of Court*, the *Law on Organization of Procuratorate*, the *Auction Law*, the *Commercial Bank Law*, the *Negotiable Instrument Law*[38] and the *Guarantee Law* which serves as a part of the essential *Real Rights Law* does not give such provisions. Are all the above-mentioned laws unconstitutional? Some scholars believe that, the possible interpretation is that, maybe the legislature does not take this as an issue that must be specially emphasized. In other words, "on the basis of the *Constitution*" is an undoubtable common view and premise, is a factual state, and requires no value judgment.[39]

The Writer agrees with the opinion of Professor TONG Zhiwei. To enact a law on the basis of the *Constitution* is a self-evident thing, and it does not matter whether the words "this Law is hereby enacted in accordance with the *Constitution*" are contained in laws. However, the practice to write such words in laws for the purpose of stating its basis has been formed in China, and the more important a law is, the more necessary such words are.[40] Therefore, the Writer also agrees with Professor HAN Dayuan, which has, from the viewpoint of legislative techniques, demonstrated the necessity to add such words in the Draft when the Draft is improved.[41] From the fifth-deliberation draft, Article 1 of the *Real Rights Law (draft)* provides "this Law is hereby enacted in accordance with the *Constitution*".

4.4 How Should Protection on Real Rights Meet the Requirements of Article 12 of the *Constitution*

4.4.1 Essence of Issue: Constitutionality of Protection Method for Real Rights

From the viewpoint of right protection in civil law, the provisions "The socialist public properties are sacred and inviolable" in Article 12 of the *Constitution* are an issue about right protection. In civil law, the claim for right protection includes primary claim and secondary claim.[42] The claim for real right provided in Chapter 3 "Protection on Real Rights" of the *Real Rights Law (draft)* is the primary claim for real rights, and the corresponding secondary claim is the claim for compensation for damage, removal of obstacles, elimination of dangers, apology and tort injunction as provided in the tort law for protection on real rights. The Writer believes that, the

---

[38]Han (2006).
[39]Han (2006).
[40]See Tong (2006).
[41]Han (2006).
[42]Yang (2005).

issue whether the *Real Rights Law* complies with Article 12 of the *Constitution* is the issue about constitutionality of protection method for real rights. Though this analysis has gone beyond the visual field of "unconstitutional doctrine", in consideration of the fact this is also the hot issue in the civil law circles, the Writer hereby performs the interpretation obligation of civil law, and thus carries out careful and comprehensive analysis.

4.4.2   Legislative Technique Issue About "Socialist Public Properties Are Sacred and Inviolable"

In the civil legislation at that time, the term "real rights" was not used. It is generally believed in civil law that, the provisions in the Chapter "Property Ownership and Property Rights Relating to Property Ownership" of *General Principles of the Civil Law* are actually the provisions about real rights. However, the property right in civil law has particular connotation, and means the right which takes the property interests as contents and directly embodies a certain physical interest. It is a concept corresponding to non-property right. The property rights are the set of several civil rights, so that the property law contains several systems in civil law, such as real rights law, obligatory rights law, intellectual property law and succession right law, etc. The "unconstitutional doctrine" also requires that the "relationship between public (state, collective) real rights and real rights of citizens" should be discussed firstly, which indicates that, on the basis of the common view, real rights are different from property, and the property is the upper seat concept of real rights.

As the fundamental law, the *Constitution* should fully provide "The socialist public properties are sacred and inviolable"; as a basic civil law generated in a special historical period, it is very necessary to add "The state properties are sacred and inviolable" into the provisions "The Civil Law of the People's Republic of China adjusts the property relationship and personal relationship between citizens, between legal persons and between citizen and legal person" of Article 2 *General Principles of the Civil Law*. However, as a part of the property law, the *Real Rights Law* can't go beyond its authority and give provisions on issues about the whole property protection, and can at most provide "The socialist public real rights are sacred and inviolable". On the basis of the *Constitution*, we should also provide "The lawful private real rights of citizens are inviolable".

This conclusion is obtained by the Writer after carefully and comprehensively studying the standing of the *Real Rights Law* in the whole civil law and legal system. However, the Writer also realizes that, at the "time of right explosion", new properties are emerging in an endless stream, and we can't expect that the provisions of the *Constitution* "The socialist public properties are sacred and inviolable" will be implemented by enumerating the socialist public "real rights", "obligatory right", "copyright", "trademark right" and "patent right" as sacred and inviolable, because the property rights can't be fully listed. At the level of legislative techniques, even if no comprehensive enumeration is given, it is obviously inappropriate to provide such an article in all possible laws and regulations. Therefore, from the viewpoint of legislative techniques of the whole civil law, it is impossible for the words "The socialist public properties are sacred and inviolable" and the words "The socialist public real rights are sacred and inviolable" to be written in the *Real Rights Law*, and this only is the consideration at the level of legislative techniques. However, this does not mean that, Article 12 of the *Constitution* can't be implemented in *Real Rights Law* field.

4.4.3 Characteristics of Legislative Techniques of Dual Protection Mechanism in Civil Law

4.4.3.1 Characteristics of Legislative Techniques of Claim for Real Right

Though the *Real Rights Law* is a right law rather than a right protection law, it also involves the issue about the protection given by claim for real right. The claim for real right is a claim arising from real rights, and can be applied when the ownership and jus in re aliena are infringe upon or may be infringed upon. With respect to the protection on socialist public real rights, special attention must be paid to the two characteristics of claim for real right: The first is that the claim for real right is not restricted by limitation of action; the second is that, as compared with the claim in tort, the claim for real right does not take fault as a requisite. With respect to the protection provided in civil law for real rights, either public real rights or private real rights, the claim for real right is the highest protection. Logically, the so-called "highest" means that it is impossible to reach any higher level. Therefore, in the system of claim for real right, we can't expect that it will develop the special protection on socialist public properties by itself. This is not an issue about standpoint, but an issue about legislative techniques caused by characteristics of legal system.

4.4.3.2 Characteristics of Legislative Techniques for Claim in Tort

1. Application Standard for Imputation Principle in Tort Law

The controversy on claim for real right and claim in tort is a hot issue in the course of the enactment of *Real Rights Law*. Some scholars proposed that, the claim for real right should be replaced by claim in tort, and as for the characteristic that fault is not a requisite of claim for real rights, the no-fault principle may be applied.[43] What is similar to this opinion is the question implied by "unconstitutional doctrine": Can we apply the no-fault liability principle for all infringement on "socialist public properties", so as to make them "sacred and inviolable"? The Writer believes that, the above-mentioned two opinions are misunderstanding on systematic function and application standard of imputation principle in tort law. The imputation principle in tort law is the core of tort law theory, while the core of imputation is the criterion. The criterion and basis for imputation of tort liabilities are three legal value judgment factors confirmed by law: fault, damage result and equitable factors. The imputation of tort means that, in light of different situations of tort and on the basis of different legal value judgment factors, the tort liabilities are allocated to the person who is liable for damage.[44] More specifically, the imputation principle is based on "behavior criterion" rather than "object criterion". In China, the imputation principle system for tort liabilities is composed of fault liability principle, presumed-default liability principle and no-fault liability principle, and the equitable liability principle is not an imputation principle. This system is divided on the basis of "behavior criterion". Therefore, it is impossible to distinguish between public real rights and private real rights on the basis of different owners. Similarly, the above-mentioned thinking that the claim for real right should be replaced with the claim in tort based on no-fault liabilities principle is also a decomposition of imputation principles for tort law, and thus is questionable.

2. Exploration into Possibility to Use "Tort Injunction" to Specially Protect Public Properties

In the field of intellectual property rights, China has introduced the "injunction" protection as provided in TRIPS. The Writer believes that, this is a different protection mode provided on the basis of different object, and in the field of intellectual property rights, such special tort liability as destruction of infringing products is also applied. Then, can we use the "injunction" protection to achieve the purpose of implementing Article 12 of the Constitution?

The injunction means a measure taken to prevent the rights from being damaged and infringed. It is provided in Paragraph 1 of Article 162 of the *Opinions on Several Issues Relating to Implementation of General Principles of the Civil Law of the People's Republic of China (for trial implementation)* that "In a litigation, in case it is necessary to stop the infringement, remove the obstacles or eliminate the dangers, the people's court may, at the request from the party concerned or by virtue of its powers and duties, give a ruling in advance".[45] The tort injunction is a compulsory measure whereby the court, at the request from the party concerned,

---

[43]See Wei (2013).
[44]See Yang (2004).
[45]Yang (2005).

orders the infringing party to cease a tort which is being implemented or is about to be implemented, so as to prevent the right holder from being infringed upon. The purpose of tort injunction is to protect the right holder against the infringement which is being implemented or is about to be implemented, so as to prevent the occurrence of irretrievable damage. As compared with the claim for damage compensation, the claim for injunction can be realized quickly and in time, can save the long litigation period faced by claim for damage compensation, and can protect the interests of injured person in time and prevent the increase of damage. In order to meet the requirements for participation into WTO, the newly-revised *Patent Law*, the *Trademark Law* and the *Copyright Law* of China provide the injunction system as provided in Article 41 of TRIPS. Two judicial interpretations issued by the Supreme People's Court, namely the *Several Provisions on Issues about Legal Application for Stopping Infringement upon Patent Right before Litigation* and the *Interpretation on Issues about Legal Application for Stopping Infringement upon Registered Trademark Right and Preserving Evidences before Litigation*, also give special provisions for application of temporary injunction.

The Writer believes that, in order to improve the claim system in civil law of China, and get in line with the internationally-recognized rules, it is necessary to provide the tort injunction. It can not only be applied in the field of intellectual property rights, but also be applied in the field of real rights, personality rights and identity rights, so as to fully protect the lawful rights and interests of right holder. With respect to specific system, the tort injunction must be petitioned by the concerned party, the court will not initiate the tort injunction on its own initiative, there should be the urgency to immediately cease the infringement, remove the obstacles or eliminate the dangers, and the applicant must also provide guaranty.[46] However, it is necessary to specially point out that, though civil law of China applies the injunction in the field of intellectual property rights on the basis of an "object criterion", the basis for such "object criterion" is the attribute of the object of property right rather than attribute of owner. Therefore, such criterion is different from the criterion proposed by Prof. Gong Xiantian for public property rights and private property rights. The proposal brought forth by the Writer about using the "tort injunction" to protect real rights is based on the legal theory that the claim for damage compensation is not fully same as claim for ceasing the infringement and claim for removing the obstacles, and under emergency circumstance the tort injunction can be applied to cease the infringement and removal the obstacle. This protection is not linked with attributes of ownership system. All lawful real rights may be protected by tort injunction, and the reason therefore is as same as that for claim for real right.

---

[46]Yang (2005).

4.4.4 *Implementation of Article 12 of the* **Constitution** *Through Special Real Rights Law*

The *Law on State-owned Assets of Enterprises* was enacted in 2008 and implemented in 2009. The Writer believes that, the "socialist public properties" are not fully equal to state-owned assets, and at least also include the collective property which is an important public property. Therefore, it is advised by the Writer to enact a *Public Property Law* as special real rights law. Then, can Article 12 of the *Constitution* be implemented through the special real rights law?

4.4.4.1 Ability Issue of General Real Rights Law to Protect the State-Owned Assets

Relative to the *Law on State-owned Assets of Enterprises* or the future possible *Public Property Law*, the *Real Rights Law* is actually the general real rights law. In fact, as mentioned by Professor Zhang Qianfan, it seems that the unconstitutional doctrine scholars did not mention two provisions in the *Constitution* which are more helpful for them, namely "The foundation of the socialist economic system of the People's Republic of China is the socialist public ownership of production materials, namely the ownership by the whole people and collective ownership by laborers" (Paragraph 1 of Article 6); "The state-owned economy, namely the socialist economy under system of ownership by the whole people, is the leading force in national economy. The state protects the consolidation and development of state-owned economy" (Article 7).[47]

The Writer firmly believes that, our country is a socialist state, which is undoubtable and must be upheld. Therefore, the basic goal of the *Real Rights Law* is to "maintain the order of socialist market economy, and maintain the basic economic system of the state". In the course of the enactment of *Real Rights Law*, importance shall be attached to the embodiment of state ownership system. This is the essential requirement of socialist society in China, and is also the internal logic of the socialist legal system under which the *Real Rights Law* exists.[48] Obviously, we may not go back to such "sacredness" which violates the basic law of market economy: "The return of illegally-occupied properties of the state will not be restricted by limitation of action, no matter whether the occupier has any fault, no matter whether the occupier knows the fact, and no matter whether such properties are directly obtained or transferred for several times; in case there is dispute over the ownership of state and other persons with respect to any property and the ownership can't be determined, it shall be resumed that such property is owned by

---

[47]Zhang (2006).
[48]Ma (2017).

the state."[49] Taking the economy under system of public ownership as main part is the outstanding embodiment of ownership system structure in China, but this does not mean that the legal status in exercise of such ownership is higher than economy under other ownership system.[50] Adjusting the property relationship is the function jointly undertaken by several legal departments, and it is unpractical to let the *Real Rights Law* undertake all of such task, but such issues must be comprehensively considered in the enactment of the *Real Rights Law*.[51]

The ideal held by the "unconstitutional doctrine" scholars to achieve all goals through one battle means that they hope to achieve the purpose of protection on state-owned assets through the *Real Rights Law*, and take whether such purpose can be achieved as the criterion for judging whether the *Real Rights Law* is unconstitutional. This is not only a too high expectation, but also illogical. As the saying goes, "one might be a master in his own special field". This is also the case of law. The *Real Rights Law* is a general real rights law which "determines the ownership of properties, protects the real rights of right holders and brings the role of properties into full play". Though it can pay certain role in "maintaining the order of socialist market economy and maintaining the basic economic system of the state", its "ability is limited", and can't become the "law for protection on state-owned assets". The protection on state-owned assets may be realized by separately enacting special real rights laws, so as to develop the state-owned assets by means of industrial policy and admission to non-competitive fields.[52]

4.4.4.2 Special Real Rights Law Should Provide that the Procuratorial Organ May File Public Interest Lawsuit

Whether the state-owned properties are scared does not depend on whether the relevant words are written in the *Constitution* or other law, but depend on whether the ownership of state-owned properties is protected.[53] In fact, over recent years, the civil procedure law community held an active and positive attitude towards the protection on state-owned assets by procuratorial organs through public interest litigation. Some scholars believe that, the provisions about supervision in the general provisions of civil procedure law are opened norms, and are also authorization-type norms. They have the characteristics such as principleness, generality and originality, and may be evolved into various specific forms. Within this scope, the people's procuratorate may creatively exercise the supervision authority.[54] As for many cases about infringement on public interests, a lawful

---

[49]China Encyclopaedia (1984).

[50]Ma (2017).

[51]Zhu (2017).

[52]See Hao (2006).

[53]Gao (2017).

[54]Tang (2004).

organ which can initiate the litigation in the capacity of plaintiff can't be found. In order to fully protect the interests of people, the procuratorate should be granted the right to file the civil public interest lawsuit.[55] The focus placed by procuratorial organs on civil litigations should be gradually shifted to the civil cases which involve public interests. In the cases involving loss of state-owned assets, the procuratorial organs, as the legal supervisory organs of the state, should investigate into the civil liabilities for infringement upon socialist public properties.[56] On June 27, 2017, the NPC Standing Committee adopted the amendment to the *Administrative Litigation Law*. One paragraph is added into Article 25 of such law as Paragraph 4: "In case in the course of performance of its duties, a people's procuratorate finds that an administrative organ which undertakes the supervisory and administrative duties in the fields of protection on ecologic environment & resourced, safety of food & drug, protection on state-owned properties and transfer of right to use state-owned land illegally exercises its powers and duties or fails to exercise such duties, and thus the interests of the state or the public interests are infringed upon, such people's procuratorate shall give supervisory advices to such administrative organ, and urge such administrative organ to legally perform its duties. Where such administrative organ fails to legally perform its duties, the people's procuratorate shall legally initiate litigation in the people's court."

The Writer believes that, the fields which involve or are closely linked with the interests of the state or the public interests shall fall in the scope for which the procuratorial organ may initiate civil litigation if necessary,[57] and the cases involving loss of state-owned assets are surely covered by such scope.[58] As for the civil cases which involve the public interests, the people's procuratorates should have the authority to initiate litigation, participle into litigation and initiate retrial. The participation into civil cases which involve public interests by the procuratorates does not violate the legal principle of civil procedure, is in line with the international practices, and is urgently required by the actuality in China.[59] The legal provisions relating to state-owned assets in various countries throughout the world reveal that, there are three manners wherein the procuratorial organs initiate civil litigations: to separately initiate the litigation, to participate in initiation of litigation and to jointly file lawsuit. In consideration of the actuality that the protection on public properties is absent, it is advised by the Writer to provide in the special real rights law—*Public Property Law* in the future that, under the circumstance that the public properties are infringed upon and the right holders fail to exercise the rights, the procuratorates will be granted the right to separately initiate

---

[55]Chang (2004).

[56]Tian (2004).

[57]Jiang and Duan (2000).

[58]Yang (2000).

[59]Zhang (2004).

the civil litigation for protecting the public properties and petition the courts to issue the tort injunction. The specific system should be further studied by the civil law community and procedure law community.

References

Chang Yi, "Three Principle Thoughts on Civil Checking and Supervising", *Modern Law Science*, No. 1, 2004.

China Encyclopaedia, Encyclopaedia of China Publishing House, 1984, p. 52.

Cui Jianyuan, Li Yongfeng, "The *Real Rights Law* is the Law to Advance the Reform and Open", available at http://www.civillaw.com.cn/weizhang/default.asp?id=24961, the latest access time: August 31, 2017.

Gao Fuping, "Real Rights Law Issue or Constitution Law Issue—Reflection on whether the *Real Rights Law* is Unconstitutional", available at http://www.civillaw.com.cn/WANGkan/msfwk/index.aspx, the latest access time: August 31, 2017.

Guo Songmin, "Dose *Real Rights Law(Draft)* have hidden positions", *Reporters' Notes*, No. 4, 2006.

Han Dayuan, "Constitutional Issue of the Debate of *Real* Rights Law*Draft*", *Law Science*, No. 3, 2006.

Hao Tiechuan, "My Point of view on the Violation of Constitution by the Draft of *Real Rights Law* ", *Law Science*, No. 8, 2006.

He Zhongzhou, "*Real Rights Law*—A Century Bumpy", *China Newsweek*, No. 9, 2006.

Ji Xiuping, "On the Equal Protection of Real Rights and the Sacredness of Public Properties", Seeker, No. 5, 2006.

Jiang Wei,Duan Houshen, "On Civil Process Filed by Procuratorial Organ", *Modern Law Science*, No, 6, 2000.

Jiao Hongchang, "Constitutionality Analysis of the Real rights law Draft", *Law Science*, No. 3, 2006.

Li Shoushuang, "Both Sides Lose in the *Real* Rights Law*(Draft)*", available at http://www.iolaw.org.cn/showNews.asp?id=14664,the latest access time: August 31, 2017.

Liang Huixing, "Several Problems in Compiling Chinese Real rights law", *Chinese Journal of Law*, No. 4, 2000.

Liang Huixing, *Draft of Chinese Civil Code with Reasons*, Law Press, 2004.

Liang Huixing, *Recommended Draft of Real* Rights Law *of China*, Social Sciences Academic Press, 2000.

Liang Huixing, *Scholar-proposed Draft of Civil Code of People's Republic of China*, Law Press, 2003.

Liu Baoyu, "Combination of the Categorization of Ownership and the Principle of Equal Protection", *Law Review*, No. 6, 2005.

Lv Juan, "Lang-Gu Dispute in Law community", *Law & Life*, No. 2, 2006.

Ma Junju, "The Aim and Function of the Real Rights Law and Erossion of State Assets", available at http://www.civillaw.com.cn/weizhang/default.asp?id=24962, the latest access time: August 31, 2017.

Meng Qinguo, "Recommended Draft of Real rights law of China", *Law Review*, No. 5, 2002.

Ji Okamura, *Civil Law and Socialism*, translated by LIU Renhang, ZHANG Mingci, China University of Political Science and Law Press, 2003.

Tang Weijian, "On Several problems of the Scope of Civil Checking and Supervising", *Modern Law Science*, No. 1, 2004.

Tian Pingan, "Two Thoughts on Civil Checking and Supervising",*Modern Law Science*, No. 1, 2004.

Tong Zhiwei, *"Draft Real Rights Law* Revisited: Constitutional Issues and Their Solutions", *Law Science*, No. 7, 2006.

Tong Zhiwei, "How Should the Real Rights Law Draft Pass the Door of the Constitution", *Law Science*, No. 3, 2006.

Wang Liming, *Recommended Draft of Real rights law of China and Explanation Thereon*, China Legal Publishing House, 2001.

Wang Liming, *Scholar-proposed Draft of Civil Code of China and the Legislation Reasons*, Law Press, 2005.

Wang Liming, *The draft of Chinese civil code and its interpretation*, China Legal Publishing House, 2004.

Wei Zhenying, *Separating Civil Liability from Obligation*, Peking University Press, 2013.

Xu Guodong, *Green Civil Code Draft*, Social Sciences Academic Press, 2004.

Xu Jian, "The *Real Rights Law* should Assimilate the Reform Achievements over the Last Decade", *Natural Resource Economics of China*, No. 4, 2006.

Yang Lixin, "Checking and Supervising on Civil and Administrative litigations and Judicial Justice", *Chinese Journal of Law*, No. 4, 2000.

Yang Lixin, Cao Yanchun, "On the Claim System of Protection of the Civil Right and Their Inner Relation", *Journal of Henan Administrative Institute of Politics and Law*, No. 4, 2005.

Yang Lixin, "Comment on the Distinct Chinese Features of Real Law Draft", *Journal of Henan Administrative Institute of Politics and Law*, No. 3, 2006.

Yang Lixin, "Closing Words of the Symposium on the *Real Rights Law* and the Theory of Constructing Socialist Harmonious Society in China", available at: http://www.civillaw.com.cn/weizhang/default.asp?id=24985, the latest access time: August 31, 2017.

Yang Lixin, *On Tort Law(the 2nd Edition)*, People's Court Press, 2004, pp. 110–111.

Zhang Qianfan, "Uses and Abuses of the Constitution: How to Deal with the Constitutional Problems of the Real rights law Draft", *Law Science*, No. 3, 2006.

Zhang Wusheng: "On the People's Procuratorate's Authority of Starting Retrial and Supervising Other Civil Trial Activity", *Modern Law Science*, No, 1, 2004.

Zhu Jingwen, "Thinking on the Controversy over the *Real Rights Law (Draft)*", available at: http://www.civillaw.com.cn/weizhang/default.asp?id=25384,the latest access time: August 31, 2017.

Zhu Jingwen, "Understanding from Argument of *Draft of Real* Rights Law, available at: http://www.civillaw.com.cn/weizhang/default.asp?id=25384, the latest access time: August 31, 2017.

Chapter 5
Constitutionality of Legal Interpretation—Taking Interpretation of Article 166 and 167 of the *Real Rights Law* as an Example

Easement is a new system in the *Real Rights Law* of China. In Chapter 14 of the *Real Rights Law*, 1 4 articles are used to give the framework provisions for the basic issues about easement. From the viewpoint of legal interpretation, the Writer analyzes the possible constitutionality-related doubts in Article 166 and 167 of the *Real Rights Law*, in the hope that the academic circle will pay attention to the defects in legislative techniques of the *Real Rights Law*, and formulate the corresponding countermeasures.

5.1 Possible Doubt Existing in Article 166 and 167 of the *Real Rights Law*

It is provided in Article 166 of the *Real Rights Law* that: "When the dominant tenement as well as the right to the contracted management of land, the right to use land for construction or the right to use house site thereon is partially transferred, and if the easement is involved in the transferred part, the transferee shall enjoy the easement at the same time." The analysis on structure of this Article reveals that, the first part of this Article actually describes two legal facts, namely the partial transfer of "dominant tenement" and the partial transfer of "the right to the contracted management of land and the right to use land for construction". It is provided in Paragraph 4 of Article 10 of the *Constitution* that: "No organization or individual may appropriate, buy, sell or otherwise engage in the transfer of land by unlawful means. The rights to the use of land may be transferred according to law." Therefore, any provision about transfer of land is unconstitutional. In general, the literal meaning of laws shall be interpreted in accordance with the common meaning of words and phrases, because laws are established for all social members, and most of legal concepts come from the words used in daily life. The literal meaning obtained on the basis of general use of language constitutes the starting

© China University of Political Science and Law Press 2020
Z. Wang, *On the Constitutionality of Compiling a Civil Code of China*,
https://doi.org/10.1007/978-981-13-7900-0_5

point of interpretation, and become the boundary of interpretation.[1] The comparative analysis on the above-mentioned articles reveals that, the partial transfer of "dominant tenement" obviously violates the provisions of the *Constitution*. There are also similar doubts in the provisions about partial transfer of "servient tenement" in Article 167 of the *Real Rights Law*.

It is well known that, the enactment of the *Real Rights Law* is full of twists and turns. After the said law was submitted for deliberation as Volume 2 of the *Civil Law (draft)* at the end of 2002, it was amended for eight times and finally adopted. It goes without saying that the *Real Rights Law* is enacted on the basis of the *Constitution*.[2] After the "unconstitutional event" in 2005, and from the Fifth-deliberation Draft, it is clearly stated that "This Law is hereby enacted on the basis of the *Constitution*." To study the relevant articles in every *Real Rights Law (draft)* is an important historical interpretation method, which can make sure the legislative policies and legislative purpose of the legislature during enactment of a law.[3] What Article 184 and 185 of the First Deliberation Draft provide is the partial transfer of "the right to the contracted management of land and the right to use land for construction", and what Article 178 and 179 of the Second Deliberation Draft provide are the division and partial transfer of "the right to the contracted management of land and the right to use land for construction". From the Third Deliberation Draft, namely the "draft for solicitation of public opinions", Article 176 and 177 use the terms "dominant tenement" and "servient tenement", adopt the expression "partial transfer of dominant tenement/servient tenement as well as the right to the contracted management of land, the right to use land for construction and the right to use house site on dominant tenement/servient tenement", and add the provisions about partial transfer of "the right to use house site". In the easement part of the *Summary of Opinions from People throughout the Country for Draft of the Real Rights Law*[4] issued by NPC, no opposition was given towards this issue. The subsequent "fourth-deliberation draft", "fifth-deliberation draft", "sixth-deliberation draft" and "seventh-deliberation draft" also adopt this expression. It should be noted that, the final "deliberation draft" deleted the provisions about partial transfer of "the right to use house site",[5] adopted the current

---

[1]See Karl (2005, p. 219).

[2]Wang (2006).

[3]See Wang (2001, p. 226).

[4]See "Advices on the Draft of Real rights law from the Masses" and "Advices on the Draft of Real rights law from the Masses (Continued)", *The People's Congress of China*, No. 15, 16, 2005.

[5]For the cause for the deletion of the provisions about partial transfer of "the right to use house site", the Writer thinks that they are in conflict with Article 153 of the *Real Rights Law*: "the acquisition, exercise and transfer of the right to use house site are subject to the *Land Administration Law* and other laws and relevant national regulations". However, subject to Paragraph 4, Article 2 of the *Land Administration Law*: "after selling and leasing the house, if the rural villagers re-apply for the home site, the application will not be approved." In essence, it is prohibited to independently transfer the home site, and it can only be transferred pursuant to "land subject to house" based on the house transfer.

expression, and was finally adopted. Thus it can be seen that, in the whole process and at the last phase of deliberation of the *Real Rights Law*, Article 166 and 167 have been carefully deliberated, so that such a low-level mistake would not be made.

In fact, the above-mentioned doubt is at the level of literal interpretation. The legal interpretation must start with literal interpretation. As long as the meaning of words in law is clear and will not generate any ridiculous result, the law shall be firstly interpreted on the basis of literal meaning.[6] This is the generally-recognized legal interpretation rules. If the literal interpretation leads to contradiction or may distort the true meaning of law, the reasoning interpretation should be carried out. In principle, no interpretation method may give the interpretation conclusion which is against the result of literal interpretation, unless the literal meaning conflicts with the true intention and legislative purpose of articles. At that time, the exceptional interpretation must meet the purpose of law and keep in line with the spirit of law.[7] Though Professor ZHU Suli determines that, it is impossible to bring forth a perfect interpretation method for law at logical level or analysis level,[8] the Writer believes that, this is only a macro judgment, and will not prevent use from carry out interpretation for doubts involved in Article 166 and 167 of the *Real Rights Law*. As for interpretation of law, it is necessary to adopt the interpretation which leads to the validity of articles as much as possible within the permitted scope of literal interpretation. As for the doubts involved in Article 166 and 167, the validity is firstly embodied in constitutionality, so as to ensure the authority and validity of legal system. The constitutionality interpretation means that the legal norms at lower level will be interpreted on the basis of the *Constitution* and legal norms at higher level, so as to maintain the consistency of legal order.[9] The requirement of interpretation is: among the interpretations which may be obtained on the basis of literal meaning and context, the interpretation which meets the principles of the *Constitution* and can be maintained should be selected.[10] Hereinafter, aiming at the validity and reasonableness of contents of articles, and under the interpretation theory, Article 166 and 167 of the *Real Rights Law* will be studied.

5.2 Path Analysis of Legal Interpretation

On the basis of literal interpretation, to constitutionally interpret Article 166 and 167 of the *Real Rights Law*, there are two interpretation approaches available: The first is to extensively interpret the concept "transfer", so as to obtain the reasonable

---

[6]See Kong (2004).
[7]See Liang (1995, p. 246).
[8]Su (1998).
[9]See Liang (1995, pp. 230–231).
[10]See Karl (2005, p. 221).

literal meaning other than "sales"; the second is to, on the basis of the system factors of the *Real Rights Law*, carry out the systematic interpretation for "dominant/servient tenement", so as to obtain the reasonable literal meaning other than "land". The so-called system factors include external system and internal system. The former is the formulation system for laws, and the latter is the internal structure, principle and value judgment of legal order.[11]

Extensive interpretation is an interpretation method whereby the literal meaning of articles is extended under the circumstance that the literal meaning is too narrow and can't represent the legislative intention, so as to correctly interpret the meaning of law.[12] The extensive interpretation is based on the precondition that all terms will be interpreted as plurality, and may not go beyond the possible scope of literal meaning. In addition, if the results obtained by extensive interpretation go beyond the possible scope of literal meaning, such interpretation may not be applied as laws.[13] According to the basic rules of literal interpretation, when a same concept is used in the same law or different laws, in principle, such concept shall be interpreted in the same way,[14] unless the legislature intentionally changes the connotation. By comparing the provisions of Article 147 of the *Real Rights Law* "In case the buildings, fixtures and their affiliated facilities are transferred, exchanged, used as equity contributions or endowed, the right to use land for construction occupied by the aforesaid buildings, fixtures and their affiliated facilities shall be disposed of concurrently." With the provisions of Article 32 of the *Urban Real Estate Administration Law*: "When the real estate is transferred or mortgaged, the ownership of the housing and the use right of land occupied by such housing will simultaneously be transferred or mortgaged", it is clear that, the concept "transfer" in the *Urban Real Estate Administration Law* is intentionally divided by the legislature into "transfer, exchange, contribution or endowment" in the *Real Rights Law*. It is provided in Article 37 of the *Urban Real Estate Administration Law* that: "Transfer of real estate means the behavior that the real estate right holder transfers the real estate to others by means of sales, donation or other legal means." It is thus clear that, the word "transfer" in Article 147 of the *Real Rights Law* is equivalent to the word "sales" in Article 37 of the *Urban Real Estate Administration Law*.

In order to extensively interpret the concept "transfer" in the *Real Rights Law*, the most valuable attempt is to consider whether the conversion of collective-owned land into state-owned land can be deemed as transfer of land. In the *Real Rights Law*, the concept "transfer" is used for 62 times, the concept "sales" is used for 2 times, and among the articles, the article which has the relatively high reference value for the purpose of interpretation is Article 28: "Where a real right is created, changed, transferred or eliminated for a legal document of the people's court or arbitration commission or a requisition decision of the people's government, etc.,

---

[11]See Wang (2001, pp. 223–226).

[12]See Liang (1995, p. 222).

[13]See Karl (2005, p. 219).

[14]See Liang (1995, p. 214).

the real right shall become effective upon the effectiveness of the legal document or the requisition decision of the people's court." In such provisions, the change in real right which may be caused by "legal document of the people's court or arbitration commission" include "creation, change, transfer or elimination", then whether the "requisition decision of people's government" can be deemed as "transfer" will not affect the descriptive manner used by such article. Therefore, there is the logical room for separate analysis. It is provided in Paragraph 1 of Article 42 of the *Real Rights Law* that: "To meet the needs of public interests, collectively-owned lands, premises owned by entities and individuals or other real estate may be expropriated in accordance with the power scope and procedures provided by laws." It is provided in Paragraph 2 that: "As for the expropriation of collectively-owned land, it is necessary to, according to law and in full amount, pay such fees as land compensation fees, placement subsidies, compensations for the above-ground fixtures of the lands and seedlings, arrange for social security fees for the farmers whose land is expropriated, secure their livelihood and safeguard their legitimate rights and interests." It is provided in Paragraph 4 of Article 2 of the Land Administration Law that: "The state may make expropriation or requisition on land according to law for public interests, but shall give compensations accordingly." It is provided in Article 51 that: "The standards for land compensation and method of resettlement for land expropriated for building large and medium-sized water conservancy projects and hydroelectric power projects shall be determined separately by the State Council." The comparison of provisions of the above-mentioned articles reveals that, what is paid for expropriation of land is "compensation" rather than the equal consideration in "sales". Therefore, the so-called attempt of extensive interpretation has gone beyond the scope of "transfer" under literal interpretation and should not be adopted. In addition, from the viewpoint of effect of change in real rights, the expropriation of land is an original obtainment of rights, and will eliminate the rights originally attached to the land. Therefore, the result is neither "transfer" nor "change", but the elimination of ownership of collective land and the creation of ownership of state-owned land. This result is described as "conversion" in laws, and such descriptive method has been established in the *Land Administration Law* and the *Urban Real Estate Administration Law* and is also used in the first sentence of Article 43 of the *Real Rights Law* "The state provides special protection for farm lands, strictly restricts the conversion of farm lands into lands for construction and controls the aggregate quantity of lands for construction.". Therefore, the extensive interpretation which regards the inclusion of collective-owned land into state-owned land as "transfer" is not acceptable.

Since it is impossible to clarify the connotation of concept "transfer" through extensive interpretation so as to meet the requirements of "constitutionality" of the transfer of "dominant/servient tenement", the only possible interpretation route left is to carry out the systematic interpretation of the concept "dominant/servient tenement".

5.3 Goal of Legal Interpretation

5.3.1 Adjustment Object of Chapter 14 "Easement" in the Real Rights Law

Maybe many readers are too impatient to remind the Writer that, it is provided in Paragraph 1 of Article 156 of the *Real Rights Law* that: "An easement holder shall be entitled to make use of the real estate of someone else according to the contract so as to increase the efficiency of his own real estate." It is provided in Paragraph 2 that: The expression of "real estate of someone else" as mentioned in the preceding Paragraph shall be the servient tenement, and the expression of "one's own real estate" shall be the dominant tenement. The rule of literal interpretation is that, after a daily expression becomes a legal term, it shall be interpreted in accordance with the special meaning in law.[15] Therefore, it seems that the issue is simple and clear. The real estate includes not only land but also other real estate, so that these two articles involve no problem. However, that is not the case. It is necessary to carry out the systematic interpretation on the provisions of Chapter 14 "Easement" in the *Real Rights Law*, identify the adjustment object pre-set by the legislation, and then give the answer.

It is provided in Article 161 of the *Real Rights Law* that: "The term of easement shall be stipulated by the parties concerned, however, it can not exceed the remnant term of the right to the contracted management of land, the right to use land for construction or any other usufructuary right." It is provided in Article 162 that: "In case a land owner enjoys or assumes the easement, when the right to the contracted management of land or the right to use house site is established, the holder of the right to the contracted management of land or the right to use house site may continue enjoying or assuming the established easement." It is provided in Article 163 that: "In case the right to the contracted management of land, the right to use land for construction and the right to use house site or any other usufructuary right on the land has already been created, the land owner shall not establish any easement without consent of the aforesaid usufructuary right holder." The right to the contracted management of land and the right to use house site provided in the usufructuary rights volume of the *Real Rights Law* are the usufructuary rights which take land as object. In practice, the right to use land for construction is mainly attached to land, and the right to use land for construction established "aboveground or underground" provided in Article 136 is actually the layered right to use land for construction which takes space as object.[16] It is thus clear that, as a subordinated usufructuary right, the original intention of the legislation is to establish such easement on land and space.

---

[15]See Liang (1995, p. 214).
[16]See Yang (2007).

We may also use the historical interpretation method again, so as to identify the value judgment and purpose of legislature when enacting the law. This will be helpful for understanding on literal interpretation, and define the scope of activities of literal interpretation.[17] In the enactment of the *Real Rights Law*, the draft proposed by scholars served as important academic foundation. It is provided in Paragraph 2 of Article 192 of the *Real Rights Law (draft)* presided over by Professor WANG Liming that: "In case the exercise of easement is related to a divided part of land according to its nature, such easement shall only exist with respect to such part of land."[18] It is provided in Article 483 of the *Real Rights Law (draft)* presided over by Professor LIANG Huixing that: "After the dominant tenement is divided, for the sake of convenience and interests of divided parts, the use right of adjacent land shall still exist in every part. However, in case the use right of adjacent land is only related to a divided part of land according to its nature, such right shall only exist with respect to such part of land. After the servient tenement is divided, the burdens undertaken for use right of adjacent land shall still exists in divided parts. However, in case such burdens are only related to a divided part of land according to the nature of use right of adjacent land, such burdens shall only be undertaken by the relevant part of land."[19] It is thus clear that, for either the legislature or semi-legislature, though the nominally-designed easement takes real estate as object, the land is essentially taken as the only thinking object and the prototype of legislative adjustment.

Though the conclusion different from that obtained from simple interpretation is obtained above, the interpretation of legislative purpose still may not go beyond the restriction of literal interpretation, because literal meaning is not only the starting point of legal interpretation, but also the ending point of legal interpretation.[20] the Writer also always believes that, real estate should not only include land and space, but also include buildings, so as to keep consistent with the provisions "① Building and other attachment on land" in Item 1 of Paragraph 1 of Article 180 of the *Real Rights Law*. Therefore, it is necessary to determine the object of establishment of easement.

5.3.2 Systematic Interpretation of "One's Own Real Estate"

In Article 156 of the *Real Rights Law*, the concepts "real estate of someone else" and "one's own real estate" are used. Interpreted on the basis of literal meaning, the latter may be understood as the real estate of which the "ownership" is enjoyed, and may also be understood as the real estate of which the "usufructuary rights" are

---

[17]See Liang (1995, p. 220).

[18]Wang (2005).

[19]Liang (2004, p. 286).

[20]Wang (2001, p. 220).

enjoyed, which must be determined on the basis of the method of systematic interpretation. Though the systematic interpretation can not be separately taken as the only or main basis for interpretation of law, the consistency of wording between legal system and concept can be better maintained by interpreting the meaning of norms on the basis of standing of a law in the legal system.[21] In other parts of the *Real Rights Law*, Article 39 provides "The owner of a a real estate or chattel has the rights to possess, use, seek profits from and dispose of the real property or movable property according to law."; the first paragraph of Article 40 provides that "The owner shall have the right to establish the usufructuary right and guaranty right on his/her own real estate or movable properties"; the first sentence of Paragraph 2 of Article 194 provides that "the obligor establishes the pledge by using his/her own properties", and Article 218 provides that "the obligor establishes the pledge by using his/her own properties". In consideration of the consistency of wording in laws, the words "one's own real estate" should be understood as the real estate of which the "ownership" is enjoyed by him.

The word "one's own" corresponds to the easement right holder. Article 162 and Article 164 of the *Real Rights Law* clearly regard land owner as easement right holder, while Article 161 sets the restriction "remaining term of usufructuary rights" for "term of easement", which should be understood as the restriction on easement established by usufructuary rights holder. As a result, it seems that the legislature has taken land owner as the main adjustment object of easement right holder. Under the constitutional provisions implemented by our country that the public can't transfer the land, the future social economy and life will surely take the establishment of easement between usufructuary rights holders as the main embodiment. As for the different conclusion obtained through this pure theoretical deduction, it is necessary to use the sociological interpretation in light of social policies. The key point of sociological interpretation method is to predict the social effect which may be caused by every interpretation, and then determine which social effect better meet the social purpose.[22] After the reform of housing system, the housings of most of citizens of China are private housings rather than public housings, and housings have also become the important properties of many enterprises and institutions. From the viewpoint of legislative purpose "to settle disputes and make the best use", in the social and economic life in China in the future our country, the land owner can't and should not act as easement right holder. Therefore, the Writer believes that, the building owner and land usufructuary right holder should be taken as subject of easement right holder. The adjustment object of Chapter 14 "Easement" of the *Real Rights Law* should not be limited to land and space, and should also include building.

---

[21]See Liang (1995, pp. 217–218).
[22]See Liang (1995, p. 241).

5.3.3 Goal of Legal Interpretation

The above-mentioned two clarify the connotation of articles of law, but also lead to the possible contradiction between original legislative intention and legal interpretation, namely the issue involving selection of interpretation goal. As for goal of legal interpretation, there has always been the controversy between subjective theory and objective theory. According to the subjective theory, the goal of legal interpretation is to explore into the subjective intention of the legislature at the time of legislation. According to the objective theory, the goal of legal interpretation is to explore into the reasonable meaning of law. The Writer believes that, with respect to the *Real Rights Law*, there should not be too much difference between objective goal and subjective goal, otherwise the legislation itself will involve serious delay problem. Therefore, it is necessary to at least believe that, with respect to the *Real Rights Law*, subjective and objective legal interpretation goals should be unified. Therefore, hereinafter, the Writer will explore into a true legislative intention which can meet the subjective goal of the legislature and the objective goal of the society social needs. In other words, the law should have the reasonable meaning.

5.4 True Legislative Intension of Article 166 and 167 of the *Real Rights Law*

5.4.1 Analysis on Meaning and Characteristics of Legislative Techniques

Professor Karl Larenz believes that, when exploring into the meaning of a phase or wording in a text, the context of law (namely "context relationship") is indispensable.[23] The indivisibility of easement is actually the extension of subordinative nature of easement.[24] Therefore, as for exploration into true meaning of indivisibility-related provisions, it is of great significance to compare the provisions on attributes of easement in the *Real Rights Law*, and the interpretation conclusion should be applied to the subordinative nature and indivisibility of easement in the same manner.

It should be noted that, the first portion of Article 164 and Article 165 of the *Real Rights Law* give the provisions "The easement may not be separately transferred/ mortgaged. In case the right to the contracted management of land or the right to use land for construction is transferred/mortgaged", and the words "dominant tenement/servient tenement" are not used. According to the analysis above, "dominant tenement/servient tenement" is the concept of real estate which include

---

[23]See Karl (2005, p. 220).
[24]Wang (2003).

land, space and building, and from the viewpoint of legal theory, the transfer or mortgage of building will lead to the transfer of easement or burden thereon. Therefore, we can't explain why Article 164 and Article 165 of the *Real Rights Law* fail to use the words "In case the dominant tenement/servient tenement as well as the right to the contracted management of land and the right to use land for construction are transferred/mortgaged" by reference to the provisions of Article 166 and Article 167. This contradiction on the newly-emerging interpretation is the starting point for exploration into real legislative intention of Article 166 and Article 167 of the *Real Rights Law*.

Maybe Article 169 of the *Real Rights Law* can point out the legislative characteristics of the *Real Rights Law* for us: "The alteration or cancellation registration shall be timely executed for the alteration, transfer or elimination of the registered easement." It can be concluded through analysis on such article together with the above-mentioned provisions "The easement may not be separately transferred/mortgaged" in Article 164 and Article 165 of the *Real Rights Law*, the so-called "transfer" of "a registered easement" actually means the transfer of auxiliary usufructuary rights owing to transfer of primary usufructuary rights. This reminds us that, in the aspect of legislative techniques, the *Real Rights Law* attaches more importance to expressing the legislative intention through articles, "more importance attached to purpose and less importance attached to expression", so that the necessary interpretation room is left for legal application.

5.4.2 Inspiration of Comparative Interpretation

Comparative interpretation is a legal interpretation method whereby the foreign legislation and case law is used as an interpretation factors to interpret the meaning and contents of laws. Its purpose is to take the foreign legislation and case law as a factor which must be considered in legal interpretation,[25] so as to correctly interpret the current legal norms. This is of special importance for interpretation of the *Real Rights Law* of China. Though the *Real Rights Law* of China has the vivid Chinese characteristics,[26] the systems of modern civil law still may not be denied and ignored. In general, however, no written legislative reason is prepared for legislation in China. Therefore, the *Interpretation of the Real Rights Law of the People's Republic of China* (hereinafter referred to as "*Interpretation of Real rights law*") prepared by the Legal Affairs Commission under the Standing Committee of NPC is important legislative interpretation material.

According to the introduction in the *Interpretation of Real Rights Law*, Article 166 and Article 167 of the *Real Rights Law* were drafted by reference to the

---

[25]See Wang (2005).
[26]See Yang (2006).

legislations of countries such as Germany, France, Switzerland and Japan etc.[27] Article 1025 [Division of Dominant Tenement] and Article 1026 [Division of Servient Tenement] of the *Civil Code of Germany*, Article 700 of the *Civil Code of France*, and Article 743 [Division of Dominant Tenement] and Article 744 [Division of Servient Tenement] of the *Civil Code of Switzerland* use the words "divided" for land, while Paragraph 2 of Article 282 of the *Civil Code of Japan* uses the words "situations of division or partial transfer of land". In addition, Article 856 and Article 857 of the *Civil Code* of Taiwan use the words "divided" for land, and Article 1437 [Indivisibility of Easement] of the *Civil Code of* Macau also uses the words "divided by several owners" for land. It is thus clear that, the legislations mainly pay attention to the impact on validity of easement by the legal fact that the land is divided, and the *Civil Code* of Japan also considers the division of land and partial transfer of land.

5.4.3 Conclusion of Teleological Interpretation

The so-called teleological interpretation is an interpretation method whereby the intention of a law is interpreted on the basis of purpose of legal norm. The function of teleological interpretation is to maintain the systematicness and stability of legal order, and implement the legislative purpose.[28] In addition to the purpose of law as a whole, the teleological interpretation also covers the normative purpose of specific articles and specific systems. In the *Interpretation of Real Rights Law*, Article 166 and Article 167 are interpreted as follows: "Such articles are the provisions about partial transfer of the right to the contracted management of land and the right to use land for construction on dominant/servient tenement." These two articles embody the "indivisibility of easement", which means that the easement exists in the whole dominant tenement and servient tenement, and may not be severed or partially exist. Even if the servient tenement or dominant tenement is divided, the easement still exists in every part of actually divided dominant tenement and servient tenement." The interpretation for these two articles mentions the "partial transfer of dominant/ servient tenement as well as the right to the contracted management of land and the right to use land for construction on dominant/servient tenement". Thereafter, the *Interpretation of Real Rights Law* gives explanation by giving example: As for dominant tenement, the example is given as follows: "For the purpose of water intaking, Party A establishes the water-intaking easement on the land of Party B. Thereafter, Party A divides his own dominant tenement into two parts, respectively transfers them to Party C and Party D, and gets such transfer registered" (hereinafter referred to as "Example 1"); as for servient tenement, the examples are given as follows: "Party A establishes the water-intaking easement on the land of Party B.

---

[27]Hu (2007, p. 356).
[28]See Liang (1995, pp. 226, 230).

Thereafter, Party B divides his land into two parts for Party C and Party D" (hereinafter referred to as "Example 2"), and "Party A and Party B agree to establish the passage easement on the land of Party B. Thereafter, as the servient tenement right holder, Party B transfers the <u>use right</u> of his <u>land to</u> Party C and Party D" (hereinafter referred to as "Example 3").[29]

The expression of the *Interpretation of Real Rights Law* reveals that, the expression of partial transfer of dominant tenement/servient tenement is not avoided, the purpose of wording in articles is to embody the "indivisibility of easement" through the provisions "partial transfer of the right to the contracted management of land and the right to use land for construction on dominant/servient tenement", and the legislative thinking is clear. The Example 1 describes the situation that the dominant tenement is divided and transferred, the Example 2 describes the situation that the servient tenement is divided, and the Example 3 describes the division and partial transfer of "land use right". Therefore, they all focus on "division" rather than "transfer", which is consistent with the above-mentioned conclusion of analysis on main legislations as well as the expression in the *Real Rights Law (draft)*, First Deliberation Draft and Second Deliberation Draft. In consideration of the legislative characteristics "more importance attached to purpose and less importance attached to expression", though the wordings and examples in the *Interpretation of Real Rights Law* are not given in strict accordance with the legal terms, we can still find that the legislative purpose of such two articles is to highlight the "indivisibility of easement" under the circumstance that the "dominant/servient tenement" is divided. This is the interpretation conclusion obtained by the Writer that the subjective goal and objective goal are unified.

5.4.4 Repeated Inspection for Conclusion of Legal Interpretation

The legal interpretation is not a one-way operation in logic. After the interpretation conclusion is obtained, it is still required to carry out the necessary repeated inspection, covering legislative purpose and constitutionality. The exploration into legislative purpose will help clarify the doubts in laws. Even if the doubts have been clarified, it is still necessary to carry out verification on the basis of purpose of legal norm.[30] The finally-obtained interpretation result should be reviewed so as to confirm whether the requirements of the *Constitution* are met,[31] and finally the constitutionality interpretation should be carried out so as to confirm whether the basic value judgment in the *Constitution* is met.[32]

---

[29]Hu (2007, pp. 355–157).
[30]See Wang (2001, p. 242).
[31]See Huang (2001).
[32]See Liang (1995, p. 245).

On the basis of the conclusion obtained above, the partial transfer of "dominant tenement/servient tenement" mentioned in Article 166 and Article 167 of the *Real Rights Law* does not involve land and space, and only[33] involves building. The legal interpretation is a kind of thinking led by intention of law. Every method has different function, but also has restriction; though they are different from each other, various interpretation methods should supplement each other, so as to obtain the reasonable result.[34] The reasonable legislative purpose deduced above essentially surpasses the subjective legislative purpose of the legislature as obtained through analysis above, but still falls within the scope of literal interpretation. This kind of interpretation complies with the provisions of the *Constitution*, and its extensive conclusion also better meet the purpose of sociological interpretation, so that it is believable and meets the requirement of repeated inspection on legal interpretation. It is thus clear that, in essence, the doubts in Article 166 and Article 17 of the *Real Rights Law* should be determined as defect in legislative techniques.

5.5   Fixed Thinking that "Real Estate Equals Land" and Remedy for Defect in Legislative Techniques

5.5.1   Fixed Thinking About Land in Volume of Usufructuary Rights in the Real Rights Law

Either the analysis based on systematic interpretation or the last repeated inspection reveals that, the root cause of such legislative doubts is that, there is the fixed thinking mode about land in drafting of the Chapter "Easement" and even the Volume "Usufructuary Rights" of the *Real Rights Law*—"The real estate equals land". The legislative philosophy still stay in the philosophy of classical civil law which believes that land absorbs building, and does not regard building as object for establishment of usufructuary rights. In fact, as for real estate other than land, building and space, such as trees which have not been separated from land, the "other real estate" provided in Article 42 is not considered by the *Real Rights Law*, except for quotation thereof by Article 184 in Volume "Usufructuary Rights". However, it is provided in Article 5 of the Real Rights Law that: "The types and contents of real rights shall be provided by laws." What this article has established is the strict Numerus Clausus. In the course of drafting of the *Real Rights Law*, a relevant legislative program was proposed to ease the principle of Numerus Clausus, but was subsequently denied. The pawn right (vadium mortuum) and right to residency which were provided in the *Real Rights Law (draft)* have been

---

[33]Space is subject to land. Even if no explicit provisions are laid down in the laws, from the perspective of natural interpretation, we should believe that the provisions for banning the transfer of land in the *Constitution* are applicable for space.

[34]See Wang (2001, p. 240).

successively excluded from real rights. This will lead to the situation that the court can't find any law as basis when facing any case involving such property rights, and another side effect is that the application scope of usufructuary rights in China is limited to land and space. The above analysis reveals that, only when the building is include into the objects of easement, can the dilemma in interpretation brought forth by Article 166 and Article 167 of the *Real Rights Law* be relieved. In China, the public ownership system is implemented for land, but the buildings can be privately owned. Owing to this difference between object system and right type, the application scope of usufructuary rights will be greatly decreased. What is special is the pawn right (vadium mortuum) system, which bears the dual functions for use benefits and fund facility, has the advantages that other usufructuary rights and guaranty rights don't have, is the excellent heritage of traditional civil law system in China, and should not be gave up without major reasons. In the future, when establishing the usufructuary right system for building in China, it is necessary to take the mortgage right system as basis, carry out improvement gradually, and finally establish the usufruct right system for building.

5.5.2 Remedy for Defect in Legislative Techniques for Article 166 and 167 of the Real Rights Law

The remedy for defects in legislative techniques for Article 166 and Article 167 of the *Real Rights Law* should be determined from the viewpoint of judicial practice and judicial interpretation. In judicial practice, the application scope of Article 166 and Article 167 of the *Real Rights Law* shall be restrictively interpreted on the basis of the legislative purpose. This means that, the provisions about "real estate" in Paragraph 2 of Article 156 shall be taken as basic provisions, and the restriction in Article 8 of the *Real Rights Law* shall be applied: "In case there are other special provisions on property rights in other relevant laws, such provisions shall apply." The special provisions of other laws mentioned shall be the provisions of Paragraph 3 of Article 2 of the *Land Administration Law*: "Neither entity nor individual may misappropriate, buy, sell or otherwise illegally transfer the land. land use right may legally transfer.", so as to preclude the possibility to apply Article 166 and Article 167 of the *Real Rights Law* to partial transfer of ownership of land, correct the legislative defects and implement the legislative intention.

Judicial interpretation is a legal document with Chinese characteristics, and its feature is to form the doctrine of judicial law under legislative system. The doubts involved in these two articles can be included into the scope of the interpretation of Supreme People's Court. As for the contents of interpretation, it is advised by the Writer that, the partial transfer of ownership and usufructuary rights of real estate involved in such two articles should be classified and clarified, and the fixed thinking mode that "the real estate equals land" in the volume of usufructuary rights in the *Real Rights Law* should be reviewed, so as to determine the independent status of building as object for establishment of usufructuary rights.

References

Hu Kangsheng, *Interpretation of the Real Rights Law of People's Republic of China*, Law Press, 2007.

Huang Maorong, *Law Methods and Modern Civil Law*, China University of Politic Science and Law Press, 2001, p. 288.

Karl Larenz, *Methodology of law*, Translated by CHEN Aie, Commercial Press, 2005.

Kong Xiangjun, *Legal Interpretation Methods and Case Studies*, People's Court Press, 2004, p. 325.

Lian Huixin, *Civil Law Hermeneutics*, China University of Politic Science and Law Press, 1995.

Liang Huixing, *Draft of Chinese Civil Code with Reasons (Real Rights Volume)*, Law Press, 2004, p. 286.

Su Li, "The Difficulty of Interpretation", at *Legal Hermeneutics*, edited by LIANG Zhiping, Law Press, 1998, p. 61.

Wang Liming, *On the Real Rights Law*, China University of Politics Science and Law, 2003, p. 496.

Wang Liming, *Scholar-proposed Draft and Legislation reasons of Chinese Civil Code: Real Rights Law Volume*, Law Press, 2005, p. 293.

Wang Zejian, "Comparative Law and Interpretation and Application of Law", available at WANG Zejian, *Civil Law Theories and Case Studies (Volume 2)*, China University of Politics Science and Law Press, 2005, p. 16.

Wang Zejian, *Legal Thinking and Civil Law Cases,* China University of Politic Science and Law Press, 2001.

Wang Zhu, "On Constitutionality of *General Principles of Civil Law* and *Real Rights Law (Draft)*", *Case Study*, NO.3, 2006.

Yang Lixin, "Comment on the Distinct Chinese Features of Real Law Draft", *Journal of Henan Administrative Institute of Politics and Law*, No. 3, 2006.

Yang Lixin, "On Setting up General Concept conoepe and Sesterm", *Journal of Henan Administrative Institute of Politics and Law*, No. 1, 2007.

Chapter 6
Constitutionality of Legislative Procedure—Taking Constitutionality Interpretation for Legislative Procedure of the *Tort Liability Law* as an Example

The *Tort Liability Law* of China was adopted at the 12th Meeting of Standing Committee of 11th NPC on December 26, 2009. Since such law has always been regarded as a basic civil law which stands side by side with the *Real Rights Law* and the *Contract Law*, the fact that it was not deliberated and adopted by NPC has aroused great controversy in the public and academic circle. In face of such controversy, Wang Shenming, the deputy director of the Legal Affaires Commission under the NPC Standing Committee gave the explanation at the news release conference held by the General Office of the NPC Standing Committee as follows: "Through repeated study, the NPC Law Committee and the Legal Affaires Commission under NPC Standing Committee believe that, from actual contents, the *Tort Liability Law* is actually enacted on the basis of the laws such as *General Principles of the Civil Law*. *General Principles of the Civil Law* was enacted in 1986, and thereafter some relevant laws were enacted. The *Tort Liability Law* is the refinement, supplementation and improvement of the laws such as *General Principles of the Civil Law*. According to the provisions of the *Constitution* and the *Legislation Law*, the Standing Committee has the authority to adopt the *Tort Liability Law*."[1] The explanation given by the deputy director Wang Shenming can only indicate that the Legal Affaires Commission of NPC Standing Committee believes that the procedure for adoption of the *Tort Liability Law* by the NPC Standing Committee meets the provisions of the *Constitution* and the *Legislation Law*, though it fails to directly state whether the *Tort Liability Law* is a basic civil law within the meaning of the *Constitution*. The advice given by Professor XU Xianming during grouped deliberation of the *Tort liability Law (draft)* in the NPC

---

[1] See "Press Conference of the General Office of the Standing Committee of National People's Congress at December 26", available at http://www.npc.gov.cn/npc/zhibo/zzzb8/node_5851.htm, the latest access time: August 31, 2017.

Z. Wang, *On the Constitutionality of Compiling a Civil Code of China*, https://doi.org/10.1007/978-981-13-7900-0_6

Standing Committee for submitting the *Tort liability Law (draft)* to NPC for deliberation and the reasons for such advice reveal that,[2] it is still necessary to give detailed explanation for such issue.

6.1   Background Reason for Unconstitutional Process Risk Is Compilation Mode of Volume by Volume

6.1.1   Review *"Wholesale to Retail" Mode Whereby the* Civil Code *Is Compiled Volume by Volume*

At the beginning of 1980s, the third drafting of civil code was initiated in China. From the *Draft of the Civil Law of the People's Republic of China (draft for solicitation of opinions)* (August 15, 1980) (hereinafter referred to as *"Third Deliberation Draft 1 of the Civil Law"*), the *Draft of the Civil Law of the People's Republic of China (draft 2 for solicitation of opinions)* (April 10, 1981) (hereinafter referred to as *"Third Deliberation Draft 2 of the Civil Law"*) and the *Draft of the Civil Law of the People's Republic of China (draft 3)* (July 31, 1981) (hereinafter referred to as *"Third Deliberation Draft 3 of the Civil Law"*) to the *Draft of the Civil Law of the People's Republic of China (draft 4)* (May 1, 1982) (hereinafter referred to as *"Third Deliberation Draft 4 of the Civil Law"*), the Civil Law Drafting Team under the Legal Affaires Commission of NPC Standing Committee always carried out the drafting under the mode whereby the *Civil Code* would be compiled as a whole. When the draft was to be submitted and adopted, the speech given by the NPC chairman PENG Zhen changed the process. According to the memory of Professor JIANG Ping, the main contents of such speech include: We have known the basic direction of rural reform. However, as for the issues how the reform will be carried out in cities, which approach will be adopted for state-owned enterprises, and whether the planned economy or market economy will be developed, no decision or clear direction is given. Under the circumstance that no direction is determined for urban reform, is it practicable to enact a complete, systematic and inclusive civil code? In such case, if we enact an inclusive civil code, maybe it can't meet the actuality and will even restrain the reform.[3] Thereafter, the legislative plan was changed, and the legislature decided to adopt the legislative plan that civil single laws will be enacted separately and then the *Civil Code* will be enacted after conditions are satisfied,[4] namely the "wholesale to retail" mode whereby the *Civil Code* will be compiled volume by volume. It is conceivable that, if the *Third*

---

[2]See "Xu Xianming Suggest that the *Tort Liability Law (Draft)* should be submitted to NPC for Deliberation", available at: http://www.npc.gov.cn/npc/xinwen/tpbd/cwhhy/2009-12/23/content_1531743.htm, the latest access time: August 31, 2017.

[3]See Jiang (2017, 2008).

[4]See Liang (2001).

Deliberation Draft 4 of the Civil Law can be adopted by NPC in the form of "wholesale", just like the *1979 Criminal Code*, the unconstitutional process risk which may arise from "retail" will not occur.

6.1.2 Unconstitutional Process Risk Involves Contents and Procedure

The unconstitutional process risk mentioned by the Writer means that, in the course of compilation of the *Civil Code* volume by volume, there may exist two unconstitutional risks in the two aspects of contents and procedure. In the aspect of contents, since every volume was adopted at different time, there may exist the difference in legislative basis and expression. The *Constitution* of China has been revised in 1988, 1993, 1999 and 2004 for four times since its enactment in 1982, so that the basis for drafting of various volumes of the *Civil Code* at different time, namely the text of the *Constitution*, may also be slightly different. In particular, the change in expression about basic economic system will impose relatively high impact on drafting of volumes of the *Civil Code*. What was involved in the "unconstitutional event" relating to the *2005 Real Rights Law (draft)* is this unconstitutional risk. In the aspect of procedure, since the *Civil Code* can't be adopted in one shot, or be adopted successively volume by volume just as the *Civil Law of the Republic of China* in a relatively-short time period,[5] there exists the procedural risk that the legislature fails to deliberate various volumes of the *Civil Code* in accordance with the legislative procedure provided in the *Constitution*.

6.1.3 Process Constitutionality Is Necessary for Drafting of Various Volumes of the Civil Code

After the legislature decided not to seek for the adoption of the *Civil Code* as a whole, it should realize the unconstitutional process risks arising from this mode whereby the *Civil Code* is drafted volume by volume. Then, the constitutionality requirement for the compilation of *Civil Code* volume by volume should be no lower than or even higher than the requirements for the compilation of *Civil Code* as a whole. In order to ensure that the *Civil Code* can be drafted in accordance with the legislative procedure provided in basic laws, two legislative routes can be designed in theory.

---

[5]About the drafting process of the *Civil Law of Republic of China*, see Xie (2000).

The first route is "basic law codification mode", which means that every volume will be adopted in accordance with the basic laws procedure, and finally the *Civil Code* will be formed through codification. The unconstitutional process risk of this mode mainly lies in the aspect of contents. The second route is "non-basic law codification mode", which means that every volume will be adopted in accordance with the non-basic laws procedure, and finally the *Civil Code* will be formed through codification in accordance with the basic laws procedure. The unconstitutional process risk of this mode lies in such two aspects as contents and procedure. It is pitiful that, the issue about constitutionality of legislative procedure has not been the focus of the civil law community.[6] From the viewpoint of the adoption procedure for various volumes of the *Civil Code*, it also can't be clearly determined that the legislature made any planned arrangement for this issue. The controversy on legislative procedure of the *Tort Liability Law* is merely one of the embodiments for such lack of planned arrangement.

6.2 Non-basic Law Status of the *Tort Liability Law* and Constitutionality of Legislative Procedure

6.2.1 *"Constitutionality Presumption" Is Basic Orientation of Constitutionality Interpretation for Legislative Procedure of the* Tort Liability Law

The so-called constitutionality presumption means that, in the course of constitutionality judgement, the statute law is firstly logically presumed as compliant with the *Constitution*, unless there are evidences which can forcibly prove that such provision obviously goes beyond the reasonable limit and thus violates the *Constitution*.[7] The "constitutionality presumption" for legislative procedure of the *Tort Liability Law* is the basic orientation of constitutionality interpretation for legislative procedure of the *Tort Liability Law*. As for the legislative procedure that the *Tort Liability Law* was adopted by the NPC Standing Committee, we should answer the question "Is the *Tort Liability Law* a basic law within the meaning of the *Constitution*?" From the basic orientation of constitutionality presumption, we should firstly try to demonstrate that the *Tort Liability Law* is not a basic law within the meaning of the *Constitution*. Only if such conclusion can't be obtained through any demonstration in line with the provisions of the *Constitution*, will we regard the *Tort Liability Law* as a basic law within the meaning of the *Constitution*.

---

[6]As for the selection of basic law mode of codification and non-basic law mode of codification, see the analysis of Chapter 10.

[7]About the introduction of presumption of constitutionality, See Wang (2009).

6.2.2 General Principles of the Civil Law *Is Basic Civil Law Within Meaning of the* Constitution

The so-called "basic law" within the meaning of the *Constitution* means a law which is enacted and amended by NPC and provides or adjusts the fundamental and comprehensive relationship in a certain aspect of social life, of which the authority is only second to that of the *Constitution* and higher than that of all other laws. *General Principles of the Civil Law* of China has not only the unique name and structure, also the special historical standing. Its status as a basic law should be further analyzed and confirmed.

After the decision to compile the *Civil Code* volume by volume was made, the *Succession Law* in the *Third Deliberation Draft 4 of the Civil Law* was firstly adopted,[8] and then the drafting of the *General Provisions of Civil Law* was initiated. In June 1985, the NPC Legal Affairs Commission held a series of symposiums on the *General Provisions of Civil Law*; On July 10, 1985, the NPC Legal Affairs Commission drafted the official *General Provisions of Civil Law the People's Republic of China (draft for discussion).*[9] Thereafter, through deliberation, the *General Provisions of Civil Law* was changed to *General Principles of the Civil Law*. It is thus clear that, the name *General Principles of the Civil Law* was not decided after fully discussion, but was agreed up in a relatively short time,[10] for the purpose of summarizing the special style and contents of such law.

With respect to the contents of *General Principles of the Civil Law*, the contents of Chapter 1 "Basic Principles", Chapter 2 "Citizens (Natural Persons)", Chapter 3 "Legal Persons", Chapter 4 "Juristic Act and Agency", Chapter 7 "Limitation of Action" and Chapter 9 "Supplementary Provisions" are the contents of "General Provisions"; Section 1 "Property Ownership and Property Rights Relating to Property Ownership" of Chapter 5 "Civil Rights" are the contents of "Real Rights Volume", Section 2 "Obligatory Rights" include some contents of "General Provisions of Obligation Law" and subsequent the *Contract Law*, Section 3 "Intellectual Property Rights" gives the basic outline of intellectual property rights law of China, and Section 4 "Personal Rights" actually does not contain the contents about identity right, but contains the main contents of "Personality Rights"; Chapter 6 "Civil Liabilities" adopts the mode that both the breach liabilities and tort liabilities are provided (the former was subsequently included into the *Contract Law,* and the latter is the embryo of the *Tort Liability Law*); Chapter 9 "Legal Application for Foreign-related Civil Relationship" are the contents of conflict law. It is obvious that, *General Principles of the Civil Law* are far beyond the scope of the *General Provisions of Civil Law* in the aspect of contents and has established

---

[8]See Liu (1988).

[9]He et al. (2003).

[10]See Wei (2006).

the basic structure of the *Civil Code*, and the only problem is that the contents of the chapter "Civil Rights" are slightly simple. Therefore, we may confirm that, *General Principles of the Civil Law* is the transitional basic civil law under the mode that the *Civil Code* is enacted volume by volume.

6.2.3   *The* Tort Liability Law *Is Not Basic Civil Law Within Meaning of the* Constitution

It is provided in Paragraph 3 of Article 62 of the *Constitution* that: "The National People's Congress shall exercise the following powers and duties: …③ Enact and amend the basic criminal laws, basic civil laws, basic laws of state organs and other basic laws; …" It is provided in Paragraph 2 of Article 7 of the *Legislation Law* that: "The National People's Congress enacts and amends the basic criminal laws, basic civil laws, basic laws of state organs and other basic laws." Judged on the basis of the literal meaning of the *Constitution* and the *Legislation Law*, the *Tort Liability Law* adopted by the NPC Standing Committee should be determined as non-basic law.

This is not the first time that such situation occurs. Before the *Tort Liability Law*, four civil laws known as components of the *Civil Code* were also adopted by the NPC Standing Committee: ① The *Foreign-related Economic Contract Law (invalidated)* was adopted at the 10th Meeting of Standing Committee of 6th NPC on March 21, 1985; ② The *Technical Contract Law (invalidated)* was adopted at the 21st Meeting of Standing Committee of 6th NPC on June 23, 1987; ③ The *Adoption Law* was adopted at the 23rd Meeting of Standing Committee of 7th NPC on December 29, 1991; ④ The *Guarantee Law* was adopted at the 14th Meeting of Standing Committee of 8th NPC on June 30, 1995.

It can be deduced that, the legislature has unconsciously select the legislative route whereby every volume of the *Civil Code* is adopted in accordance with the non-basic law procedure, and finally the *Civil Code* is formed through codification. It should be clarified that, all the laws enacted by NPC may not be "basic law". The *Marriage Law*, the *Succession Law*, the *Contract Law* and the *Real Rights Law* adopted by NPC are really not basic civil laws within the meaning of the *Constitution*,[11] but non-basic laws. The legislative practice in China reveals that, NPC often firstly enacts the non-basic laws, and then enacts the basic laws.

---

[11] Such deduction is astringent for the civil law scholars. It is due to the poor appropriateness of the *Tort Liability Law*, a basic protection law of civil rights, adopted by the NPC Standing Committee.

6.2.4 *The* **Tort Liability Law** *Adopted by NPC Standing Committee Is Procedurally Constitutional*

The *2002 Civil Law (draft)* may be taken as the official document for the determination of contents of the *Civil Code*. Such draft contains 9 volumes, including Volume 8 "Tort Liability Law". Other documents of the NPC Legal Affairs Commission also reveal that, the deliberation of Volume 8 "Tort Liability Law" as a part of the *Civil Code* is deemed as the first deliberation of the *Tort Liability Law*. Therefore, we can also conclude that, the *Tort Liability Law* is a part of future *Civil Code* rather than the *Civil Code* itself.

From the viewpoint of constitutionality, the Writer believes that, the basic criminal and civil laws within the meaning of the *Constitution* should mean the *Criminal Code* and the *Civil Code*. As a transitional basic civil law, *General Principles of the Civil Law* is the basic civil law within the meaning of the *Constitution*. However, as a component of future *Civil Code*, the *Tort Liability Law* may be adopted by the NPC Standing Committee since it is not a basic civil law within the meaning of the *Constitution*. This legislative procedure complies with the provisions of the *Constitution* and the *Legislation Law*. The concerns in academic circle on adoption of the *Tort Liability Law* by the NPC Standing Committee mainly arose from the fact that over the ten years before the *Tort Liability Law* was adopted, the *Contract Law* and the *Real Rights Law* were adopted by NPC, while the *Tort Liability Law* which has the same status was adopted by the NPC Standing Committee, and is an issue about appropriateness rather than constitutionality.

References

He Qinhua, Li Xiuqing, Chen Yi, *Overview of the Civil Code (Draft) of PRC (Volume 2)*, Law Press, 2003, pp. 623–624.

Jiang Ping, "From Legal Pragmatism to Legal Conceptualism ", Recording of the Lecture at China University of Political Science and Law, at May 10, 2008.

Jiang Ping, "Three decades of Rule of Law in China", available at: http://hn.rcdnct.cn/c/2008/05/29/1519093_1.htm, the latest access time: August 31, 2017.

Liang Huixing, "Observations on Drafting a Civil Code", *Modern Law Science*, No. 2, 2001.

Liu Supingn, *Succession Law*, China Renmin University Press, 1988, p. 87.

Wang Shucheng, " Waking of Constitutional Methodology—Deriving from the Constitutionality", *ZheJIANG Academic Journal*, No. 1, 2009.

Wei Zhenying, "Review of the Participation to the Drafting of *General Principles of the Civil Law*", *Case Study*, No. 1, 2006.

Xie Zhenmin, *Legislative History of Republic of China (Volume 2)*, China University of Political Science and Law Press, 2000, pp. 753–801.

Chapter 7
Constitutionality of Legal Application—Taking the Determination and Legislative Prospect of Essential Tort Law as an Example

Some scholars believe that, all the laws adopted by NPC and its Standing Committee can be deemed as basic civil laws.[1] What can be deduced from this opinion is that, whether the *Tort Liability Law* is adopted by NPC as a basic civil law will not affect the application of such law. The Writer can't agree with such opinion. As mentioned above, the demonstration of constitutionality of legislative procedure for the *Tort Liability Law* reveals that, the *Tort Liability Law* is not a basic civil law within the meaning of the *Constitution*, and the *Real Rights Law*, and the *Contract Law* which is deemed as basic civil law by default is also faced with such dilemma. With the promulgation of the *General Provisions of Civil Law*, this dilemma relating to status of law will bring about more complicated problem relating to application of law. In the following sections, this Writer will start with the status of the *Tort Liability Law* as a non-basic law, interpret the problem relating to application of law brought about by the dilemma in status of law, try to find the application-of-law norm route for the transitional period when the *Civil Code* is being compiled, and forecast the constitutionality of legislation of essential tort law in future.

7.1 Impact on Systems in Essential Tort Law by the *Tort Liability Law*

7.1.1 Essential General Tort Law and Special Tort Law

Formal law and essential law are two basic forms of law. The difference between general tort law and special tort law is the difference in essence rather than form. The *Tort Liability Law* is a formal tort liability law, while the tort liability norms in

---

[1]Zhu (2011).

© China University of Political Science and Law Press 2020
Z. Wang, *On the Constitutionality of Compiling a Civil Code of China*,
https://doi.org/10.1007/978-981-13-7900-0_7

all current legal systems[2] constitute the essential tort liability laws. *General Principles of the Civil Law* is a basic civil law within the meaning of the *Constitution*, and the tort liability norms therein, together with the *Tort Liability Law*, constitute the essential general tort laws. The tort liability norms in laws other than *General Principles of the Civil Law* and the *Tort Liability Law* accordingly constitute the essential special tort laws.[3] From the viewpoint of legislative techniques of tort laws, since it is impossible to separately enact a law titled as "Special Tort Law", no formal special tort law will occur. Therefore, the essential special tort law is hereinafter referred to as special tort law.

In addition, the difference between general tort law and special tort law is different from the difference between general tort and special tort. The former establishes the rules for application of essential legal norm, while the latter applies different imputation principles for different types of torts. Therefore, the contents of Chapter 4 through Chapter 11 of the *Tort Liability Law* are provisions about special tort on one hand, and are essential general tort laws on the other hand.

7.1.2 Impact on Essential Tort Laws by Promulgation of the Tort Liability Law

Since the *Tort Liability Law* was adopted by the NPC Standing Committee rather than the NPC, we can judge that, it is not a basic civil law within the meaning of the *Constitution*.[4] This status makes it relatively difficult to evaluate the impact of the *Tort Liability Law* on the original system of special tort laws. We may not regard the provisions of special tort laws which are different from the *Tort Liability Law* as invalid, and also may not carry out judgment simply in accordance with the basic rule "a new law shall prevail over an old law". More concretely, since the *Tort Liability Law* is not a basic civil law within the meaning of the *Constitution*, its impact on essential tort laws involves two aspects:

The first is the impact on determination of essential general tort laws. The essential general tort laws include the *Tort Liability Law* and the tort liability norms in *General Principles of the Civil Law* which are deemed as valid through validity judgment. If the provisions of the *Tort Liability Law* are inconsistent with the

---

[2]Subject to the arrangements of Legislature, the *Tort Liability Law* adjusts the tort of state organs and its employees in the civil activity. For the adjustment scope of the *State Compensation Law*, the provisions of the *State Compensation Law* are applied. Therefore, the *State Compensation Law* does not belong to tort law. See Wang (2010a, pp. 161–162).

[3]According to some scholars, the general laws and special laws are distinguished mainly based on the application scope of laws (such as scope of person, matter, time and territory). Therefore, they have the relativity. See Zhang (2007). In addition, some scholars regard the distinguishing of general laws or "common laws" and special laws as the rules of concurrence of articles of law in the same rank for analysis. See Huang (2007).

[4]Wang (2010c).

relevant provisions of *General Principles of the Civil Law*, the issue about judgment on the validity of relevant articles of *General Principles of the Civil Law* will be involved.

The second is the impact on judgment of validity of special tort laws. Owing to the promulgation and implementation of the *Tort Liability Law*, great change has occurred to the essential general tort laws. Such change is mainly embodied in three aspects, namely the increase in number of articles of essential general tort law, the concretion of contents and the modification in some rules. This will greatly affect the validity of existing special tort laws, and will also define the boundary for amendment and enactment of special tort laws in the future.

In the following section, the basic rules for judgment on validity of special tort laws will be discussed on the basis of the above-mentioned two aspects.

7.2 Basic Types of Special Laws and General Laws in Current Legal System of China

In the current legal system of China, the whole application of laws has seldom drawn attention as an issue about legislative technique, and generally the judgment is made on the basis of legal theory and in accordance with the provisions of the *Legislation Law*. The Writer only focuses on the whole application of a law or the provisions relating to civil liabilities in such law. According to the style whereby the application norm for a current law of China is provided, it is advised by the Writer that, the application norm for law may be divided into four levels, namely absolutely general law, absolutely special law, relatively general law and relatively special law. Generally, the applicability of first three legal norms will be expressly provided through legislation, and a law which does not provide the application norm will be a relatively special law. Most of the departmental laws are relatively special laws. These four levels of application norm are detailed as follows.

7.2.1 Absolutely General Law

According to the provisions of the *Constitution* and the *Legislation Law*, the "criminal, civil, state organ and other basic laws" which must be enacted by NPC are absolutely general laws. The so-called absolutely general law means that, such law is a general law in all events, and all other laws are special laws relative to such law. The *Criminal Code* and *General Principles of the Civil Law* are the generally-accepted basic criminal law and basic civil law within the meaning of the *Constitution*, and thus are absolutely general laws. As the components of the separately-enacted *Civil Code*, though the *1980 Marriage Law*, the *Succession Law* and the *Adoption Law* give no express provisions, since the contents thereof basically don't overlap those of *General Principles of the Civil Law*, they essentially pay the role of absolutely general laws. Article 49 of the *2001 Marriage Law* expressly provides the civil liability norms in the *Marriage Law* as absolutely general law: "In case there are other provisions on illegal acts and legal liabilities relating to marriage and family in other laws, such provisions shall apply." This is for the first time in the legislative history in China that the application norm of absolutely general law is provided by civil legislation. In the future when the *Succession Law* and the *Adoption Law* are amended, the express provisions about its status as an absolutely general law should be added.

7.2.2   Absolutely Special Law

The so-called absolutely special law means that, such law or the provisions relating to civil liabilities in such law are special law in all events, and all other laws are general laws relative to such law; other laws will apply only when no provision is given in such law. In the current legal system of China, the status of absolutely special law is provided in two manners, namely "In case this Law gives no provisions" and "Unless there are other provisions in this Law". The law wherein these two legislative techniques are most intensively embodied is the *Law on Protection of Rights and Interests of Consumers*. It is provided in Article 2 of such law that: "In case a consumer purchases or uses any commodity or accepts any service for meeting the needs of living consumption, his/her rights and interests shall be protected by this Law; where this Law gives no provisions, his/her rights and interests shall be protected by other relevant laws and regulations." It is provided in Article 3 that: "In case a business operator provides consumers with the commodities produced or sold by it or the services, such business operator shall comply with this Law; in case this Law gives no provisions, such business operator shall comply with other relevant laws and regulations." It is provided in Article 48 that: "Under any of the following circumstances, unless there are other provisions in this Law, a business operator which provides commodities or services shall undertake the civil liabilities in accordance with the provisions of other relevant laws and regulations: …" According to these two modes, the *Law on Protection of Rights and Interests of Consumers* is an absolutely special law. Those which adopt the mode "In case this Law gives no provisions" also include Article 2 of the *Non-government-funded Education Promotion Law*, Article 13 of the *Law on Exclusive Economic Zone and Continental Shelf* and Paragraph 3 of Article 2 of the *Law on Diplomatic Personnel Stationed Abroad*. Those which adopt the mode "Unless there are other provisions in this Law" also include Article 94 of the *Insurance Law* and Article 64 of the *Agricultural Law*.

It must be pointed out that, in the field to which the special law is applied, maybe there also exist the laws which are more special relative to absolutely special laws. For example, in the field of food/drug-related dispute, the *Food Safety Law* and the *Drug Administration Law* are the more special laws relative to the *Law on Protection of Rights and Interests of Consumers*. In addition, with respect to rules of application of laws, this relative absoluteness can be further intensified. For example, the provisions relating to food and drugs for babies and infants are more special as compared with the *Food Safety Law* and the *Drug Administration Law*. It is thus clear that, an absolutely general law will encounter the *Constitution* when going upwards, but an absolutely special law may encounter more special norms in special field when going downwards.

7.2.3 Relatively General Law

It is provided in Article 8 of the *Real Rights Law* that: "In case there are other special provisions on real rights in other relevant laws, such provisions shall apply." The words "other special provisions" here are different from the words "other provisions" in Article 49 of the *Marriage Law*, and the word "special" is added specially. It is provided in Article 5 of the *Tort Liability Law* that: "In case there are other special provisions on tort liabilities in other relevant laws, such provisions shall apply." According to the interpretation given by the legislature, the provision of Article 5 of the *Tort Liability Law* is enacted by reference to the mode used in Article 8 of the *Real Rights Law*.[5] In fact, among the currently valid laws in China, besides the *Real Rights Law* and the *Tort Liability Law*, only Article 2 of the *Law of the Application of Law for Foreign-related Civil Relations* adopts the mode "Unless there are other special provisions", which means that the legislature intentionally adopted the same special legislative techniques for such three laws, so as to indicate the application relationship with *General Principles of the Civil Law*.

With respect to the legislative process of the *Real Rights Law*, it is provided in Article 8 of "draft for 7th deliberation" and final "draft for adoption" that: "In case there are other provisions on real rights in other laws, such provisions shall apply." Obviously, the finally-adopted words "other special provisions" in Article 8 of the *Real Rights Law* are specially added. The Writer believes that, the *Real Rights Law*, the *Tort Liability Law* and the *Law of the Application of Law for Foreign-related Civil Relations* have made relatively great breakthrough in legislative techniques for relationship between general laws and special laws. The problem about validity relationship between *General Principles of the Civil Law* as a basic civil law within the meaning of the *Constitution* and the *Real Rights Law*, the *Tort Liability Law* or the *Law of the Application of Law for Foreign-related Civil Relations* is considered. By adding the restrictive word "special", i t s ensured that the relevant provisions of the *Real Rights Law*, the *Tort Liability Law* and the *Law of the Application of Law for Foreign-related Civil Relations* can replace the relevant provisions of *General Principles of the Civil Law*, so that the problem about validity relationship between *General Principles of the Civil Law* and the *Real Rights Law*, the *Tort Liability Law* or the *Law of the Application of Law for Foreign-related Civil Relations* is avoided.

---

[5]Wang (2010a, p. 22).

In summary, the Writer believes that, owing to the above-mentioned special legislative techniques, the *Real Rights Law*, the *Tort Liability Law* and the *Law of the Application of Law for Foreign-related Civil Relations* have become the relatively general laws which are different from absolutely general laws. The so-called relatively general law means the law has both the status of general law and the status of special law, but mainly acts as a general law in a certain field. Relative to absolutely general laws, a relatively general law is applied as a special law; relative to other laws (including other relatively general laws), a relatively general law has the status of general law in a certain field.

Determining the status of the *Tort Liability Law* as a relatively general law is of great significance for determining the essential tort liability law. As a relatively general law, the *Tort Liability Law* is a special law relative to *General Principles of the Civil Law*. In case of any conflict between the articles of these two laws, the new law or the special law, namely the *Tort Liability Law* shall apply. Relative to other laws, the *Tort Liability Law* is a general law in the tort law field; if there is any conflict between the *Tort Liability Law* and the tort liability norm in any other current law, the application of such law or such norm will depend on whether such law is an absolutely special law.

In this sense, just like Article 8 of the *Real Rights Law*, Article 5 of the *Tort Liability Law* and Article 2 of the *Law of the Application of Law for Foreign-related Civil Relations*, the words "other provisions" in "In case there are other provisions in other laws, such provisions shall apply" as provided in Article 123 of the *Contract Law* shall be interpreted as "other special provisions". If the *Contract Law* is amended in the future, such article should also be amended accordingly, so as to ensure the consistency in legislative techniques for application norm between such law and the *Real Rights Law*, the *Tort Liability Law* or the *Law of the Application of Law for Foreign-related Civil Relations*. The future possible *Personality Rights Law* and the *General Provisions of Obligation Law* also should give the similar provisions relating to relatively general law.

7.2.4   Relatively Special Law

Most of the departmental laws are not basic laws within the meaning of the *Constitution*, and have not oriented itself as absolutely special laws, just like the *Law on Protection of Rights and Interests of Consumers*. Therefore, with respect to the status in application-of-law rules, they are relatively special laws. The so-called relatively special law means that, it acts as a general law only relative to absolutely special law; under other circumstances, it acts as special law relative to absolutely general laws and relatively general laws. Generally, no validity conflict will occur between relatively special laws. If any validity conflict occurs, such situation should be handled in accordance with the general provisions about validity conflict in the *Legislation Law*.

7.3 Contents Determination of Essential General Tort Law

7.3.1 Application Norm for Situation that the Provisions of the Tort Liability Law Are Inconsistent with the Provisions of General Principles of the Civil Law

Contents determination of essential general tort law is the precondition for validity judgment on special tort laws. Its essence is the issue about validity judgment for articles about tort law norms in the *Tort Liability Law* and *General Principles of the Civil Law*. When the provisions of the *Tort Liability Law* are inconsistent with those of *General Principles of the Civil Law*, the result of validity judgment includes two situations, namely the situation that the provisions of *General Principles of the Civil Law* are applied, and the situation that the provisions of the *Tort Liability Law* are applied.

The situation that the provisions of *General Principles of the Civil Law* are applied involve two situations: The first situation is that, the *Tort Liability Law* does not contain the tort liability norms provided in *General Principles of the Civil Law*, and thus the provisions of *General Principles of the Civil Law* should still be applied; the second situation is that, the provisions of the *Tort Liability Law* are not as detailed as the corresponding tort liability norms in *General Principles of the Civil Law*, there is no essential validity conflict between them, and thus the provisions of *General Principles of the Civil Law* should still be applied.

The situation that the provisions of the *Tort Liability Law* are applied involves four situations: The first situation is that the *Tort Liability Law* changes the provisions of *General Principles of the Civil Law*; the second situation is that the *Tort Liability Law* further clarifies the provisions of *General Principles of the Civil Law*, and the courts can directly apply the *Tort Liability Law* rather than *General Principles of the Civil Law*; the third situation is that the *Tort Liability Law* further typifies the provisions of *General Principles of the Civil Law*, including the situation that new types are added; the fourth situation is that the *Tort Liability Law* changes the orientation of relevant articles of *General Principles of the Civil Law*, and this situation is main applied in equitable liabilities.

7.3.2 Validity Type and Application Norm for Tort Liability Norms in General Principles of the Civil Law

On the basis of the application norm determined above, the tort liability norms in *General Principles of the Civil Law* may be divided into six types.

7.3.2.1   As for the Tort Liability Norms in *General Principles of the Civil Law* Which Are Not Involved in the *Tort Liability Law*, The Provisions of *General Principles of the Civil Law* Should Be Applied

The tort liability norms in *General Principles of the Civil Law* which are not involved in the *Tort Liability Law* may be divided into three situations:

First, the general type of tort as provided in *General Principles of the Civil Law*. Though comparing to other countries' legislation, the *Tort Liability Law* is a legislation which enumerates more types of tort, a few general torts enumerated in *General Principles of the Civil Law*, including some general torts which are not provided in the part about tort liabilities in *General Principles of the Civil Law* are still not contained in the *Tort Liability Law*. Therefore, the provisions of *General Principles of the Civil Law* should still be applied. Specifically speaking, the following three torts are involved: The first is the tort that the guardian fails to perform duties or infringes upon the lawful rights and interests of person under guardianship, which is provided in Article 18 of *General Principles of the Civil Law*; the second is the joint and several liabilities for illegal agency behavior, which are provided in Article 67 of *General Principles of the Civil Law*; the third is the tort liabilities for infringement upon intellectual property rights and unfair competition behavior, which are provided in Article 118 of *General Principles of the Civil Law*. Though the intellectual property right laws and anti-unfair competition laws have given specific provisions on such tort, the above-mentioned article still has the general protection effect for discovery right and other scientific/technical achievement right.

Second, the provisions of *General Principles of the Civil Law* corresponding to the "regressive article" in the *Tort Liability Law*. The so-called "regressive article" means that the provisions of the *Tort Liability Law* are simpler than the corresponding tort liability norms in *General Principles of the Civil Law*, and when applying such provisions, the court must separately or jointly apply the relevant provisions of *General Principles of the Civil Law*. The most typical is the provisions of Article 19 of the *Tort Liability Law*: "As for infringement upon properties of other persons' properties, the loss of properties shall be calculated on the basis of the market price when such loss occurs or other method." As compared with Article 117 of *General Principles of the Civil Law*,[6] only the principle for calculation method for damage compensation under the circumstance of full damage is given,

---

[6]There are three paragraphs in article 117 of *General Principles of the Civil Law*. Paragraph 1 provides that: "Anyone who encroaches on the property of the state, a collective or another person shall return the property; failing that, he shall reimburse its estimated price." Paragraph 2 provides that: "Anyone who damages the property of the state, a collective or another person shall restore the property to its original condition or reimburse its estimated price." Paragraph 2 provides that: "If the victim suffers other great losses therefrom, the infringer shall compensate for those losses as well".

and the provisions on partial compensation, return of properties, restoration of original state and compensation for other huge loss are not given for partial damage.

Third, the general provisions in *General Principles of the Civil Law*. The *Tort Liability Law* does not provide the limitation of action and application rules for foreign-related civil relations laws, and this should be understood as the intentional arrangement made by the legislature. The provisions relating to limitation of action include Articles 135–141 of *General Principles of the Civil Law*. The Article 141 serves as referral clause, so that the provisions relating to limitation of action in other special tort laws may be applied. As for the rules for application of foreign-related civil relationship law, the *Law of the Application of Law for Foreign-related Civil Relations* shall apply.[7]

7.3.2.2   As for the Tort Liability Norm for Which There Is no Essential Difference Between the Provisions of the *Tort Liability Law* and *General Principles of the Civil Law*, It Is More Appropriate to Apply the Provisions of the *Tort Liability Law*

As for the tort liability norm for which there is no essential difference between the provisions of the *Tort Liability Law* and *General Principles of the Civil Law*, the provisions of the *Tort Liability Law* should be applied. There are two reasons therefore: First, *General Principles of the Civil Law* were enacted at the beginning of 1980s, and the idioms used at that time, such as "citizen" and "unit", now have been inappropriate; second, the *Tort Liability Law* specially adjusts the tort liabilities, and the relationship among relevant articles are closer than *General Principles of the Civil Law*, and in the compilation of the *Civil Code* in the future, the relevant articles of *General Principles of the Civil Law* may be amended. Specifically speaking, that involves the following three aspects:

First, the application rules for joint and several liabilities provided in the *Tort Liability Law* and joint obligation provided in *General Principles of the Civil Law*. Article 87 of *General Principles of the Civil Law* is the provisions on joint obligation. Before the enactment of the *Tort Liability Law*, there was no provision about joint and several liabilities in legal system of China, and in judicial practice, the provisions about joint obligation were applied to joint and several liabilities. This situation also exists in the *Civil Code* of Taiwan. The judicial practice in both sides of the Taiwan Strait reveals that, no too many problems have occurred with respect to application, but this problem must be further clarified in the aspects of theory and legislation. Professor Qiu Congzhi has specially pointed out that, in theory, it can't be said that there is no room for discussion over the issue whether the joint and several liabilities defined in law are joint obligations or unreal joint

---

[7]In Article 44 of the *Law of the Application of Law for Foreign-related Civil Relations*, the general provisions are laid down for the foreign-related law application of tort liability. In Article 45 and Article 46, the special enumeration provisions are laid down for the foreign-related law application of product liability and infringement upon personality rights.

and several liabilities.[8] Article 13 of the *Tort Liability Law* clarifies the provisions about outward undertaking rules for joint and several liabilities, and Article 14 clarifies the provisions about inward apportionment rules and recovery right for joint and several liabilities. Though this clarification is not thorough owing to that fact that the claim for apportionment of joint and several liabilities are not included,[9] it is not essentially different from the provisions of Article 87 of *General Principles of the Civil Law*, and changes the original application rules. Therefore, in judicial application, the provisions of the *Tort Liability Law* shall be applied.

Second, the undertaking for tort liabilities provided in the *Tort Liability Law* and *General Principles of the Civil Law*. As compared with Paragraph 1 of Article 134 of *General Principles of the Civil Law*, Paragraph 1 of Article 15 of the *Tort Liability Law* deletes the typical breach liabilities, namely "⑥ Repair, rework or replacement" and "⑧ compensation for breach of contract", and changes the relative sequence of "eliminating the effect, restoring the reputation" and "apologizing". With respect to the latter, the legislature gave no explanation, and the Writer believes that maybe such adjustment is made for the sake of aesthetics,[10] and will not affect the application rules for such two civil liabilities. Paragraph 2 of Article 15 of the *Tort Liability Law* is not essentially different from Paragraph 2 of Article 134 of *General Principles of the Civil Law*, but the former limits the single application or joint application to tort liabilities and thus is more specific. In addition, Article 15 of the *Tort Liability Law* does not provide the civil sanction as provided in Item 3 of Paragraph 2 of Article 134 of *General Principles of the Civil Law*. The above-mentioned comparison reveals that, there is no essential difference between Article 15 of the *Tort Liability Law* and Article 134 of *General Principles of the Civil Law* in the aspect of types of tort liabilities. Since Article 15 of the *Tort Liability Law* provides eight civil liabilities, it is more appropriate to apply the provisions of the *Tort Liability Law* in judicial practice.

Third, the adjustment made by the *Tort Liability Law* to sequence and contents of defense system provided in *General Principles of the Civil Law*. Both the *Tort Liability Law* and *General Principles of the Civil Law* give provisions on defense. As for the provisions about force majeure, act of rescue, justifiable defense and fault of injured person,[11] there is no essential difference in contents between them. However, in the aspects of sequence and contents, relatively large adjustment has been made. In *General Principles of the Civil Law*, the system for fault of injured person is provided in Article 131, and, together with the provisions about joint tort

---

[8]Qiu (2004).

[9]Wang (2010e).

[10]Unfortunately, the Legislature fail to stipulate the "elimination of effect" and "restoration of reputation" as two forms of tort liability respectively, which shows the hurry in the legislation process.

[11]The system of intentional act of injured person in Article 27 of the *Tort Liability Law*: "If the harm is [solely] due to the injured person's intentional [act], the actor shall not bear liability." This is the new rule, and exists as the general tort law naturally.

in Article 130, constitutes the formal tort liability apportionment system;[12] and together with Article 132, constitutes the tort liability reduction system.[13] In *General Principles of the Civil Law*, the force majeure system is provided in Article 107 in "General Provisions for Civil Liabilities", exists as the general defense for civil liabilities, and is naturally applicable in the field of tort liabilities. In *General Principles of the Civil Law*, the act of rescue and justifiable defense systems are respectively provided in Article 129 and Article 128 in the part of tort liabilities. As compared with the provisions of Chapter 3 of the *Tort Liability Law*, such law firstly provides the system of fault of injured person in Article 26, adds the system of intentional act of injured person in Article 27 and the system of third-party reason in Article 28 as compared with *General Principles of the Civil Law*, and subsequently provides three defenses, namely force majeure, justifiable defense and act of rescue. This change is the new style formed after defining the fault of injured person as defense, itemizing the force majeure, and finally changing the sequence of relevant articles. However, since there is no priority among these defenses with respect to application, this change has no impact on tort liability norm. However, since two defenses are added in Chapter 3 of the *Tort Liability Law*, and these six defenses are provided under the title "Exculpatory or Extenuating Circumstances" of in Chapter 3, it is simpler to select defenses for application. In the judicial application, the *Tort Liability Law* should be applied.

7.3.2.3 As for the Situation that the *Tort Liability Law* Further Clarifies the Tort Liability Norms in *General Principles of the Civil Law*, The Provisions of the *Tort Liability Law* Should Be Applied

The situation that the *Tort Liability Law* further clarifies the tort liability norms in *General Principles of the Civil Law* is one of the legislative purposes of the *Tort Liability Law*. Specially, this is embodied in the following six aspects:

First, the general articles of tort liabilities. Paragraph 2 of Article 6 of the *Tort Liability Law* clarifies that the presumed-default liability principle is the independent imputation principle for tort liabilities. Article 7 amends the ambiguous provisions of Paragraph 3 of Article 106 of *General Principles of the Civil Law*. The concept "citizen" used in Paragraph 2 of Article 106 of *General Principles of the Civil Law* does not meet the orientation of civil subject in current legal system, so that when the imputation principle for tort liabilities is applied in judicial practice, Article 6 and Article 7 of the *Tort Liability Law* should be applied.

Second, the emotional damage compensation system. It is generally believed that, the "damage compensation" for infringement upon personality rights as

---

[12]Certainly, the formation of this structure may be occasional. For the formation process of this style, see Wang (2009, pp. 57–61).

[13]Wang (2008).

provided in Paragraph 1 of Article 120 of *General Principles of the Civil Law* include emotional damage compensation, and Article 22 of the *Tort Liability Law* clearly provides the conditions for application of emotional damage compensation: "If [one] infringes on another's personal rights or interests, causes serious emotional harm, the victim may claim solatium for emotional harm." In judicial practice, the provisions of the *Tort Liability Law* should be applied.

Third, the liabilities for harm caused by domesticated animals. Article 127 of *General Principles of the Civil Law* provides the damage caused by domesticated animals. However, such article is divided into three parts by two semicolons, and the relationship among such three parts is not so clear. Especially, there is doubt on whether the provisions of the third part "In case the damage is caused by fault of a third party, such third party shall undertake the civil liabilities" refer to ground for exemption or unreal joint and several liabilities. The provisions of Article 78 of the *Tort Liability Law* are equivalent to the first and second parts of Article 127 of *General Principles of the Civil Law*, and the gross negligence of injured person is added as a ground for extenuating liabilities. The provisions of Article 83 of the *Tort Liability Law* are equivalent to the last part of Article 127 of *General Principles of the Civil Law*, and confirm that the unreal joint and several liabilities will be applied for damage caused by domesticated animals arising from third-party fault.

Fourth, the product liabilities. Article 122 of *General Principles of the Civil Law* gives the basic provisions for product liabilities, including the liabilities of manufacturer and seller and the liabilities of transporter and storekeeper. Article 43 of the *Product Quality Law* provides the liabilities of producer and seller as unreal joint and several liabilities, but fails to provide the liabilities of transporter and storekeeper. Article 43 of the *Tort Liability Law* defines the unreal joint and several liabilities to be undertaken by producer and seller for defective products, and Article 44 provides the recovery right of producer and seller towards third party whose fault has made the product defective. In judicial application, the provisions of the *Tort Liability Law* should be applied.

Fifth, the special rules to be applied when the infringed party does not exist. Paragraph 2 of Article 44 of *General Principles of the Civil Law* gives the provisions on change in subject of rights and obligations arising from division or merger of enterprises legal person, and such provisions are applied in the situation that the infringed party is an entity. Paragraph 1 of Article 18 of the *Tort Liability Law* specifically provides the rules for change in right subject arising from death of injured person or division/merger of infringed entity. In judicial application, the provisions of the *Tort Liability Law* should be applied.

Sixth, the tort liabilities and indemnity liabilities for damage caused by act of rescue. Article 109 of *General Principles of the Civil Law* gives the general provisions on tort liabilities and indemnity liabilities for damage caused by act of rescue, and the second sentence of Article 23 of the *Tort Liability Law* further defines the rules for make-up liabilities of beneficiary: "If the tortfeasor flees or is unable to bear liability, and the victim claim indemnity, the beneficiary shall pay for appropriate relief."

7.3.2.4   As for the Situation that the *Tort Liability Law* Further Typifies or Adds Any New Type of the Tort Liability Norms in *General Principles of the Civil Law*, The Provisions of the *Tort Liability Law* Should Be Applied

The situation that the *Tort Liability Law* further typifies or adds any new type of the tort liability norms in *General Principles of the Civil Law* involves the following four aspects:

First, the joint and several liabilities for joint tort. Article 130 of *General Principles of the Civil Law* is the general provisions on joint and several liabilities undertaken for joint tort. Article 8, Paragraph 1 of Article 9, Article 10 and Article 11 of the *Tort Liability Law* divides the joint and several liabilities undertaken for joint tort into four specific types, namely joint and several liabilities for joint tortfeasors, joint and several liabilities for instigator or helper, joint and several liabilities for joint dangerous actors and joint and several liabilities for undividable damage caused by occasional combination of several sufficient causes. It should be noted that, the scope of joint and several liabilities undertaken for joint tort is gradually expanded in the continental legal system.[14] The provisions of Article 8 of the *Tort Liability Law* limit the joint tort to the subjectively joint tort, and are more conservative as compared with Paragraph 1 of Article 3 of the *Judicial Interpretation on Personal Damage Compensation*. If any breakthrough is realized in judicial practice, the generalized provisions in Article 130 of *General Principles of the Civil Law* may be applied.

Second, the ultra-hazardous liabilities. Article 123 of *General Principles of the Civil Law* give provisions on ultra-hazardous liabilities and grounds for exemption. Chapter 9 of the *Tort Liability Law* extensively provides the ultra-hazardous liabilities. Article 69 is the general article for no-fault liabilities for damage caused by ultra-hazardous activity. Article 72 and Article 73 distinguish between the no-fault liabilities for damage caused by ultra-hazardous objects and the no-fault liabilities for damage caused by ultra-hazardous act, and provide different defenses. In addition, Article 76 also gives the special provisions for defenses to be used by ultra-hazardous actor towards unauthorized trespasser. As compared with "high-speed means of transport" provided in Article 123 of *General Principles of the Civil Law*, the field of liabilities for traffic accident is limited to "high-speed track conveyance" in Article 73, and the liabilities for traffic accident of motor vehicle are excluded. For such liabilities, the provisions of Chapter 6 "Liability for Motor Vehicle Traffic Accidents" of the *Tort Liability Law* are applied.

Third, the real estate and facilities fall off, fall down, and collapse. Article 126 of *General Principles of the Civil Law* gives the unified provisions on presumed-default liabilities for damage caused by the real estate and its attachment

---

[14]Wang (2009, pp. 40–46).

falling down, falling off and collapsing. Article 85 and Article 86 of the *Tort Liability Law* respectively provides the presumed-default liabilities for damage caused by the real estate and its attachment falling down, falling off as well as the tort liabilities for damage caused by building, structure or any other facility collapsing.

Fourth, the liabilities for damage caused by underground construction facility. Article 125 of *General Principles of the Civil Law* provides the presumed-default liabilities for damage caused by underground facilities of constructor, Paragraph 1 of Article 91 of the *Tort Liability Law* gives the similar provisions, and Paragraph 2 adds the provisions for presumed-default liabilities for damage caused by underground facilities of administrator. Such article further itemizes the types.

7.3.2.5 As for the Situation that the Orientation of Tort Liability Norms Is Changed Owing to the Change of Position in the *Tort Liability Law* and *General Principles of the Civil Law*, the Provisions of the *Tort Liability Law* Should Be Applied

The tort liability norms of which the orientation is changed owing to change in position in the *Tort Liability Law* and *General Principles of the Civil Law* mainly involve equitable liabilities and relevant articles. In the drafting of *General Principles of the Civil Law*, owing to the impact arising from amendment of obligation law of Yugoslavia in 1970s as well as the *1922 Civil Code* and the *1964 Civil Code* of USSR, the provisions about tort liabilities for damage caused by person with non-full capacity for civil conducts in Article 133 of *General Principles of the Civil Law* are not placed in the contents about special tort, but specially placed following Article 132 "Equitable Liabilities" as the restrictive article for the application of equitable liabilities.[15] The *Tort Liability Law* cuts off the relationship between these two tort liability norms. On one hand, the equitable liabilities are defined as generally-applied equitable indemnity liabilities, and are provided in Article 24; on the other hand, the tort liabilities for damage caused by person with non-full capacity for civil conducts return to the traditional orientation of civil law, are provided in Article 32, and together with the tort liabilities and equitable liabilities for unconsciously-caused damage provided in Article 33, constitute the complete tort liabilities system for damage caused by person with non-full capacity for civil conducts. This is mainly because that the orientation is changed owing to change in position of such articles.[16] In judicial application, the provisions of the *Tort Liability Law* should be applied.

---

[15]See Wang (2008).

[16]Except the orientation change due to the change of position, Article 32 of the *Tort Liability Law* is slightly different from Article 133 of *General Principles of the Civil Law* in the contents. This is another reason for referring to Article 32 of the *Tort Liability Law* in the judicial application.

7.3.2.6 As for the Situation that the *Tort Liability Law* Changes the Tort Liability Norms in *General Principles of the Civil Law*, The Provisions of the *Tort Liability Law* Should Be Applied

The situations that the provisions of the *Tort Liability Law* should be applied since the *Tort Liability Law* has changed the tort liability norms in *General Principles of the Civil Law* include:

First, the scope of personal damage compensation. It is provided in Article 119 of *General Principles of the Civil Law* that: "Anyone who infringes upon a citizen's person and causes him physical injury shall pay his medical expenses and his loss in income due to missed working time and shall pay him living subsidies if he is disabled; if the victim dies, the infringer shall also pay the funeral expenses, the necessary living expenses of the deceased's dependents and other such expenses." It is provided in Article 16 of the Tort Liability Law that: "[One who] infringes on another, causes physical injury, shall compensate for the reasonable expenses of medical care, nursing, and transportation, etc. for the purpose of therapy and restoring good health, as well as the income lost owing to missed work. [One who] causes disability shall also pay expense for prostheses and compensation for disability. [One who] causes death shall also pay funeral expenses and compensation for death." Through comparison, it is clear that, the *Tort Liability Law* does not provide "necessary living expenses of the deceased's dependents", but expressly provides the compensation for disability and compensation for death. It is provided in Article 4 of the *Circular of Supreme People's Court on Several Issues relating to Application of the Tort Liability Law of the People's Republic of China* (F.F. [2010] No. 23) that: "When the people's court applies the *Tort Liability Law* in trial of civil dispute cases, in case there is any dependents supported by the injured person, the people's court shall, in accordance with the provisions of Article 28 of the *Interpretation of Supreme People's Court for Several Issues Relating to Application of Law in Trial of Personal Damage Compensation Cases*, include the living costs of dependents into the compensation for disability or compensation for death." These provisions further have complicated this issue. Though the specific rules for application of law are to be clarified by legislative interpretation or judicial interpretation, it can be confirmed that the *Tort Liability Law* really changes the scope of personal damage compensation as provided in *General Principles of the Civil Law*.[17]

Second, the components of no-fault liabilities for environmental pollution. It is provided in Article 124 of *General Principles of the Civil Law* that: "Any person who pollutes the environment and causes damages to others in violation of state provisions for environmental protection and the prevention of pollution shall bear civil liability in accordance with the law." It is provided in Article 65 of the *Tort Liability Law* that: "If environmental pollution causes harm, the polluter shall bear tort liability." The comparison reveals that, the *Tort Liability Law* deletes the

---

[17]The preliminary analysis on this issue, see Wang (2010b).

illegality component provided in *General Principles of the Civil Law*, and keeps consistent with the environmental protection laws.

7.3.3 Collateral Issue: Basic Rules for Validity Judgment for Tort Liability Norms in Existing Judicial Interpretation

The issue about contents determination of essential general tort law is the issue about validity of tort liability norms in the judicial interpretation issued by the Supreme People's Court before the *Tort Liability Law* came into effect. The Writer believes that, the validity of tort liability norms in existing judicial interpretation depends on the validity of articles of *General Principles of the Civil Law*. Specially, three situations are involved:

Firstly, in case the *Tort Liability Law* does not directly involve the tort liability norms in *General Principles of the Civil Law* which are taken as basis for the judicial interpretation, then in principle, the tort liability norms provided by such judicial interpretation should still be valid, and the validity of the involved articles of *General Principles of the Civil Law* should be determined by reference to the above-mentioned first validity type.

Secondly, in case the Tort Liability Law confirms or does not change the tort liability norms in *General Principles of the Civil Law* which are taken as basis for the judicial interpretation, then in principle, the tort liability norms provided by such judicial interpretation should still be valid, and the validity of the involved articles of *General Principles of the Civil Law* should be determined by reference to the above-mentioned second, third and fourth validity types.

Thirdly, since the *Tort Liability Law* changes the tort liability norms in *General Principles of the Civil Law* which are taken as basis for the judicial interpretation, then in principle, the tort liability norms provided by such judicial interpretation should not be valid any longer, and the validity of the involved articles of *General Principles of the Civil Law* should be determined by reference to the above-mentioned fifth and sixth validity types.

7.4 Rules for Validity Judgment for Special Tort Law

7.4.1 Two Basic Modes for Validity Judgment for Special Tort Law

The mode for validity judgment for special tort law can be understood as making judgment in the manner which is similar to the article "In case there are other provisions in other laws, such provisions shall apply". Through careful study, the

Writer believes that the *Tort Liability Law* affects the validity of existing special tort laws in the following two modes:

The first mode, known as "whole judgment of law mode", means that, the *Tort Liability Law* changes the rules of general tort law established by *General Principles of the Civil Law*, and thus the validity of relevant special tort law is changed. The validity judgment for most of the special tort laws is carried out under this mode. Its basic rule is that, the tort liability norms provided in all laws other than *General Principles of the Civil Law* and the *Tort Liability Law* shall be judged by taking the following provisions as basic standard, namely the provisions "In case there are other special provisions in other laws, such provisions shall apply" in Article 5 of the *Tort Liability Law*.[18]

The second, known as "referral clause judgment mode", means that, the *Tort Liability Law* confirms the validity of existing special tort laws and reserves the space for legislation of special tort laws in the future through the rules for application of other laws as provided in referral clause. The validity judgment under this mode is carried out for only a few special tort laws. Its basic rule is that, though the tort liability norms provided in laws other than *General Principles of the Civil Law* and the *Tort Liability Law* are judged as invalid in accordance with the "whole judgment of law mode", they obtain the legal validity owing to the referral clause expressly provided in the *Tort Liability Law*. Frankly speaking, the "referral clause judgment mode" is the exception and supplementation of "whole judgment of law mode".

7.4.2   Basic Rule for Validity Judgment for Special Tort Laws Under Whole Judgment of Law Mode

7.4.2.1   Rules for Judgment for "Other Provisions" Provided in Article 5 of the *Tort Liability Law*

As mentioned above, what the Article 5 of the *Tort Liability Law* provides is the orientation mode of relatively general article: "In case there are other provisions in other laws, such provisions shall apply." Different from Article 49 of the *Marriage Law* which only provided "other" provisions, the above-mentioned article provides two restrictions, namely "other" provisions and "special" provisions. Since the whole *Tort Liability Law* is a general tort law, all the "other special provisions" judged on the basis of Article 5 of the *Tort Liability Law* are valid special tort laws. Therefore, how to judge that "there are other special provisions" is especially important.

---

[18]Such perspective is similar to the scope of "law norms" called by the scholars in Taiwan Province of China. See Huang (2007).

1. Judgment Rules for "Other" Provisions

The so-called "other" provisions should be understood as that, other laws also provide the tort liability norms. Specially, the following types are involved:

First, the provisions for type of tort, namely the principle and components of imputation. For example, it is provided in Article 28 of the *Electronic Signature Law* that: "In case the electronic signer or electronic signature relier incurs losses owing to civil activity carried out by it on the basis of the electronic signature authentication services provided by the electronic authentication service provider, and the authentication service provider can't prove that it is without fault, then it shall undertake the compensation liabilities."

Second, the special provisions for form of tort liabilities. For example, it is provided in Article 58 of the *Product Quality Law* that: "In case any social organization or social intermediary agency gives any guaranty for product of a product, but such product fails to meet the quality requirements guaranteed and thus the consumer incurs losses, the producer and seller of such product shall undertake the joint and several liabilities."

Third, the special provisions for defenses. For example, it is provided in Paragraph 1 of Article 58 of the *Railway Law* that: "A railway transport enterprise shall be liable to compensation for any personal injury or fatality due to traffic accident or other operational accident. It shall hold no liability for compensation for any personal injury or fatality due to force majeure or due to the fault of the aggrieved person oneself." Paragraph 2 explains the "injured person's cause" by means of enumeration: "Personal injury or fatality resulting from passing the railway track at a level crossing or via a pedestrian cross-walk in violation of relevant regulations or from walking, sitting or lying on the railway track shall be deemed injury or fatality caused by the fault of the aggrieved person one-self."

Fourth, the special provisions for scope of damage compensation. For example, it is provided in Paragraph 1 of Article 20 of the *Anti-unfair Competition Law* that: "In case the business operator violates the provisions of this Law and thus damages the infringed business operator, the infringing business operator shall undertake the damage compensation liabilities (where it is difficult to calculate the loss incurred by the infringed business operator, the amount of compensation shall be the profit obtained by the infringing party during the period of tort), and shall undertake the reasonable expenses paid by the infringed business operator for investigation into the unfair competition behavior of infringing business operator which has infringed upon its lawful rights and interests."

2. Judgment Rules for "Special" Provisions

Under the whole judgment of law mode, the word "special" means that the whole law is a special law relative to the *Tort Liability Law*. Relative to the *Tort Liability Law* which is a relatively general law, in accordance with the validity norm system among four kinds of laws as analyzed above, all other relatively general laws, relatively special laws and absolutely special laws are special laws. Since there is a situation that there are other provisions in other laws but there is no corresponding provision in the *Tort Liability Law*, the "special" provisions involve the following three situations:

First, no matter whether the *Tort Liability Law* provides, another absolutely special law gives the provisions. Let's take the typical absolutely special law, namely the *Law on Protection of Rights and Interests of Consumers,* as an example. The punitive compensation provided in Paragraph 2 of Article 55 of such law belongs to this situation: "In case a business operator knows that the commodities or services are defective but still provides them to consumers, and thus causes death or serious injury to consumers or other injured persons, the injured persons shall have the right to require such business operator to make compensation in accordance with the provisions of Article 49 and Article 51 of this Law, and shall have right to claim for punitive compensation up to two times the amount of loss incurred."

Second, the *Tort Liability Law* gives no provision, and another non-absolutely general law gives provisions.[19] This situation involves other relatively general law and relatively special law. As for other relatively general laws, let's take the *Real Rights Law* as an example. Paragraph 2 of Article 21 thereof provides the compensation liabilities of registration authority for error in registration: "In case any other person is damaged owing to any error in registration, the registration authority shall undertake the compensation liabilities. After making the compensation, the registration authority may recover such compensation from the person which has caused such error in registration." This paragraph provides a special unreal joint and several liabilities.[20] As for relatively special laws, let's take the *Product Quality Law* as an example. Since the *Tort Liability Law* has not defined the products and defects, the provisions of Article 2 and Article 46 of the *Product Quality Law* shall be applied.

Third, the *Tort Liability Law* gives the general provisions, and another relatively special law gives the special provisions. Paragraph 1 of Article 86 of the *Tort Liability Law* give provisions on liabilities for damage caused by collapse of defective real estate of owner and contractor: "If a building, structure or any other facility collapses, causes harm to another, the builder and the constructor shall bear joint and several liabilities. After the builder or constructor compensated [to the victim], if there is any other liable person, [the builder or constructor] has the right to claim indemnity from the other liable person." The provisions of Paragraph 1 of Article 69 of the *Construction Law* cover the joint and several liabilities of construction supervisor: "In case a construction supervisor colludes with the owner or contractor, plays tricks and reduce the quality of works, it shall be ordered to make correction, shall be fined, and shall get its qualification class reduced or its qualification certificate revoked; where there is any illegal gain, such gain shall be confiscated; where any loss is caused, it shall undertake the joint compensation liabilities; where a crime is constituted, the criminal liabilities shall be legally investigated."

---

[19]Under such circumstance, the special rule of *General Principles of the Civil Law* as the absolutely general law is no longer judged, for this issue belongs to the general tort law.

[20]Yang (2010).

7.4.2.2   Rules for Validity Judgment when There Is Conflict Between Special Tort Law and General Tort Law

It should be pointed out that, the essential change made by the *Tort Liability Law* to *General Principles of the Civil Law* are mainly embodied in the scope of personal damage compensation and the component of no-fault liabilities for environmental pollution, and as special tort laws, all the tort liability norms in the legislations before the *Tort Liability Law* was adopted must keep consistent with *General Principles of the Civil Law*, so that the special tort laws which are subject to validity judgment owing to the existence of validity conflict only exist in these two fields.

1. Scope of Personal Damage Compensation

Before the *Tort Liability Law* was enacted, in the middle of 1990s, the original *Product Quality Law*, the *Law on Protection of Rights and Interests of Consumers* and the *State Compensation Law* provided the scope of personal damage compensation in accordance with the basic spirit of Article 119 of *General Principles of the Civil Law*, and such compensation items were not change when the *Product Quality Law* was amended in 2000 and the *State Compensation Law* was amended in 2001. As mentioned above, the *Law on Protection of Rights and Interests of Consumers* is an absolutely special law, and the *Tort Liability Law* is also different from the *State Compensation Law* in the aspect of application scope. Therefore, only the provisions of Paragraph 1 of Article 44 of the *Product Quality Law* conflict with Article 16 of the *Tort Liability Law* in the aspect of validity: "In case the injured person is injured owing to any defect in product, the infringing party shall make compensation for expenses such as medical expenses, nursing expenses during medical treatment period, and income reduced by lost working time; where disability is caused, the infringing party also shall pay the expenses of life support devices, living allowances and disability compensation of disabled person as well as the necessary living expenses of persons supported; where death of the injured person is caused, and shall pay the funeral expenses, death compensation as well as the necessary living expenses of the deceased's dependents." It is clear through comparison that, the item "necessary living expenses of the deceased's dependents" is not listed in Article 16 of the *Tort Liability Law* any longer. A s mentioned above, owing to the provisions of Article 4 of the *Circular of Supreme People's Court on Several Issues relating to Application of the Tort Liability Law of the People's Republic of China* (F.F. [2010] No. 23), this issue become uncertain. However, it is clear that, there is no reason for the compensation items of product liabilities to be different from the general provisions of the *Tort Liability Law*. Therefore, such article will not be applied any longer in judicial practice.

2. Legal Effect of Environmental Pollution Caused by Third-Party Fault

Article 68 of the *Tort Liability Law* provides the unreal joint and several liabilities for environmental pollution caused by third-party fault: "If the environmental pollution is caused by a third party's fault, causes harm, the victim may claim compensation from the polluter, and may claim compensation from the third party.

After the polluter paid compensation [to the victim], it has the right to claim indemnity from the third party." However, Paragraph 1 of Article 90 of the *Marine Environment Protection Law* gives the exceptional provisions for exempting the polluter from liabilities and imposing such liabilities on third party: "The liable party for marine environmental pollution shall eliminate the danger, and make compensation for losses; where the marine environmental pollution is caused by intentional conduct or negligence of any third party, such third party shall eliminate the danger and undertake the compensation liabilities." The authoritative interpretation given by the legislature reveals that, the legislature hopes to "grant to the infringed party the right to select the object of compensation" through Article 68 of the *Tort Liability Law*.[21] Therefore, the provisions about taking third-party fault as ground for exemption in Paragraph 1 of Article 90 of the *Marine Environment Protection Law* will not be applied any longer in judicial practice.

7.4.3 Basic Rule for Validity Judgment for Special Tort Laws Under Referral Clause Judgment Mode

7.4.3.1 Basic Rules for Referral Clause Judgment Mode

The referral clause means the clause which have no independent normative connotation (even the meaning of interpretation rules), but simply refer to specific norm, and a judge must determine its effect on the basis of the purpose of specific norm referred by it.[22] On the basis of the specificity of clause referred by referral clause, the referral clause may be divided into opened referral clause and closed referral clause. The so-called opened referral clause means the referral norm which only gives the provisions such as "In case there are other provisions in other laws, such provisions shall apply law". For example, it is provided in Article 85 of the *Real Rights Law* that: "Where there is any provision on the handling of contiguous relationship, such provision shall apply; where there isn't any provision on it, the contiguous relationship shall be handled in light of the local customs." Since the referral object is not specifically determined, when applying such clause, the court must only make formal judgment for the tort liability norms in other laws. The legislature may also amend or add the referred articles by amending laws or enacting new laws.

The so-called closed referral clause means the clause which clearly provides the referring object, and in the course of application, the court may only find the referred clause in the laws which are specifically provided by such referral clause. The legislature can only amend the referred clause by amending such laws, and may not add the referred clauses through new legislation. In legislative techniques, there

---

[21]See Wang (2010a, pp. 341–342).
[22]Su (2004, p. 35).

are two situations, namely the situation that the book title mark is used and the situation that no book title mark is used. The situation that the book title mark is used is represented by the provisions in Paragraph 2 of Article 113 of the *Contract Law:* "In case the business operator has any fraudulent conduct in provision of commodities or services to consumer, it shall undertake the damage compensation liabilities in accordance with the provisions of the *Law of the People's Republic of China on Protection of Rights and Interests of Consumers*." The situation that no book title mark is used is represented by the provisions in Article 114 of the *Real Rights Law*: "The finding of drifted, buried or concealed object shall be dealt with by reference to the provisions relating to lost and found objects. In case there are other provisions in the laws such as law for preservation of antiques, such provisions shall apply." From the viewpoint of stability and compatibility of legislation, it is advised not to use the book title mark.

7.4.3.2   Opened Referral Clause in the *Tort Liability Law*

The opened referral clause in the *Tort Liability Law* can be divided into always-opened referral clauses and exceptionally-opened referral clauses on the basis of referral mode. The so-called always-opened referral clause means that the contents which are intentionally reserved by the *Tort Liability Law* and to be provided by other laws, so as to achieve the referral purpose by giving description in article of the *Tort Liability Law*. The so-called exceptionally-opened referral clause means that the *Tort Liability Law* gives general provisions on an issue, but exceptionally permits other laws to give special provisions on such issue, so as to achieve the referral purpose by using the words "In case there are other provisions in other laws".

1. Always-Opened Referral Clause[23]

There are always-opened referral clauses in the *Tort Liability Law*[24]:

First, the provisions relating to no-fault liability principle in Article 7: "If an actor damages another's civil rights or interests, no matter the actor is at fault or not, in case that a provision of law requires him to bear tort liability, then that provision

---

[23]Professor Karl Larenz calls such incomplete article form which requires the further enrichment of content or detailed description of concept or type of application in other articles as the "explanatory article". See Karl (2003, p. 138).

[24]Subject to Article 64 of the *Tort Liability Law*: "The legal rights and interests of medical institution and its medical personnel are protected by law. [One who] upsets the medical order, disturbs work and life of medical personnel, shall bear legal liability according to law." "According to law" here is mainly quoted from Article 40, the *Practicing Physician Law*: "those who hamper the practicing of the physician according to law, insult, slander, threaten or beat the physician or infringe on the personal freedom of the physician, and disturb the normal work and life of the physician will be punished according to the public security management punishment law. If a crime is constituted, the criminal responsibility will be investigated according to the law." However, this regulation is not the tort liability code.

shall govern." Such clause applies to the no-fault liabilities provided in the *Tort Liability Law*, and also refers the no-fault liability torts expressly provided in other laws. For example, it is provided in Paragraph 2 of Article 84 of the *Animal Epidemic Prevention Law* that: "If the provisions of this Law are violated, and thus any animal disease is spread and other persons incur personal injury or property damage, the civil liabilities shall be legally undertaken." It is provided in Paragraph 3 of Article 32 of the *Mineral Resource Law* that: "If the exploitation of mineral resources causes any loss to the production and living of other persons, the compensation shall be made and the necessary remedial measures shall be taken."

Second, the provisions relating to burden of proof for polluter with respect to defense in Article 66: "When a dispute arises about an environmental pollution, the polluter shall bear the burden of proving exculpatory or extenuating circumstances stipulated in laws and the lack of causal relation between its act and the harm." Article 92 of the *Marine Environment Protection Law*, Article 63 of the *Law on Prevention and Control of Air Pollution* and Article 85 of the *Law on Prevention and Control of Water Pollution* give the provisions on defense cause.

Third, the provisions relating to rules for application of legal compensation limit for ultra-hazardous liabilities in Article 77: "To bear ultra-hazardous liability, if other laws provide compensation limitation, then that law shall govern." The *Civil Aviation Law* and the *Maritime Law* in the current legal system of China as well as the *Warsaw Pact* participated in by China respectively provide the compensation limit for ultra-hazardous liabilities. It should be pointed out that, since administrative regulations are not laws, the provisions relating to compensation limit for ultra-hazardous liabilities in administrative regulations are not the objects of such referral clauses.

2. Exceptionally-Opened Referral Clause[25]

The exceptionally-opened referral clause in the *Tort Liability Law* is the provisions about force majeure in Article 29: "If the harm to another is caused by force majeure, [the actor] shall not bear liability. If other laws contain [such] rules, then that law shall govern." In the current laws of China, there are two categories of such exceptionally-opened referral clause for force majeure: The first category is that the force-majeure-based ground for exemption is fully or partially excluded. For example, it is provided in Paragraph 1 of Article 48 of the *Post* Law that: "A postal enterprise shall not be liable for making compensation for losses to receipt mail caused by: ① a force majeure, except for losses to an insured receipt mail caused by a force majeure; ..." It is provided in Article 70 of the *Tort Liability* Law that: "If a nuclear accident occurs to a civilian nuclear facility, cause harm to another, the operator of the civilian nuclear facility shall bear tort liability, except it can be proved that the harm is caused by force majeure such as war or is intentionally

---

[25]Some scholars define the attached provisions, inserted exclusion regulation or separately added negative element and other circumstances in the same article as the "restrictive article". See Huang (2007, pp. 167–168).

caused by the injured person." Therefore, the defense based on force majeure for damage caused by civilian nuclear facility is only limited to war and situations similar to war. It is provided in Article 71: "If civilian aircrafts cause harm to another, the operator of the civilian aircraft shall bear tort liability, except it can be proved that the harm is intentionally caused by the injured person." Therefore, the force majeure is not a defense for damage caused by civilian aircraft.

The second category is environmental protection laws. It should be pointed out that, the above-mentioned Article 66 of the *Tort Liability Law* as an always-opened referral clause is actually also the referral object of Article 29. On the basis of the provisions in Paragraph 2 of Article 92 of the *Marine Environment Protection Law* and Article 63 of the *Law on Prevention and Control of Air Pollution*, the force-majeure-based ground for exemption is only limited to "natural disaster which is fully caused by force majeure", and the precondition is given as follows: "the damage of environmental pollution can't be prevented after the reasonable measures are taken in time". It is provided in Paragraph 2 of Article 85 of the *Law on Prevention and Control of Water Pollution* that: "In case the damage of water pollution is caused by force majeure, the pollutant-discharging party shall not be required to undertake the compensation liabilities; unless there are other provisions in other laws." The provisions of Article 86 of the *Law on Prevention and Control of Environmental Pollution Caused by Solid Wastes* are similar to those of Article 66 of the *Tort Liability Law*. It is provided in Article 64 of the current *Environmental Protection Law* that: "In case any damage is caused by polluting the environment and disturbing the ecology, the tort liabilities shall be undertaken in accordance with the relevant provisions of the *Tort Liability Law of the People's Republic of China*." Since the *Environmental Protection Law* is a general law in the field of environmental pollution liabilities, unless the special environmental tort law expressly provides that the force-majeure-based defense cause is only limited to "damage fully caused by irresistible natural disaster" and gives the condition that "the damage of environmental pollution can't be prevented after the reasonable measures are taken in time", the provisions of the *Tort Liability Law* shall apply.

7.4.3.3 Closed Referral Clause in the *Tort Liability Law*[26]

The closed referral clause in the *Tort Liability Law* is the provisions about legal application of liabilities for traffic accident of motor vehicles in Article 48: "If a motor vehicle causes harm in a traffic accident, [the tortfeasors] shall bear compensatory liability according to related rules in the *Law on Road Traffic Safety*." The said provisions mainly refer to the provisions in Article 76 of the *Law on Road Traffic Safety*.

---

[26]In some theories, this article form may be divided into the "explanatory article". See Su (2004, p. 138).

It should be noted that, it is provided in Article 27 of the *Tort Liability Law* that "If the harm is [solely] due to the injured person's intentional [act], the actor shall not bear liability." While it is provided in Paragraph 2 of Article 76 of the *Law on Road Traffic Safety* that: "In case the loss of traffic accident is caused by intentionally collision with motor vehicle by non-motor vehicle driver or pedestrian, the motor vehicle driver is not required to undertake the compensation liabilities." As a result, there is conflict between Article 27 of the *Tort Liability Law* and Paragraph 2 of Article 76 of the *Law on Road Traffic Safety*. The Writer believes that, the referral provision of Article 48 of the *Tort Liability Law* only means that the liabilities composition, but the defense is not referred.[27]

7.4.4 Collateral Issue: Validity of Tort Liability Norms in Administrative Regulations

It is provided in the *Provisions of Supreme People's Court on Quotation of Normative Legal Documents such as Laws and Regulations in Judgment Instruments (F.SH.[2009] No. 14)* that: "The civil judgment instruments shall apply laws, legal interpretations or judicial interpretations. The administrative regulations, local regulations, autonomous regulations or separate regulations which must be applied may be directly applied." Among the current administrative regulations of China, there are many tort liability norms, especially in the field of medical damage liabilities. After the *Tort Liability Law* comes into effect, how to judge whether the administrative regulations are "must be applied" is a collateral issue about judgment on validity of special tort law under the whole judgment of law mode.

It is provided in Paragraph 1 of Article 88 of the *Legislation Law* that: "The validity of laws is higher than that of administrative regulations, local regulations and rules." Therefore, if the tort liability norms in administrative regulations conflict with the *Tort Liability Law*, the *Tort Liability Law* shall apply. Therefore, the tort liability norms in the *Regulations for Handling of Medical Accidents*, including the authentication procedure, shall not be applied, and the latter has been confirmed by Article 3 of the *Circular of Supreme People's Court on Several Issues Relating to Application of the Tort Liability Law of the People's Republic of China* (F.F. [2010] No. 23).

It should be pointed out that, though such administrative regulation may not be applied in determination of tort liabilities, they will not get invalidated owing to implementation of the *Tort Liability Law*, and other norms shall still be valid as administrative regulations.

---

[27] As to the detailed explanation, see Wang (2012).

7.5 Impact on Essential Tort Law by the *General Provisions of Civil Law*

The tort liability norms in the *General Provisions of Civil Law* mainly include the generalized norms of the *Tort Liability Law,* and the newly-added norms which are mainly distributed in Chapter 8 "Civil Liabilities" and also distributed in Chapter 9 "Limitation of Action".

7.5.1 Generalization of Norms in the Tort Liability Law

The generalization of the norms in the *Tort Liability Law* mainly involves the following aspects:

First, the generalization of the apportionment rules for general multi-party tort liabilities. Article 177 of the *General Provisions of Civil Law* takes out the final liabilities apportionment rule for proportional liabilities contained in Article 12[28] of the *Tort Liability Law* and provide such rule as a general rule: "When more than two persons undertake the proportional liabilities according to law, in case the proportion of liabilities can be determined, they shall respectively undertake the corresponding liabilities; in case it is difficult to determine the proportion of liabilities, they shall equally undertake the liabilities." This is praiseworthy. The first two paragraphs of Article 178 of the *General Provisions of Civil Law* integrate the rules for apportionment of outward liabilities provided in Article 13 of the *Tort Liability Law* and the rules for apportionment of inward final liabilities provided in Article 14, Paragraph 3 considers the two main application scope (namely tort liabilities and breach liabilities) and provides that "The joint and several liabilities shall be provided by laws or agreed upon by parties concerned.", so as to generalize the rules of joint and several liabilities and eliminate the defect that there are no rule for joint and several liabilities in civil law of China and the provisions about joint obligations in Article 87 of *General Principles of the Civil Law* have to be used.[29] In the future, the *General Provisions Volume of Civil Code* may also further integrate the inward liability apportionment rules for proportional liabilities provided in Article 177 and for joint and several liabilities provided in Paragraph 2 of Article 178.[30]

Second, the generalization of main tort liabilities. Paragraph 1 of Article 179 of the *General Provisions of Civil Law* is the provisions on main civil liabilities.

---

[28]Article 12 of the Tort Liability Law provides that: "If two or more persons engage in tortious acts separately, cause a single harm, in case that the extent of responsibility can be determined, each one bears corresponding liability; in case that the extent of responsibility can not be determined, compensatory liability is borne equally".

[29]Similar issue about application of law exists in Taiwan district, see Qiu (2004, p. 394).

[30]See Wang (2010d).

Eventually, such paragraph fails to establish the liability "to repair the ecological environment" provided in the *General Provisions of Civil Law (draft) (first-deliberation draft for solicitation of public opinions)*, and fails to fully meet the legislative intention of the newly-added basic green principle "The civil activities carried out by civil subjects shall be favorable for saving resources and protecting ecological environment" in Article 9 of such law. It is advised that, the *Tort Liabilities Volume of Civil Code* should enrich Chapter 8 "Liabilities for Environmental Pollution" of the *Tort Liability Law*[31] into "Liabilities for Polluting Environment and Damaging Ecology",[32] and provide the application of the liability to "repair the ecological environment".[33] It should be noted that, the general provisions "In case the punitive compensation is provided for in other laws, such provisions shall apply." have been added into Paragraph 2 of Article 179 of the *General Provisions of Civil Law*, and there will be the legislative trend to expand the application scope in the future.

Third, the generalization of three defenses for tort liabilities. Article 180 integrates the contents of Article 107 and Article 153 of *General Principles of the Civil Law*, unifies the provisions on force majeure, and applies it as a defense in the whole civil liability system. Subsequently, the *General Provisions of Civil Law* provides two defenses (namely justifiable defense and act of rescue) in Article 181 and Article 182, of which the contents are slightly adjusted as compared with Article 30 and Article 31 of the *Tort Liability Law*. It is advised that, in the future, such important defense cause as self-help behavior should be added into the *General Provisions Volume of Civil Code*.[34]

Fourth, the generalization of liabilities for damage incurred by samaritan. Article 183 of the *General Provisions of Civil Law* gives the provisions on liabilities for damage incurred by samaritan, of which the contents are slightly adjusted as compared with Article 23 of the *Tort Liability Law*, and for which the structure used to arrange the provisions of Article 109 of *General Principles of the Civil Law* in Section 1 "General Provisions" of Chapter 6 "Civil Liabilities" is still adopted.

---

[31]The title of Chapter 8 of the *Tort Liability Law* uses the word "pollution of environment", but the article in Chapter 8 uses the word "pollute the environment", It need to be pointed out that the word "pollute the environment" is more accurate. The future *Tort Liability Volume of Civil Code* should use the word "pollute the environment".

[32] 《环境保护法》第64条规定因污染环境和破坏生态造成损害的，应当依照《中华人民共和国侵权责任法》的有关规定承担侵权责任. Article 64 of the *Environment Protection Law* provides that the liability for polluting the environment and destroying the ecology should refer to the *Tort Liability Law*.

[33]Refer to the *Interpretations of the Supreme People's Court about Several Issues of Applicable Laws in the Hearing of Environmental Civil Public Welfare Lawsuit Case* (Fa Shi [2015] No. 1), Article 15, Articles 20–24.

[34]Article 23 of Volume 8 "Tort Liability Law" of the *Civil Law of the People's Republic of China (draft)* (December 23, 2002) has stipulated the "self-help". However, this article is not retained in the subsequent draft.

Fifth, the generalization of priority rules for tort liabilities. Taking the priority of tort liabilities in Article 4 of the *Tort Liability Law* as compilation object, Article 187 of the *General Provisions of Civil Law* provides the "priority rules for civil liabilities".

In the future, it is unnecessary to repeat the above-mentioned generalized norms in the *Tort Liabilities Volume of Civil Code*.

7.5.2 Newly-Added Tort Liability Norms in the General Provisions of Civil Law

The tort liability norms newly added into the *General Provisions of Civil Law* mainly include the following aspects:

First, provisions on exemption of liabilities for damage caused by voluntary emergency rescue are added. At the last phase, Article 184 was added into the *General Provisions of Civil Law*: "In case the rescued person is damaged owing to voluntary emergency rescue, the rescuing person will not undertake the civil liabilities." Such article does not give the exceptional provision for intentional conduct or gross negligence,[35] it is really inappropriate to enact them in a hurry. It is advised that the Supreme People's Court should issue the judicial interpretation as soon as possible, and correct such legislative mistake in the course of compilation of the *Civil Code* in the future.

Second, the tort liabilities for infringement upon personality interests of heroes and martyrs are added. Article 185 of the *General Provisions of Civil Law* provides that: "Civil liabilities shall be undertaken for the damage to name, portrait, reputation or honor of heroes and martyrs if such damage infringe upon social public interests." This is the typical legislative embodiment of implementation of the provisions "carry forward the core values of socialism" provided in Article 1 of such law.[36] Through comparison with the provisions in Paragraph 1 of Article 3 of the *Judicial Interpretation on Emotional Damage Compensation*,[37] we can find that they have the similar scope of protection. Article 185 of the *General Provisions of*

---

[35]See Shi (2017, pp. 437–438).

[36]See Shi (2017, p. 440).

[37]Item 1 of article 3 of the *Interpretation of the Supreme People's Court on Problems regarding the Ascertainment of Compensation Liability for Emotional Damages in Civil Torts* provides that: The people's court shall accept according to law cases arising from any of the following infringements related to the death of a person that caused mental suffering to the close relative of the deceased, and brought to the court by the relative for claiming emotional damages: (1) infringement upon the name, portrait, reputation or honor of a deceased person by insulting, libelling, disparaging, vilifying or by other means contrary to the societal public interests or societal morality.

Civil Law highlights the infringement upon "heroes and martyrs" and the damage to "social public interests", and in the future, the corresponding public interest litigation system should be established. The provisions of such articles are occasional, and the reputation right dispute case for Langya Shan Five Heroic Men[38] which aroused great controversy in the course of enactment of the *General Provisions of Civil Law* has obviously driven the establishment of such provisions. The judicial application of such article in the Reputation Dispute Case (PENG Jiahui vs China Narrative) published in the *Gazette in the Supreme People's Court* in 2002[39] can be taken for reference.

Third, the limitation of action for tort liabilities is added. The *General Provisions of Civil Law* provides two starting points for calculation of special limitation of action, and they are actually the special protection system for disadvantaged infringed party. It is provided in Article 190 that: "The limitation of action of claim of a person without capacity of civil conduct or with limited capacity of civil conduct against his/her legal agent shall be calculated from the date on which such legal agency is terminated." It is provided in Article 191 that: "The limitation of action for damage compensation claim for sexual abuse on minors shall be calculated from the date on which the age of injured person reaches 18 years." These two articles about special limitation of action in the *General Provisions of Civil Law* indicate that in the future, the *Tort Liabilities Volume of Civil Code* should give special provisions regarding non-full capacity actor (especially minors) being infringed upon by legal representative or sexual abused. On the basis of this legislative thinking, during the compilation of the *General Provisions Volume of Civil Code* in the future, it is also advised by the Writer that, the third sentence of Article 11 ("In case the party concerned whose personal freedom is illegally restricted requests for revocation of marriage, such request shall be lodged within one year after the date on which the personal freedom is restored.") in the *Marriage Law* should be taken as reference. On the basis of Article 191, the following provision is added: "In case of illegal restriction on personal freedom and sexual abuse, the limitation of action for damage compensation claim shall be calculated from the date on which the personal freedom is restored."

The above-mentioned tort liability norms which are added into the *General Provisions of Civil Law* during the compilation of Civil Code should be coordinated with the *Tort Liabilities Volume of Civil Code*.

---

[38]The *Supreme People's Court Publishes 4 Typical Cases about the Protection of the Personality Rights and Interests of Heroes and Martyrs like Langya Shan Five Heroic Men*, October 19th 2016.

[39]*Reputation Dispute of Peng Jiahui vs China Narrative, the Bulletin of Supreme People's Court of the People's Republic of China*, No. 6 2002.

7.5.3 Relatively Low Impact on Essential Tort Law by the General Provisions of Civil Law

After the *General Provisions of Civil Law* was promulgated and implemented, the judgment scope for essential general tort law include three laws, namely the *General Provisions of Civil Law*, *General Principles of the Civil Law* and the *Tort Liability Law*. Since the rule "a new law shall prevail over an old law" is applied to the relationship between the *General Provisions of Civil Law* and *General Principles of the Civil Law*,[40] the relationship between the *General Provisions of Civil Law* and the *Tort Liability Law*,[41] and the impact on general tort laws by the *General Provisions of Civil Law*, the rule that "a new law shall prevail over an old law" can be applied comprehensively. On the basis of the above rules, the essential contents of "old general tort laws" composed of *General Principles of the Civil Law* and the *Tort Liability Law* can be determined firstly, and then the relationship between tort law norms in the *General Provisions of Civil Law* and "old general tort laws" will be treated in accordance with the rule that "a new law shall prevail over an old law", and finally the "new general tort laws" will be established. After the "new general tort laws" are established, the "new special tort laws" will be determined on the basis of the above-mentioned validity rules for "old special tort law".

On the basis of the above analysis, the tort liability norms in the *General Provisions of Civil Law* can be divided into two categories, namely the generalized norms of the *Tort Liability Law* and the newly-added norms. The generalization is only slight adjustment for specific rules, so that as for the *Tort Liability Law*, such two categories fall into the application scope of the rule "a new law shall prevail over an old law". In principle, we can believe that, owing to their priority over the corresponding rules and newly-added rules in the *Tort Liability Law,* the tort liability norms in the *General Provisions of Civil Law* will not exceed the impact of tort liability norms in *General Principles of the Civil Law* as adjusted by the *Tort Liability Law*. Therefore, the "new general tort law" is essentially the slight adjustment to those tort liability norms which are generalized by the *General Provisions of Civil Law* and the addition of a few new tort liability norms, and the impact on special tort law may be ignored, so that the whole essential tort law also remains basically stable.

---

[40]Li (2017).

[41]*Report of the Legal Committee of the 12th National People 's Congress on the Deliberation of the General Provisions of Civil Law of the People' s Republic of China (Draft)*, adopted at the Second Meeting of the Fifth Presidium Meeting of the 12th National People 's Congress on March 12th 2017.

7.6 Legislative Prospect for Essential Tort Law in Future

According to the legislative mode whereby the *Civil Code* is enacted volume by volume and the legislative document that the legislature has issued, in the future, maybe the *Personality Rights Law* will be enacted, and the *General Provisions of Obligation Laws* will also be enacted. *General Principles of the Civil Law* will also finally step down from the stage of history. Even if the situation that the *Tort Liability Law* may be amended in the course of compilation of the *Civil Code* is not considered, only the above-mentioned legislative activities in the future will have the relatively material impact on the general tort laws and then the special tort laws. Therefore, it is also very important to study these two issues in advance.

7.6.1 Possible Change to General Tort Laws in Future

7.6.1.1 Possible Impact on General Tort Laws by Enactment of the *Personality Rights Law* and the *General Provisions of Obligation Law*

If the *Personality Rights Law* is enacted in the future, it will inevitably contain some tort liability norms, and this is consistent with the close relationship between the *Personality Rights Law* and the *Tort Liability Law*. In the future, if the *General Provisions of Obligation Laws* is enacted, the tort obligations and tort liabilities will surely be involved, especially the relationship with damage compensation liabilities. It is thus clear that, the enactment of the *Personality Rights Law* and the *General Provisions of Obligation Law* will surely impact the general tort law to a certain extent. The Writer believes that, this impact may involve two situations: The first is to establish new general tort law norms. This situation is mainly embodied in the *Personality Rights Law*, whereby the type of infringement upon personality rights, special civil liabilities and tort liability apportionment rules are provided. The second is to amend the existing provisions of general tort law. This situation often occurs in the *General Provisions of Obligation Law*, such as the improvement of multi-party obligation system. Generally, the possible impact on the general tort laws by the enactment of the *Personality Rights Law* and the *General Provisions of Obligation Law* is incremental.

7.6.1.2 Possible Impact on General Tort Law by Abolishment of *General Principles of the Civil Law*

Different from the incremental impact on the general tort laws by the enactment of the *Personality Rights Law* and the *General Provisions of Obligation Law*, the possible impact on the general tort laws by the abolishment of *General Principles of the Civil Law* will be decremental. Though the *General Provisions of Civil Law* retains the chapter "Civil Liabilities", it only retains the general provisions and forms of civil liabilities, and does not provide any specific tort civil liability norm. In light of the analysis above, the current tort liability norm in *General Principles of the Civil Law* which will be deleted mainly includes two categories of norms which are not provided in the *Tort Liability Law*": The first category is the general type of torts provided in the part about tort liabilities in *General Principles of the Civil Law*, namely the general articles about infringement upon intellectual property rights and unfair competition behavior in Article 118. After such article is deleted in the future, Paragraph 2 of Article 2 and Paragraph 1 of Article 6 of the *Tort Liability Law* may be applied. The second category is the "regressive article" in the *Tort Liability Law*, that is the provisions about property damage compensation in Article 19, which corresponds to Article 117 of *General Principles of the Civil Law*. After such article is deleted in the future, it is advised to amend Article 19 of the *Tort Liability Law* or through the "judicial interpretation for properties damage compensation" issued by the Supreme People's Court.

7.6.2 Legislative Room and Legislative Techniques for Special Tort Laws in Future

One of the purposes of enactment of general tort laws is to determine the basic principles and overall framework of tort liability norms, and reserve the legislative room for future special tort laws in a planned manner. Either the enactment or amendment of special tort laws must be carried out in the legislative room reserved in the general tort laws. In order to ensure the validity of tort liability norms in special tort laws, it is necessary to apply certain legislative techniques. Therefore, the legislative room and legislative techniques under two modes should be determined respectively on the basis of the two different modes for judgment of validity of special tort laws as mentioned above.

7.6.2.1 Future Legislative Room and Legislative Techniques for Special Tort Laws Under Whole Judgment of Law Mode

As for future legislative room and legislative techniques for special tort laws under whole judgment of law mode, it is necessary to distinguish between non-absolutely special law and absolutely special law.

The non-absolutely special laws can supplement or improve the general tort laws, but may not go against or distort the legislative intention of general tort laws. The supplementation of norms means to supplement the tort liability norms which are not provided by the general tort laws, which often involves the provisions on special limitation of action. The improvement of norms means to further improve the tort liability norms provided by the general tort laws, which involves three situations: The first is to embody the abstract provisions in the general tort laws, such as providing the specific equitable liabilities; the second is to clarify the ambiguous provisions in the general tort laws, such as providing the property damage compensation rules; the third is to typify the general tort laws or add new types, such as providing the vicarious liabilities of other user.

The absolutely special laws may give the special provisions which are different from those of the general tort laws, so as to reflect the special protection on special populations. For example, the *Law on Protection of Rights and Interests of Consumers* give special provisions on the types of tort liabilities,[42] the calculation of damage compensation, and the system of punitive compensation.[43] The laws on protection of disadvantaged populations to be amended or enacted in the future, such as the *Law on Protection of Disabled Persons*, the *Law on Protection of Rights and Interests of Women*, the *Law on Protection of Rights and Interests of Elderly Persons*, the *Law on Protection of Minors*, may give special provisions on the calculation of damage compensation and the conditions for application of emotional damage compensation.

7.6.2.2   Future Legislative Room and Legislative Techniques for Special Tort Laws Under Referral Clause Judgment Mode

As for future legislative room and legislative techniques for special tort laws under referral clause judgment mode, it is necessary to distinguish between opened referral clause and closed referral clause. As mentioned above, there are 4 opened referral clauses in the *Tort Liability Law*, and the legislative room reserved for every referral clause and the corresponding legislative techniques are as follows:

First, the referral clause provided in Article 7 for no-fault liability principle. In the future, as long as they are really applied to no-fault liabilities, the torts provided in departmental laws may be determined as valid as special tort law. However, it should be noted that, in the current legal system of China, though no fault requisite is expressly provided for the tort liability norms in most of the departmental laws, the fault liability principle is applied. In the future, if the legislature can improve the normalized nature of legislative techniques for tort liability norms in departmental laws, the determination of validity of such special tort laws will be supported.

Second, the referral clause provided in Article 29 for force majeure. In the future, the exceptional provisions for force majeure in special tort laws may include two categories: The first is to preclude the force majeure as ground for exemption; the second is to impose conditions for the application of force majeure as ground for exemption.

---

[42]See Wang (2014).

[43]For this legislative development, the predictive suggestions of the Writer before the modification of the *Law on Protection of Rights and Interests of Consumers* are realized. See Wang (2011).

Third, the referral clause provided in Article 66 for burden of proof of polluter for defense. In the future when the current environmental protection laws are amended and new environmental protection laws (such as the *Law on Prevention and Control of Light Prevention*) are enacted, the particular defense may be provided on the basis of the characteristics of different types of different pollution, provided that the basic rules established by the *Tort Liability Law* may not be violated.

Fourth, the referral clause provided in Article 77 for application rules for legal compensation limit for ultra-hazardous liabilities. In the future, in case the special tort laws provide the types of ultra-hazardous liabilities and apply the no-fault liability principle, then the legal compensation limit may and should be provided. More importantly, it is necessary to incorporate the current administrative regulations, such as the statute limit of compensation for ultra-hazardous liabilities given in the *Reply of State Council on Issues Relating to Damage Compensation Liabilities for Nuclear Accidents*, into the corresponding laws.

The only closed referral clause in the *Tort Liability Law* is Article 48, and the referral object of such article is the *Law on Road Traffic Safety*. Therefore, in the future, the amendment of tort liability norms for traffic accidents of motor vehicles can be realized by amending Article 76 and relevant articles the *Law on Road Traffic Safety*.

References

Huang Maorong, *Law Method and Modern Civil Law*, Law Press, 2007.

Karl Larenz, *Methodology of Law*, translated by Chen Aie, the Commercial Press, 2003, p. 138.

Li Jianguo, the *Explanation of the Daft of the General Provisions of Civil Law of the People's Republic of China*, at the Fifth Session of the Twelfth National People's Congress on March 8th, 2017.

Qiu Congzhi, *General Rules of Obligation Volume of Newly Revised Civil Law* (Volume II), China Renmin University Press 2004.

Shi Hong, ed. *Clauses Interpretation, Legislation Reasons and Relevant Provisions of the General Principles of Civil Law of People's Republic of China*, Peking University Press, 2017.

Su Yongqin, *Economic Rationality in Autonomy of Private Law*, China Renmin University Press, 2004.

Wang Zhu, "An Investigation into the History of 'Fair Liability' of Chinese Tort Law", *Journal of Gansu Political and Legal College*, No. 2, 2008.

Wang Zhu, *Theory of Apportionment of Tory Liability*, China Renmin University Press 2009.

Wang Shengming, *Interpretations of the Tort Liability Law of the People's Republic of China*, China Legal Publishing House, 2010a.

Wang Zhu, "On the Abolishment of the Living expenses of Dependent Person", *Chinese Social Science Today*, Nov. 4th, 2010b.

Wang Zhu, "Interpretation of Constitutionality of the Legislative Procedure of Tort Liability Law", *Legal Science Monthly*, No. 5, 2010c.

Wang Zhu, "On the Method of Determining Ultimate Liability in Apportionment of Tort Liability between Multiple Tortfeasors", *Studies in Law and Business*, No. 6, 2010d.

Wang Zhu, "On the Right of Contribution in Joint and Several Liability– With Comment on the Mode of Redistribution of the Share of Insolvent Jointly and Severally Liable Tortfeasor", *Law Science*, No. 3, 2010e.

Wang Zhu, "On the Determination of Tort Law in Substance and Legislation Prospect", *Journal of Sichuan University (Social Science Edition)*, No. 3, 2011.

Wang Zhu, " Study on Application of Comparative Fault in Special Tortious Acts—Based on Stipulations from Chapter Six to Ten of Tort Liability Law", *Journal of Henan Administrative Institute of Politics and Law*, No. 1, 2012.

Wang Zhu, "Analysis of the Liability of Marketing Participators of Defective Food and Pharmaceutical Product in China's Torts Law—Comments on Relevant Provisions of Opinions of the Supreme People's Court Concerning Certain Issues of Food and Pharmaceutical Product", *Renmin University Law Review*, No. 1, 2014.

Yang Lixin, "On the Nature of Damage Compensation for Wrongful Registration of Real Estate", *Modern Law Science*, No. 1, 2010.

Zhang Wenxian, *Jurisprudence*, Law Press, 2007, p. 141.

Zhu Yan, *Tort Law*, Law Press, 2011, p. 72.

Part III
Road Map for Compilation of *Civil Code* Under Pragmatic Thinking

On the basis of "pragmatic thinking" and with respect to the compilation of *Civil Code* in the future, either in the aspect of design of legislative procedure or in the aspect of setting of volumes and chapters, the writer will bring forth the legislative advices which are different from the generally-accepted opinions in academic circle. With respect to legislative procedure, the "pragmatic thinking" does not presume that the deliberation ability of legislature can surely meet the needs arising from compilation of *Civil Code*, but pays more attention to the impact on compilation of *Civil Code* by actual deliberation ability of legislature, and brings forth the "codification mode for non-basic laws" for the compilation of *Civil Code*; with respect to setting of volumes and chapters, the "pragmatic thinking" does not rely on the legislative route for drafting of *Civil Code*, but maintains the status of *General Principles of the Civil Law* as basic civil law, and proposes to realize the updating of the *General Provisions of Civil Law* and the *General Provisions of Obligation Law* in the framework of the *General Provisions Volume of Civil Code*.

Chapter 8 Design of Legislative Procedure for Compilation of *Civil Code* under "Non-basic Law Codification Mode".

Chapter 9 Analysis on the Orientation of the Compilation of General Provisions of Civil Law and Comment on Its Contents.

Chapter 10 Big Data Analysis on Deletion or Retention of Several Legal Norms in the *General Provisions of Civil Law*

Chapter 11 View on Formal Compilation Techniques for Articles of *Civil Code* from the *General Provisions of Civil Law*.

Chapter 12 Setting of Chapter "Obligation and Liabilities" in the *General Provisions Volume of Civil Code* for Providing the System "General Provisions of Obligation Law".

Chapter 13 Compiling Background and Structural Adjustment of the *Tort Liabilities Volume of Civil Code*.

Chapter 8
Design of Legislative Procedure for Compilation of *Civil Code* Under "Non-basic Law Codification Mode"

8.1 Make an Inventory of the Resources Available for the Compilation of *Civil Code*

Since *2002 Civil Law (Draft)* was deliberated, remarkable achievements have been made in China's civil law jurisprudence, providing more resources for the compiling efforts of the *Civil Code*. To be specific.

8.1.1 The Common Growth of Academics and Legislation

16 years ago, Professor Yang Zhenshan argued that "So far, there is not any scholar who has deeply and systematically studied the thoughts of famous German civil scholars such as Savigny or Jhering, or the influence of the German BGB itself, nor any scholar who has deeply and systematically studied the theories and practices of American real rights law, contract law, or tort law."[1] Looking back upon the three grand debates in the history of *Civil Code* compilation, it is obvious that every debate was a strong push to the development of theories of jurisprudence.[2] In the past 16 years, regarded by some scholars as "the fourth grand debate in the history of *Civil Code* compilation," it cannot be denied that the drafting efforts for *Civil Code* have also helped to improve the theoretical system of civil law, despite the fact that

---

[1]Yang (2003).
[2]Feng (2002).

This chapter is derived in part from an article published in the Peking University Law Journal, 3:1, 197–226 (2015), available online: https://www.tandfonline.com/doi/full/10.1080/20517483.2015.1049001.

there has been no fundamental change in the theoretical study of civil law in China. This is another example of "wading across the stream by feeling the way," a perfect embodiment of Chinese characteristics. As Professor YI Jiming pointed out, it is really hard to distinguish the threshold between the third and fourth attempts to draft *Civil Code*.[3] In fact, the theories of civil law grow out of the legislative experiences in the past 30 years. Therefore, it is not justified that the *Civil Code* can only be drafted after China's civil law theories become mature. Instead, this is a reciprocal process where civil law develops both academically and legislatively.

8.1.2 Accumulation of Materials and Reserve of Talents

In contrast to the severe lack of material available during the first three attempts of drafting *Civil Code*,[4] the research materials and publications available to the fourth attempt can only be described as "innumerable." Besides countless published academic monographs, papers and doctoral dissertations devoted to this specific topic, a complete list of *Civil Codes* from countries and regions all over the world has also been introduced, triggering a magnificent wave of translating these civil codes into Chinese.[5] Different from Chinese texts translated from English versions in the 20th Century, this round of translation campaigns has turned to the original versions, greatly improving the accuracy of the Chinese versions. In terms of the preparation of the academic materials, the talent pool essential to the process of *Civil Code* compilation, comprised of individuals of all ages and at all levels, is in the preliminary stages of formation. Most of these individuals have backgrounds in overseas education and are highly proficient in foreign languages. These all represent the tremendous advances as compared to 15 years ago.

8.1.3 Further Promotion of the Legislative Procedure

Based on the *2002 Civil Law (Draft)*, the Legislature passed the *Real Rights Law* in 2007, the *Tort Liability Law* in 2009, and the *Law on Choice of Law for Foreign-*

---

[3]Yi (2014).

[4]The main resources for the first attempt to draft civil code came from *Compiled Material of Civil Law* edited by Commission of Legal Affairs of the Central Government in 1953, including part 1 and 2 regarding of the Soviet Union, part 3 regarding of the countries of people's democracy, part 4 regarding the newly founded People's Republic of China, part 5 regarding China before the founding of the People's Republic, and parts 6 and 7 regarding capitalist countries. *Compiled Documents of Civil Law of People's Republic of China* edited by Teaching and Research Office of Beijing College of Political Science and Law and published by Beijing College of Political Science and Law Press in 1956. In the third attempt to draft the civil code, *Selected Documents of Civil Law of the World* (Law Press, 1983.) were published.

[5]It is represented by *Translated Works of Foreign Civil Laws* translated by Professor Xu Guodong.

Related Civil Relationships in 2010. As China finishes its drive to build a market economy and a complete configuration of civil law, a system that integrates laws already enacted would be a precursor for the future *Civil Code*.[6] More importantly, China's *Civil Code*, procedurally, still remains in the process of being drafted according to the process outlined in the *Legislation Law*.

8.2   The Legislature Is Still Too Overloaded to Deliberate the Texts of *Civil Code* in an Appropriate Manner

Single laws that constitute the future *Civil Code* have, on average, about 80 Chinese characters in every single Article.[7] To be specific:

Character statistics table of civil laws

Legislation	Character number	Article number	Average character number
Succession law	3080	37	83
General principles of the civil law	12905	156	83
Guarantee law	7925	96	83
Adoption law	2507	34	74
Marriage law	4115	51	81
Contract law	32809	428	77
Real rights law	19097	247	77
Tort liability law	6887	92	75
General provisions of civil law	15808	206	77

According to basic statistics, every single law (including drafts) has, on average, 80–120 Chinese characters in one Article. Considering the raw data regarding the historical deliberation capacity of NPC and its Standing Committee in terms of numbers of laws and articles, it is easy to estimate whether the Legislature of China has the capacity to adopt the *Civil Code* in accordance with the legislative procedures. This can be done by analyzing the volume of text deliberated by the 6th[8] to the 12th NPC and its Standing Committee.

---

[6]Sun (2012).

[7]This statistics includes the sequence number, such as "The First Chapter" and "The First Section".

[8]The 5th National People's Congress existed from March 1978 to June 1983. Considering instability of legislative activities shortly after the end of Cultural Revolution and the existing *Constitution* enacted in 1982, according to Article 58 of *Constitution* that states "The National People's Congress and its Standing Committee exercise the legislative power of the state", the author's statistics begins from the 6th National People's Congress.

According to the database of the official website of NPC, the following are the number of articles and laws deliberated by the 6th to 12th NPC and its Standing Committee (the differences among laws [including drafts] and Articles are omitted):

Legal deliberation capacity table of NPC and its standing committee

NPC sessions	Article of legislation (draft)		Number of legislation adopted	
	NPC	Standing committee	NPC	Standing committee
6th	367	1263	6	40
7th	924	1888	12	48
8th	1264	3935	21	76
9th	536	3743	4	72
10th	331	3368	4	69
11th	134	2809	2	120
12th	363	2869	3	150
Average number	559	2840	8	82

The usual deliberation capacity determines that since the 6th NPC, one NPC can deliberate 8 Laws, totalling 600 articles on average. One Standing Committee can deliberate 71 laws (including drafts), totalling 2800 articles. As for a single law, the maximum number of Articles passed by the legislature of China is often less than 300. Only in rare cases have they passed more than 300 Articles—in 1997, the 5th Session of the 8th NPC amended and passed the *Criminal Code* (452 Articles) and in 1999 the 2nd Session of the 9th NPC passed the *Contract Law* (428 Articles). The *2002 Civil Law (Draft)* had 1209 Articles, and it is foreseeable that the number of Articles in the future *Civil Code* will exceed 1200.

Since the end of 2002, NPC launched the first deliberation on a draft civil code. It was expected that the draft would be enacted by NPC after being deliberated twice by the Standing Committee of NPC.[9] Statistics show that the normal capacity of the Legislature can only guarantee the draft be deliberated by the Standing Committee of NPC, not NPC. Even when first deliberated by the Standing Committee of NPC, with the magnitude of the text and the highly complicated structure, the work of deliberation of the *Civil Code* is unlikely to be finished by a single Standing Committee. In order to reduce the difficulty the legislature is faced with in their efforts to deliberate the draft, optimized methods for deliberation should be sought under the framework of the *Constitution*, the *Legislation Law*, the *Rules of Procedure for the NPC*, and the *Rules of Procedure for the Standing Committee of NPC*.

---

[9]Para. 1 of Art. 27 of *Legislation Law*: A legislative bill placed on the agenda of a meeting of the Standing committee shall, as a rule, be put to vote after deliberation at three meetings of the Standing Committee.

8.3 It Is Suggested that an Expert Committee for the Compilation of *Civil Code* Supported by the Standing Committee of NPC Be Established

A positive interaction between the Legislature and the academic community is an important precondition that decides whether *Civil Code* can enter into the legislative agenda. As long as the Legislature does not respect or trust the academic community, any legislative attempts to create a uniform civil code would be a many-year endeavor of assembling legal documents.[10] It is suggested that an official "Expert Committee for the Compilation of *Civil Code*" ("Expert Committee") sponsored by the Standing Committee of NPC be established, so that the identity of experts can be recognized[11] and their efforts respected. To be specific.

8.3.1 Participants in the Compilation of the Civil Code Should Be in the Form of Groups Instead of Individuals

In comparative law, although there are cases that a particular civil code was drafted by an individual, such as Eugen Hubel and the *Swiss Civil Code*,[12] René David and the *Ethiopian Civil Code*,[13] the author still believes that an Expert Committee with participants in the form of groups is more suitable. In this case, the work of the Expert Committee will not be constrained by the personal limitations of individual scholars. Also the three complete proposed versions of the draft of *Civil Code*,[14] drafted by the research panels, have shown that this is a good way to overcome personal limitations.

8.3.2 Characteristics of the Expert Committee

Some scholars have described the characteristics of the Expert Committee as such: (1) it needs to be led by scholars, oriented by academic studies, organized in the form of a substantial entity, devoted full-time to its mission and diversified in its

---

[10]Zhang (2004a).

[11]Xu (2003).

[12]See Chen (2008).

[13]See Xia (2008).

[14]They are: Liang (2004), Wang (2005) and Xu (2004).

power[15]; (2) in terms of professional composition, professors, judges and lawyers/ notaries should each make up one third of the members; (3) in terms of geographic distribution, there should be at least one representative from the six major regions of China—Eastern China, the Central South, the Southwest, the Northwest, Northern China, and the Northeast[16]; (4) in terms of age composition, it is suggested that the old, the middle-aged, and the young should be involved, with the young scholars serving as members of the Secretariat.

8.3.3 Constitution of the Mechanism of the Expert Committee

With the current regimes for research and personnel management, it is suggested that the Expert Committee be formed by personnel seconded from other entities, and that their service last until the Civil Code is completely compiled. Since many experts are scholars who have presided or participated in the drafting work of the proposed versions of *Civil Code*, they are able to integrate the advantages of the "scholar-proposed draft" with the "indoor draft".[17] Or by a more preferred tactic, as the *Decision to Rule by Law* mentions: "…explore the option of assigning the drafting work to a third party," in which NPC directly assigns the drafting work to the Expert Committee.

In order to improve efficiency, it is suggested that a clear division of work be defined, with specific volumes assigned to specific groups in the following way: the first group, responsible for the drafting of personality rights protection law, should determine the legislative program of personality rights protection as soon as possible; the second group, responsible for amending the *Marriage Law*, the *Adoption Law* and the *Succession Law*, should integrate the amendments of *Succession Law* left unfinished by the 11th NPC into the compilation of the *Civil Code*, and determine at the same time the amendments and compilation of the *Marriage Law* and the *Adoption Law*; the third group, responsible for the drafting of the *Legislation Scheme of Civil Code of the People's Republic of China* ("*Legislation Scheme of Civil Code*"), will explore, the possibility of codifying the *General Provisions of Civil Law*, the *Real Rights Law*, the *Contract Law*, the *Tort Liability Law*, and the *Law on Choice of Law for Foreign-Related Civil Relationships*, integrating the part of "Obligations in General" in the *Civil Code*, and deciding whether those articles of *Guarantee Law* should be kept.

---

[15]Fang and Zhang (2003).

[16]Xu (2003).

[17]Xu (2003).

8.3.4   A Secretariat Should Be Set up in the Expert Committee

It is suggested that a Secretariat be established, consisting of young scholars with doctorate degree in law,[18] and bar examination certificate. Young scholars with overseas education backgrounds should also be included in order to increase the diversity and fairness of the personnel composition. The main tasks of the Secretariat would be: (1) to systematically assemble civil law documents[19] and produce collections of materials on comparative law[20]; (2) to prepare a "glossary" similar to that of the *German BGB* and the *Ethiopian Civil Code*, to guarantee the accuracy and consistency of terms and to avoid overlapping and confusion[21]; (3) to keep official minutes of discussions—although these minutes will be different from those of formal meetings and will have no binding effect on the interpretation of judicial application, with their theoretical value[22] they will become valuable documents for historical interpretation and academic research in the future study of civil law; (4) to make remarks on drafts, based on the texts produced by the Expert Committee at different stages, which can be modified later into "Legislative Justification Books" after the *Civil Code* is enacted[23]; (5) to establish an official website for the Expert Committee by actively applying modern technology, which would publish different versions of drafts and documents concerned, collect feedback from the general public, and forward this feedback to the Expert Committee for reference.

8.3.5   The Preparatory Work of the Expert Committee

The preparatory work of the Expert Committee is to promptly facilitate the Legislature to enact the *Personality Rights Law* and amend the *Marriage Law*, the *Adoption Law* and the *Succession Law*. As a part of the *Civil Code*, the *Personality Rights Law* was deliberated at the end of 2002, and it was the only draft deliberated which failed to be adopted. Like the deliberation procedure of the *Civil Code*, it is necessary to enact the *Personality Rights Law* as soon as possible, unless it is reported by the Chairman Meeting to the Standing Committee of NPC to terminate the deliberation procedure as provided in Article 39 of the *Legislation Law*.

---

[18]Xu (2003).

[19]Fang (2003).

[20]In 1995, Office of the Standing Committee of NPC produced *Compiled Documents of the World's Civil Laws* (Vol. 1–4).

[21]Wei (2011a).

[22]Zhang (2004b).

[23]Although the Legislature seldom issue the *Legislation Justification*, if the Legislation Justification can be issued by the Expert Committee, it would be of great significance.

According to the model of the codification of non-basic laws, it is acceptable for the Standing Committee of NPC to enact this law. The draft amendment of the *Succession Law* has preliminarily come into shape. It is necessary to integrate the existing judicial interpretations into the *Marriage Law* and link the relevant administrative provisions to the *Adoption Law*. These two can be integrated into the *Marriage and Family Volume*. Since the specific technical practices are not the focus of this paper and there remain uncertainties in the scheme of legislatures, the author is not going to elaborate on this issue.

8.4 It Is up to the Standing Committee of NPC to Deliberate and Enact the *Legislation Scheme of Civil Code*

In order to unify the guiding principles and legislative techniques, it is suggested that the *Legislation Scheme of Civil Code* be drafted by the Expert Committee, then deliberated and adopted by the Standing Committee of NPC.

8.4.1 Legislation Scheme of Civil Code *in Comparative Law*

With regards to comparative law, before the *Civil Code* was drafted in many countries, such as some Latin American countries, Holland, and Spain, a "medium" was prepared which outlined the plans for drafting the law. It was called the *Legislation Scheme of Civil Code* or other titles to that same effect. Before the draft of *Civil Code* enters the stage of approval, such propositioned procedural design will help to solve many issues in advance concerning principles or policies, and avoid repeated discussions and disputes over the same issues in meetings at various levels.[24]

In 1928, before the *Civil Code of the Republic of China* was drafted, Hu Hanmin, Lin Sen and Sun Ke, members of the KMT Political Committee pointed out that "since the civil law has long not been enacted, it is up to the Legislative Institute to compile the *Civil Code*. However, the principles of legislative procedure should be decided by the Central Committee. It is proposed that a draft version of the *Legislation Scheme for 'General Rules of Civil Volume'* be prepared and forwarded for decision." Later, the 167th Session of the KMT Political Committee appointed Wang Conghui, Cai Yuanpei, and Dai Chuanxian, together with the above-mentioned three members who made the proposal, to scrutinize the legislation scheme. In their efforts, the legislation principles for the *Obligation Volume*,

---

[24]Wei (2011b).

the *Real Rights Volume*, the *Domestic Relations Volume* and the *Succession Volume* were deliberated and confirmed.[25]

In the former Soviet Union, from which the legislative tradition of China's civil law originated, the Supreme Soviet also enacted the *Legislative Scheme of Civil Code of the Soviet Union and Union Republics* in 1961 and 1991 as a guiding document for drafting of the *Civil Code*.

8.4.2   *It Is Suggested that the* Legislation Scheme of Civil Code *Also Be Drafted*

In his tenure as Representative to NPC, Professor Liang Huixing made an official proposal that a working group be formed to draft the *Legislation Scheme of Civil Code* which would clarify legislative principles, and would provide a guiding ideology, basic principles, basic rules, and structural outlines. This was done in the hope that the *Civil Code* of China would be drafted featuring rigorous logic, complete system, progressive significance, and contents that reflect both the domestic conditions of China and the international trend.[26] Before that, Professor Liang Huixing drafted the *Legislation Scheme of Contract Law of the People's Republic of China* in 1994,[27] the *Legislation Scheme of Real Rights Law of the People's Republic of China*,[28] and the *Compendium of Civil Code of the People's Republic of China (Draft)*[29] in 1998. If the future *Civil Code* of China is to be exquisite and progressive, the *Legislation Scheme of Civil Code* should be drafted prior to the efforts to compile the *Civil Code*, so that the legislative process will be carried out in a more accurate and efficient way.[30]

8.4.3   *Main Contents of the* Legislation Scheme of Civil Code

The author holds that the *Legislation Scheme of Civil Code* should include the following contents:

First, the guiding ideology must be established. This includes the legislative political ideas in view of building the socialist legal system with Chinese characteristics, legislative economic ideas in view of promoting the development of the

---

[25]Xie (2000).

[26]Liang (2017c).

[27]Liang (2017a).

[28]Liang (2017b).

[29]Liang (2001).

[30]Xu (2007).

socialist market economy, and legislative technical ideas supported by the model of the codification of non-basic laws.

Second, the scope of regulation by the scheme must be established. This would aim to define the relations of private law between subjects with equal status regulated by the *Civil Code*, establish the legislative system combined with civil and commercial laws, and clarify its relations with intellectual property rights law, labor law, social law, and economic law.

Third, the framework of volumes/chapters and the main contents must be established. It is suggested that the outline of *2002 Civil Law (Draft)* stay unchanged, with slight adjustment to the sequence of the volumes. To be specific, the *Personality Rights Volume* should be put in the second volume to highlight the protection over personality rights.[31]

Fourth, the basic legislative scheme of civil code must be established. It is suggested that the scheme be made up of three parts: a scheme for drafting legislative program of personality rights protection,[32] a scheme to amend the existing law, and the *Scheme for Codifying Civil Laws of People's Republic of China ("Scheme for Codifying Civil Laws")*.

8.5   *Scheme for Codifying Civil Laws* with Less Than 400 Articles Should Be Drafted

Since it is estimated that the future *Civil Code* has more than 1200 Articles, the regular deliberation procedure could not guarantee the appropriate deliberation over the *Civil Code* in such a short time, according to the above analysis about the deliberation capacity of NPC. Therefore, it is necessary to explore a new mode of deliberation that may help to reduce the difficulty of deliberation and ensure that the *Civil Code* can be enacted in a quality and constitutional way. It is suggested that a cap on the articles be set, and that NPC only deliberate a maximum of 400 articles. Specifically, the *Civil Code* can be drafted on the basis of the *Scheme for Codifying Civil Laws* prepared by the Expert Committee under the framework of the *Legislation Scheme of Civil Code* passed by the Standing Committee of NPC. *The Scheme for Codifying Civil Laws* should highlight the following aspects.

---

[31]The legislative body has considered the sequence. It is evident in the enumeration sequence of civil rights and interests in Paragraph 2 of Article 2 of the *Tort Liability Law*: "the civil rights and interests mentioned in this Law shall include the personal and property rights and interests such as right to life, right to health, right to name, right to reputation, right to honor, right to portrait, right to privacy, right to marital autonomy, guardianship, right to ownership, usufructuary right, guarantee right, copyright, patent right, trade mark right, discovery right, equity right and succession right".

[32]It is advised by the Writer to set up the Chapter "Tort Liabilities for Infringement upon Personality Rights and Interests" in the *Tort Liability Volume of Civil Code*, see Wang (2017b).

8.5.1 Coverage of the Legislation Scheme for Codifying Civil Laws *Should Be Confined to Private Law*

The *Legislation Scheme for Codifying Civil Laws* will focus on the compilation of the existing private laws.[33] In other words, it will only deal with the relationship between the *Civil Code* and the supplementary civil single laws (namely, commercial law and intellectual property rights law), and leave the policy-oriented special civil law in the field of special civil law.[34] In short, the efforts to codify will not go beyond the scope of *General Principles of the Civil Law*, the *Marriage Law*, the *Succession Law* and the *Adoption Law*; instead, it will substitute the contents of *General Principles of the Civil Law* with those of the *Guarantee Law*, the *Contract Law*, the *Real Rights Law*, the *Tort Liability Law*, the *General Provisions of Civil Law* and the *Law on Choice of Law for Foreign-Related Civil Relationships*, and absorb the contents concerning other private laws by judicial interpretations. If the Legislature decides to continue drafting the *Personality Rights Law*, it will then substitute the relevant part of *General Principles of the Civil Law*.

8.5.2 Legislation Scheme for Codifying Civil Laws *Should Suggest that the Contents of the* General Provisions of Obligation Law *Be Provided in the* General Provisions Volume of Civil Code

Some scholars are of the opinion that compared to issue about whether the *Personality Rights Law* should be compiled as an independent volume, the arrangement of the *General Provisions of Civil Code* and the *General Provisions of Obligation Law* is more important with regard to the wholeness of the system.[35] The author holds that pragmatically, the contents of *General Provisions of Obligation Law* should be included in the *General Provisions Volume of Civil Code*.[36] This is out of the following considerations: (1) since the *2002 Civil Law (Draft)* does not have a general provisios of obligation volume, it would require a complicated legislative procedure if it is decided that *General Provisions of*

---

[33]Yi (2014).

[34]As to the distinguish between "supplementary special civil law", "policy-oriented special civil law" and "administrative special civil law", see Xie (2013).

[35]Mao (2013).

[36]The Writer has advised that the "*General Provisions of Civil Law*" should not be set separately, but *General Principles of the Civil Law* should be modified, which acts as Volume 1. Besides, in *General Principles of the Civil Law*, the content of "*General Provisions of Obligations Law*" is retained. After the *General Provisions of Civil Law* is adopted, the theoretical basis of such advice is still applicable, and it is retained in the *General Provisions of Civil Law* in the legislation planning. See Wang (2012).

Obligation Law should be drafted and forwarded to the Standing Committee of NPC for deliberation according to Article 24 of *Legislation Law*; (2) if the *General Provisions of Obligation Law* is to be drafted as an independent law, it will be inevitable that the *Contract Law* will need to be amended, which would be a significant workload. Besides, the abstract principles elaborated in the *General Provisions of Obligation Law* cannot directly apply to the judicial practices; (3) the contents of *General Provisions of Obligation Law* is applied to the *Contract Volume* and *Tort Liability Volume*, so it's better to be put in the *General Provisions Volume of Civil Code*.

According to the pragmatic design mentioned above, the *Legislation Scheme for Codifying Civil Laws* will touch approximately 100 articles of *General Principles of the Civil Law* in the following ways: (1) correcting and improving about five articles concerning general principles in civil law; (2) adding about ten articles concerning object of right[37]; (3) optimizing about ten articles concerning civil subjects; (4) optimizing about twenty articles concerning general provisions of obligation law; (5) deleting about ten articles in "Chapter 8: Application of Law in Civil Relations with Foreigners"; (6) deleting about twenty-five articles, except those concerning general principles of obligation, in "Chapter 5: Civil Rights"; (7) deleting about twenty articles in "Chapter 6: Civil Liability." *The General Provisions of Civil Law* has accomplished the above amendment and improvement. The future *Legislation Scheme for Codifying Civil Laws* will decide whether the articles in *General Principles of the Civil Law* which have no corresponding provisions in the *General Provisions of Civil Law* should be kept when *General Principles of the Civil Law* is abolished.[38]

8.5.3 Make a Once-and-for-All Attempt to Amend *the* Specific Provisions Volumes of Civil Code *Through the* Legislation Scheme for Codifying Civil Laws

There are approximately 300 articles in the *Legislation Scheme for Codifying Civil Laws*, whose functions include: (1) abolishing the *Guarantee Law*, transferring its "Chapter 2: Guarantee" and "Chapter 4: Deposit" into the *Contract Volume* of *Civil Code*, and optimizing the regulations concerned—in all, the articles provided total about one hundred; (2) substantially amending the *Contract Law*, the *Real Rights Law, the Tort Liability Law*, and the *Law on Choice of Law for Foreign-Related Civil Relationships*, the articles provided total about seventy; (3) optimizing and

---

[37]The *General Provisions of Civil Law* does not stipulate the "civil rights object", which belongs to the to-be-added content of the *General Provisions Volume of Civil Code*.

[38]See the Comparative Table between the *General Principles of Civil Law* and the *General Provisions of Civil Law*, Wang (2017a).

amending the *Succession Law*, the articles provided total about thirty; (4) After amending the *Marriage Law* and the *Adoption Law*, merging them into *Marriage and Family*, the articles provided total about fifty; (5) deleting the first chapters and supplementary provisions of the existing single civil laws, the articles provided total about thirty; (6) conceptually and systematically unifying, the existing civil laws, the articles provided total about twenty.

8.6 Substantially Codify the Civil Laws Through the *Legislation Scheme for Codifying Civil Laws* Enacted by NPC

8.6.1 Nature of Codification Through the Legislation Scheme for Codifying Civil Laws *Is to Exercise the Right to Amend Basic Laws Provided by the* Constitution

In recent years, the Legislature in China has begun attempts to amend a number of laws at one meeting: on August 27, 2009, *Decision to Amend a Number of Laws by the Standing Committee of NPC* listed amended 53 laws with 95 articles; on June 29, 2013, December 28, 2013 and August 31, 2014, the Standing Committee of NPC amended 12, 7, and 5 laws respectively. On April 24, 2015, the 14th meeting of the 12th NPC Standing Committee adopted four decisions to respectively amend 5 laws,[39] 5 laws,[40] 6 laws[41] and 7 laws.[42] Since 2016, this amendment mode is continuing.

These positive attempts have successfully amend a number of laws, and also served as a breakthrough to the traditional practice of only amending one law *at one time*. NPC's deliberation of the *Legislation Scheme for Codifying Civil Laws* is, by nature, exercising its right to amend basic laws provided by Paragraph 3 of Article 62 of the *Constitution* in the model of codifying non-basic laws—amending a number of civil single laws at one time.[43]

---

[39]*Standing Committee of National People's Congress on Amendment of Five Laws Including the Metrological Law of People's Republic of China*.

[40]*Decision of Standing Committee of National People's Congress on Amendment of Five Laws Including the Compulsory Education Law of People's Republic of China*.

[41]*Standing Committee of National People's Congress on Amendment of Six Laws Including the Electric Power Law of People's Republic of China*.

[42]*Standing Committee of National People's Congress on Amendment of Seven Laws Including the Port Law of People's Republic of China*.

[43]Nominally, the *Scheme for Codifying Civil Laws* is like the "Semi-law Decisions". In nature, it should be deemed as the law amendment decision. For the "semi-law decisions", see Wang (2011).

8.6.2 Deliberation in a Volume-by-Volume Manner for Two Times Will Reduce the Workload of the Standing Committee of NPC

At the 31st meeting of the Standing Committee of the 9th NPC held on December 23 to 28, 2002, the achievements were remarkable: 1209 Articles of "2002 *Civil Law (Draft)*" were preliminarily deliberated, *Law on the Promotion of Private Education, Agriculture Law (Amendments), Grassland Law (Amendments), Amendment to Criminal Code (4th Edition)*, and *"Interpretation on Applicable Subjects Provided in Chapter 9 of Dereliction of Duty of Criminal Code"* were adopted; *Ordinance of Customs Official Rank* (Draft), *Port Law (Draft)*, the *Law of Radioactive Pollution Prevention and Control (Draft)*, and the *Decision on the Management of Forensic Examination by the Standing Committee of NPC (Draft)* were preliminarily deliberated; deliberation of *Administrative Permission Law (Draft)* and the *Law of Citizen's Identity Card* were continued, and a series of "quasi-legal decisions" and personnel appointment were adopted.[44]

The author has every reason to be confident that the Standing Committee of NPC and its subordinate departments will make a full preparation prior to the meeting being convened to guarantee the quality of its deliberation, but a 1209-Article *2002 Civil Law (Draft)* apparently goes beyond the deliberation capacity of any NPC Standing Committee in history. Given the fact that the focus of deliberation is the *"Volume 2: Real Right Law"* and is this draft is partially assembly of law, it is acceptable that other chapters of *2002 Civil Law (Draft)* only be deliberated formally. If, indeed, the Standing Committee of NPC is required to substantially deliberate the *Legislation Scheme for Codifying Civil Laws*, procedures concerned need to be redesigned.

It is suggested that the Secretariat of the Expert Committee draft, on the basis of the *Legislation Scheme for Codifying Civil Laws*, the *Civil Code of People's Republic of China (Draft and Modification Descriptions)*, to ensure correspondence between every article of the future *Civil Code* with the existing laws and the *Legislation Scheme for Codifying Civil Laws*. In terms of specific deliberation procedures, it is suggested that the Standing Committee of NPC deliberate the *Legislation Scheme for Codifying Civil Laws* more than twice before it is forwarded to NPCs. The version deliberated by the Standing Committee of NPC will be published on the official website of the Expert Committee for public opinion, which will serve as a source of reference for the next round of deliberation. If necessary, multiple deliberations can be arranged until the *Legislation Scheme for Codifying Civil Laws* reaches a point of maturation.

---

[44]*Brief Introduction to the 31st Meeting of the Standing Committee of the 9th NPC*, Website of NPC: http://www.npc.gov.cn/npc/cwhhy/content_304789.htm, the latest access item: May 15, 2015.

8.6.3 *Codify the Civil Law Through the* Legislation Scheme for Codifying Civil Laws Enacted by NPC

Compared to the deliberation capacity of the Standing Committee of NPC, NPC which convenes once a year is even more questionable. According to the agenda of the 12th NPC, every year the meeting lasts for about ten days. In these ten days, three days are devoted to deliberating government work reports, planning reports and budget reports, three days to deliberating reports of the Standing Committee of NPC and reports from of the Supreme People's Court and the Supreme People's Procuratorate, and one day to adopting those reports. The remaining time for deliberating laws does not exceed three days. With more than 1200 articles, the *Civil Code* cannot be deliberated and enacted democratically and appropriately within three days.

It is suggested that after the Standing Committee of NPC has deliberated the *Legislation Scheme for Codifying Civil Laws* at least twice, both the *Civil Code of People's Republic of China (Draft and Modification Descriptions)* and the *Legislation Scheme for Codifying Civil Laws* should be printed and distributed to the representatives of NPC before January 1st[45] of the year in which the two texts are to be deliberated. Distributed together with them are also documents that explain how the *Legislation Scheme for Codifying Civil Laws* corresponds with the *Civil Code of People's Republic of China (Draft and Modification Descriptions)*, and illustrate that the deliberation over the former has the de facto equal validity as the latter. While deliberating the *Legislation Scheme for Codifying Civil Laws*, NPC may focus on newly added provisions of substantial significance according to the *Decision to Rule by Law* that states "voting can be made separately for important articles or sections."

The way of substantially codifying civil laws by deliberating the *Legislation Scheme for Codifying Civil Laws* by NPC has the following benefits: (1) since the *Legislation Scheme for Codifying Civil Laws* is drafted on the basis of the *Legislation Scheme of Civil Code* adopted by the Standing Committee of NPC, its basic contents are relatively established; (2) deliberation based on the existing single civil laws will help to remove any obstacles or difficulties in the process of deliberation, reduce the workload, guarantee the time devoted for deliberation, and further the quality of deliberation; (3) the *Legislation Scheme for Codifying Civil Laws* is relatively mature after being deliberated at least twice by the Standing

---

[45]Paragraph 1 of Article 6 of the *Rules of Procedure for the National People's Congress of the People's Republic of China* states: "The Standing Committee of the National People's Congress shall, one month before the meeting of the National People's Congress is convened, inform deputies to the Congress of the date of the meeting and important issues to be discussed during the meeting, and distribute drafts of laws for deliberation to them at the meeting." Considering both the difficulty in deliberating a civil code, and the customs and habits of Chinese people during the period between New Year's Day and the Spring Festival, to guarantee the quality of deliberation, it is suggested that documents of the *Civil Code of People's Republic of China (Draft and Synopsis)* and Scheme for Codifying Civil Code be distributed to Deputies before New Year's Day.

Committee of NPC and also after soliciting public opinions; (4) the NPC's adoption of the *Legislation Scheme for Codifying Civil Laws* represents their exercise of legislative power under the *Constitution*, which, in this analysis, removes the risk of potential controversy over its constitutionality.

References

Chen Huabin, "Exploration and Analysis on Swiss Civil Code", *Research on Rule of Law*, No. 6, 2008.

Fang Shaokun, Zhang Pinghua, "Three Ground Works for Legislating Civil Code", *Seeker*, No. 1, 2003.

Feng Lixia, "Three Grand Debate Over A Number of Major Issues Concerning Legislation of Civil Code", *Law and Social Development*, No. 4, 2002.

Liang Huixing, "Synopsis of Civil Code of the People's Republic of China (Draft)", reprinted in XU Guodong, *Debate on Drafting Methods of Civil Code of China*, China University of Political Science and Law Press, 2001.

Liang Huixing, *Proposed Version of Civil Code and Its Justifications*, Law Press, 2004.

Liang Huixing, *Legislation Scheme for Contract Law of the People's Republic of China*, available at http://www.iolaw.org.cn/shownews.asp?id=447, the latest access time: August 31, 2017a.

Liang Huixing, *Legislation Scheme for Property Right Law*, available at http://www.iolaw.org.cn/showArticle.aspx?id=2159, the latest access time: August 31, 2017b.

Liang Huixing, *Suggestions on Correcting Arbitrariness in Legislating Civil Code*, available at http://www.iolaw.org.cn/shownews.asp?id=179, the latest access time: August 31, 2017c.

Mao Shaowei, "Need of Prudence in Seeking a New Civil Code—Rethinking the Value, Structure and System of Civil Code", *Peking University Law Journal*, No. 6, 2013.

Sun Xianzhong, "Systemization and Scientification of Legislative Efforts of China's Civil Law", *Tsinghua Law Review*, No. 6, 2012.

Wang Liming, *Expert Proposed Version of Civil Code and Justification for Legislation*, Law Press, 2005.

Wang Zhu, "How many currently valid laws are there in our country?", Social Science, No. 10 2011.

Wang Zhu, "Study on the Legislative Mode of 'General Rules of Obligations Law' in Pursuing Pragmatic Methods of Drafting Civil Code", *Journal of Sichuan University (Social Science Edition)*, No. 3, 2012.

Wang Zhu, ed. *Compiling Comparative Table of the General Provisions of Civil Law and Clause Interpretation*, Peking University Press, 2017a, pp. 367–370.

Wang Zhu, "Compiling Background and Structure Adjustment of Tort Liability Part of Civil Code", *Journal of National Prosecutors College*, No. 4, 2017b.

Wei Leijie, "Issues of Compilation of Civil Code", *Journal of the East China University of Politics and Law*, No. 2, 2011a.

Wei Leijie, "Technical Considerations for Compiling Civil Code", *ECUPL Journal*, No. 2, 2011b.

Xia Xinhua, "*Rene David and Civil Code of Ethiopia*", *West Asia and Africa*, No. 1, 2008.

Xie Hongfei, "Establishment of Relations Between Civil Code and Special Civil Law", *Social Sciences in China*, No. 2, 2013.

Xie Zhenmin, *Legislative History of Republic of China (Volume 2)*, China University of Political Science and Law Press, 2000, pp. 753–801.

Xu Guodong, "Seriously Re-thinking of the Organizing Methods of the 4th Drafting of Civil Code of PRC", *Law Science*, No. 5, 2003.

Xu Guodong (ed.), *Draft of Green Civil Code*, Social Sciences Academic Press, 2004.

Xu Guodong, "Legislative Procedure of Civil Code", published in XU Guodong, *Civil Code and Civil Law Philosophy*, China Renmin University Press, 2007.

Yang Zhenshan, "Several Major Issues in Drafting Civil Code", *Tribune of Political Science and Law*, No. 1, 2003.

Yi Jiming, "Unification of Private Laws and the Future of Civil Code in the Eyes of History", *Social Sciences in China*, No. 5, 2014.

Zhang Jianwen, "A Study on Necessity of Compiling Civil Code from the Perspectives of Politicization and Anti-Politicization", *Hebei Law Science*, No. 6, 2004a.

Zhang Xinbao, "Technical Problems of Civil Code Legislation", *Law Science Magazine*, No. 2, 2004b.

Chapter 9
Analysis on the Orientation of the Compilation of the *General Provisions of Civil Law* and Comment on Its Contents

9.1 Introduction

Since the founding of PRC, the Party and the State initiated the work for the enactment of *Civil Code* for four times respectively in 1954, 1962, 1979 and 2001.[1] No actual effect was achieved in the first and second times of the enactment for various reasons. When the third time of the enactment was initiated, owing to the fact that China just entered into the new period of reform and opening up, the conditions for the enactment of a complete civil code were not satisfied. Therefore, in accordance with the working idea of "enact the civil single laws one by one when it is mature", it was decided to firstly enact the civil single laws.[2] The so-called transfer from "wholesale" to "retail" is an analogy made by the legal circle in China for the historical trend of the enactment of *Civil Code* since the founding of PRC by using the commercial terms, and means the situation that, after the *Civil Law of the People's Republic of China (draft 4)* (May 1, 1982) (hereinafter referred to as "*Fourth Draft in Third Compilation of Civil Law*") was enacted, the Legislature did not seek for the enactment of *Civil Code* as a whole, but enacted every volume of the *Civil Code* respectively.[3] Concretely speaking, before the *Fourth Draft in Third*

---

[1]Zhang (2017b).

[2]Li (2017).

[3]According to the search of the Writer in CNKI, The earliest scholars who proposed the analogy of "wholesale" and "retail" in the doctrine may be the late Professor Cai Dingjian. He thought: "In the legislative approach, we should 'retail' other than 'wholesale'. For those social relations that could have been adjusted by uniform law, due to the maturity of the different parts of these social

---

This chapter is derived in part from an article published in the Peking University Law Journal, 5:2, 387–429 (2017), available online: https://www.tandfonline.com/doi/full/10.1080/20517483.2017.1427184.

Compilation of Civil Law, the Legislature took the drafting and enactment of *Civil Code* as a whole as the legislative objective, namely the so-called "wholesale". Thereafter, the Legislature abandoned the legislative plan to enact the *Civil Code* as a whole, and on the basis of *Succession Volume* in the *Fourth Draft in Third Compilation of Civil Law*,[4] NPC enacted the *Succession Law* in 1985, and then enacted *General Principles of the Civil Law* in 1986. These laws, together with the *Marriage Law* enacted in 1980, may be deemed as the first batch of legislative results achieved in the third time of the compilation of *Civil Code*. On this basis, the legislature enacted the *Adoption Law* in 1991, enacted the *Guarantee Law* in 1995, and enacted the *Contract Law* in 1999. These laws may be deemed as the second batch of legislative results achieved in the third time of the compilation of *Civil Code*.

At the end of 2002, the NPC Standing Committee deliberated the *2002 Civil Law (draft)*, which was the attempt of "wholesale" in the fourth time of the enactment of *Civil Code*, but was criticized by many scholars because such enactment became a mere formality.[5] Thereafter, on the basis of the "retail" mode, the Legislature enacted the *Real Rights Law* in 2007 and enacted the *Tort liability Law* in 2009. In 2011, WU Bangguo, the former chairman of the NPC Standing Committee, declared "the formation of socialist legal system with Chinese characteristics",[6] which can be deemed as a milestone in "retail" phase of the fourth time of the compilation of *Civil Code*.

Reviewing the legislative activities relating to the *Civil Code* carried out since the founding of PRC, the Writer believes that, the difference between the so-called "wholesale" and "retail" is not only reflected in the aspect whether the object of the enactment is *Civil Code* as a whole or each volume of the *Civil Code*, and more importantly, but also reflected in the macro-concept of the "establishment of *Civil Code* system" in "wholesale" or the micro-concept of "settlement of problems" in "retail".

The compilation of *Civil Code* carried out in accordance with the *Decision to Rule by Law* should be regarded as the legislative process whereby the fourth time of the compilation of *Civil Code* transfers from the "retail" phase to the "wholesale" phase. Whether the *General Provisions of Civil Law* enacted on March 15, 2017 is "wholesale" and/or "retail" is the key to the accurate orientation of legislative activities relating to the *General Provisions of Civil Law* and the accurate master of the compilation of *Civil Code*.

Since the *Decision to Rule by Law* uses the phrase of "compile the *Civil Code*", it should be regarded as "wholesale" rather than "retail". At the level of legislative planning, the difference between concepts contained in "wholesale" and "retail"

---

relations and the urgency of the actual needs is different, Where there is more mature conditions and more urgent needs, we should enact the civil single laws, and then codify them into Civil Code." See Cai (1986).

[4]See Liu (1988).

[5]Liang (2003).

[6]Wu (2011).

will directly decide that the draft legislation takes the orientation of "establishment of system" or "settlement of problems". Briefly speaking, whether the compilation of *Civil Code* is "wholesale" or "retail" depends on the "concept" rather than the "object". The concept of "wholesale" can lead to the enactment of a substantial civil code, while the concept of "retail" may only lead to the assembly of civil single laws. On the basis of the embodiment of legislative concept in contents of law, the difference between the concepts "wholesale" and "retail" is further reflected in the enactment of *the General Provisions of Civil Law*. In this chapter, under the framework of "wholesale" and "retail", the Writer tries to determine the orientation of the compilation of *the General Provisions of Civil Law*, and briefly analyze the relevant legislative contents.

9.2 From "Retail" to "Whosale": The Compilation of *Civil Code* in Two Steps

9.2.1 *"Retail": Enact the* Civil Code *Volume by Volume*

On January 28, 2015, the NPC Legal Affairs Commission held the Symposium for the Compilation of *Civil Code*, implementing the decision to compile the *Civil Code* in the *Decision to Rule by Law*. The attending scholars reached a consensus on firstly enacting *the General Provisions of Civil Law* as *General Provisions Volume of Civil Code*.[7] However, there was still a lot of controversy on setting of chapters and sections of the *Specific Provisions Volumes of Civil Code*, especially on the issue whether *Personality Rights Law* should be compiled as a separate volume. During the deliberation of *the General Provisions of Civil Law (draft)*, the Legislature gave the statement "*Civil Code* will be composed of the *General Provisions Volume* and the *Specific Provisions Volumes* (currently including the *Contract Volume,* the *Real Rights Volume,* the *Tort liability Volume,* the *Marriage and Family Volume* and the *Succession Volume,* etc.)",[8] so as to provide certain room for the academic community to discuss over the issue whether the *Personality Rights Law* should be compiled as a separate volume.

9.2.1.1 *General Principles of the Civil Law*: Detailed Retail of the Rules with General Provisions Nature and Brief Wholesale of the Rules with Specific Provisions Nature

Against the special historical background, *General Principles of the Civil Law* are mainly composed of the rules with general provisions nature, including all contents

---

[7]Yang (2015).

[8]Li (2016a), the document at the Fifth Session of the Twelfth National People's Congress.

of Chapter 1 "Basic Principles", Chapter 2 "Citizen (Natural Persons)", Chapter 3 "Legal Persons", Chapter 4 "Civil Juristic Acts and Agency", Chapter 7 "Limitation of Action" and Chapter 9 "Supplementary Provisions", as well as Section 1 "General Provisions" and Section 4 "Formation of Civil Liabilities" of Chapter 6 "Civil liabilities", a total of 96 articles and slightly more than 3/5 of all the 156 articles of *General Principles of the Civil Law*. These articles may be deemed as detailed retail of the rules with general provisions nature, because though *General Principles of the Civil Law* tries to constitute the basic framework of the rules with general provisions nature, it does not try to integrate the *Marriage Law* and the *Succession Law* which have been enacted earlier; in addition, the rules with general provisions nature are designed on the basis of the micro concept of "settlement of problems", so as to meet the urgent needs of judicial practices.

In *General Principles of the Civil Law*, Chapter 5 "Civil Rights" as well as Section 2 "Civil Liabilities for Breach of Contract" and Section 3 "Civil liabilities for Tort" of Chapter 6 "Civil liabilities" contain 58 articles, slightly less than 2/5 of all the 156 articles of *General Principles of the Civil Law*. These articles may be deemed as the brief wholesale of the rules with specific provisions nature, because though *General Principles of the Civil Law* contains less provisions about the rules with specific provisions nature, they aim to establish the civil rights system of real rights,[9] creditor's rights, intellectual property rights, personality and identity rights and establish the civil liabilities system based on liabilities for breach of contract and tort liabilities, which indicates the macro-concept "establishment of system".

Owing to the legislative orientation relating to detailed retail of the rules with general provisions nature and brief wholesale of the rules with specific provisions nature in the subsequent 30 year's judicial practice, *General Principles of the Civil Law* on one hand maintained the retail position of the rules with general provisions nature, and on the other hand set up the framework for the *Contract Law*, the *Real Rights Law* and the *Tort liability Law* to replace the corresponding contents of the *General Principles of the Civil Law* by means of retail of the rules with specific provisions nature. During the enactment of *the General Provisions of Civil Law*, the Legislature decided that, since the contents relating to contract, ownership, other property rights and civil liabilities in *General Principles of the Civil Law* must be further refined and systematically integrated in the course of compilation of every part of the *Civil Code*, *General Principles of the Civil Law* will not be abolished after the *General Provisions of Civil Law* is enacted.[10] It is thus clear that, the legislative orientation of *General Principles of the Civil Law* as to briefly "wholly sell the rules with specific provisions nature" will remain unchanged until the compilation of *Civil Code* is completed.

---

[9]Due to specific historical reasons, the concept of Property was deemed as a Capitalism concept when *General Principles of the Civil Law* was drafted. Thus, Section 1 of this Chapter uses the phrase of "Property Ownership and Related Property Rights".

[10]Li (2017).

9.2.1.2 Completed Retail of the Rules with Specific Provisions Nature: Civil Single Laws

On the basis of contents, the current civil single laws system of China can be divided into the system of *General Principles of the Civil Law* and the system of *Marriage, Family and Succession law*. The system of *Marriage, Family and Succession law* includes the *Marriage Law*, the *Adoption Law* and the *Succession Law*. Influenced by *Civil Code* of former Soviet Union, the *Marriage and Family Law* of China has not been included into the unified civil law system for long time, the *Marriage Law* and *Succession Law* were enacted before the enactment of *General Principles of the Civil Law*. The system of *General Principles of the Civil Law* takes *General Principles of the Civil Law* as core, and is composed of the *Real Rights Law*, the *Contract Law*, the *Tort liability Law* and the *Guarantee Law*. Among these laws, the *Guarantee Law* is relatively special. When the said law was enacted in 1995, the main purpose was to improve and update the system of the guarantee law in *General Principles of the Civil Law*, so that both the real right guarantee and creditor's right guarantee were involved. However, the *Real Rights Law* enacted in 2007 also gives comprehensive provisions on real right guarantee, and it is provided in Article 178 of the said law that "In case of any discrepancy between the provisions of the *Guarantee Law* and the provisions of this Law, the provisions of this Law shall apply." Therefore, Chapter 1 "General Rules", Chapter 2 "Security", Chapter 6 "Deposit" and Chapter 7 "Supplementary Provisions" of the *Guarantee Law* remain in full force and effect, while three kinds of real right guarantees, namely mortgage, pledge and lien, are governed by the provisions of the *Real Rights Law*. In principle, the contents of the *Real Rights Law*, the *Contract Law* and the *Tort liability Law* supersede the relevant provisions of *General Principles of the Civil Law*.[11]

9.2.1.3 Undecided Retail of the Rules with Specific Provisions Nature: *Personality Rights Law*

The civil right system constituted through the brief wholesale of the rules with specific provisions nature by *General Principles of the Civil Law* reveals that, the legislative room has been reserved for the *Personality Rights Law*, and the *Personality Rights Law* also appears in the *2002 Civil Law (draft)* as the fourth volume. During the drafting of the *General Provisions of Civil Law*, there was less hope for the *Personality Rights Law* as a separate volume owing to potential political risk.[12] However, at the Seminar on Legislative Recommendations of

---

[11]It should be noted that the *Tort Liability Law* is enacted by the Standing Committee of NPC other than NPC, the relationship between the *Tort Liability Law* and *General Principles of the Civil Law is special.* See Wang (2010).

[12]Professor Liang Huixing said: "It's easy to see that there's some causal relationship between the two times Color Revolution of Ukraine and the Personality Rights Volume of Ukraine *Civil Code*". See Liang (2016b).

Personality Rights Volume of Civil Code held on May 24, 2017 in Suzhou, the representatives of three major participants in the compilation of *Civil Code*, namely China Law Society, Supreme People's Court and Supreme People's Procuratorate reached a consensus on the enactment of *Personality Rights Law* as an independent volume,[13] so that the debate will continue. The *General Provisions of Civil Law* only lists various kinds of personality rights in three articles (namely Articles 109–111), and the contents are too simple. No matter whether *Personality Rights Law* will be separately enacted as an independent volume in the future, it is necessary to give more detailed provisions on protection of personality rights in *Civil Code*.

However, owing to the deadline of 2020 for the compilation of *Civil Code*,[14] it is not so realistic to separately "retail" the *Personality Rights Law*. If the *Personality Rights Law* enacted as an independent volume is finally realized, it should also be included into the *Civil Code* in 2020 when the *Civil Code* is "wholly sold".

9.2.2 *"Wholesale": To Codify the Civil Single Laws into the* Civil Code

9.2.2.1 Ideal Route: Change from "Retail" to "Wholesale"

If in the fourth time of the enactment of *Civil Code*, the legislative planning of the third time of the compilation whereby the "wholesale" is changed to "retail" will still be adopted, then maybe the final result of legislation will be an assembled civil code.[15] The legislature believes that, the compilation of *Civil Code* is not the enactment of a brand new civil code from scratch, but the scientific sorting out of current civil legislations; is not a simple assembly of civil legislations, but the amendment of those provisions which fail to meet the actual situations and the enactment of new provisions aiming at new situations and new problems emerging in economic and social life.[16] Then, the final result of legislation should be a substantially codified civil code.[17] Therefore, the decision to compile the *Civil Code* given in the *Decision to Rule of Law* substantially contains the requirement for transfer from "retail" to "wholesale".

---

[13]"Seminar on *Legislative Proposal of Personality Rights Volume of Civil Code* Held in Suzhou Campus", http://news.sina.com.cn/o/2017-05-28/doc-ifyfqqyh8824254.shtml.
[14]Li (2017).
[15]See Jiang (2003a, b).
[16]Li (2017).
[17]Li (2006).

9.2.2.2 Actual Difficulty: There Is no Legislative Planning in Place

The transfer from "retail" to "wholesale" requires us to determine what the scope of "retail" is and when we will enter into the "wholesale" phase. With respect to the planning for the compilation of *Civil Code*, it is advised by Professor Liang Huixing to directly compile the *Civil Code* as a whole; it is advised by Professor WANG Liming to compile the *Civil Code* in three steps, namely "*the General Provisions of Civil Law—Personality Rights Law—Civil Code*"; it is advised by Professor Sun Xianzhong to compile the *Civil Code* in two steps, namely "*the General Provisions of Civil Law—Civil Code*".[18] Unfortunately, NPC and its Standing Committee did not make a clear legislative planning.[19] In fact, they only decided to firstly enact *the General Provisions of Civil Law*, which is less controversial, but did not make clear whether *the General Provisions of Civil Law* should retail or wholly sell the rules with general provisions nature.

If there is enough time, we may update and retail all civil single laws one by one and then codified them into the *Civil Code*. There are more conditions for the amendment of the *Succession Law* initiated before the expiration of tenure of the 11th NPC to be completed as soon as possible.[20] The actual difficulty is that, the Legislature has set the legislative objective to complete the compilation of *Civil Code* in 2020, but has not made a legislative planning. The Writer believes that, we should not remain in the "retail" phase any more, but enter into the "wholesale" phase as soon as possible. If the *General Provisions of Civil Law* is oriented as "firstly wholesale" of the rules with general provisions nature, then the macro-concept "establishment of system" rather than the micro-concept "settlement of problems" shall apply.

9.2.2.3 The *General Provisions of Civil Law*: Legislation with Relatively Low Cost-Efficiency Which Would Have Been Avoided

With respect to the legislative costs, *the General Provisions of Civil Law* was finally adopted by NPC (rather than its Standing Committee) in accordance with the legislative procedure for basic civil laws as provided in the *Constitution* after the NPC Standing Committee has carried out the deliberation and publicly solicited opinions for three times and has also discussed and amended a lot of work drafts, so that the legislative costs reach the highest level.

---

[18]"The Compiling of Chinese Civil Code: A Historical Emergent Task and Epochal Initiative", *China Law Review Volume*, No. 4, 2015.

[19]For the detailed discussion about this question, see Wang (2014b).

[20]Yang and Yang (2012).

The *General Provisions of Civil Law* has come into force at October 1st, 2017. However, it is very likely that it will become invalid at October 1st, 2020[21] owing to the implementation of the *Civil Code*. As a result, it will only exist for three years. The legislative controversy reflected in the enactment of the *General Provisions of Civil Law* reveals that, it is impossible to ensure that the rules with general provisions nature contained in the *General Provisions of Civil Law* will not be substantially amended in the future. In the legislative history of China, there has never been a law with such a short life.

As the legislation with the shortest life obtained at the legislative costs of the highest level, the *General Provisions of Civil Law* updates the rules with general provisions nature in *General Principles of the Civil Law*, but leads to the difficulty in application of law owing to the dilemma that *the General Provisions of Civil Law* and *General Principles of the Civil Law* coexist. It seems that it is wiser to avoid the difficulty in application of law arising from the coexistence of *the General Provisions of Civil Law* and *General Principles of the Civil Law* by postponing the updating of the rules with general provisions nature for three years. More importantly, under the precondition that the deadline of 2020 is set, the updating of the rules with general provisions nature will waste the insufficient time for the compilation of *Civil Code*, which will indirectly affect the legislative quality of the *Civil Code*. From the viewpoint of cost-efficiency, we have to acknowledge that this is the legislation with relatively low cost-efficiency which would have been avoided.

9.2.3   *"Wholesale in Two Steps": Compilation of the* Civil Code *in Two Steps*

9.2.3.1   Essence of the Compilation of *Civil Code* in Two Steps Is to Wholly Sell the *Civil Code* in Two Steps

The Writer believes that, the compilation of *Civil Code* in two steps should be interpreted as "to wholly sell the *Civil Code* in two steps". In details, the first step is the "firstly wholesale" of the rules with general provisions nature. The finally-adopted articles of the *General Provisions of Civil Law*s should be regarded as the substantial updating of the rules with general provisions nature. More importantly, the *General Provisions of Civil Law* enacted as a basic civil law meets the requirements of legislative procedure whereby the rules with general provisions nature is firstly wholly sold.

The second step is the "subsequent wholesale" of the rules with specific provisions nature. According to the orientation of the compilation of *Civil Code*, the draft in current phase should be the draft of *Civil Code* rather than the draft of the *Specific Provisions Volumes of Civil Code*. However, since the rules with general

---

[21]According to the legislative custom of specific civil laws of China, if the law is enacted by NPC at March, it generally takes effect on October 1.

provisions nature has been firstly wholly sold, the remaining work is "subsequent wholesale" of the rules with specific provisions nature.[22] In accordance with the legislative plan, the draft of *Specific Provisions Volumes of Civil Code* will be completed and submitted to the NPC Standing Committee for deliberation in 2018, and the compilation of *Civil Code* will be finally completed in 2020.[23]

9.2.3.2   "The Compilation of *Criminal Code*": Re-orientation of the Amendment of *Criminal Code* in 1997

Let's review the legislative background for amendment of *Criminal Code* in 1997. After the promulgation of *Criminal Code* in 1979, the NPC Standing Committee successively enacted 25 criminal single laws, and provided additional criminal rules in 107 non-criminal laws during the period from 1981 to 1997 before the amendment of the 1997 *Criminal Code* was completed.[24] In 1997, the Legislature, on the basis of these criminal single laws and additional criminal rules, fully amended the *1979 Criminal Code*. Before the amendment, the 1979 *Criminal Code* has only 192 articles; after the amendment, the *1997 Criminal Code* contains 452 articles; the layout of "General Rules" is not substantially changed, and the main change is that the "Specific Rules" are enriched and improved. According to Annex 1 and Annex 2 of the *1997 Criminal Code*, 15 criminal single laws were abolished,[25] and the provisions relating to criminal liabilities in 8 criminal single laws are not applicable any longer.[26]

---

[22]"The Founding of the Task Group of the *Specific Provisions Volumes of Civil Code*, and the Task Group Commence to Work Orderly." https://www.chinalaw.org.cn/Column/Column_View. aspx?ColumnID=82&InfoID=20623. "China Civil Law Forum 2017 Held in Beijing", http:// www.iolaw.org.cn/showNews.aspx?id=59650.

[23]Li (2017)

[24]Zhao (2012).

[25]Including: *Interim Regulations of the People's Republic of China on Punishing Soldiers' Violation of Duty, The Decision to Severely Punish the Criminals who Severely Damage the Economy, The Decision to Severely Punish the Criminals who Severely Damage the Social Security, Supplementary Provisions on the Punishment of Smuggling, Supplementary Provisions on the Punishing the Crime of Corruption and Bribery, Supplementary Provisions on Punishing State-Secret-Divulgence Related Crime, Supplementary Provisions on Punishing Precious and Endangered Wild Animals Crime, The Decision to Punish the Insult to the National Flag and National Emblem of the People's Republic of China, Supplementary Provisions on Punishing the Crime of Digging Ancient Cultural Sites and Ancient Tombs, Decision on Punishing Hijacking Aircraft Criminals, Supplementary Provisions on the Punishment of Counterfeiting Trademarks, Decision on the Punishment of Infringement of Copyright, Decision on Punishing Violations of Company Law, On the Decision to Deal with Labor Reformers and Re-education through Labor who Escaped or Re-commit a new crime.*

[26]Including: *Decision on Anti-Drug, Decision on the Punishment of Criminals who Smuggle, Produce, Sell and Disseminate obscene articles, Decision to Severely Punish the Criminals of Trafficking, Kidnapping of Women, Children, Decision on Prohibition of Prostitution and Whoring, Supplementary Provisions on Punishing Tax Evasion and Tax Crimes, On the strict*

Thus, the comprehensive amendment of *Criminal Code* by NPC in 1997 was carried out as follows: centering around the *1979 Criminal Code*, all criminal single laws were compiled into the new *Criminal Code*, so as to realize the codification of basic criminal laws. If we compare the coexistence of the 1979 *Criminal Code* and criminal single laws with the coexistence of *General Principles of the Civil Law* and civil single laws today, maybe it is more appropriate to call the amendment of the *1997 Criminal Code* as the compilation of *Criminal Code*.

9.2.3.3 Compilation of *Civil Code*: To Amend *General Principles of the Civil Law* into the *Civil Code* by Reference to the Compilation of *Criminal Code*

如果不制定《民法总则》,那么在民法典编纂过程中,就应该按照"零售"改"批发"的既定策略,由《民法通则》提供"民法总则"的零售内容,由各部民事单行法提供"民法分则"的零售内容,然后"批发"为《民法典》。制定了《民法总则》之后,未来的"民法总则"的内容就应该由《民法总则》来提供。这就出现了《民法总则》《物权法》《合同法》《侵权责任法》《婚姻法》《继承法》《收养法》等各部民事单行法作为一个序列与《民法通则》并行的态势。

If the *General Provisions of Civil Law* is not enacted, then during the compilation of *Civil Code*, it is necessary to, in accordance with the preset strategy whereby the "retail" will be changed to "wholesale", get the retailed system of the general provisions volume of civil code from *General Principles of the Civil Law*, get the retailed system of the specific provisions volumes of civil code from civil single laws, and then "wholly sell" them as the *Civil Code*. After the *General Provisions of Civil Law* was enacted, the rules with general provisions nature should be provided by the *General Provisions of Civil Law*. This will lead to the situation that, the *General Provisions of Civil Law*, the civil single laws including the *Real Rights Law*, the *Contract Law*, the *Tort liability Law*, the *Marriage Law*, the *Succession Law* and the *Adoption Law* coexist with *General Principles of the Civil Law*.

It should be noted that, the *Legislation Law* only provides three kinds of legislative activities, namely enactment, amendment and abolishment,[27] and the compilation of *Civil Code* must be converted into a combination of such three legislative activities. The Writer believes that, under the above-mentioned situation, in the legislative activities for the compilation of *Civil Code*, *General Principles of the Civil Law* shall be taken as the object of compilation, and various civil single

---

provisions of the organization, delivery of others to steal the country (border) crime, Supplementary Provisions on Severely Punishing the Crime of Organization, delivery of others to steal the country (side), Decision on Punishing the Crime of Destroying Financial Order, Decision on Punishing Fraudulent, Forged and Illegal Sale of VAT Invoices.

[27]It is provided in the *Legislation Law* that: "This Law shall be applicable to the enactment, revision and nullification of laws, administrative regulations, local regulations, autonomous regulations and separate regulations".

laws shall be included into *General Principles of the Civil Law* by means of amendment and respectively supersede the corresponding parts of *General Principles of the Civil Law*. Such compilation activities can to the greatest extent maintain the continuity since the enactment of *General Principles of the Civil Law* in 1986 as "Basic Civil Law", just as the continuity between the *1997 Criminal Code* and *1979 Criminal Code*.

Specifically, *General Principles of the Civil Law* has the position equivalent to that of the *1979 Criminal Code*, while the future *Civil Code* has the position equivalent to that of the *1997 Criminal Code*. Therefore, when compiling the *Civil Code*, NPC shall follow the legislative procedure used for the amendment of *Criminal Code* (namely the compilation of *Criminal Code*), and exercise the amendment right rather than enactment right as provided in Paragraph 3 of Article 62 of the *Constitution*: "The National People's Congress shall exercise the following powers and duties: … (3) To enact and amend the basic civil laws."

9.2.3.4 Legislative Orientation of the Fourth Compilation of *Civil Code* Is to Transform from "Retail" to "Wholesale"

The above analysis reveals that, the compilation of *Civil Code* is the last phase of fourth drafting of *Civil Code* which follows the transfer from "wholesale" to "retail" in the third drafting of *Civil Code*. The decision to compile the *Civil Code* given in the *Decision to Rule by Law* realizes the historical transfer from "retail" to "wholesale", and outlines the historical route and direction (namely "wholesale"—"retail"—"wholesale") since the third drafting of *Civil Code*.

On the basis of the above analysis, the compilation of *Civil Code* which starts with the enactment of *the General Provisions of Civil Law* involves the following legislative orientations: Firstly, the "wholesale" of the *Civil Code* shall be taken as the objective. Secondly, the compilation of *Civil Code* in two steps is the wholesale of the *Civil Code* in two steps, namely "*General Provisions Volume—Specific Provisions Volumes*". Thirdly, the *General Provisions of Civil Law* not only involves "updating and retail", but also involves the "firstly wholesale".

9.3 "Both Wholesale and Retail Carried Out": Orientation of the Compilation of the *General Provisions of Civil Law*

9.3.1 "Both Wholesale and Retail Carried Out": Dual Orientation of the General Provisions of Civil Law

As the comprehensive updating of general provisions in *General Principles of the Civil Law*, the enactment of *the General Provisions of Civil Law* indicates the ending of "retail" phase; as the comprehensive provisions of the rules with general provisions nature, the enactment of the *General Provisions of Civil Law* also indicates the beginning of "wholesale" phase. Therefore, the *General Provisions of Civil Law* has the dual orientation of "retail" and "wholesale". By using the commercial terms, the Writer calls it as "both wholesale and retail carried out", involving "updating and retail" and "firstly wholesale".

9.3.1.1 "Updating and Retail" of the Rules with General Provisions Nature: The Enactment of the *General Provisions of Civil Law* Ends the Retail Task

The enactment of *the General Provisions of Civil Law* should be interpreted as follows: the Legislature does not agree to directly amend the rules with general provisions nature in *General Principles of the Civil Law* as the *General Provisions Volume of Civil Code*, and hopes to settle the conflict between *General Principles of the Civil Law* and the *Contract Law* by the *General Provisions of Civil Law*, amend the system of invalid and revocable juristic acts and improve the general rules relating to civil subject and limitation of action. Therefore, the *General Provisions of Civil Law* is actually the upgrading of *General Principles of the Civil Law*,[28] and is the "updated retail" of the *General Provisions of Civil Law*. The enactment of the *General Provisions of Civil Law* also indicates the ending of "retail".

9.3.1.2 "Firstly Wholesale" of the *General Provisions of Civil Law*: First Step of the Compilation of *Civil Code* in "Two Steps"

Though the *2002 Civil Law (draft)* has contained the first volume of "General Provisions", the Legislature specially stated that "the *General Provisions of Civil Law of the People's Republic of China (draft)* was firstly deliberated at the 21st Meeting of the 12th NPC Standing Committee on June 27, 2016."[29] This can only be interpreted as that, the legislature does not think that the *2002 Civil Law (draft)* is a substantial "wholesale", and the purpose of enactment of *the General Provisions of Civil Law* is the "firstly wholesale" of the contents of the *General Provisions Volume of Civil Code*.

---

[28]Zhang (2017b).

[29]"The Full Text of the General Provisions of Civil Law (Draft)", http://www.npc.gov.cn/npc/flcazqyj/2016-07/05/content_1993342.htm.

9.3.2 The Stereotype of "Updating and Retail": The Explanation of "Other Special Provisions" in Article 11 of the General Provisions of Civil Law

Obviously the Legislature has not fully consciously entered into the "wholesale" legislative status, so that the "retail" stereotype is reflected during the enactment of the *General Provisions of Civil Law*, which is most obviously reflected in the Article 11 of the *General Provisions of Civil Law*.

9.3.2.1 The Explanation on "Other Special Provisions" in Article 11 of the General Provisions of Civil Law

Article 11 of *the General Provisions of Civil Law* provides that: "In case other laws give other special provisions on civil relationship, such provisions shall apply." To explain such provision is the key for evaluation on the legislative orientation "updating and retail" of *the General Provisions of Civil Law*.

The survey on the *Civil Codes* which have imposed relatively great impact on China, the words "In case there are other provisions in laws, such provisions shall apply" are used as the Referral Clause for specific rules, and this whole judgement of law mode which provide "other (special) provisions" is seldom used in civil legislation in such countries. This difference in legislative techniques should be interpreted as caused by the fact that, the *Civil Code* of other countries are enacted in short time under the legislative planning, and there is no such special need on coordination of relationship between *General Principles of the Civil Law* and civil single laws as that in China which is originated from the 30-year legislation course.

In the civil legislative history of China, Article 123 of the *Contract Law* adopts the whole judgment of law mode for the first time: "In case other laws give other provisions on contract, such provisions shall apply." In 2001, Article 49 was added by the *Decision on Amendment of Marriage Law of the People's Republic of China* issued by the NPC Standing Committee: "In case other laws give other provisions on juristic acts and legal liabilities relating to marriage and family, such provisions shall apply." These two laws use the phrase of "other provisions". Thereafter, Article 8 of the *Real Rights Law* and Article 5 of the *Tort liability Law* use the phrase of "other special provisions": "In case other relevant laws give other special provisions on real rights (or tort liabilities), such provisions shall apply", so as to coordinate the relationship between these two laws and *General Principles of the Civil Law*.[30]

It should be noted that, as a basic civil law, *General Principles of the Civil Law*, does not provide the priority of special law based on the whole judgement of law mode. Similar to the orientation of basic civil laws, it should be interpreted as not

---

[30]Wang (2011).

required by legislative techniques. The *General Provisions Volume of the 2002 Civil Law (draft)* contains no similar clause. However, Article 10 of *the General Provisions of Civil Law of the People's Republic of China (draft for solicitation of opinions)* dated January 29, 2016 provides "In case other laws give other provisions on civil relationship, such provisions shall apply." Article 11 of the *General Provisions of Civil Law of the People's Republic of China (draft for solicitation of opinions for first deliberation)* dated July 5, 2016 (hereinafter referred to as "*First Deliberation Draft*") provides "In case other laws give other special provisions on civil relationship, such provisions shall apply" and adopts the same legislative technique as the *Real Rights Law* and the *Tort liability Law*, and this technique was maintained in the subsequent *Second Deliberation Draft* and *Third Deliberation Draft*. Only when the *General Provisions of Civil Law* was finally adopted, it seemed likely that the Legislature realized the position of *the General Provisions of Civil Law* as a basic civil law, deleted the word "other" and changed the words into "special provisions", so as to create a new legislative provision.

Strictly speaking, Article 11 of *the General Provisions of Civil Law* is the true meaning of the provisions "In case of any discrepancy between the special provisions and general provisions enacted by a same legislature, the special provisions shall prevail" in Article 92 of the *Legislation Law*. Therefore, the Writer believes that, Article 11 of the *General Provisions of Civil Law* mainly arise from the accidental combination of the expression habit of retailed legislation since the enactment of the *Contract Law* (especially since the enactment of the *Real Rights Law)* and the literal adjustment on latest phase of legislation process, and involves no other meaning. This reveals that, the legislature drafted the *General Provisions of Civil Law* under the stereotype of "updating and retail". In the future when the *Civil Code* is being compiled, it is advised to delete the said article by reference to the treatment for *General Principles of the Civil Law*.[31]

9.3.2.2 Relationship Among the Updated and Retailed *General Provisions of Civil Law*, *General Principles of the Civil Law* and Other Civil Single Laws

With respect to the relationship between the *General Provisions of Civil Law* and *General Principles of the Civil Law*, the legislature has expressly stated that: "In case of any discrepancy between the *General Provisions of Civil Law* and *General Principles of the Civil Law*, the provisions of the *General Provisions of Civil Law* shall prevail in accordance with the principle that a new law shall prevail over an old law."[32] In accordance with this provision, the legislature directly applied the judgment rule "a new law shall prevail over an old law" for the *General Provisions*

---

[31]See Shi (2017).
[32]Li (2017).

of Civil Law and *General Principles of the Civil Law* both of which are the basic civil laws under the *Constitution*.

With respect to the relationship among the *General Provisions of Civil Law*, the *Contract Law*, the *Real Rights Law* and the *Tort liability Law*, the legislature has expressly provided that the rule "a new law shall prevail over an old law" shall apply.[33] In the aspects of contents, there is less overlap among the *General Provisions of Civil Law,* the *Succession Law*, the *Marriage Law* and the *Adoption Law*. The Writer believes that, the words "other special provisions" in Article 11 of the *General Provisions of Civil Law* mainly aim to coordinate the relationship between general civil law and special civil law. In the aspect of contents, the civil single laws are general civil law rather than special civil law, so that the rule "a new law shall prevail over an old law" shall still apply.

9.3.3 Content Arrangement for "Firstly Wholesale": Comparison on Settings of Chapters and Sections in the General Provisions of Civil Law and General Principles of the Civil Law

Except for the newly-added Chapter 4 "Unincorporated Organization", for almost every chapter or section of the *General Provisions of Civil Law*, the corresponding contents can be found in *General Principles of the Civil Law*.[34] There are some concerns in the academic community that, the *General Provisions of Civil Law* is only an "amendment" of *General Principles of the Civil Law*.[35] The Writer believes that, in the aspect of contents, the *General Provisions of Civil Law* is the "firstly wholesale" of the contents of the *General Provisions Volume of Civil Code*.

9.3.3.1 Chapter 1 of the *General Provisions of Civil Law* Is Oriented to the First Chapter of the *General Provisions Volume of Civil Code*

It is provided in Article 1 of the *General Provisions of Civil Law* that: "In order to protect the lawful rights and interests of civil subject, to regulate the civil relationships, to maintain the social and economic order, to get adapted to the development of socialism with Chinese characteristics and carry forward the socialist

---

[33]"Report of the Legal Committee of the 12th National People's Congress on the Deliberation of the General Provisions of Civil Law of the People's Republic of China (Draft)", adopted at the Second Meeting of the Fifth Presidium Meeting of the 12th March 2017.

[34]See "Comparative Table Between the Chapter Settings of the General Principles of Civil Law and the General Provisions of Civil Law", Wang (2007).

[35]Liu (2016).

core values, this Law is hereby enacted in accordance with *Constitution*." This is also the first law which provides "carry forward the socialist core values" in the clause of legislative purpose since the issuance of the *Guiding Opinions on Further Integrating Socialist Core Values into Legal Construction* by the General Office of CCCPC and the General Office of the State Council on December 25, 2016.

The said chapter contains other provisions, which include not only the basic principle relating to principle of equality, principle of autonomy of will, principle of fairness, principle of good faith, principle of public order and fine custom and the newly-added green principle in Article 4 through Article 9, but also Article 2 "Object of Adjustment", Article 3 "No Infringement upon Civil Rights and Interests", Article 10 "Sequence of Legal Authorities of Civil Law", Article 11 "Precedence of Special Law" and Article 12 "Territorial Validity of Civil Law". In consideration of the fact that the contents of Chapter 1 of the *General Provisions of Civil Law* are not limited to "basic principles", the legislature finally did not use "Basic Principles" as the title of Chapter 1 of the *General Provisions of Civil Law*, but adopted use the title "Basic Provisions".[36] Its contents are richer and more concrete than Chapter 1 of *General Principles of the Civil Law*, and meet the legislative orientation "firstly wholesale" of Chapter 1 of the *General Provisions Volume of Civil Code*.

9.3.3.2 Chapter 2–4 Establish the Framework of Civil Subject System of *Civil Code*

Chapter 2 of *General Principles of the Civil Law* adopts the title of "Citizen (Natural Persons)" which has the meaning of historical transfer, and Chapter 2 of the *General Provisions of Civil Law* directly uses the concept of "natural persons". In the aspect of contents, this chapter contains four sections, namely "Capacity for Civil Rights and Capacity for Civil Acts", "Guardianship", "Declaration of Missing and Declaration of Death" and "Individually-owned Business and Leaseholding Farm Household". The characteristics are as follows: Firstly, the guardianship system which should have been covered by the *Marriage and Family Volume of Civil Code* is remained in the *General Provisions of Civil Law*; secondly, the rules for two special civil subjects, namely individually-owned business and leaseholding farm household are remained; thirdly, the rules for individual partnership which would be included in the specific provision of the *Contract Volume of Civil Code* are not provided in the *General Provisions of Civil Law*.

Chapter 3 "Legal Persons" contains four sections, namely "General Provisions", "Profit-making Legal Persons", "Non-profit-making Legal Persons" and "Special

---

[36]"Report of the Legal Committee of the 12th National People's Congress on the Deliberation of the General Provisions of Civil Law of the People's Republic of China (Draft)", adopted at the Second Meeting of the Fifth Presidium Meeting of the 12th March 2017.

Legal Persons". There is great changes as compared with *General Principles of the Civil Law*, and the change is mainly reflected as follows: Firstly, the division method based on "enterprise legal person" and "non-enterprise legal person" in *General Principles of the Civil Law* is changed, the division method based on "association legal persons" and "foundation legal persons" in the traditional Continental Law System is also not adopted, but adopts the "profit-making" standard. Secondly, since it is difficult to divide the legal persons such as institutions and rural collective economic organizations, urban collective economic organizations, and grass root mass autonomous organizations in accordance with the profit-making standard, the category "special legal persons" is established. Thirdly, the rules for joint operation (a type of civil subject at the initial development stage of market economy) are not provided in the *General Provisions of Civil Law*.

In the newly-added Chapter 4 "Unincorporated Organization", the third type of civil subject other than natural person and legal person is clearly recognized, which covers individual proprietorship, partnership enterprise, and unincorporated professional service institution. This declarative confirmation of the type of civil subject is fully implemented in the *General Provisions of Civil Law*, as represented by Article 2 "Object of Adjustment": "The civil law adjusts the personal relationship and property relationship between equal subjects (namely natural persons, legal persons and unincorporated organizations)."

9.3.3.3 Following the Legislative Tradition, Chapter 5 Provides "Civil Rights" Rather Than "Civil Right Objects"

1. Special Orientation of Chapter 5 of "Civil Rights" of *General Principles of the Civil Law*

Owing to its special orientation of general principle, *General Principles of the Civil Law* has to not only "retail" in details the rules with general provisions nature, but also briefly "wholly sell" the rules with specific provisions nature. Therefore, Chapter 5 "Civil Rights" is set instead of the chapter of "civil right objects (properties)".[37] Such chapter is divided into four sections, briefly wholesale the rules with specific provisions nature, and provide the basic contents of property rights, creditor's right, intellectual property rights, personality and identity rights. Such chapter is arranged after Chapter 4 "Civil Juristic Acts and Agency" in *General Principles of the Civil Law*, which indicates the very strong Chinese characteristic.[38]

---

[37]Equivalent to the Chapter 2 of "Property, Animals" of Volume 1 of the *General Provisions, Chapter 3 of Japanese Civil Code and Chapter 3 of Civil Code of Taiwan area of China use the title of "property"*.

[38]Li (2016b).

2. The Main Contents of Chapter 5 "Civil Rights" of the General Provisions of Civil Law

During the legislation process, some scholars proposed to provide the civil rights from the viewpoint of civil right object. This can not only avoid the provisions given simply for declaration of rights, but also correct the systematic defect that the civil right objects are not clearly defined in the current civil law and establish the corresponding relationship with civil subjects.[39] However, the *General Provisions of Civil Law* finally adopts the structure of *General Principles of the Civil Law*,[40] and provides the "civil rights" rather than "civil right objects".

Chapter 5 "Civil Rights" of the *General Provisions of Civil Law* is divided into two sections, namely "Types of Civil Rights" and "Acquisition and Exercise of Civil Rights". As compared with *General Principles of the Civil Law*, the articles in the first section simplify the corresponding contents of *General Principles of the Civil Law* and add new types; and new rules systems are added in the second. It is advised that, this chapter in the future *General Provisions Volume of Civil Code* should also be divided into two sections, so as to make the system clearer.[41]

As for the types of civil rights, for the purpose of highlighting the precedence of personality and identity rights,[42] the *General Provisions of Civil Law* firstly provides the personality and identity rights, and then provides the property rights. Concretely speaking, Articles 109–111 provide personality rights, Article 112 provides identity rights, Articles 113–117[43] provide real rights, Articles 118–122 provide creditor's rights, Article 123 provides intellectual property rights, Article 124 provides succession rights, Article 125 provides investment rights, and Article 126 miscellaneously provides other legal civil rights and interests. In addition, two referral clauses are provided. Article 127 is the referral clause for special protection on data and network-based virtual properties, and Article 128 is the referral clause for special protection on disadvantaged groups such as minors, elderly, disabled, women and consumers, etc.

---

[39]Yao (2017).

[40]Xue (2017).

[41]The *General Provisions of Civil Law of P.R.C. (Draft)* of January 29th 2016 used to set Chapter 8 of "the Exercise and Protection of the Civil Rights", the first half of "the Exercise of the Civil Rights" is the embryonic form of the second half of the Chapter 5 of "Civil Rights".

[42]It is provided in Article 2 of *General Principles of the Civil Law* that: "The Civil Law of the People's Republic of China shall adjust property relationships and personal relationships between civil subjects with equal status, that is, between citizens, between legal persons and between citizens and legal persons." While it is provided in Article 2 of the *General Provisions of Civil Law* that: "The Civil Law shall adjust the personal relationships and the property relationships between civil subjects with equal status, that is, between natural persons, between legal persons and between unincorporated organizations." In comparison, the two legislations exchange the order of the personal relationships and the property relationships. See Xu (2002).

[43]It is provided in Article 113 of the *General Provisions of Civil Law* that: "The property rights of civil subjects enjoy the equal protection of law." This article is applied to all types of property rights. But from the source of the article, this would have been the provisions of property rights. See the analysis later.

In the section relating to acquisition and exercise of civil rights, Article 129 provides the acquisition of civil rights, Article 130 provides the voluntary and lawful exercise of civil rights, Article 131 provides that the obligations shall be performed for the exercise of rights, and Article 132 provides the prohibition on abuse of rights.

It should be noted that, most of the articles in Chapter 5 "Civil Rights" of the *General Provisions of Civil Law* have the relatively strong declarative meaning, and can't be directly applied as judgment standard. In a sense, setting the chapter "Civil Rights" rather than the chapter "Civil Right Objects" is also a makeshift under the situation that the legislative planning for *Personality Rights Law* and *General Provisions of Obligation Law* is not clear. If the Legislature does not carry out any substantial legislative activity in the field of *Personality Rights Law* and *General Provisions of Obligation Law*, then the provisions on personality rights and creditor's rights in Chapter 5 "Civil Rights" of the *General Provisions of Civil Law* may also be applied as the simplest basic provisions. If the legislative mode of civil right objects is adopted, on one hand, there will be controversy and difficulty in expression of personality right objects; on the other hand, the dilemma that the *Personality Rights Law* and *General Provisions of Obligation Law* are not compiled in the *Civil Code* may also occur.

3. Civil Right Objects of Absolute Rights are Provided in the Form of Civil Rights

It is provided in Article 115 of the *General Provisions of Civil Law* that: "The properties include real estate and chattel. In case it is provided in laws that right shall be the object of property right, such provision shall apply." It is provided in Paragraph 2 of Article 123 that: "Intellectual property rights are the exclusive rights legally owned by right holder in the following objects." It is thus clear that, since no provision on civil right object is provided in the *General Provisions of Civil Law*, there is certain problem in logic. Therefore, the civil rights are provided in the part of absolute property rights instead of civil right objects, and such provisions are provided before Chapter 6 "Civil Juristic Acts" in the *General Provisions of Civil Law*.

As for the institutional supply, the listing of objects of intellectual property rights meets the orientation of intellectual property rights of the future *Civil Code*.[44] However, that is too simple for real rights. It is hoped that the relevant provisions on properties and objects of property rights will be strengthened in the future *Real Rights Volume of Civil Code*.

---

[44]See Li and Ni (2017), He and Xiao (2017).

9.3.3.4 Chapter 6 and Chapter 7 Provide the Civil Juristic Acts and Agency in Details

In Chapter 4 of *General Principles of the Civil Law*, the Civil Juristic Acts and Agency are provided respectively in two sections. In combination of the relevant provisions of *General Principles of the Civil Law* and the *Contract Law*, the *General Provisions of Civil Law* divides and refines these two systems. Chapter 6 "Civil Juristic Acts" is divided into four sections, namely "General Provisions", "Intention Expressed", "Validity of Civil Juristic Acts" and "Conditional Civil Juristic Acts and Civil Juristic Acts with Time Period)", and Chapter 7 of "Agency" is divided into three sections, namely "General Provisions", "Entrusted Agency" and "Termination of Agency".

The main changes in the contents of the *General Provisions of Civil Law* relating to Civil Juristic Acts include: Firstly, Article 133 does not emphasize the legality requirement of civil juristic acts, but focus on the intention expressed.[45] Secondly, with respect to the types of revocable civil juristic acts, Article 149 and Article 150 provide the new types such as third-party fraud and menace, and Article 151 combines "taking advantage of other's difficulties" and "obviously unfair acts" into a type equivalent to "excessive profit acts" as provided in Germany laws.[46] Thirdly, as for the revocable civil juristic acts, the "right of revocation" rather than the "right of modification" is provided. Fourthly, Article 152 provides the exclusion period of three-month or one-year and different starting points for different situations under which the civil juristic acts can be revoked, and provides the maximum exercise period of five years.

In the *General Provisions of Civil Law*, "Agency" is provided in an independent chapter, rather than taken as an affiliated system of juristic acts.[47] The main characteristics of Chapter "Agency" are as follows: Firstly, no provision is given on unnamed agency, and such agency shall be governed by the provisions of Article 402 and Article 403 of the *Contract Law*.[48] Secondly, appointed agency is not listed as a separate type, but a special statutory agency. Thirdly, the provision "In case the authorization given in authorization letter is not clear, the principal shall bear the civil liabilities for third parties, and the agent shall bear the liabilities jointly and severally" in Paragraph 3 of Article 65 of *General Principles of the Civil Law* is not provided.

---

[45]It is provided in Article 54 of General Principles of the Civil Law that: "A civil juristic act shall be the lawful act of a citizen or legal person to establish, change or terminate civil rights and obligations." It is provided in Article 133 of the General Provisions of Civil Law that: "A civil juristic act shall be the act of civil subjects to establish, change or terminate civil rights and obligations through intention expressed".

[46]See Dieter (2007).

[47]Zhang (2017b).

[48]The Unnamed Agency was provided in The First Deliberation Draft to the Third Deliberation Draft, but was deleted at the final deliberation of NPC.

9.3.3.5 Chapter 8 Tries to Set up the Framework of Civil Liabilities of the *Civil Code*

Chapter 8 "Civil liabilities" of the *General Provisions of Civil Law* follows the tradition to provide the general provisions of civil liabilities in the *General Provisions Volume of Civil Code*, but the provisions provided are relatively complicated, and lack of systematic planning, mainly contain the contents in the following four aspects:

Firstly, the provisions in Article 176 on performance of civil obligations and undertaking of civil liabilities as well as the provisions in Article 179 on undertaking of civil liabilities are equivalent to Article 106 and Article 134 of *General Principles of the Civil Law*, and the rule on precedence of civil liabilities is provided in Article 187. These three rules are the general rules for civil liabilities.

Secondly, Article 177 and Article 178 generalize the rules on proportional liabilities and joint and several liabilities in Articles 12–14 of the *Tort liability Law*, and Article 186 generalizes the concurrence rules of liabilities for breach of contract and liabilities for tort liabilities provided in Article 122 of the *Contract Law*, which obviously aims to supplement the concurrence rules of obligation with several creditors and concurrence rules of claim in *General Provisions of Obligation Law*.

Thirdly, the provisions on force majeure in Article 180, the provisions on justifiable defense in Article 181 and the provisions on act of rescue in Article 182 generalize the main types of defenses,[49] rather than provide the self-relief.[50] Otherwise, the type of self-help should be provided intentionally.[51] The "liabilities for damage to person who acts bravely for a just cause" provided in Article 183 of the *General Provisions of Civil Law* actually follow the orientation of the rules with general provisions nature of Article 109 in Section 1 "General Provisions" of Chapter 6 "Civil liabilities" of *General Principles of the Civil Law*.

Fourthly, different from the orientation of the above articles as "wholesale of the rules with general provisions nature", the rule for exemption of liabilities for damage caused by voluntary emergency rescue as provided in Article 184 and the rule for liabilities for damage to personality interest of heroes and martyrs as provided in Article 185 involve the obvious characteristic of "retail of the rules with specific provisions nature".

In the future, it is necessary to systematically integrate Chapter 8 of the *General Provisions Civil Law* in the *General Provisions Volume of Civil Code* and refine the contents of Article 184 and Article 185 in the *Tort liability Volume of Civil Code*.[52]

---

[49]Wang (2017c).
[50]Yao (2017).
[51]Yang (2017a).
[52]Zhang (2017c).

**9.3.3.6   Adjustment Made in Chapter 9 Through Chapter 11 to Other
Contents of *General Principles of the Civil Law***

Chapter 9 "Limitation of Action" of the *General Provisions of Civil Law* fully
improves the system of limitation of actions. In Chapter 10 of the *General
Provisions of Civil Law*, the system of period calculation is separated from Chapter
9 "Supplementary Provisions" of *General Principles of the Civil Law*, and constitutes the relatively complete system of period together with the system of limitation of action. In the future, the system of limitation of action and system of
period calculation can be further integrated into one chapter of *General Provisions
Volume of Civil Code*.

In addition, since the *Law of Choice of Law for Foreign-Related Civil
Relationships* was enacted in 2010, the *General Provisions of Civil Law* does not
repeat the relevant contents of Chapter 8 "Application of Law for Foreign-related
Civil Relations" of *General Principles of the Civil Law*.

9.4   "Wholesale as Main Business and Retail as Side Business": Analysis on Contents of the *General Provisions of Civil Law*

9.4.1   "Wholesale as Main Business and Retail as Side Business": Legislative Function of the General Provisions of Civil Law

Normally, the legal rules compiled into the future *General Provisions Volume of
Civil Code* should be the result of extraction of common factors of civil and
commercial rules.[53] In the future, most of the rules of the *General Provisions of
Civil Law* will be compiled into the *General Provisions Volume of Civil Code*, and
a few rules will directly or indirectly constitute the *Specific Provisions Volumes of
Civil Code*. Using the commercial terms again, the Writer describes this legislative
phenomenon by using the commercial term "wholesale as main business and retail
as side business" again.

9.4.1.1   "Wholesale as Main Business": Most of the Articles Will Be
Compiled into the *General Provisions Volume of Civil Code*

Though most of the articles of the *General Provisions of Civil Law* will be compiled into the *General Provisions Volume of Civil Code*, such articles can be

---

[53]Wang and Guan (2017).

divided into "definite wholesale" category and "tentative wholesale" category on the basis of whether such articles need to be further amended in the future. The so-called "definite wholesale" means that most of the articles of the *General Provisions of Civil Law* involve no controversy in the enactment of the *General Provisions of Civil Law*, and have been basically determined and will not be substantially amended in the future *General Provisions Volume of Civil Code*. The so-called "tentative wholesale" means that a few articles of the *General Provisions of Civil Law* involve controversy during the enactment, and will be further determined or even be substantially amended in the *General Provisions Volume of Civil Code* in the future.

9.4.1.2 "Retail as Side Business": A Few Articles Will Directly or Indirectly Constitute the Rules with Specific Provisions Nature

Though the legislature has realized and expressly proposed that, some rules involving real rights, contract, tort liabilities, marriage and family and succession may be settled in the compilation of the *Specific Provisions Volumes of Civil Code*,[54] a few articles still directly or indirectly constitute the rules with specific provisions nature in the *General Provisions of Civil Law*. This is obviously linked with the fact that there is no clear legislative planning for the compilation of *Civil Code* and the legislature fails to show sufficient restraint. More importantly, this is also linked with the urgent response made by the Legislature to the following demands: Firstly, to reflect the political determination: this is mainly reflected in "retail" of the rule for equal protection on civil property rights and the rule for fair and reasonable compensation for expropriation of private properties in the *Real Rights Volume of Civil Code*. Secondly, to make response to public opinions: this is mainly reflected in "retail" of the rule for exemption of liabilities for damage to rescued person caused by voluntary emergency rescue and the rule for liabilities for damage to personality rights and interests of heroes and martyrs in the *Tort liability Volume of Civil Code*. Thirdly, to meet the practical needs: this is mainly reflected in "retail" of the guardianship system in the *Marriage and Family Volume of Civil Code* and the guardian appointed by testament in the *Succession Volume of Civil Code*. In addition, the needs to carry forward the legislative tradition and reflect the academic development also lead to the fact that the *General Provisions of Civil Law* "retails" some contents of the rules with specific provisions nature.

---

[54]Li (2017). "Report of the Legal Committee of the 12th National People's Congress on the Deliberation of the General Provisions of Civil Law of the People's Republic of China (Draft)", adopted at the Second Meeting of the Fifth Presidium Meeting of the 12th March 2017.

9.4.2 *"Wholesale as Main Business": Evaluation on Progress of the Wholesale Process*

9.4.2.1 Rules Subject to "Definite Wholesale" in the *General Provisions of Civil Law*

In the *General Provisions of Civil Law*, the relatively typical rule subject to "definite wholesale" is limitation of action. As compared with Chapter 7 of *General Principles of the Civil Law*, Chapter 9 of the *General Provisions of Civil Law* has been duly adjusted by the following means:

Firstly, to change some rules: Paragraph 1 of Article 188 of the *General Provisions of Civil Law* has changed the general limitation of action from two years to three years. With respect to the effect of suspension of the limitation of action, Article 194 changes the rule for calculation of remaining limitation of action in *General Principles of the Civil Law* to re-calculation of six-month limitation of action, so as to prolong the limitation of action to a certain extent and protect the right holders in face of matters for suspension of limitation of action.

Secondly, to delete some rules: By combining the rules in Article 135 and Article 137 of *General Principles of the Civil Law*, Article 188 of the *General Provisions of Civil Law* deletes the provisions relating to one-year special short limitation of action in Article 136 of *General Principles of the Civil Law*.[55]

Thirdly, to clarify some rules: By reference to the *Provisions on Limitation of Action for Civil Cases*, Article 189 of the *General Provisions of Civil Law* clarifies the calculation of limitation of action for installment debt, Article 193 clarifies the adversarialism for limitation of action, Article 196 clarifies the claims to which the limitation of action is not applicable, and Article 197 clarifies the statutory limitation of action.

Fourthly, to distinguish some rules: In Article 198 and Article 199 of the *General Provisions of Civil Law*, the limitation of action of arbitration and exclusion period are distinguished.

Fifthly, to add some rules: In light of the unreasonable situations in calculation of limitation of action for cases wherein the statutory agents infringe upon the rights and interests of principals[56] and the cases wherein the minors suffer sexual invasion[57] and by reference to the experience in comparative law, it is provided in Article 190 of the *General Provisions of Civil Law* that: "The limitation of action for a person without capacity for civil conduct or a person with limited capacity for civil conduct to claim against his/her statutory agent shall be calculated as of the date on which such statutory agency terminates." It is provided in Article 191 that:

---

[55]Wang (2017b).

[56]See Shi (2017, p. 453).

[57]Liang (2017a).

"The limitation of action for minors to claim compensation for sexual invasion shall be calculated as of the date on which the injured party reaches the age of 18 years."

9.4.2.2   Rules Subject to "Tentative Wholesale" in the *General Provisions of Civil Law*

In the *General Provisions of Civil Law*, the rules subject to "tentative wholesale" mainly include the rules of age standard for person with limited capacity for civil conduct and the rules of types and sequence of legal authorities of civil law.

1. Age Standard for Person with Limited Capacity for Civil Conduct

It is provided in Paragraph of Article 12 of *General Principles of the Civil Law* that: "A minor under the age of 10 shall be a person having no capacity for civil conduct and shall be represented in civil activities by his agent ad litem." Ten years old is the relatively reasonable age standard for limited capacity for civil conduct in 1980s in China, but is somewhat high nowadays.[58] During the enactment of the *General Provisions of Civil Law*, though there was certain controversy, the standard was determined as 6 years in *First Deliberation Draft* through *Third Deliberation Draft*, and was finally changed to 8 years as a compromise.[59]

The opinions against the age standard from 10 years to 6 years are mainly brought forth from the viewpoint of protection on interests of minors.[60] The Writer believes that, the safety in transactions shall also be considered. It is provided in Article 6 of the *Opinions on General Principles of the Civil Law* that: "In case any person with no capacity for civil conduct or with limited capacity for civil conduct accepts rewards, donations, or remunerations, no other person may claim the invalidity of the above-mentioned conducts by the reason that the person has no capacity for civil conduct or with limited capacity for civil conduct." On one hand, it is provided in Article 144 of the *General Provisions of Civil Law* that: "The civil juristic acts carried out by a person without capacity for civil conduct will be invalid." On the other hand, it is provided in Articles 19, 22 and 145 that the purely-profitable civil juristic acts carried out by persons with limited capacity for civil conduct will be valid, which actually confirms that the purely-profitable civil juristic acts carried out by persons without capacity for civil conduct will be invalid.

It is provided in Article 11 of the *Compulsory Education Law*: "When children have reached the age of six, their parents or other statutory guardians shall send them to school to receive and complete compulsory education; as for the children in areas where the conditions are unfavorable, the initial time of schooling may be

---

[58]Guan (2016).

[59]"Report of the Legal Committee of the 12th National People's Congress on the Deliberation of the General Provisions of Civil Law of the People's Republic of China (Draft)", adopted at the Second Meeting of the Fifth Presidium Meeting of the 12th March 2017.

[60]See Shi (2017, pp. 42–45).

postponed to 7 years old." As for the civil subjects which deal with minors, taking 6 years old corresponding to the schooling time as the age standard[61] will make the expectation on validity of civil juristic acts clearer. It is advised that, the age standard for person with limited capacity for civil conduct should be reduced to 6 years in the *General Provisions Volume of Civil Code* in the future.

2. Types and Sequence of Legal Authorities of Civil Law

It is provided in Article 6 of *General Principles of the Civil Law* that: "All civil activities shall comply with the laws. In case no relevant provisions are given in laws, the state policies shall be complied with." The legal authorities of civil law discussed during the enactment of the *General Provisions of Civil Law* include legislations, customs, legal theory and state policies. In comparison, there is less controversy on exclusion of state policies[62] and inclusion of customs[63] as legal authorities, but there is more controversy on inclusion of legal theory as legal authorities.[64] Finally, it is provided in Article 10 of the *General Provisions of Civil Law* that: "The civil disputes shall be settled in accordance with the legislations; in case no relevant provisions are given in legislations, the customs may apply, provided that the public order and fine custom may not be violated." A general survey of legislations in various countries reveals that, legal theory is provided as the third legal authorities in most countries. In the judicial practices in China, though the legal theory is not expressly referred to in judgment, the actual application of legal theory in judicial practices can't be avoided under the legislative guideline "broad rather than refined". Therefore, it is advised that the legal theory should be provided as the third legal authorities in *General Provisions Volume of Civil Code* in the future and the supplementary legislative authority should be granted to courts, so as to fill the legal loophole and eliminate the disadvantages in positive laws and customary laws.[65]

9.4.3 *"Retail as Side Business": Evaluation on Impact of "Retailed Articles"*

As for the future *Specific Provisions Volumes of Civil Code*, namely the *Real Rights Volume,* the *Contract Volume,* the *Tort liability Volume,* the *Marriage and Family Volume and* the *Succession Volume,* the *General Provisions of Civil Law* has directly or indirectly "retailed" a few articles. The evaluation is carried out as follows.

---

[61]Chen (2016).

[62]Yang (2015a).

[63]Yao and Liang (2016).

[64]Zhang (2017a).

[65]Chen (2017b).

9.4.3.1 Marriage and Family Volume of Civil Code

1. Guardianship System is Provided in the *General Provisions of Civil Law* as Tradition

Since the *1980 Marriage Law* was enacted before the *1986 General Principles of the Civil Law*, the guardianship system which would be included in the *Marriage Law* has to be provided in the Section "Natural Persons" of *General Principles of the Civil Law*. Still following the tradition of *General Principles of the Civil Law*, the *General Provisions of Civil Law* provides the guardianship system in Section "Natural Persons", improving the guardianship system by taking the family guardianship as basic guardianship, social guardianship as supplementary guardianship and state guardianship as last guardianship.[66]

In addition, the *General Provisions of Civil Law* generalizes two guardianship systems provided in special laws. One is the system of elderly self-determined guardianship as provided in Article 26 of the *Law on Protection of Rights and Interests of the Elderly*, which has achieves relatively good effect in practices. Article 33 of the *General Provisions of Civil Law* converts it into a negotiation-based guardianship system applicable to adults with full capacity for civil conduct. The other is the provision "The injuring party whose guardianship has been revoked shall continue to bear the corresponding care and support expenses" in Paragraph 2 of Article 21 of the *Anti-Domestic-Violence Law* and the provision "The parents whose guardianship has been revoked shall continue to bear the foster expenses in accordance with laws" in Article 53 of the *Law on Protection of Minors*, which are converted into the provision in Article 37 of the *General Provisions of Civil Law* that the legal obligation of foster will not be exempted by the revocation of guardianship.

From the viewpoint of the *General Provisions of Civil Law*, the guardianship system shall be included into *Marriage and Family Volume*, so as to bring the guardianship function of family into full play.[67] The *Marriage and Family Volume of Civil Code* proposed by the *Civil Code Compilation Project Team of China Law Society* contains 7 chapters, namely general provisions, marriage, conjugal relationship, divorce, relationship among parents, children and other close relatives, adoption and guardianship.[68] In the future, it is advised to include the guardianship system into *Marriage and Family Volume of Civil Code*.

2. Obligations Between Parents and Children Are Not Covered by Guardianship System

It is provided in Paragraph 1 of Article 26 of the *General Provisions of Civil Law* that: "The parents have the obligation to foster, educate and protect their minor

---

[66]Li (2017).
[67]Liu (2016).
[68]Xia (2017).

children." In the Section "Guardianship", the said article separately provides the legal obligations of parents to foster, educate and protect minor children, distinguishes such obligations from guardianship of other guardians, and establishes the system of paternity to a certain extent.

It is provided in Paragraph 2 of the said article that: "The adult children have the obligation to support and protect their parents." Different from the *Marriage Law* and the *Law on Protection of Rights and Interests of the Elderly* which only provide the support obligation, the *General Provisions of Civil Law* also provides the obligation of adult children to protect their parents. The Writer believes that, by providing such obligation of protection, the *General Provisions of Civil Law* aims to ensure that the adult children will better protect the rights and interests (especially personal safety) of their parents. However, if the obligation of protection is established by full reference to the paternity system between parents and children, then unfavorable consequences may occur under certain circumstances. For example, it is necessary to clarify in practices in the future that, when the parents are infringed upon, whether the infringer may be exempted from liabilities by claiming that the adult children fail to fulfill the obligation of protection. In the future, it is advised to clarify this rule as the obligation of adult children to protect their parents who have fully or partially lost the capacity for civil conducts.

What needs to be pointed out is that, this article gives the provisions on obligations between parents and children, which are not covered by guardianship system. Even if the guardianship system is included in the *General Provisions Volume of Civil Code* as tradition, the provisions of this article should also be included in the *Marriage and Family Volume of Civil Code*.

2. Impact on Marriage Relationship by Revocation of Declaration of Death

It is provided in Article 51 of the *General Provisions of Civil Law* that: "The marriage relationship of a person who has been declared as dead shall terminate as of the date on which the death of such person is declared. In case the declaration of death is revoked, the marriage relationship shall automatically recover as of the date on which the declaration of death is revoked, unless the spouse has married again or declares in writing to the marriage registration authority that he/she is not willing to recover such marriage relationship." The words "unless the spouse declares in writing to the marriage registration authority that he/she is not willing to recover such marriage relationship" in the second sentence in this article aim to avoid the tedious procedure that "The spouse who is not willing to recover the marriage relationship has to get such relationship recovered and then go through the divorce procedure",[69] but indirectly establish a new registration item for marriage registration authority under the *Marriage and Family Volume of Civil Code*.

---

[69]See Shi (2017, p. 106).

9.4.3.2 Succession Volume of Civil Code

1. Protection on Interests of Fetus

Article 28 of *Succession Law* adopts the restrictive doctrine for protection on interests of fetus: "At the time of the partitioning of heritage, reservation shall be made for the share of an unborn child. The share reserved shall, if the baby is stillborn, be dealt with in accordance with statutory succession." Since the new Article 16 of the *General Provisions of Civil Law* adopts the generalization doctrine with respect to legislative purpose, it would have adopt the provisions similar to those in Article 7 of the *Civil Code* of Taiwan area in China: "The fetuses shall be limited to those which are alive at birth in the future, and will be deemed as already born with respect to the protection on their individual interests." However, the said article focuses much attention on listing of partitioning of heritage: "With respect to protection on interests of fetus such as succession of heritage, acceptance of gift and etc., a fetus shall be deemed as having the capacity for civil rights. However, if the fetus is a dead body at birth, its capacity for civil rights shall be deemed as nonexistent at first." It seems that this article provided the capacity of fetus for civil rights,[70] but actually it is limited to the partitioning of heritage. As for the word "etc.", though the Legislature believes that "No specific scope is defined, so that there is room left for legislation in this aspect in the future",[71] the *General Provisions of Civil Law* missed the good opportunity to "wholly sell" the rules based on generalization doctrine for protection on interests of fetus, but actually "retailed" the rules for reserved portion of succession for fetus in the *Succession Law*.

2. Guardian Appointed by Testament

Article 29 of the *General Provisions of Civil Law* establishes the system of guardian appointed by testament: "In case the parents of a person under guardianship act as the guardian, the said parents may appoint the guardian by means of testament. "The purpose of this article is to ensure that the parents can appoint the person who is trustworthy and is the most favorable for protection on rights and interests of children under guardianship as the guardian by giving a testament,[72] because the appointment by parents is usually the most favorable arrangement for minors,[73] and can also reduce the workload of people's court in appointing guardian.[74]

What needs to be pointed out is that, the provisions of this article expand the testament system in *Succession Law* which is only applicable to the succession of

---

[70]Yang (2017b).

[71]See Shi (2017, p. 35).

[72]See Shi (2017, p. 66).

[73]Wang (2017d).

[74]Liang (2016a).

properties. Since the testament system in *Succession Law* only involves the positive burden arising from transfer of heritage and the guardian appointed in accordance with the provisions of this article is actually a passive burden, it is also necessary to further clarify whether the guardian so appointed has the right to refuse such appointment. In addition, Chapter 5 of the *Succession Law* establishes the order of precedence "legacy support—testament/bequest—statutory succession".[75] It is also necessary to provide the rules for bequest-support agreement which involve the burden of appointed guardian and its precedence over testament or bequest which involve the burden of appointed guardian in details in the *Succession Volume of Civil Code* in the future.

9.4.3.3 Property Volume of Civil Code

Some constitution law scholars have pointed out that, in the socialist country where the public ownership system remains dominant, actively avoiding the inherent contradiction between the social nature of public ownership system and the private nature of civil law and effectively coordinating the relationship between the civil law and the *Constitution* will not only provide an extensive stage for the *Civil Code* to play its role, but also comply with the provisions relating to public ownership system in the *Constitution*, and will be an issue which should be carefully considered during the compilation of *Civil Code*.[76]

1. No Powerful Political Determination in the *Real Rights Law*

During the drafting of the *Real Rights Law*, two principled provisions were not clearly given owing to the lack of powerful political determination. One is the principle for equal protection on property rights. It is also the important point of controversy with respect to the unconstitutional event of the *2005 Real Rights Law (draft)*,[77] and finally the equal protection is not expressly provided in Article 4 of the *Real Rights Law*: "The state, collective and private property rights as well as the real rights of other right holders are protected by laws and may not be infringed upon by any individual or entity."

The other is the principle for fair and reasonable compensation for expropriation of private properties. Before the *Constitution* was amended in 2004, it was provided in Paragraph 3 of the Article 13 that: "For the purpose of public interests, the State may expropriate land in accordance with the laws." In 2004, the said paragraph was amended as: "The state may, for the public interest, expropriate or take over private

---

[75]It is provided in Article 5 of the *Succession Law* that: "Succession shall, after its opening, be handled in accordance with the provisions of statutory succession; where a will exists, it shall be handled in accordance with testamentary succession or as legacy; where there is an agreement for legacy in return for support, the former shall be handled in accordance with the terms of the agreement".

[76]Qin (2016).

[77]About this constitutionality controversy, see Wang (2006).

property of citizens for public use, and pay compensation in accordance with the law." However, the principle for amount of compensation was not provided. Article 42 of the *Real Rights Law* gives the principle for compensation for the land owned by collectives as well as the housing and other real estate owned by entities and individuals which are expropriated for the purpose of public interests and in accordance with the authority and procedure provided by laws, and Article 44 gives the principle for compensation for the real estate or movable properties owned by entities and individuals which are expropriated for the purpose of rescue and disaster relief and in accordance with the authority and procedure provided by laws. However, the principle for fair and reasonable compensation was not established.

2. Political Determination in the *Opinions on Protecting Property Rights*

As for the compilation of *Civil Code*, the political factors are the most important, and when a code is issued, there should be an appropriate political environment.[78] On November 4, 2016, the CPC Central Committee and the State Council issued the *Opinions on Improving Property Right Protection System and Legally Protecting Property Rights* (ZH.F. [2016] No. 28, hereinafter referred to as "*Opinions on Protecting Property Rights*"). It is pointed out in Article 3 "Improvement of Legal System for Equal Protection on Property Rights" of the *Opinions* that: "We shall accelerate the compilation of *Civil Code*, improve the legal systems relating to real rights, contract and intellectual property rights, delete the unfair provisions of laws and regulations, and take the equal protection as the basic principle for normalizing property relationship. We shall improve the legal system for market subjects based on corporate organization forms and investor's liabilities, sort out and abolish the law and administrative regulations for market subjects which are enacted on the basis of different ownership systems, sort out the departmental rules and normative documents, and equally protect various market subjects. It is pointed out in Article 4 "Improvement of Property Expropriation System" that: "We shall improve the legal system for expropriation of properties such as land and housing, reasonably determine the scope of public interests for which the expropriation may be carried out, never excessively extend the public interests, and refine the legal authority and procedure for expropriation. We shall follow the principle of timely and reasonable compensation, improve the state compensation system, further clarify the scope, form and standard of compensation, and give fair and reasonable compensation to those persons whose properties have been expropriated."

3. Implementation of the *Opinions o n Protecting Property Rights* by the *General Provisions of Civil Law*

The first deliberation draft of the *General Provisions of Civil Law* dated July 5, 2016 contains no provisions on equal protection of property rights, and only provides in Article 123 that: "The income, savings, housing, articles for daily use,

---

[78]Allan (2005).

production tools, investment and other property rights legally owned by civil subjects are protected by laws." After the *Opinions on Protecting Property Rights* were issued on November 4, 2016, the second deliberation draft dated November 18, 2016 immediately preliminary implements this important political determination, and gives the provisions relating to equal protection on real rights in Article 114: "The real rights of civil subjects are equally protected by laws, and may not be infringed upon by any entity or individual." In the third deliberation draft dated December 17, 2016, under the precondition that the provisions relating to equal protection on real rights are remained, Article 112 adopts the more broad statement "private property rights": "The private property rights of natural persons are protected by laws." Finally, Article 113 of the *General Provisions of Civil Law* expands the equal protection on real rights to the property rights of civil subjects: "The property rights of civil subjects are equally protected by laws." This is the first time in the civil legislative history of China that clear provisions are provided for equal protection.[79] It is advised that "property rights" in such article should be amended to "property rights and interests" in the future, so as to cover all kinds of property rights and interests.

Similarly, with respect to the principle for fair and reasonable compensation for expropriation of private properties, no relevant provision was provided in the first deliberation draft and the second deliberation draft of the *General Provisions of Civil Law*. However, as advised by some members of NPC Standing Committee, departments, NPC deputies and scholars,[80] such provision was added into the third deliberation draft, and was finally adopted as Article 117 of the *General Provisions of Civil Law*: "In case any real estate or movable property is expropriated for the purpose of public interests and in accordance with the authority and procedure provided by laws, the fair and reasonable compensation shall be given." It is advised to use the statement "private property" in the future in accordance with the statement of 2004 Amendment to the *Constitution*.

4. Great Constitutional Significance of "Continuing from the Preceding and Introducing the Following"

It should be noted that, the principle for equal protection on property rights provided in Article 113 of the *General Provisions of Civil Law* and the principle for fair and reasonable compensation for expropriation of private properties provided in Article 117 of the *General Provisions of Civil Law* not only have the function to "retail" the important principled provisions of the *Property Volume of Civil Code*, but also have the great constitutional significance of "continuing from the preceding and introducing the following".

The so-called "continuing from the preceding" means that these two articles are actually the implementation of the corresponding articles of the *Constitution*. Briefly speaking, as supported by the political determination in the *Opinions on*

---

[79]Zhang (2017b).

[80]Li (2016a), the document at the Fifth Session of the Twelfth National People's Congress.

Protecting Property Rights, the legislature believes that the words "The public properties of socialism are sacred and inviolable" in Paragraph 1 of Article 12 of the *Constitution* will not surely deduce the conclusion that the property rights of civil subjects can't be equally protected by laws, and such equal protection can be embodied by the public-welfare litigation for the protection of state-owned assets as initiated by people's procuratorate under the *Law on State-owned Assets in Enterprises* and the *Administrative Procedure Law*.[81] In addition, the words "For the purpose of public interests, the State may expropriate the private properties of citizens in accordance with the laws and give compensation" in Paragraph 3 of the Article 13 of the *Constitution* shall also deduce the fair and reasonable compensation.

The so-called "introducing the following" means that, the future *Property Volume of Civil Code* shall implement the political determination in the *Opinions on Protecting Property Rights*; the protection on property rights of civil subjects shall be designed in accordance with the legislative thoughts for equal protection; the principle for fair and reasonable compensation shall be implemented for expropriation of private properties.

9.4.3.4 Contract Volume of Civil Code

The *General Provisions of Civil Law* "retails" the rules of the future *Contract Volume of Civil Code* in a relatively indirect manner. The general provisions of the *Contract Volume* will be applied as the system of general provisions of obligation law. And the "individual partnership" will be provided as named contract in the specific provisions of the *Contract Volume*.

3. General Provisions of the *Contract Volume* will be Applied as the System of General Provisions of Obligation Law

If the *General Provisions of Obligation Law* will not be enacted according to the current legislative plan, then the system of general provisions of obligation law will have to be divided and included into the *General Provisions Volume of Civil Code* and the general provisions of *Contract Volume of Civil Code*.[82] the *General Provisions of Civil Law* provides the concept of creditor's right and the causes of

---

[81]The legislative expression based on the political determination of the *Opinions on Protecting Property Rights* actually responds the core controversy of the constitutionality of the *Real Rights Law*, avoids the political controversy of the future possible amendment of the Article 12 of the *Constitution*. See Wang (2006).

[82]笔者个人建议是将 "债法总则" 的内容与《民法总则》上 "民事责任" 章合并, 规定为《民法典·总则编》的 "债与责任" 章. 参见王竹:《民法典起草实用主义思路下的 "债法总则" 立法模式研究,《四川大学学报》(哲学社会科学版) 2012 年第 3 期. The Writer's suggestion is to combine the contents of the *General Provisions of Obligation Law* and the Chapter of "Civil Liabilities", so as to form a new Chapter of "Obligations and Liabilities" in the *General Provisions Volume of Civil Code*. See Wang (2012).

obligation in Article 118, and then provides four typical causes for obligation (namely Contract, Tort, Negotiorum Gestio and Unjust Enrichment) respectively in a single article among Articles 119–122, but even the "claim for obligation" is not provided,[83] which indicates that the supply of systems is insufficient. In the future, the system of general provisions of obligation law can only be realized by using the corresponding rules in the general provisions of *Contract Volume of Civil Code*.[84]

In consideration of the arrangement whereby the civil right objects are replaced by Chapter 5 "Civil Rights" of the *General Provisions of Civil Law* as well as the provisions in Chapter 8 "Civil liabilities" relating to proportional liabilities and joint and several liabilities, in the future, it is unnecessary to provide object of obligation and obligation with multiple-party in the system of general provisions of obligation law. In consideration of the structure of the *Contract Law*, "Types of Obligation" may be reserved to the legal theory, and "Validity of Obligation", "Performance of Obligation", "Transfer of Obligation" and "Termination of Obligation" may respectively apply the rules of Chapters 3–6 "Validity of Contract", "Performance of Contract", "Modification and Transfer of Contract" and "Termination of Rights and Obligations under Contract" of the *Contract Law*.

2. Unprovided "Individual Partnership" will be Provided in the Specific Provisions of the *Contract Volume of Civil Code* as Named Contract

The "individual partnership" is not provided in the *General Provisions of Civil Law*, and the "unincorporated organizations" provided in Paragraph 2 of Article 102 in Chapter 4 "Unincorporated Organizations" include individual proprietorship, partnership enterprise and professional service institution without legal personality. Only the partnership enterprise rather than the individual partnership is included.[85] In nature, the individual partnership system is not a civil subject system, but a named contract. Owing to the urgent demand on individual partnership as a form of participation in market economy at the initial stage of reform and opening-up and the lack of relevant provision on partnership contract in the *1981 Economic Contract Law*, the relevant provisions were given in *General Principles of the Civil Law*. It is advised to provide the partnership contract in the specific provisions of the *Contract Volume of Civil Code* in the future.

9.4.3.5   Tort Liability Volume of Civil Code

The main impact imposed by the *General Provisions of Civil Law* on the *Tort liability Volume of Civil Code* is that, for the purpose of making response to hot cases over recent years and in accordance with the requirement of the NPC deputies that the legislation shall carry forward the socialist core values, the rule for

---

[83]Wang (2017b).
[84]Wang (2017a).
[85]Zhu (2017).

exemption of liabilities for damage caused by voluntary emergency rescue was added during the deliberation of the third deliberation draft, and the rule for liabilities for damage to personality interest of heroes and martyrs was added during final deliberation.

1. Exemption of Liabilities for Damage to Rescued Person Caused by Voluntary Emergency Rescue

It is provided in Article 184 of the *General Provisions of Civil Law* that: "A person shall not bear civil liabilities if he acts voluntarily to help another in emergency and inflicts losses on the one being helped." The legislative purpose of such article is to avoid the adverse impact on the public arising from hot events such as PENGyu Case,[86,87] but the legal facts described in such article indicate that the provisions are not related to core controversy on determination of evidences and free evaluation of evidence in PENGyu Case,[88] and are more linked with the Glass Doll Case in Taiwan area of China,[89] so that the legislative accuracy is relatively low.[90]

The provisions in Article 184 of the *General Provisions of Civil Law* are not originally created by China. In the Anglo-American legal system, this is a typical Good Samaritan Law.[91] In the Continental legal system, however, it is included into emergency voluntary service. For example, it is provided in Article 680 of the *Civil Code of Germany* that: "In affair management, for the purpose of avoiding any immediate danger which he/she may incur, the actor shall only undertake liabilities for his/her intentional conduct or gross negligence."[92] Article 175 of the *Civil Code* of Taiwan area of China gives the similar provisions: "In affair management, for the purpose of avoiding any immediate danger which may occur to his/her life, body or property, the actor shall not be liable to make compensation for damage caused by such management, unless ill intention or gross negligence is involved."

What is worth of careful study is that, the purpose of this article when it was proposed was to clearly "give the provisions on exemption of liabilities". This means that, unless gross negligence is involved, the rescuer shall not undertake civil liabilities. However, during the solicitation of opinion on the third deliberation draft, it was advised by some NPC deputies and CPPCC members to delete "unless gross negligence is involved", because they thought that, such words are against the provisions for carrying forward the socialist core values; and since acting bravely

---

[86]People's Court of Gu Lou District of Nan Jing City: The Civil Judgment of the First Instance of the Dispute of Personal Injury Compensation between the Plaintiff Ms. Xu and the Defendant Mr. Peng (2007) Gu Civil Court of 1, Number 212.

[87]See Shi (2017, p. 437).

[88]See Wang Yaxin: "fact of judgment", "fact of media" and society in the transforming stage reflected by civil judicature, *Cross-Strait Law Review*, No. 24. Wu Zeyong: "The boundary of the Free Evaluation of the Evidence", *Cross-Strait Law Review*, No. 30.

[89]See Wang (2009).

[90]Wang (2014a).

[91]Li (2014).

[92]Translated by Chen (2010).

for a just cause is encouraged, no regret shall be left in laws. In addition, they also thought that it would be difficult to define the gross negligence. Through the wrestling in deliberate and final adoption, the words "unless gross negligence is involved" were finally deleted.[93]

It should be regretfully pointed out that, the provisions of this article fail to settle the social moral crisis brought about by PengYu Case as expected by NPC deputies and CPPCC members, and cause new problem in application of laws. The reason is that, such provisions do not belong to the rules with general provisions nature, and were temporarily drafted by the legislature at the last phase of legislative procedure without any legislative survey; the legislative advice given by NPC deputies and CPPCC members involves the problem that the social justice is replaced by purpose justification.[94] The Writer believes that, the controversy on the words "unless gross negligence is involved" was caused by the fact that the possibility to undertake appropriate indemnity liabilities is excluded by relevant discussion. It is advised to amend this rule in the future *Tort liability Volume of Civil Code*, and by reference to the liabilities for excessive defense as provided in Paragraph 3 of Article 182 of the *General Provisions of Civil Law*,[95] Paragraph 2 is added as follows: "In case any unnecessary damage is caused by improper or excessive measures taken in the emergency rescue, the rescuer shall bear the appropriate civil liabilities."

2. Liabilities for Damage to Personality Rights and Interests of Heroes and Martyrs

In the last deliberation of the *General Provisions of Civil Law*,[96] the following provisions were added into Article 185: "Civil liabilities shall be undertaken for the damage to name, portrait, reputation or honor of heroes and martyrs if such damage infringe upon social public interests." This article has strong political significance and meaning of the times.[97] This article was enacted against the social background that, in order to always remember the immortal feats of heroes and martyrs in the war of resistance against Japanese aggression, carry forward the spirit of patriotism and gather all forces for realization of great rejuvenation of the Chinese nation, the NPC Standing Committee adopted the *Decision on Establishment of Martyr's Day* on August 31, 2014. Thereafter, the Ministry of Civil Affairs issued the first (300 persons) and second (600 persons) lists of famous heroes and martyrs who tenaciously struggled and sacrificed their life for the country in the war of resistance against Japanese aggression respectively on September 1, 2014 and August 24, 2015.

---

[93]See Shi (2017, p. 438).

[94]Liang (2017b).

[95]It is provided in Paragraph 3 of Article 182 in the *General Provisions of Civil Law* that: "The measures in a Act of Rescue is taken improperly or exceeding the necessary limits, causing the harm which should have been avoided, the actor of Rescue shall bear the proper civil liabilities".

[96]"Report of the Legal Committee of the 12th National People's Congress on the Deliberation of the *General Provisions of Civil Law* of the People's Republic of China (Draft)", adopted at the Second Meeting of the Fifth Presidium Meeting of the 12th March 2017.

[97]Chen (2017a).

As the rule for judicial practices, the application of tort liabilities for damage to personality rights and interests of heroes and martyrs has been clarified in the reputation dispute case (PENGJiahui vs. China Narrative) published in the *Gazette in the Supreme People's Court* in 2002.[98] If the Legislature only hopes to clarify this rule, it should have provided it in the *Tort liability Law* in 2009. It is thus clear that, Article 185 of the *General Provisions of Civil Law* obviously aims to make response to the serial reputation dispute cases relating to Langya Shan Five Heroic Men which have caused great controversy during the enactment of the *General Provisions of Civil Law*.[99]

The provisions of this article are similar to Paragraph 1 of Article 3 of the *Judicial Interpretation on Compensation for Mental Damage*: "After the disease of a natural person, in case his/her close relatives incur emotional suffering owing to the following torts and initiate a litigation in people's court for compensation for emotional damage, the people's court shall legally accept such request: (1) Damage the name, portrait, reputation or honor of the deceased by means of insult, libel, defamation, vilification or any other mean which violates social public interests or social morals;" However, the said judicial interpretation is only applicable to the diseased, namely the martyrs as provided in Article 185 of the *General Provisions of Civil Law*,[100] and is not applicable to the heroes who are still alive.[101] As for the word "etc.", the legislative meaning is to include other outstanding persons who have made great contribution to the construction of socialism with Chinese characteristics and defense of nation,[102] namely the natural persons who bear the social and public interests such as model workers and moral models, whether deceased or alive. By this token, the core element of this article is to impose liabilities for behaviors which damage the social and public interests by infringing upon the name, portrait, reputation or honor of heroes and martyrs, rather than simply protect the personality interests of martyrs.

The Writer believes that, according to the manner for initiation of civil litigation as provided in this article, the close relatives of the deceased may initiate the litigation on the basis of Article 7 of the *Judicial Interpretation on Compensation for Emotional Damage*, or a member of a hero group may initiate the litigation with

---

[98]Reputation Dispute of PENG Jiahui vs. China Narrative, *the Gazette in the Supreme People's Court*, 2002.

[99]"The Supreme People's Court publishes 4 Typical Cases about the Protection of the Personality Rights and Interests of Heroes and Martyrs like Langya Shan Five Heroic Men", October 19th 2016.

[100]See Article 2 of the *Regulation of Martyr Praise* and Article 2 of the *Regulation of Military Pensions Priority*.

[101]See Paragraph 2 of Article 8 of the *Ordinance of the Reward for the People's Police* and Paragraph 1 of Article 8 of the *Ordinance of the Discipline for People's Liberation Army*.

[102]See Shi (2017, p. 440).

respect to the rights and interests in jointly-owned "name, portrait, reputation or honor".[103] In addition to private interest litigation, this article may be extended to cover the public interest litigation initiated in accordance with Article 55 of the *Civil Procedure Law*.[104] The applicable rules are to be clarified in the future *Tort liability Volume of Civil Code*.

References

Allan Watson, The Making of the Civil Law, translated by LI Jingbing and YAO Xinhua, China Legal Publishing House, 2005, p. 130.

Cai Dingjian, "On the Relationship of Rule of Law and Reform", *Legal Research*, No. 2 1986.

Chen Weizuo, *German Civil Code (Edition 3)*, Law Press, 2010, p. 274.

Chen Huabing, "On the Structure, Innovation and Perfection of the General Principles of Civil Law (Draft) of China", *Journal of Comparative Law*, No. 5, 2016.

Chen Huabin, "The Commentary on the Provisions of 'Civil Liabilities' of the *General Provisions of Civil Law*", *Journal of Law Application,* No. 9, 2017a.

Chen Weizuo, "Swiss Civil Code: A Brave and Confident Civil Code", *The People's Congress of China*, No. 5, 2017b.

Dieter Medicus, *General Theory of German Civil Law*; Law Press, 2007, pp. 538–542.

Guan Shufang, "Protection of the Rights and Interests of Minors in Compiling Civil Code", *Journal of China Youth College for Political Sciences*, No. 6, 2016.

He Hua, Xiao Zhiyuan, "Commentary and Analysis on the Clauses about Intellectual Property in the General Principles of Civil Law and the Prospect of Future Legislation", *Intellectual Property*, No. 5, 2017.

Jiang Ping, "On the Formulating of an Open Civil Code", *Tribune of Political Science and Law*, No. 1, 2003a.

Jiang Ping, "On the Formulating of an Open Civil Code Again", *The Jurist*, No. 4, 2003b.

Li Yongjun, "Paving the Way of Civil Code Taking Root in Native China", *The People's Congress of China*, No. 14, 2006.

Li Hao, "On the Samaritan in Common Law", *Journal of East China University of Political Science and Law*, No. 4, 2014.

Li Shishi, "The Explanation of the Daft of the General Provisions of Civil Law of the People's Republic of China", June 27th, 2016a.

---

[103]The common interests of the Name shared by the Heroes and Martyrs, should be interpreted as the honorary title of the same hero martyr group, the image, reputation and honorary title are co-owned. See Yang (2007).

[104]It is provided in Paragraph 1 of Article 55 of the Civil Procedure Law that: "For the act of damaging the social public interests such as environment pollution and infringement upon multiple consumers, the statutory organs and related organizations may bring a lawsuit to the People's Court." The newly added Paragraph 2 in 2017: "If the People's Procuratorate find the facts of damaging the social public interests such as destruction of the ecological environment and resource protection, infringement upon multiple consumers in Food and Medicine area, When there is no statutory organs and related organizations or such statutory organs and related organizations refuse to bring a lawsuit, the People's Procuratorate may bring a lawsuit to the People's Court. If the statutory organs and related organizations agree to bring a lawsuit, the People's Procuratorate may support such lawsuit".

Li Yongjun, "Commentary on Chapter of Civil Rights in the General Principles of Civil Law", *The Jurist*, No. 5, 2016b.

Li JianGuo, "The Explanation of the Daft of the General Provisions of Civil Law of the People's Republic of China", at the Fifth Session of the Twelfth National People's Congress on March 8th, 2017.

Li Yufeng, Ni ZhuLiang, "Significance and Influence of the Clauses about Intellectual Property in the General Principles of Civil Law", *Intellectual Property*, No. 5, 2017.

Liang Huixing, "Loose and Complied Civil Code Is Not Appropriate for China's National Condition", *Tribune of Political Science and Law*, No. 1, 2003.

Liang Huixing, "Key Problems on the Legislation of the General Principles of Civil Law (the First Volume)", *Chinese Lawyer*, No. 7, 2016a.

Liang Huixing, "The Personality Right can't be as a Separated Part in Chinese Civil Code", *Academic Journal of Zhongzhou*, No. 2, 2016b.

Liang Huixing, "The Formulating of the General Principles of Civil Law of China", *Northern Legal Science*, No. 1, 2017a.

Liang Huixing, "Understanding and Application of Important Clauses of the General Principles of Civil Law", *Journal of Sichuan University (Social Science Edition)*, No. 4, 2017b.

Liu Jingwei, "The General Principles of Civil Law Should not be the Revised Version of the General Provisions of Civil Law", *Law Science*, No. 10, 2016.

Liu Suping, ed., *Inheritance Law*, China Renmin University Press, 1988, p. 87.

Qin Qianhong, "Constitutional Problems in Compiling Civil Code", *Journal of National Procurators College*, No. 6, 2016.

Shi Hong, ed. Clauses Interpretation, Legislation Reasons and Relevant Provisions of the General Principles of Civil Law of People's Republic of China, Peking University Press, 2017.

Wang Zhu, "On the Constitutionality of the General Provisions of Civil Law and the Real rights law (draft)", Renmin University Law Review, No. 3, 2006.

Wang Zhu, ed. *Compiling Comparative Table of the General Principles of Civil Law and Clause Interpretation*, Peking University Press, 2007, pp. 1–2.

Wang Zejian, *Tort Law*, Peking University Press, 2009, p. 95.

Wang Zhu, "The Constitutionality of Legislative Procedures of the *Tort Liability Law*", *Law Sciences*, No. 5, 2010.

Wang Zhu, "On the Determination of Tort Law in Substance and Legislation Prospect", *Journal of Sichuan University (Social Science Edition)*, No. 3, 2011.

Wang Zhu, "A Research on the Legislative Mode of the *General Provisions of Obligation Law* under the Pragmatic Thought of the Drafting of Civil Code, *Journal of Sichuan University (Social Science Edition)*, No. 3, 2012.

Wang Lei, *Friendship Behavior in the Perspective of Civil Law*, Peking University Press, 2014a, pp. 181–184.

Wang Zhu, "The Legislative Procedure to Formulate Civil Code in the Mode of Codification of Nonbasic Law", *Peking University Law Journal*, No. 6, 2014b.

Wang Liming, "On the Legislation of Contract Part of Specific Provisions of Civil Law". *China Legal Science*, No. 2, 2017a.

Wang Zhu, "Big Data Analysis on Whether to Keep or Eliminate Several Law Norms of the General Principles of Civil Law (Draft)", *Journal of Sichuan University (Social Science Edition)*, No. 1, 2017b.

Wang Zhu, "Compiling Background and Structure Adjustment of Tort Liability Part of Civil Code", *Journal of National Prosecutors College*, No. 4, 2017c.

Wang Zhuqing, "On the Legislation of National Guardianship for Minors and on the System Design of Guardianship in the Marriage and Family Part of Civil Code". *Hebei Law Science*, No. 5, 2017d.

Wang Yi, Guan Shufang, "Six Relationships that Need Dealt with in Compiling Civil Code", *Law Science Magazine*, No. 1, 2017.

Wu Bangguo, "The Speech on the Symposium of a Socialist Legal System with Chinese Characteristics", *People's Daily*; January 1st, 2011.

Xia Yinlan, "On the Legislation of Marriage and Family Part of the Specific Provisions of Civil Law", *China Legal Science*, No. 3, 2017.

Xu Guodong, "A Re-Study of Personal Relationships", *China Legal Science*, No. 4, 2002.

Xue Jun, "The General Principles of Civil Law: Background, Problems and Prospect", *Journal of East China University of Political Science and Law*, No. 3, 2017.

Yang Lixin, *The Theory and Application of the Right of Co-Ownership,* Law Press, 2007, pp. 257–259.

Yang Lixin, Yang Zhen, "The Proposal of Draft Amendment of Inheritance Law of People's Republic of China", *Journal of Henan University of Economics and Law*, No. 5, 2012.

Yang Lixin, "General Chapter in China's Civil Code should provide the Rules of Law", *Seeking Truth*, No. 4, 2015a.

Yang Lixin, "On the Unity of Validity Rules of Juristic Act in the General Principles of Civil Law", *Law Science*, No. 2015b, (5).

Yang Lixin, "Act of Rescue for the General Principles of Civil Law to Formulate Civil Liability and Content Adjustment", *Legal Forum*, No. 1, 2017a.

Yang Lixin, "Concept Definition and Theoretical Basis of Partial Capacity for Civil Rights in the General Principles of Civil Law", *Law Science*, No. 5, 2017b.

Yao Hui, "Expression of Rights in Civil Code", *Journal of CUPL*, No. 2, 2017.

Yao Hui, Liang Zhanxin, "Sources of Law in the General Principles of Civil Law and the Types", *Journal of Law Application*, No. 7, 2016.

Zhang Minan, "Triumphs and Failures of Article 10 of the General Principles of Civil Law", *Research on Rule of Law*, No. 3, 2017a.

Zhang Mingqi, "The Formulating of the General Provisions of Civil Law of the People's Republic of China", *China Legal Science*, No. 2, 2017b.

Zhang Xinbao, "On the Legislation of Tort Liability Part of the Specific Provisions of Civil Law", *China Legal Science*, No. 3, 2017c.

Zhao Bingzhi, "The Reform of Chinese Criminal Law for Hundreds of Years—to Mark the Centennial of the Revolution of 1911", *Tribune of Political Science and Law*, No. 1, 2012.

Zhu Guangxin, "Systematic Thinking on Adding the Typical Contracts Types of Civil Code", *SJTU Law Review*, No. 1, 2017.

Chapter 10
Big Data Analysis on Deletion or Retention of Several Legal Norms in the *General Provisions of Civil Law*

Through comparison between the *General Provisions of Civil Law* and *General Principles of the Civil Law*, we can find that, the *General Provisions of Civil Law* retains the main structure and contents of the system of general provisions in *General Principles of the Civil Law,* but adds, deletes or amends the specific rules; in addition, some contents are controversial to a certain extent. The big data analysis can not only impact the operation of judicial practice,[1] but also provide better evidence support and justification for legislative activities.[2] Hereinafter, the Writer tries to, on the basis of the big data report for judicial application of *General Principles of the Civil Law*, bring forth the advices on deletion or retention of relevant norms.

10.1 Overview of Big Data Analysis on Judicial Application of the Legal Norms of the *General Provisions of Civil Law*

10.1.1 Judicial Application of the Legal Norms Relating to the General Provisions of Civil Law *Covered by System of Cause of Action*

The current *Provisions on Cause of Action for Civil Cases* (F. [2011] No. 42) provide 10 class-1 causes of action and 43 class-2 causes of action. Part 1 "Dispute over Personality Rights" through Part 9 "Dispute over Tort Liabilities" are unfolded

---

[1]See Drury D. Stevenson & Nicholas J. Wagoner, *Bargaining in the Shadow of Big Data*, 67 Fla. L. Rev. 1337. John O. McGinnis & Russell G. Pearce, *The Great Disruption: How Machine Intelligence Will Transform the Role of Lawyers in the Delivery of Legal Services*, 82 Fordham L. Rev. 3041.
[2]Hu (2015).

© China University of Political Science and Law Press 2020
Z. Wang, *On the Constitutionality of Compiling a Civil Code of China*,
https://doi.org/10.1007/978-981-13-7900-0_10

in accordance with the structure of specific provisions of civil and commercial laws. Except for Part 1 "Dispute over Personality Rights", Part 2 through Part 8 respectively correspond to the *Marriage Law*, the *Adoption Law*, the *Succession Law*, the *Real Rights Law*, the *Contract Law*, the intellectual property right laws, *Anti-unfair Competition Law*, the *Anti-monopoly Law*, the labor laws, the *Maritime Law*, the commercial laws as well as the *Tort Liability Law*. Only "32. Cases concerning the declaration of missing status or presumed death of citizens", "33. Cases about determination of citizen without civil capacity or with limited civil capacity" and "35. Cases about guardianship subject to special procedure" under Part 10 "Causes of Action for Cases Subject to Special Procedure" are directly related to the *General Provisions of Civil Law*.[3]

On the basis of the "general provisions–specific provisions" structure of the *Civil Code*,[4] the legal norms of the system of general provisions of civil law may be applied in the causes of action relating to the system of specific provisions of civil law, and such causes of action involved are extensive and discrete, so that it is not strange that there is no directly-corresponding cause of action for most of the legal norms of the system of general provisions of civil law. This arrangement in the *Provisions on Cases of Action for Civil Cases* is also relatively reasonable, but makes it difficult to evaluate the system supply of the *General Provisions of Civil Law*. As a result, the application of a legal rule in actual practice can't be understood directly through the number of cases involved in a certain cause of action and the application of legal norm, but can only be understood through full-sample analysis by using big data analysis method.[5]

10.1.2   Difference in Big Data Analysis Methods for Deletion, Retention and Addition of Legal Norm

Since the *General Provisions of Civil Law* does not clearly provide the relationship between such law and *General Principles of the Civil Law*, and the relationship between it and *General Principles of the Civil Law* can't be directly determined by Article 11 of the *General Provisions of Civil Law* "In case there are other provisions in other laws, such provisions shall apply", there comes the necessity to compare *General Principles of the Civil Law* with the *General Provisions of Civil Law*, so as to determine the deletion, retention and addition of legal norms.

---

[3]If the article 109 and 110 is the general enumeration of general personality right and types of personality rights, the cause of action should correspond to part one "dispute over personality rights".

[4]A dispute still exists in whether the *Civil Code* is the "general provisions-specific provisions" structure or "general provisions-specific provisions-liability provisions" in the future. It mainly relates to the orientation of the *Tort Liability Law*. However, no effect is left on the basic judgment of the orientation of the *General Provisions of Civil Law*.

[5]Liu (2015).

The so-called issue about deletion means the issue that, because of various considerations, it is unnecessary for a norm in *General Principles of the Civil Law* to be provided in the *General Provisions of Civil Law*, and thus it is also unnecessary to further discuss over retention or amendment of such norm. The so-called issue about retention means that, a legal norm in *General Principles of the Civil Law* is retained and the further issue is about its retention or amendment. The so-called issue about addition means a rule which is not contained in *General Principles of the Civil Law* is added into the *General Provisions of Civil Law*. The exploration into these issues is mainly about the improvement of the *General Provisions of Civil Law*.

In fact, the study on the issue about deletion or retention by using the big data analysis method is to analyze the application of an existing article in judicial practice, so as to determine the system needs contained in such article, and thus evaluate whether the new legislation can respond to such system needs. The study on the issue about addition by using the big data analysis method is to simulate the effect of an article when being applied in judicial practice. The big data study method used hereinafter is to analyze the application of relevant articles of the *General Principles of Civil Law*, so that it can only settle the issue about deletion and retention of articles of the *General Provisions of Civil Law*, but can't deeply discuss the issue about addition, such as the design of personality right norm.

10.1.3 Samples and Indicator for Big Data Analysis on Deletion or Retention of Legal Norms in the General Provisions of Civil Law

The samples of this big data analysis are all the judgment documents published by China Judgments Online during the period from January 1, 2014 to December 15, 2015, involving 12,435,889 judgment documents. According to the study carried out by IBM, the magnitude of data in big data is different in different industries and regions. Even if the magnitude of PB (Petabyte) or ZB (Zetabyte) can't be reached, more than half of the interviewees believe that the data can be referred to as big data if the magnitude is between TB (Terabyte) and PB (Petabyte),[6,7] After the words and data were acquired by the Legal Big Data Laboratory under Law School of Sichuan University, the data in every judgment document are slightly more than 100 K, and the total quantity of data is about 1.5 TB, reaching the magnitude

---

[6]The computer adopts the binary system, the data unit is Byte. KB (kibibyte) is equivalent to 1024 bytes. The next unit is MB (mebibyte), which is equivalent to 1024 KB. By analogy, TB, PB, EB, ZB are 2^{30}, 2^{40}, 2^{50}, 2^{60}, 2^{70} bytes. If 1024 is slightly made to 1000, it is 10^3. The threshold order of magnitudes TB of big data is slightly more than 10^{12} bytes.

[7]IBM Institute for Business Value (2012).

required by big data analysis.[8] In addition, the more than 12.4 million judgment documents are at the same order of magnitude as the number of cases tried by court system of China every year over recent years,[9] and the corresponding conclusion of big data analysis can not only objectively reflect the real situations in judicial practice, but also help readers establish the relatively intuitive impression.

The Writer firstly counted the "total times of application" of 156 articles of *General Principles of the Civil Law* as basis of civil judgment[10] and the "top-10 causes of action with respect to times of application".[11] The writing hereinafter is based on this statistics. Selecting "total times of application" as the "general indicator" for study is based on the following considerations:

Firstly, if the times of application of an article in judgment are relatively high, this at least indicates that the system needs contained in such article in judicial judgment are relatively high,[12] so that the Legislature should pay attention to the issue about deletion or retention of such article. Hereinafter, the articles which enjoy relatively high times of application but have been deleted from the *General Provisions of Civil Law* are discussed.

Secondly, if the times of application of an article in judgment are relatively low, this can only indicate that there are less needs on such article in judicial judgment, but can't necessarily indicate that the system needs contained in such article are low. However, with respect to the articles which have been deleted from the *General Provisions of Civil Law*, if the relatively clear supporting opinions can be obtained from the analysis on times of application, they will be shown hereinafter, so as to provide the empirical basis for legislative decision.

---

[8]In the setting of order of magnitudes of big data, even if the angle is slightly different, Professor Bai Jianjun also has similar empirical viewpoints: "if the total is 10,000,000 or above, the increase of sample proportion does not work actually." See Bai (2015).

[9]The people's courts at all levels tried 13,810,000 cases in 2014 and 16,730,000 cases in 2015. Refer to Zhou (2015, 2016).

[10]Article 4, the *Provisions of Supreme People's Court on Quotation of Normative Legal Documents such as Laws and Regulations in Judgment Instruments* (F.SH. [2009] No. 14) has defined the scope of judgment basis of civil judgment instruments: "The civil judgment instruments shall quote laws, legal interpretations or judicial interpretations. The administrative regulations, local regulations, autonomous regulations or separate regulations which must be applied may be directly quoted".

[11]If the applicable causes of action are less than 10, only the actually applicable causes of action are calculated.

[12]Main considerations of this judgment: firstly, the relatively high times of application may be partially due to the relatively large absolute number of main applicable causes of action of this article. It shows that the judicial application demand of this article is relatively high. Secondly, in the judgment, some judges do not quote all legal norms which should apply. This possible fact can only deduce that this article has a relatively high judicial demand. Thirdly, some articles of law have the behavior norm or judgment norm nature. The relatively low times of application do not affect its value as the behavior norm, and can only deduce the higher system demand.

Thirdly, whether an article can be replaced by another article may be analyzed by comparing the situation that the "article to be replaced" is applied alone with the situation that the both articles are applied together. If in most of the situations, both the "article to be replaced" and "replacing article" are applicable, then the system supply can be realized by improving the "replacing article"; otherwise the "article to be replaced" should be retained.

Selecting "times of application" and "top-10 caused of action" as the special indicators for studying the general provision nature of legal norms is based on the consideration that it is necessary to use a relatively clear indicator to show the general provision nature of a legal norm,[13] and the "top-10 causes of action" is a simple indicator which can reflect in a centralized manner the application of an article in judicial practice. The preliminary study reveals that, the percentage of times of application for top-10 causes of action in total times of application (hereinafter referred to as "Percentage of Top-10 Causes of Action") is highly linked with the general provision nature of article. The total times of application of 156 articles in *General Principles of the Civil Law* are 1,511,425, while the total times of application for top-10 causes of action reach 1,276,775, accounting for 84.47% of total times of application. However, as for the articles of which the general provision nature is relatively strong, such as the core articles about basic principle, juristic act and agency system in *General Principles of the Civil Law*, the Percentage of Top-10 causes of action is relatively low.

Application of articles with relatively strong general provision nature in *general principles of the civil law* for top-10 causes of action

Article number	Contents	Percentage of top-10 causes of action (%)	Total number of cases
Article 3	Basic principle	69.91	452
Article 4	Basic principle	43.06	21782
Article 5	Basic principle	51.93	45926
Article 6	Basic principle	42.21	2722
Article 7	Basic principle	43.57	1042
Article 54	Juristic act	43.66	2469
Article 55	Juristic act	49.09	4123
Article 56	Juristic act	50.07	769
Article 57	Juristic act	47.09	4738
Article 58	Juristic act	49.49	3263
Article 59	Juristic act	62.54	1041

(continued)

[13]This description of "general provision nature" does not represent that this rule should be stipulated in the *General Provisions of Civil Law*. It may be stipulated in the general provisions of the *Property Law* or the general provisions of the *Contract Law* or even other legislations which adopt the "general provision-specific provision" structure. Within the scope of sample of this chapter, it is embodied as the general provision nature of the *General Provisions of Civil Law*.

(continued)

Article number	Contents	Percentage of top-10 causes of action (%)	Total number of cases
Article 60	Juristic act	55.82	421
Article 61	Juristic act	52.12	1485
Article 62	Juristic act	56.58	843
Article 63	Agency	60.18	6032
Article 64	Agency	57.83	479
Article 65	Agency	62.39	827
Article 66	Agency	57.54	2414
Average proportion of top-10 causes of action		53.06	

The above table reveals that, the provisions about basic principles in Articles 3–7, except for Article 3 "Equality Principle" of which the percentage of Top-10 Causes of Action is about 70%,[14] the percentage of Top-10 Causes of other articles is 40–50%; the provisions about juristic act in Articles 54–62 and the provisions about agency in Articles 63–66,[15] except for a few articles of which the percentage of Top-10 Causes of Action is about 60%, the percentage of Top-10 Causes of most articles is 40–50%. The Average Proportion of Top-10 Causes of Action for the above-mentioned articles with relatively strong general provision nature is 53.06%. It is thus clear that, as for the rules of which the percentage of Top-10 Causes of Action is less than 70%, especially those of which the percentage of Top-10 Causes of Action is 40–50%, the general provision nature is stronger. Therefore, the legislature should pay attention to the articles in the *General Provisions of Civil Law* of which the percentage of Top-10 Causes of Action is too high, and consider the necessity of such articles in the *General Provisions of Civil Law*.

---

[14]No. 1 cause of action for which the principle of equality is applicable is "dispute over liabilities for traffic accident of motor vehicle", and the times of application are 146, accounting for 31.9%. Relatively great effects are left on the proportion of application. The Writer is surprised at it. However, according to experience of the Writer, for the cause of action or articles if the cases are fewer than 200, the big data analysis cannot be done. For the articles or causes of action, if the cases are more than 1000, the effects of big data analysis are relatively good. Therefore, the further analysis can be done only after the data size meets the standard in the future.

[15]In the remaining articles of Section 2 "Agency", Chapter 4 "Civil Juristic Acts and Agency" in *General Principles of the Civil Law*, Articles 67–69 are only applicable for the entrusted agency. However, the enumeration provisions of Article 70 have restricted its applicable scope of cause of action.

10.2 Three Categories of Controversial Issues About Retention or Deletion in the *General Provisions of Civil Law* for Which the Big Data Analysis Can Be Carried Out

According to the above-mentioned setting for full-sample indicator analysis, the Writer believes that, in three categories of controversial issues, it is necessary and also possible to make the judgment on deletion or retention in light of the results of legal big data analysis.

10.2.1 Issue About Deletion or Retention of Three Special Civil Subject Systems

Owing to the special drafting background and time characteristics of *General Principles of the Civil Law*, Chapter 2 "Citizen (Natural Persons)" contains Section 4 "Individually-owned Business and Leaseholding Farm Households" and Section 5 "Individual Partnership", and Chapter 3 "Legal Person" contains Section 4 "Joint Operation". The *General Provisions of Civil Law* retains Section 4 "Individually-owned Business and Leaseholding Farm Households" in Chapter 2 "Natural Persons" but deletes "Individual Partnership". Chapter 3 "Legal Persons" distinguishes between "profit-making legal person" and "non-profit-making legal person", and deletes "joint operation".

The Writer believes that, the core issue about deletion or retention of these three civil subject systems is the social needs. This can be studied in light of the results of big data analysis. If the legislature believes that a certain legal system is no longer required by the society at least in the traditional civil law field, then such system may be deleted decisively. The typical example is the "joint operation" which acts as civil subject system. If the legislature believes that though a certain system may gradually disappear in long term,[16] such system is still required in short term, then

---

[16]The "individually-owned business and leaseholding rural household" systems are retained in the *General Provisions of Civil Law*. The "individually-owned business and leaseholding rural household" systems were once deleted in Chapter 2 "Natural Person", Volume 1 "General Provisions", the Draft of Civil Code in 2002. Some scholars think that the concept of "household contractual management" should be abandoned in the Chinese laws, and the individual of rural collective economic organization member acts as the main subject of land contractual management right. Refer to Zhou (2009). Some scholars think that the rural land contractual management household is breaking up, and the individualism system construction should be stuck to in the future. Refer to Shen (2016). In addition, on April 30, 2015, at the seminar of civil subject legislation issue of the Expert Proposal of General Provisions of Civil Law of Civil Code of the People's Republic of China (Draft for Comment) held in Southwest University of Political Science & Law, Professor Xu Mingyue and Professor Sun PENG thought that the leaseholding farm household was not necessary any more. However, Professor Ma Junju thought that the

such system must be retained, and be adjusted appropriately, so as to bring its role into full play. The typical example is "individually-owned business and lease-holding rural household" system. If the legislature believes that, a certain system still has value and is also applied in actual practice, and it can be ensured that such rule will be given in any other volume in the course of compilation of *Civil Code*, then the sufficient supply of system should be given in the *General Provisions of Civil Law*; otherwise, the situation that no law can be taken as basis will occur in judicial practice. The typical example is "individual partnership".

10.2.2 Issue About Deletion or Retention of Relatively-Short Special Limitation of Action

Paragraph 1 of Article 99 of Volume 1 "General Provisions" of the *2002 Civil Law (draft)* has ever provided a relatively-short special limitation of action, but such contents are deleted in the *General Provisions of Civil Law*. Through comparison, the relatively-short special limitation of action is mainly applied to the claim for obligations most of which are related to daily life.[17] Articles 2271–2279 of the *Civil Code of France*,[18] Article 196 of the *Civil Code of Germany*, Article 170 of the *Civil Code of Japan* and Articles 126 and 127 of the *Civil Code of Taiwan* which have relatively great impact on the compilation of *Civil Code* and civil law theory in China provide the relatively-short special limitation of action. Whether the relatively-short special limitation of action, As a traditional system of continental legal system, is not required in judicial practice in China or is omitted in legislation should be analyzed in light of the results of big data analysis.

10.2.3 Issue About Deletion or Retention of Core Systems of Obligation Law

The *General Provisions of Civil Law* provides the "civil rights" rather than the "object of civil right" in Chapter 5 by carrying forward the style in *General Principles of the Civil Law*. In addition, owing to its orientation, the *General Provisions of Civil Law* may not unfold such system in the same style as used by Chapter 5 "Civil Rights" in *General Principles of the Civil Law*. Therefore,

---

individually-owned business and leaseholding farm household were designed based on the national conditions in the initial stage of the reform, and the changes took place in the current conditions. If the concept of individually-owned business and leaseholding farm household is still adopted in the future, it is relatively backward. Refer to Chen (2015).

[17]Karl (2013).

[18]The modified *Civil Code of France* has deleted the relatively-short special limitation of action.

a special unbalanced legislative phenomenon may occur: Even if the downsized Chapter "Civil Rights" provides the system supply at the same strength for every type of civil right, owing to the system supply from current laws to the *Specific Provisions of Civil Code* is different and the system supply in the future is not clear, then the supply of some systems may become sufficient.

Concretely speaking, the identity right provided in Article 112 of the *General Provisions of Civil Law* is protected by laws. Articles 114–117 provide the real rights, Article 123 provides the intellectual property rights, Article 124 provides the succession right, and Article 125 provides the investment rights. It should be pointed out that, whether the above-mentioned types of civil rights are enumerated will not have great impact on system supply, and only meets the requirement of a logical exhaustiveness, because they are supported by current laws. According to the explanation given by the legislature that "The *Civil Code* will be composed of general provisions volume and other volumes (At present, the volumes determined include the *Contract Volume*, the *Real Rights Volume*, the *Tort Liabilities Volume*, the *Marriage and Family Volume* and the *Succession Volume*)",[19] the *General Provisions of Obligation Law* has been cancelled. If the provisions relating to obligatory rights in Articles 118–122 are compared with the above-mentioned provisions relating to real rights, intellectual property rights, identity right, succession right and investment rights, the conclusion that it is necessary to supply the basic systems for "obligatory right" in the *General Provisions of Civil Law* will be obtained.

It is provided in Paragraph 1 of Article 118 of the *General Provisions of Civil Law* that: "The civil subjects legally enjoy obligatory right." This paragraph has no actual meaning of norm. It is provided in Paragraph 2 of such article that: "The obligatory right is the right of right holder to request for any act or omission from particular obligor owing to contract, tort, negotiorum gestio, unjustified enrichment or other provisions of law." The provisions are used to improve Paragraph 1 of Article 84 of *General Principles of the Civil Law*, and especially clarify that "tort" is one cause of obligation. Article 119 of the *General Provisions of Civil Law* is the provision relating to contracts, Article 120 is the provision relating to tort liabilities, Article 121 and Article 122 are respectively equivalent to the provision relating to negotiorum gestio in Article 93 and the provision relating to unjustified enrichment in Article 92 of *General Principles of the Civil Law*.

The comparison with *General Principles of the Civil Law* reveals that, the provisions of Article 118 of *General Provisions of Civil Law* have the obvious "hollowing-out" characteristic, which means that, except for the concept "obligation", there is no system supply within the meaning of the general provisions of obligation law, and even the basic provisions relating to claim for obligatory right in Paragraph 2 of Article 84 of *General Principles of the Civil Law* ("The obligatory right holder shall have the right to require the obligor to perform the obligation in accordance with the provisions of contract or laws.") are simplified and

---

[19]Li (2016a), the document at the 21st Session of the Standing Committee of the Twelfth National People's Congress.

incorporated in the concept of obligatory right. It should be pointed out that, in the downsized Chapter "Civil Rights", there is very limited room reserved for the legislature to "backfill" the system of general provisions of obligation law. Therefore, it is necessary to supply the basic systems or carry out modification for obligation law systems which are most urgently required in actual practice in light of the results of big data analysis, so as to avoid the situation that no law can be taken as basis.

10.3 Big Data Analysis on Deletion or Retention of Three Special Civil Subject Systems

10.3.1 The Writer Agrees to Delete the "Joint Operation" as a Civil Subject System

The "joint operation" provided in *General Principles of the Civil Law* is actually the description of three joint operation modes between enterprises, and has no essential meaning of norm. As for the "legal-person joint operation" provided in Article 51 of such law, since the qualification of legal person is obtained, the relevant provisions should be applied to "legal-person joint operation" as independent legal person. *The* "joint operation in partnership" provided in Article 52 has been essentially replaced by the provisions of the *Partnership Enterprise Law*. The "cooperative joint operation" provided in Article 53 will not generate any new incorporated organization, and will also not generate any other organization which carries out activities in its own name. In essence, it is the application of the *Contract Law*. Actually, these three definitions can be concluded from the provisions of the *Decision of the Supreme People's Court on Several Issues Relating to Trial of Cases Involving Dispute over Joint Operation Contract (F.(J.)F. (1990) No. 27)*: Item (1) in "2. Jurisdiction of dispute case about joint operation contract"[20] and "3. Determination of subject qualification for joint operation contract".

In judicial practice, Article 51 of *General Principles of the Civil Law* have only been applied for 28 times, Article 52 of *General Principles of the Civil Law* have been applied for 253 times, and Article 53 of *General Principles of the Civil Law* have been applied for 132 times. Except for outward contract disputes over activities of joint operation, the "disputes over joint operation contract" involve 74 times, accounting for about 18%. The main difficult problem is the invalidity of

---

[20]It is explicitly specified in this point of such judicial interpretations that: "(1) the territorial jurisdiction of dispute case about joint operation contract differs due to different joint operation forms: 1. The dispute case about corporate joint operation contract is governed by the local people's court of main working body of corporate joint operation entity. 2. The dispute case about partnership joint operation contract is governed by the people's court in the registration place of partnership joint operation entity. 3. The dispute case about cooperative joint operation contract is governed by the local people's court of the Defendant."

"miscellaneous article" in joint operation contract as provided in "4. Miscellaneous article in joint operation contract" of the *Decision of the Supreme People's Court on Several Issues Relating to Trial of Cases Involving Dispute over Joint Operation Contract*,[21] and the provisions in "7. Disposal of properties after termination of joint operation contract" has been applied to many cases.

It can be concluded that, the "joint operation" as a civil subject system in *General Principles of the Civil Law* has come to the end of history. As joint operation gradually quits the historical stage, even if there are few demands on the system of joint operation as a civil subject system, such demands can also be satisfied by using the *Company Law*, the *Partnership Enterprise Law* and the *Contract Law*. Even if the joint operation is not provided as a civil subject system in the *General Provisions of Civil Law*, no problem about system supply will emerge. The Writer agrees that the rules relating to joint operation should be deleted from the *General Provisions of Civil Law*.

However, it is necessary to remind the legislature that, though the "joint operation" as a civil subject system can be deleted during the enactment of the *General Provisions of Civil Law*, we can't obtain the conclusion that joint operation has been eliminated in actual practice. In contrast, as the legal description of cooperation between enterprises, joint operation has become an important approach for modern enterprises in development and competition, and the key and difficult problems in this field have been shifted to the field of anti-monopoly law.[22] Because the anti-monopoly administrative examination rather than judicial examination is applied to the relevant disputes, they are not reflected in judicial application of corresponding rules in *General Principles of the Civil Law*. Therefore, in the field of joint operation, the *Civil Code* should also pay attention to the legislative coordination with the anti-monopoly law field.

10.3.2 The Writer Agrees to Retain "Individually-Owned Business and Leaseholding Rural Household" Systems

The definition of "individually-owned business and leaseholding rural household" given in Article 54 and Article 55 of the *General Provisions of Civil Law* is not essentially different from that in Article 26 and Article 27 of *General Principles of the Civil Law*. The provisions on "individually-owned business and leaseholding rural household" systems as given in the part of natural persons of the *General Provisions of Civil Law* confirm the industrial & commercial registration

---

[21]Shu (1990), Zhang and Wang (1997).

[22]See Jiang and Huang (2012), Jiang and Su (2014).

qualification of individually-owned business[23] and the collective land leasing qualification of rural collective economic organization which are different from natural persons, and constitute the legal basis for existence of these two systems.

With respect to times of application, Article 26 of *General Principles of the Civil Law* has been applied for 326 times, Article 27 has been applied for 43 times, and Article 28 has been applied for 180 times. The application frequency of these three articles is equivalent to that of joint operation system. The judicial application of system of individually-owned business and leaseholding rural household is mainly focused on the rules for outward undertaking of liabilities in Article 29 of *General Principles of the Civil Law*: "As for the obligations of an individually-owned business or a leaseholding farm household, in case the business is operated by an individual, such obligations shall be undertaken with the properties of such individual; in case the business is operated by family, such obligations shall be undertaken with the properties of such family." Such rules have been applied for 2190 times. The top-10 causes of action are detailed as follows:

Table of top-10 causes of action with respect to times of application of article 29 of *general principles of the civil law*

Top-10 cause of action	Times of application	Percentage (%)
1. Disputes over contract of sale	725	44.05
2. Disputes over contracts for private loan	250	15.19
3. Labor dispute	146	8.87
4. Disputes over financial loan contracts	125	7.59
5. Disputes over claims for labor remuneration in arrear	123	7.47
6. Dispute over infringement upon trademark right	101	6.14
7. Dispute over contracts	57	3.46
8. Dispute over loan contract	42	2.55
9. Disputes over contracts for contracting work	42	2.55
10. Disputes over labor services contracts	35	2.13
Total	1646	100
Percentage of top-10 causes of action	2190	75.16

Among the above-mentioned causes of action, except for the "dispute over infringement upon trademark right" which involves "trade name", most of them are contract-related disputes, and still have certain realistic significance. The literatures about the adoption of *General Principles of the Civil Law* reveal that, at that time, as for Article 29 of *General Principles of the Civil Law* which provides the rules for

---

[23]Some scholars think that the micro and small individual businesses have great burden due to the fact that the current laws and regulations uniformly stipulate the commercial registration system of individual businesses. It is suggested that the micro and small individual businesses should be exempted from the commercial registration obligation. Refer to Shi and Li (2012).

undertaking outward obligation for "individually-owned business and leaseholding rural household" and distinguishes between "personal business" and "family business", the basic spirit is "The losses shall be made up by those who have caused such losses, and the obligations shall be discharged by those who have caused such obligations." The prototype for design is individually-owned business rather than leaseholding farm households, because the latter is family business in principle.[24] Article 56 of the *General Provisions of Civil Law* distinguishes between the individually-owned business and leaseholding farm household. It is provided in Paragraph 1 that: "If operated by individual, the obligations of an individually-owned business shall be undertaken with the properties of such individual; if operated by a family, the obligations shall be undertaken with the properties of such family; if it is impossible to distinguish between individual or family, the obligations shall be undertaken with the properties of such family." It is provided in Paragraph 2 that: "The obligations of a leaseholding farm household shall be undertaken with the properties of the farmer which has engaged in rural land contractual business; in case such business is actually operated by some members of such household, the obligations shall be undertaken with the properties of such members." This distinction is praiseworthy. In the future, in the course of legislation of Article 56 of the *General Provisions of Civil Law*, it is also necessary to clarify that, the term "family properties" used does not only mean the "properties jointly owned by family" provided in Article 42 of the *Opinions on General Principles of Civil Law*,[25] but also means all "family properties", and it is also necessary to add the provisions about reserving the basic living costs of family members and the education expenses of minor children by reference to the spirit of Article 44 of the *Opinions on General Principles of Civil Law*.

It should be pointed out that, the retention of "individually-owned business system and leaseholding farm household system" in the *General Provisions of Civil Law* also has important political significance in declaring and recognizing the achievements of reform and opening-up. The expression in Paragraph 1 of Article 11 of the *Constitution* was determined in the *1999 Amendment to the Constitution*: "The non-public ownership economies within the scope provided in the law, such as individual economy and private economy, are the important components of socialist market economy." Paragraph 2 was determined in the *2004 Amendment to Constitution*: "The state protects the lawful rights and interests of non-public ownership economies such as individual economy and private economy. The state encourages, supports and leads the development of non-public ownership economies, and legally supervises over and administers the non-public ownership economies." While replacing the *Interim Regulations for Administration on Urban and Rural Individually-owned Businesses* issued in 1987, the *Regulations on Individually-owned Businesses* promulgated in 2011 once again recognizes this innovative economic form adopted since the beginning of reform and opening-up till now at the level of administrative regulations. The corresponding social

---

[24]Wang (1986).

[25]Zhang (2005).

actuality is that, by the end of September 2015, there were more than 70 million individually-owned businesses and private enterprises, absorbing the employment of 273 million persons.[26] The expression of the first sentence in Paragraph 1 of Article 8 of the *Constitution* was also determined in the *1999 Amendment to Constitution*: "As for rural collective economic organizations, the double-layer operation system which is based on household contractual management shall be implemented." If the expression in the *Constitution* relating to this basic rural economy system of China remains unchanged within a certain time period, then the leaseholding farm households will still be the subject of contractual management of rural land in China.

In light of the above-mentioned opinions, though the percentage of Top-10 Causes of Action for the core article of *General Principles of the Civil Law* (namely Article 29) is as high as 75.16% and thus indicates that the general provision nature of the system of "individually-owned business and leaseholding rural household" is relatively low, the Writer still agrees to retain the provisions about "individually-owned business and leaseholding rural household" in the *General Provisions of Civil Law*, and make the final decision on deletion or retention three years later after the compilation of *Civil Code* is completed.

10.3.3   It Is Advised to Partially and Temporarily Retain the Individual Partnership System

In *General Principles of the Civil Law*, the "individual partnership" is provided as a section in Chapter "Citizen (Natural Persons)", which has ever been appraised by scholars as a pioneering work in civil legislation.[27] However, there is no content about "individual partnership" in Chapter 2 "Natural Persons" of the *General Provisions of Civil Law*, and this is not consistent with the actuality that there are a lot of cases relating to individual partnership in actual practice and the times of application are as high as 25,589, so that it is necessary to re-evaluate the system supply. As for specific system, the individual partnership system in *General Principles of the Civil Law* may be divided into three groups of rules.

The first group is the inward relationship rules, including Articles 30–32 of *General Principles of the Civil Law*. It is provided in Article 30 that: "An individual partnership means that more than two citizens carry out joint operation and joint labor by respectively providing funds, physical materials or techniques in accordance with the agreement." Such provisions have been applied for 8020 times, and the top-10 causes of action and the times of application thereof are detailed as follows:

---

[26]http://www.saic.gov.cn/zwgk/tjzl/zxtjzl/xxzx/201510/t20151030_163438.html, the latest access time: August 31, 2017.
[27]Ma (1986).

Table of top-10 causes of action with respect to times of application of article 30 of *general principles of the civil law*

Top-10 cause of action	Times of application	Percentage (%)
1. Disputes over partnership agreements	5419	76.99
2. Disputes over contract of sale	482	6.85
3. Dispute over private loan	370	5.26
4. Disputes over labor services contracts	239	3.40
5. Dispute over contracts	169	2.40
6. Dispute over the withdrawal from partnership	96	1.36
7. Dispute over liabilities for injury suffered by service provider	88	1.25
8. Disputes over the right to life, the right to health and the right to body	83	1.18
9. Disputes over contract of lease	47	0.67
10. Disputes over contracts for carrying out of construction projects	46	0.65
Total	7039	100
Percentage of top-10 causes of action	8020	87.77

The provisions of Article 31 of *General Principles of the Civil Law* "The partners shall enter into a written agreement on matters such as amount of contribution, distribution of profits, undertaking of obligations, participation in partnership, withdrawal from partnership and termination of partnership." have been applied for 3213 times. The top-10 causes of action and times of application are as follows:

Table of top-10 causes of action with respect to times of application of article 31 of *general principles of the civil law*

Top-10 cause of action	Times of application	Percentage (%)
1. Disputes over partnership agreements	2507	85.45
2. Dispute over private loan	169	5.76
3. Dispute over contracts	60	2.04
4. Dispute over contract of sale	58	1.98
5. Dispute over the withdrawal from partnership	52	1.77
6. Dispute over unjustified enrichment	20	0.68
7. Disputes over labor services contracts	20	0.68
8. Disputes over the right of recourse	17	0.58
9. Disputes over the right to life, the right to health and the right to body	16	0.55
10. Disputes over contracts for carrying out of construction projects	15	0.51
Total	2934	100
Percentage of top-10 causes of action	3213	91.32

The provisions of Paragraph 1 of Article 32 of *General Principles of the Civil Law* "The properties invested by partners shall be jointly managed and used by partners" and the provisions of Paragraph 2 "The properties accumulated by partnership shall be jointly owned by the partners" have been applied for 2896 times:

Table of top-10 causes of action with respect to times of application of article 32 of *general principles of the civil law*

Top-10 cause of action	Times of application	Percentage (%)
1. Disputes over partnership agreements	2274	88.55
2. Dispute over private loan	77	3.00
3. Dispute over contracts	58	2.26
4. Dispute over contract of sale	43	1.67
5. Disputes over specific return of the thing	30	1.17
6. Dispute over unjustified enrichment	19	0.74
7. Disputes over co-ownership	18	0.70
8. Dispute over the withdrawal from partnership	17	0.66
9. Disputes over contract of lease	16	0.62
10. Disputes over contracts for carrying out of construction projects	16	0.62
Total	2568	100
Percentage of top-10 causes of action	2896	88.67

With respect to application of these three articles, the common characteristic is that, more than 75% of applications are linked with "dispute over partnership agreements",[28] which is similar to the situation reflected in judicial practice. In the cases involving dispute over individual partnership, the litigation claims lodged by party concerned mainly include: 1. Requiring the distribution of profits of partnership; 2. Requiring the apportionment of losses of partnership; 3. Requiring the recovery of debt of partnership which has been paid and exceeds the portion payable by it; 4. Requiring the compensation for loss arising from withdrawal from partnership; 5. Requiring the proportional distribution of properties of partnership.[29] The relatively-high absolute number and the relatively-high relative proportion indicate that the individual partnership system still has certain vitality.

The second group is the provisions relating to registration of trade name in Article 33 of *General Principles of the Civil Law*: "An individual partnership may have trade name, and shall, after being legally registered, carry out operation within the approved business scope", which have been applied for 110 times. Though the times of application are relatively low, such article has ever been the legal basis for registration of individual partnership. Though some scholars believe that the

---

[28]The No. 1 percentage of application is over 70%, it is thus clear that the nature of general provisions of individual partnership is weak.

[29]Hu (2012).

provisions of such article embody the integration of civil and commercial affairs in partnership,[30] if the legislature believes that it is unnecessary for the *Civil Code* to provide whether an individual partnership may get its trade name registered, then such article may delete.

The third group is outward relationship rules, including Article 34 and Article 35 of *General Principles of the Civil Law*. Article 34 gives the provisions on partnership, and it is provided in Paragraph 1 that: "The operating activities of an individual partnership shall be jointly decided by partners, and the partner shall have the right to implement and supervise over such activities." It is provided in Paragraph 2 that: "The partners may select a person in charge. As for the operating activities carried out by the person in charge and other persons, the civil liabilities shall be undertaken by all partners." Such article has been applied for 1853 times, and the top-10 causes of action are as follows:

Table of top-10 causes of action with respect to times of application of article 34 of *general principles of the civil law*

Top-10 cause of action	Times of application	Percentage
1. Disputes over partnership agreements	612	42.65
2. Dispute over contracts	309	21.53
3. Disputes over labor services contracts	150	10.45
4. Dispute over private loan	99	6.90
5. Dispute over contracts	54	3.76
6. Disputes over contracts for contracting work	51	3.55
7. Disputes over contracts for carrying out of construction projects	45	3.14
8. Dispute over liabilities for injury suffered by service provider	40	2.79
9. Disputes over contract of lease	38	2.65
10. Disputes over the right to life, the right to health and the right to body	37	2.58
Total	1435	100
Percentage of top-10 causes of action	1853	77.44

Paragraph 1 of Article 34 has the attribute of inward relationship, and is mainly applied to "dispute over partnership agreements", accounting for 42.65% in all judgments. Paragraph 2 of such article has obvious attribute of outward relationship, and is applied to other nine causes of action, accounting for 57.35%.

This outward relationship attribute is more obviously embodied in Article 35. This is because that, in actual practice, the dispute over individual partnership is mainly related to outward liabilities, especially the undertaking of joint and several liabilities. Paragraph 1 of Article 35 of *General Principles of the Civil Law* provides the rules for determining the shares in undertaking of outward liabilities:

---

[30]Li (2016b).

"The obligations of a partnership shall be performed by the partners with their respective properties in accordance with the contribution proportion or agreement." Paragraph 2 provides the rules for outward joint and several liabilities: "The partners shall undertake the joint and several liabilities for obligations of the partnership, unless there are other provisions in other laws. The partner which has repaid the obligation of the partnership in excess of the amount payable by him/her shall have the right to recover the excessive amount from other partners." The times of application reach 9497, and the top-10 cause of action are as follows:

Table of top-10 causes of action with respect to times of application of article 35 of *general principles of the civil law*

Top-10 cause of action	Times of application	Percentage (%)
1. Dispute over contract of sale	2557	34.30
2. Disputes over labor services contracts	1219	16.35
3. Disputes over partnership agreements	1218	16.34
4. Dispute over private loan	707	9.48
5. Disputes over claims for labor remuneration in arrear	413	5.54
6. Dispute over liabilities for injury suffered by service provider	287	3.85
7. Disputes over liability of motor vehicles traffic accidents	269	3.61
8. Dispute over contracts	264	3.54
9. Disputes over the right of recourse	262	3.51
10. Disputes over contract of lease	258	3.46
Total	7454	100
Percentage of top-10 causes of action	9497	78.49

It can be seen that, the "dispute over partnership agreements" only accounts for 16.34% in all cases, and more cases are about the undertaking of outward liabilities. In the future, the individual partnership system should pay more attention to establishment of rules for undertaking of outward liabilities.

While the individual partnership system is deleted from the *General Provisions of Civil Law*, it is provided in Paragraph 2 of Article 102 of Chapter 4 "Unincorporated Organizations" that "The unincorporated organizations include sole proprietorship enterprise, partnership enterprise, and unincorporated professional service institution." Only the "partnership enterprise" rather than "individual partnership" is included. The statistics of percentage of top-10 causes of action of individual partnership given in the above table reveal that, the percentage is 70–90%, and the general provision nature is relatively low. Essentially, the individual partnership system is not a civil subject system, but a civil contract system, and should be provided in the *Contract Volume of Civil Code* rather than the *General Provisions of Civil Law*. What the Writer worries about is that, if the individual partnership system is deleted from the *General Provisions of Civil Law*, it can't be ensured that such system will be provided in the *Contract Volume of Civil Code* in the course of compilation of *Civil Code* in the future. Therefore, it is advised to continue to apply the provisions of *General Principles of the Civil Law* after the *General Provisions of Civil Law* comes into effect, and transplant such provisions to the *Contract Volume of Civil Code* in the course of codification,[31] so as to avoid the situation that no law can be taken as basis.

10.4 Big Data Analysis on Issue About Deletion or Retention of System of Relatively-Short Special Limitation of Action

10.4.1 Relatively Low Application Rate of System of Relatively-Short Special Limitation of Action

It is provided in Article 136 of *General Principles of the Civil Law*: "The limitation of action for the following situations is one year: (1) claims for compensation for bodily injuries; (2) sales of substandard goods without proper notice to that effect; (3) delays in paying rent or refusal to pay rent; (4) loss of or damage to property left in the care of another person." Different from the general limitation of action in Article 135 which has been applied for 23,056 times, such article has only been applied for 2984 times. The top-10 cause of action, the number of corresponding cases and the main types of application are detailed as follows:

Table of top-10 causes of action with respect to times of application of article 136 of *general principles of the civil law*

Top-10 cause of action	Times of application	Number of cases involving such cause of action	Percentage (%)
1. Disputes over liability of motor vehicles traffic accidents	697	696470	0.10
2. Disputes over the right to life, the right to health and the right to body	680	145011	0.47
3. Disputes over contract of lease to housing	403	105634	0.38
4. Disputes over contract of lease	345	103039	0.33
5. Dispute over liabilities for injury suffered by service provider	139	62339	0.22
6. Disputes over liability for injury in medical treatments	134	17749	0.75
7. Disputes over contract of lease to construction equipments	56	13690	0.41

(continued)

---

[31]About the thinking of this codification process, see Wang (2014).

(continued)

Top-10 cause of action	Times of application	Number of cases involving such cause of action	Percentage (%)
8. Disputes over contract of sale	39	704497	0.01
9. Disputes over compensation for damages to property	34	77691	0.04
10. Disputes over contract of lease to land use rights	34	8783	0.39
Total	2561	1934903	0.13

The above-mentioned statistics reveal that, except for the application rate for "disputes over liability for injury in medical treatments" which is 0.75%, the application rate of other main case types is generally lower than 0.5%. It should be pointed out that, the times of application of Item 4 of Article 136 of *General Principles of the Civil Law* which is corresponding to "disputes over contract of bailment" are only 2. The relatively high application rate for "disputes over liability for injury in medical treatments" is mainly because that in such cases, some damages would be delayed, and the infringement state may be concealed for relatively long time.[32] This problem can be settled in judicial practice by improving the rule for determination of starting point of limitation of action for disputes over liability for injury in medical treatments.[33] The second highest application rate (0.47%) for "Disputes over the right to life, the right to health and the right to body" is also mainly related to this. If this factor is considered, then in actual practice, the actual needs on Article 136 of *General Principles of the Civil Law* may also be lower.

Besides the relatively low absolute application rate, as compared with Article 135 of *General Principles of the Civil Law*, its application rate is also lower.

Table of top-10 causes of action with respect to times of application of article 135 of *general principles of the civil law*

Top-10 cause of action	Times of application	Number of cases involving such cause of action	Percentage
1. Disputes over contracts for pre-sale of commercial residential housing	2935	79763	3.68
2. Disputes over contract of sale	2590	569883	0.45

(continued)

---

[32]Zhu (2005b).

[33]Article 168 of the *Opinions of the Supreme People's Court on Several Issues concerning the Implementation of the General Principles of the Civil Law* provides that: "For personal injury that is obvious, the limitation of action for compensation shall be computed from the date when the person suffers from such injury; if the injury is not found then and there, but is diagnosed after examination to be caused by the infringement by proof, the limitation of action shall be computed from the date when the condition of the injury is diagnosed".

(continued)

Top-10 cause of action	Times of application	Number of cases involving such cause of action	Percentage
3. Dispute over private loan	2112	1277463	0.17
4. Disputes over contracts for sales of commercial residential housing	1698	59801	2.84
5. Disputes over contracts for property management services	1518	218416	0.70
6. Disputes over contracts for sales of housing	1064	136759	0.78
7. Disputes over financial loan contracts	893	575300	0.16
8. Dispute over contract	647	160998	0.40
9. Disputes over contracts for carrying out of construction projects	582	98325	0.59
10. Labor dispute	547	291633	0.19
Total	14586	3468341	0.42

The comparison reveals that, the application rate of Article 136 of *General Principles of the Civil Law* is about 1/3 of that of Article 135. It is thus clear that, the application rate of four relatively-short special limitation of action systems provided in *General Principles of the Civil Law* is relatively low in actual practice. Since the relatively-short special limitation of action system is to restrict the right holder from ensuring the discharge of obligatory right through exercise of litigation right, if its application rate is even lower than the relatively-long general limitation of action, then at least there is no necessity for the existing relatively-short limitation of action system to be retained. This is because that, if the relatively-short one-year limitation of action is prolonged to three years, the situations for application of such system will be less, and the significance of special provisions will also be lowered.

10.4.2 System of Relatively-Short Special Limitation of Action Is Not Reasonable

The Writer believes that, the limitation of action system in *General Principles of the Civil Law* of China adopts the subjective legislative mode, and shall be calculated from the date on which the right holder knows or should know that its rights are damaged. The *General Provisions of Civil Law* continues to adopt this legislative mode, which is in line with the orientation of legislative activities of the compilation of *Civil Code*. According the survey carried out by scholars, the reason why *General Principles of the Civil Law* has provided a relatively-short limitation of action is because of the impact on legislation by the planned economy system. During the planned economy period, most of the contracts were concluded in the form of annual plan. In order to ensure the implementation of plans and the performance of contracts, and protect the contractual rights and interests in time, it was natural to provide the relatively-short limitation of action.[34] However, as mentioned by scholars, the general limitation of action provided in *General Principles of the Civil Law* is relatively short, and is not favorable for protection on private rights. The short-term limitation of action is further shortened on such basis, so that the principle of sacred private rights is more ignored. This legislative mode pays more attention to efficiency while ignores equality, so that the short-term limitation of action basically ignores the protection on private rights. There is no necessity for existence of short-term limitation of action which is shorter than general limitation of action.[35] With respect to the establishment of relatively-short special limitation of action system, some scholars have refuted the four situations provided in Article 136 of *General Principles of the Civil Law* one by one, saying that no reasonableness for establishment of relatively-short special limitation of action is found.[36]

10.4.3   The General Provision Nature of Relatively-Short Limitation of Action Is Relatively Weak

Though the relatively-short special limitation of action system is provided in *General Principles of the Civil Law* as a legislative tradition, the percentage of Top-10 Causes of Action indicates that its general provision nature is relatively weak.

Application of chapter 7 "limitation of action" of *general principles of the civil law* for top-10 causes of action

Article number	Topic of article	Percentage of top-10 causes of action (%)	Total number of cases
Article 135	General limitation of action	64.83	22521
Article 136	**Special limitation of action**	**88.56**	**2902**
Article 137	Starting time of limitation of action and maximum protection period	56.93	10180
Article 138	Voluntary performance beyond limitation of action	74.47	380
Article 139	Termination of limitation of action	61.66	446
Article 140	Interruption of limitation of action	64.17	8911
Article 141	**Application of limitation of action in special law**	**80.70**	**114**

---

[34]Li and Lai (2005).

[35]Hou and Li (2012).

[36]Zhu (2005a).

The table above reveals that, as for the provisions about "special limitation of action" in Article 136 and the provisions about "Application of limitation of action in Special Law" in Article 141 of *General Principles of the Civil Law*, the percentage of Top-10 Causes of Action exceeds 80%. As for Article 136, the percentage of Top-10 Causes of Action even reaches 88.56%, and its general provision nature is obviously lower. It seems that the provisions of Article 141 "In case there are other provisions in other laws, such provisions shall apply" has also pointed out the direction for the deletion of Article 136.

On the basis of the above-mentioned consideration, the Writer agrees that, the relatively-short special limitation of action system should be deleted from the *General Provisions of Civil Law*, and believes that, in the future, it is inappropriate to provide such relatively-short special limitation of action in special laws. If necessary, the special law may provide a relatively long special limitation of action.

10.5 Big Data Analysis on Issue About Deletion or Retention of Core Systems of Obligation Law

10.5.1 It Is Advised to Define the Exercise of Claim for Obligatory Right

If Article 84 of *General Principles of the Civil Law* is determined as the "article to be replaced", then the functional "replacing article" is Article 60 of the *Contract Law*. Though Paragraph 1 of Article 60 of the *Contract Law* ("The parties concerned shall fully perform their own obligations in accordance with the agreement.") gives the provisions on performance of contractual obligation from the standing point of obligor, this can't satisfy the demands on application of article about claim for obligatory right in judicial practice. This is because that, the provisions on claim for obligatory right in Paragraph 2 of Article 84 of *General Principles of the Civil Law* meet the basic expression style of claim, and also cover other types of obligatory right. Article 84 of *General Principles of the Civil Law* has been applied for 198,293 times, and has become the article with the second highest application times in *General Principles of the Civil Law*.[37] Obviously, as for most of the applications, the purpose is not to apply the concept of obligatory right defined in its Paragraph 1. All the top-10 causes of action with respect to such article are contract-related causes of action, and the situation that such article is applied together with Article 60 of the *Contract Law* to every cause of action is as follows:

---

[37]The article of the highest times of application of the *General Principles of Civil Law* is Article 108 Obligation Discharge, and it is 355,107 times. In the extremely high times of application, "dispute arising from private lending" is No. 1 and it is 215,624 times. However, the percentage of Top 10 causes of action of this rule is 88.92% and the general provision nature is relatively weak.

Table of situation for application of article 84 of *general principles of the civil law* **and situation for application of such article together with article 60 of the** *contract law*

Top-10 cause of action	Number of judgments	Application together with article 60 of the *contract law*	
		Number of judgments	Percentage (%)
1. Dispute over private loan	103049	4722	4.58
2. Disputes over contract of sale	18534	3568	19.25
3. Disputes over labor services contracts	12835	1416	11.03
4. Disputes over claims for labor remuneration in arrear	8040	388	4.83
5. Disputes over financial loan contracts	6778	1802	26.59
6. Dispute over contracts	5047	1209	23.95
7. Disputes over loan contracts	4919	777	15.80
8. Disputes over the right of recourse	2788	474	17.00
9. Disputes over contracts for property management services	2765	243	8.79
10. Disputes over contracts for carrying out of construction projects	2497	529	21.19
Total	167252	15128	9.05

The table above reveals that, among a lot of judgments which apply Article 84 of *General Principles of the Civil Law*, the judgments which also apply Article 60 of the *Contract Law* account for no more than 25% in top-10 causes of action, and account for less than 5% in many causes of action, with the average being only 9.05%. This indicates that, Paragraph 1 of Article 60 of the *Contract Law* can't fully meet the needs on system of claim for obligatory right, and in actual practice, there are high demands on Article 84 of *General Principles of the Civil Law* for judgment. In fact, the percentage of Top-10 Causes of Action with respect to Article 84 of *General Principles of the Civil Law* is as high as 83.87%, and the general provision nature is relatively weak. As a result, it would be inappropriate to provide such article in the *General Provisions of Civil Law*, and such article is placed in the *General Provisions of Civil Law* only because that the "general provisions of obligation law" has been cancelled. Therefore, it is advised by the Writer that, the *General Provisions of Civil Law* should define the mode for exercise of claim for obligatory right, so as to meet the needs of actual practice with the lowest legislative costs. It advised to add the second sentence "The obligatory right holder shall have the right to require the obligor to fully perform the obligation." following the provisions "The civil subjects legally enjoy obligatory right." in Paragraph 1 of Article 118 of the *General Provisions of Civil Law*, amend Paragraph 2 of such article into a pure article about "causes of obligations", and provides the obligatory right holder and obligor as follows: "The obligatory right arises from contract, unilateral promise, tort, negotiorum gestio, unjustified enrichment and other provisions of laws. The party which enjoys the rights is the obligatory right holder, while the party which undertakes the obligations is the obligor."[38]

10.5.2 It Is Advised to Replace the Provisions About "Joint and Several Obligations" with the Provisions About "Joint and Several Liabilities"

Article 87 of *General Principles of the Civil Law* is the provision on "joint and several obligations", and has been applied for 12,958 times, which indicates its importance. The top-10 causes of action are as follows:

Table of top-10 causes of action with respect to times of application of article 87 of *general principles of the civil law*

Top-10 cause of action	Times of application	Percentage (%)
1. Dispute over private loan	5985	53.31
2. Disputes over financial loan contracts	1293	11.52
3. Disputes over contract of sale	1066	9.49
4. Disputes over the right of recourse	907	8.08
5. Disputes over labor services contracts	703	6.26
6. Disputes over loan contracts	416	3.71
7. Disputes over claims for labor remuneration in arrear	323	2.88
8. Dispute over contracts	251	2.24
9. Disputes over contracts for education and training	148	1.32
10. Disputes over contracts for carrying out of construction projects	135	1.20
Total	11227	100.00
Percentage of top-10 causes of action	12958	86.64

In actual practice, there are very few disputes over joint and several obligatory rights, and such article is mainly applied for joint and several obligations. This is because that, though the joint and several obligations are not in the name of guaranty, it has the essence of guaranty. As a result, the joint and several obligation

---

[38]Subject to Paragraph 2, Article 105, the *General Provisions of Civil Law of the People's Republic of China (draft for solicitation of opinions for first deliberation)* on July 5, 2016: the obligatory right is the right of right holder to request for any act from particular obligor owing to contract, unilateral promise, tort, voluntary service, unjustified enrichment or other provisions of law." the cause for unilateral promise obligation is included, but the provisions for unilateral promise is deleted in the later draft.

is widely applied and become the core obligation of multiple-party.[39] Among the cases for which Article 87 of *General Principles of the Civil Law* has been applied, the expression "joint and several obligation" has been used only in the judgments of 289 cases, most of which is the quotation of "joint and several obligation" contained in Article 90 of the *Contract Law* and the "joint and several obligor" contained in Article 102 of the *Real Rights Law*, Article 17 of the *Civil Limitation of Action Provisions* and the *Enterprise Bankruptcy Law*. The fact covered by the high application rate is that, in judicial practice in China, the "joint and several obligation" in Article 86 of *General Principles of the Civil Law* is used as "joint and several liabilities".

This judicial application wherein the name is not consistent with essence is not the only phenomenon in Mainland China. In the *Civil Code* in Taiwan, except for the section "Multi-party Obligor and Obligatory Right Holder" wherein the words "joint and several obligation" are used, the words "joint and several liabilities" are used in other chapters and sections.[40] In current laws of China, on one hand, the joint and several obligations rather than the joint and several liabilities are provided in *General Principles of the Civil Law*; on the other hand, except for a few exceptions, the words "joint and several liabilities" are used in almost all legislations. However, in current laws, the specific rules for joint and several liabilities are only given in Article 13 and Article 14 of the *Tort Liability Law*, and can't be used as general provisions. The percentage of Top-10 Causes of Action of Article 87 of *General Principles of the Civil Law* is 86.64%, and it seems that the general provision nature of such article is relatively weak. This is only because that, Article 13 and Article 14 of the *Tort Liability Law* which are also taken as the basis for joint and several liabilities have been applied for 4224 times and 3538 times and such times of application are not included. The Writer believes that, the *General Provisions of Civil Law* should replace the joint and several obligations with joint and several liabilities in light of the needs of actual practice, clarify the difference between claim for apportionment and claim for recourse, and provide the "general article for apportionment of final liabilities" in a unified manner.[41]

The advices given by the Writer have been partially adopted by Chapter 8 "Civil Liabilities" of the *General Provisions of Civil Law*. It is provided in Article 177 that: "When more than two persons legally undertake the proportional liabilities, in case the proportion of liabilities can be determined, they shall respectively undertake the corresponding liabilities; in case it is difficult to determine the proportion of liabilities, they shall equally undertake the liabilities." It is provided in Article 178 that: "When more than two persons legally undertake the joint and several liabilities, the right holder shall have the right to require any or all of them to undertake the liabilities." "The proportional of liabilities to be undertaken by joint and several liable persons shall be determined on the basis of the proportion of their respective

---

[39]Qiu (2004, p. 395).

[40]Qiu (2004, p. 394).

[41]See Wang (2010).

liabilities; in case it is difficult to determine the proportion of liabilities, they shall equally undertake the liabilities. The joint and several liable persons who have actually undertaken the liabilities in excess of the proportion which must be undertaken by him shall have right to recover the excessive proportion from other joint and several liable persons." "The joint and several liabilities shall be provided by laws or agreed upon by parties concerned." The Writer believes that, though there are still some problems in these articles, they may be deemed as the embryo of general provisions for apportionment of civil liabilities. As a result, in the future *Tort Liabilities Volume of Civil Code*, the contents equivalent to Articles 12–14 of the *Tort Liability Law* may be deleted, so as to realize the generalization of general provisions for apportionment of civil liabilities.

References

Bai Jianjun, "Some Effects of Big Data on Study of Law", *Peking University Law Journal*, No. 1, 2015.

Chen Longyin, Hou Guoyue, *Summary of Seminar Meeting of Civil Subject Legislation Issue of Civil Code of China*, Journal of Southwest University of Political Science & Law, No. 5, 2015.

Hou Guoyue, Li Xiaoyu, "Legislative Conception of Special Limitation of Action of the *Civil Code* of China", *Gansu Social Sciences*, No. 3, 2012.

Hu Jing, "Analysis on Several Issues of Individual Partnership in Trial Practice", *Journal of Law Application*, No. 9, 2012.

Hu Ling, The Influence of Increasing of Big Data on Legal Practice and Theoretical Research, *Journal of XinJIANG Normal University (Edition of Philosophy and Social Sciences)*, No. 4, 2015.

IBM Institute for Business Value, *Analytics: The Real-world Use of Big Data*, October 2012, p 4. Website: https://www.ibm.com/smarterplanet/global/files/se_sv_se_intelligence_Analytics_-_ The_real-world_use_of_big_data.pdf. The latest access time: August 31, 2017.

Jiang Shan, Huang Yong, "On the Concentration Control to Joint Venture in China", *Law Science Magazine*, No. 10, 2012.

Jiang Shan, Su Jun, "On the Antitrust Regulation on Innovation of Corporation Joint Venture", *Oriental Law*, No. 2, 2014.

Karl Larenz, *General Provisions of German Civil Law (Volume 1)*, translated by Wang Xiaoye, Shao Jiandong, Cheng Jianying, Xu Guojian, Xie Huaishi, Law Press, 2013, p. 336.

Li L, Lai Xinfang, "The Time-and-Efficiency Institution of China: Weak Points and Improvement in Legislation", *Academic Research*, No. 2, 2005.

Li Shishi, *The Explanation of the Daft of the General Provisions of Civil Law of the People's Republic of China*, June 27th, 2016a.

Li Yongjun, "Design of Subject System in the Future *Civil Code* of China", *Legal Forum*, No. 2, 2016b.

Liu Jiaqi, "Paradigm Change of Legal Empirical Research in Big Data Era", *Hubei Social Sciences*, No. 7, 2015.

Ma Junju, "General Principles of Civil Law and Civil Subject Status of Partnership", *Law Review*, No. 3, 1986.

Qiu Congzhi, *General Rules of Obligation Volume of Newly Revised Civil Law (Volume II)*, China Renmin University Press 2004.

Shen Huiwen, *Death of Leaseholding Farm Household, Journal of Henan University of Economics and Law*, No. 2, 2016.

Shi Shaoxia, Li Zhen, "Exemption from Commercial Registration Obligation of Individual Businesses", *Economic Review*, No. 1, 2012.

Shu Manping, "Several Legal Problems on Bottom Profit Clauses in Joint Venture Contracts", *People's Judicture*, No. 4, 1990.

Wang Shenming, "On Individual Business and Lease Holding Farm Household", *Chinese Legal Science*, No. 4, 1986.

Wang Zhu, "On the Right of Contribution in Joint and Several Liability", *Science of Law*, No. 3, 2010.

Wang Zhu, "The Legislative Procedure to Formulate Civil Code in the Mode of Codification of Nonbasic Law", *Peking University Law Journal*, No. 6, 2014

Zhang Jianqiu, Wang Chunmei, "On Bottom Profit Clauses in Joint Venture Contracts", *Seeking Truth*, No. 2, 1997.

Zhang Xuejun, "A Study on Individual Businesses and Lease-holding Farm Households", *Contemporary Law Review*, No. 1, 2005.

Zhou Youjun, *Civil Subject in the Land Contractual Relationship*, Journal of Nanchang University (Humanities and Social Sciences) No. 1, 2009.

Zhou Qiang, *The Work Report of the Supreme People's Court*, Document of the Third Meeting of the 12th National People's Congress on March 12, 2015.

Zhou Qiang, *The Work Report of the Supreme People's Court*, Document of the Fourth Meeting of the 12th National People's Congress on March 13, 2016.

Zhu Yan, "Basic Issue of Limitation of Action", *Peking University Law Journal*, No. 2, 2005a.

Zhu Yan, "Basic Problem on Negative Limitation of Action System: A Comparative Analysis and a Study on China's Civil Legislation", *Peking University Law Journal*, No. 2, 2005b.

Chapter 11
View on Formal Compilation Techniques for Articles of *Civil Code* from the *General Provisions of Civil Law*

On January 29, 2016, the Legal Affairs Commission of NPC Standing Committee solicited opinions from various research institutions for the *People's Republic of China the General Provisions of Civil Law (draft)* (hereinafter referred to as "the *General Provisions of Civil Law (draft)*"). On May 20, 2016, the *General Provisions of Civil Law (draft)* was further amended.[1] On June 27, 2016, the *General Provisions of Civil Law (draft)* was deliberated for the first time at the 21st Meeting of 12th NPC Standing Committee. On October 30, 2016, the *General Provisions of Civil Law (draft for second deliberation)* was deliberated at the 24th Meeting of 12th NPC Standing Committee. On December 17, 2016, the *General Provisions of Civil Law (draft for third deliberation)* was deliberated at the 25th Meeting of 12th NPC Standing Committee. The comparison among five versions of the *General Provisions of Civil Law (draft)* since 2016 and the *General Provisions of Civil Law* reveals that, this compilation of the *General Provisions of Civil Law* has preliminarily formed the relatively stable compilation techniques.

Hereinafter, the formal article-compiling techniques reflected by the *General Provisions of Civil Law* will be summarized. On this basis, the Writer tries to identify the similar articles in the *General Provisions of Civil Law* and current separate civil laws corresponding to specific volumes of the future *Civil Code*, and thus determine the possibility to apply the same formal article-compiling techniques, so as to realize the formal unification of compilation of *Civil Code*.

---

[1] About the deliberation, see Liang (2016).

© China University of Political Science and Law Press 2020
Z. Wang, *On the Constitutionality of Compiling a Civil Code of China*,
https://doi.org/10.1007/978-981-13-7900-0_11

11.1 System Orientation of Formal Compilation Techniques for Articles of *Civil Code*

The compilation of *Civil Code* is different from enactment,[2] and is also different from assembly.[3] It is the integrative treatment on the basis of the current civil legal norm system.[4] The decision on the compilation of *Civil Code* in the *Decision to Rule by Law* should be understood as the political restriction on legislative authority of the Legislature. The Legislature may not formally assemble the *Civil Code*, and also may not enact the *Civil Code*. Frankly speaking, within the meaning of change of legal system, the compilation is a legislative activity between enactment and assembly.

11.1.1 Difference Between Compilation Techniques for Micro-articles and Compilation Techniques for Macro-articles

If the compilation techniques for *Civil Code* are observed from micro level and macro level, they actually include micro article-compiling techniques and macro system-compiling techniques. The micro article-compiling techniques take the articles which bear legal norms as objects, and generate the articles to be used for macro system compilation.[5] Then, under the framework of volume, chapter and section, the macro system-compiling techniques properly arrange the articles in system.

The macro compilation techniques not only involve the compilation of the *General Provisions of Civil Law*, but also involve the coordination with specific provisions volume. However, at present, the legislature has only completed the compilation of the *General Provisions of Civil Law*, so that the full view can't be realized now. Hereinafter, the micro article-compiling techniques embodied by the *General Provisions of Civil Law* will be discussed.

---

[2]Liang (2003b).

[3]See Jiang (2003).

[4]Wang (2014).

[5]Under ideal conditions, the carrier unit of compilation techniques for micro articles is "article". In other words, an article of law is corresponding to a legal norm. However, in the legislative practice, sometimes, several articles are corresponding to a legal norm, and an article is corresponding to several legal norms. The standard hierarchy orientation of article, paragraph and item should be further unified.

11.1.2   Two Types of Compilation Techniques for Micro Articles

It is provided in Paragraph 1 of Article 2 of the *Legislation Law* that: "As for enactment, amendment and abolishment of laws, administrative regulations, local regulations, autonomous regulations and separate regulations, this Law shall apply." It is thus clear that, according to the provisions of the *Legislation Law*, the legislative activities for law only include "enactment", "amendment" and "abolishment", and "compilation" is not the legislative activity within the meaning of the *Legislation Law*. Since the state of a current law is "retained" if it is not amended or abolished, essentially the "compilation" should be the combination of four legislative activities (namely retention, enactment, amendment and abolishment) to a certain extent. As for an article which bears legal norm, the legislative activities are the retention, addition, amendment and deletion of such article.

The Writer believes that, it is necessary to distinguish between formal compilation of articles and essential compilation of articles. The so-called formal compilation of articles means that, the essential contents of legal norm as object of compilation are not changed, and only the expression is adjusted. The so-called essential compilation of article means that the essential contents of legal norm as object of compilation are changed, which will surely bring about the adjustment to expression. With respect to the priority in application of article-compiling techniques, since the compilation of *Civil Code* is a restrictive legislative activity, the priority should be given to the formal compilation techniques. Only when it is necessary to change, delete or add any legal norm for sufficient reason, will the essential compilation techniques be applied.

11.1.3   Application Rules for Formal Compilation Techniques for Articles

The formal compilation techniques for articles of *Civil Code* mainly include the following two techniques: The first is to remain the expression of compilation object unchanged, and directly compile it into the *Civil Code*, which is essentially a legislative activity within the meaning of assembly. The second is to formally amend the articles of compilation object, which will not affect the legal norms but change the expression mode.

What may be ignored is that, the application of formal compilation techniques of articles is also restrictive. The compilation of *Civil Code* will not preclude the assembly of few articles, but should take assembly as the starting point for selection of compilation techniques, and every article which will not be compiled by means of assembly should have its own reasonable reason. If there is no need to formally amend the articles, the existing articles should be fully compiled into the *Civil Code* without any amendment. The formal amendment of articles may be carried out only when there is reasonable reason.

11.1.4   Object of Formal Compilation Techniques for Articles of Civil Code

The object of this compilation of *Civil Code* not only included civil laws, but also includes civil judicial interpretation. The difference between essential compilation and formal compilation of articles reveals that, the object of essential compilation is only limited to law, while the object of formal compilation includes laws and judicial interpretations. This is because that, if it is necessary to amend any article of current law, then the object of amendment shall be the law, and the judicial interpretation may only be used as reference for amendment of law. If it is necessary to abolish any article of current law, then the object of abolishment shall be the law, and the judicial interpretation shall only be the object of cleaning after the compilation of *Civil Code* is completed. If it is necessary to add any article, then the object of addition shall be the law, and the judicial interpretation may only be used as reference for addition of legal norm. The formal article compilation for the *Civil Code* should take the civil law as the primary object of compilation and take the relevant judicial interpretation as the auxiliary object of compilation, and different compilation techniques should be used for them.

11.2   Formal Article-Compiling Techniques Which Take Laws as Compilation Object

There are six formal article-compiling techniques which take laws as compilation object, which are detailed as follows.

11.2.1   Compilation Techniques Whereby Expression of Articles Remain Unchanged

Among the articles in the *General Provisions of Civil Law* which take *General Principles of the Civil Law* as compilation object, only a few remain unchanged. The provisions about unjustified enrichment in Article 122 directly use the expression of Article 92 of *General Principles of the Civil Law*. This means that the drafting organ recognizes the unjustified enrichment rules provided in General Principles of the Civil Law. However, as compared with the provisions about negotiorum gestio in Article 93 of *General Principles of the Civil Law*, in the provisions of Article 121 of the *General Provisions of Civil Law* which has the similar status, the word "discharge" is changed to "repay": "In absence of legal or contractual obligation, the person which provides voluntary service for the purpose of preventing the interests of other persons from being damaged, such person shall have the right to request the beneficiary to 'repay' the necessary expenses paid therefor." From the viewpoint of legislative techniques, this tiny change is not necessary. If this is only attributable to the personal preference of drafter, such article should remain unchanged in accordance with the restrictive rules for formal compilation of articles.

Another group of articles in which the wordings remain unchanged are the provisions about justifiable defense in Article 181 and the provisions about act of rescue in Article 182 in the *General Provisions of Civil Law*. Those provisions directly adopt the expression in Article 30 and Article 31 of the *Tort Liability Law*. In the course of compilation of *Civil Code* in the future, especially the laws to be compiled later, as for those articles to which no amendment is required, the Legislature should restrain the impulse to randomly make amendment, and directly incorporate them into the *Civil Code*, so as to avoid the occurrence of unnecessary misleading arising from historical interpretation.

11.2.2 Compilation Techniques Whereby Slight Formal Adjustment Is Made to Expression of Articles

The situations that only slight formal adjustment is made to expression of an article and the legal norm is not essentially changed are detailed as follows.

11.2.2.1 Unified Change of Wording Habits

1. The Word "his" is Changed to "his/her", so as to Declare the Gender Equality

Article 23 of the *General Provisions of Civil Law* is essentially identical with Article 14 of *General Principles of the Civil Law*, and the only difference is that the word "his" is changed to "his/her": "The guardian of a person without capacity for civil conduct or limited capacity for civil conduct shall be his/her legal representative." This amendment has the value in declaring gender equality. In fact, almost all contents relating to "natural persons" in Chapter 2 in the *General Provisions of Civil Law* are amended in this way.

It is provided in Paragraph 1 of Article 15 of *General Principles of the Civil Law* that: "The registered permanent residence of a citizen shall be regarded as his residence." From the viewpoint of application of this article-compiling technique, however, it seems that the word "his/her" is omitted in Article 25 of the *General Provisions of Civil Law*,: "The registered permanent residence of a natural person shall be regarded as residence;" The situation in Article 25 of the *General*

Provisions of Civil Law that the word "his/her" is deleted on the basis of change in wording habit without sufficient reason should be corrected.

This article-compiling technique is worth generalizing, and when the *Succession Volume of Civil Code* is compiled in the future, the word "his" in Articles 6, 11 and 33 of the *Succession Law* as well as Articles 52 and 53 of the *Opinions on the Succession Law* should be changed to "his/her".

2. "Makes …Incur Damage/Loss" is changed to "Causes Damage/Loss to …"

The use of expression mode "causes damage/loss to 'other persons'"[6] in *General Principles of the Civil Law* is related to the *General Provisions of Civil Law*, such as the provisions in Article 92 relating to unjustified enrichment and the provisions in Article 107 relating to force majeure. However, if the position of "other persons" is a relatively long expression, then the expression mode "makes …incur damage/ loss" is used. This wording considers the expression habit, but is not favorable for literal interpretation of law. The *General Provisions of Civil Law* has noticed this problem, and used the expression mode "causes damage/loss to …" by reference to the *Tort Liability Law*. The adjustment is embodied in three respects:

Firstly, Paragraph 1 of Article 164 of the *General Provisions of Civil Law* is essentially equivalent to Paragraph 2 of Article 66 of *General Principles of the Civil Law*, but the words "the principal is damaged" are changed to "causes damage to the principal".

Secondly, when compiling Article 43 of *General Principles of the Civil Law* by reference to Article 58 of the *Opinions on General Principles of Civil Law*, Paragraph 1 of Article 62 of the *General Provisions of Civil Law* adhered to the traditional expression style "causes damage/loss to other persons": "In case the legal representative causes damage to any other person owing to performance of duties, the legal person shall bear the civil liabilities."

Thirdly, when designing new rules, Paragraph 3 of Article 43 of the *General Provisions of Civil Law* actively comply with this wording norm: "In case the administrator of properties causes property losses to missing person owing to intentional conduct or gross negligence, the administrator shall undertake the compensation liabilities." This is also the good example for complying with formal compilation requirement in the course of essential compilation of articles.

In the course of compilation of Articles 42, 43, 113, 118, 408 and 410 of the *Contract Law* and Article 21 of the *Real Rights Law* in the future, such syntactical structure should be adjusted.

---

[6]The differentiation and unification of "loss" and "damage" belong to the material compilation scope of article.

11.2.2.2 Evolution and Unification of Legislative Terminology

1. Day" is Changed to "Calendar Day"

It is provided in Paragraph 1 of Article 154 of *General Principles of the Civil Law* that: "A period mentioned in the civil law shall be calculated on the basis of calendar year, month, day or hour." In Paragraphs 2–4, however, "day" is used instead of "calendar day". It is provided in Paragraph 2 that: "A period which is calculated on the basis of hours as provided shall be calculated from the time when such period is provided. A period which is calculated at days, months or years as provided shall be calculated from the day immediately after the date on which such period is provided." It is provided in Paragraph 3 that: "In case the last day of a period is Sunday or a legal holiday, the day immediately following such Sunday or legal holiday shall be taken as the last day of such period." It is provided in Paragraph 4 that: "The deadline for the last day of a period shall be Hour 24. In case there is business time, the deadline shall be the time point when the business activities are stopped." Articles 200–203 of the *General Provisions of Civil Law* has noticed this tiny difference and carried out full amendment. This is worth praising.

2. Extension of Coverage of "Legal Holiday"

It is provided in Paragraph 3 of Article 154 of *General Principles of the Civil Law* that: "In case the last day of a period is Sunday or a legal holiday, the day immediately following such Sunday or legal holiday shall be taken as the last day of such period." Such paragraph uses the expression "other legal holidays", and it should be interpreted as that the Legislature included "Sunday" into "legal holidays". It is provided in the *Provisions of the State Council on Working Time of Workers* amended in 1994 that: "Saturday and Sunday are weekly rest days." Paragraphs 2 and 3 of Article 44 of the *Labor Law* distinguish between "rest day" and "legal holiday", and provide different calculation proportion for salary: "Under any of the following circumstances, the employer shall pay to employees the salary higher than that for normal working time in accordance with the following standards: ...(2) In case the employees are arranged to work on any rest day and no compensated leave can be arranged, such employees shall be paid the salary no less than 200% of normal salary; (3) In case the employees are arranged to work on any legal holiday, such employees shall be paid the salary no less than 300% of normal salary."

It is provided in Paragraph 1 of Article 203 of the *General Provisions of Civil Law* that: "In case the last day of a period is a legal holiday, the day immediately following the expiry of such legal holiday shall be taken as the last day of such period." From the viewpoint of evolution of legislative terminology, it is acceptable to include "weekly rest days" into "legal holidays". However, from the viewpoint of coordination with the *Labor Law*, it is more appropriate to provide "weekly rest day or other legal holiday". It should be pointed out that, the "legal holidays" must be extensively interpreted in actual practice, and should also include the national or local temporary holidays decided by the State Council and local governments at various levels other than the *Law on Holiday Office for National Annual Festivals and Memorial Days*.[7] From the viewpoint of literal meaning, however, this is still different from "legal" to a certain extent, and it is advised to clarify such issue through judicial interpretation in the future.

11.2.2.3   Amendment for Historical Limitation: The Word "Citizens" Is Changed to "Natural Persons"[8]

For special historical reasons, the title "Citizens (Natural Persons)" is adopted for Chapter 2 of *General Principles of the Civil Law*, and the word "citizens" is used in every position where "natural persons" should be used. In the *General Provisions of Civil Law*, the title of Chapter 2 is changed to "Natural Persons", and the word "citizens" are replaced in the following three manners:

The first manner is to change "citizens" to "natural persons", which is mainly applied in the situation that the word "citizens" is listed together with the word "legal persons" and indicates natural persons, and is also the most frequently used manner. However, in very few situations that the word "citizens" only indicate Chinese citizens, this manner is not appropriate. For example, it is provided in Article 54 of the *General Provisions of Civil Law* that: "After being legally registered, the industrial or commercial business engaged into by a natural person shall be an individually-owned business. An individually-owned business may have its own trade name." However, in Paragraph 1 of Article 2 of the *Regulations for Individually-owned Business*, the registrants are limited to "citizens": "After being registered by industrial & commercial administration authority, the industrial or commercial business engaged into by a citizen with operational capacity in accordance with the provisions of these regulations shall be an individually-owned business." Article 27 also only permits the compatriots in Hong Kong, Macao and Taiwan to be registered as individually-owned business: "The Chinese citizens among permanent residents in Hong Kong Special Administrative Region and Macau Special Administrative Region as well as the residents in Taiwan may apply for being registered as individually-owned businesses in accordance with the relevant provisions of the state." Therefore, it is appropriate to change the "natural persons" here into "citizens".

Secondly, the word "citizens" corresponding to natural persons under the age of 18 is changed to "minors". The typical example is Paragraph 2 of Article 18 of the *General Provisions of Civil Law*: "A minor which is older than 16 years and takes his/her own labor income as main source of income shall be deemed as a person with full capacity for civil conduct."

---

[7]However, the legal basis of decision of holiday beyond the *Law on Holiday Office for National Annual Festivals and Memorial Days* is still not clear, and it should be further improved, so as to realize the seamless connection with this regulation of the *General Provisions of Civil Law* in the future.

[8]About the essential change of the chapter of "Natural Persons", see Chen (2016b).

Thirdly, "citizens" is changed to "civil subjects". It is provided in Article 113 of the *General Provisions of Civil Law*: "The property rights of civil subjects are equally protected by laws." This article corresponds to Paragraph 1 of Article 75 of *General Principles of the Civil Law*: "The personal properties of citizens include the lawful income, housing, savings, articles for daily use, cultural relics, books, trees, livestock, production materials which may be legally owned by citizens and other lawful properties." The change in wording is worth approving.

In the course of compilation of Articles 3, 16 and 31 of the *Succession Law* as well as Article 5 of the *Adoption Law* in the future, the word "citizens" should be treated accordingly. Paragraph 2 of Article 31 of the *Succession Law* contains the contents about legacy-support agreement with collective-ownership-system organization.[9] Since the situation is similar to the above-analyzed situation about individually-owned business, the word "citizens" should be retained.

11.2.3   Compilation Techniques for Punctuation Marks Are Changed—Taking the Use of Semicolon as an Example[10]

Semicolon is a punctuation mark used in a sentence, indicating the stop between coordinative-relation clauses in a multi-clause sentence, as well as the stop between first-layer clauses in non-coordinative-relation multi-clause sentence.[11] In the *General Provisions of Civil Law*, the semicolon is used between different items enumerated, and also used in the following situations.

11.2.3.1   Comma Is Changed to Semicolon

It is provided in Article 15 of *General Principles of the Civil Law* that: "The registered permanent residence of a citizen shall be regarded as his residence. In case the habitual residence is different from registered permanent residence, the habitual residence shall be regarded as residence." In Article 25 of the *General Provisions of Civil Law*, the first comma in Article 15 of *General Principles of the Civil Law* is changed to semicolon: "The registered permanent residence of a

---

[9]Paragraph 2 of article 31 of the *Succession Law* provides that: "A citizen may enter into a legacy-support agreement with an organization under collective ownership which, in accordance with the agreement, assumes the duty to support the former in his or her lifetime and attends to his or her interment after death, in return for the right to legacy."

[10]In Paragraph 2, Article 180, the *General Provisions of Civil Law*, for the definitions of force majeure, the quotation mark of Article 153, *General Principles of the Civil Law* is deleted. It is suggested that all quotation marks of Article 205, the *General Provisions of Civil Law* should be deleted subject to the use way of punctuation mark of Article 99, the *Criminal Law*.

[11]*Usage of Punctuation Marks* (GBT 15834—2011) 4.6 Semicolon.

natural person shall be regarded as residence; in case the habitual residence is different from registered permanent residence, the habitual residence shall be regarded as residence." As a result, the structure is clearer. When compiling the provisions about legal effect of invalidated or revocable civil juristic acts as provided in Paragraph 1 of Article 61 of *General Principles of the Civil Law*, Article 157 of the *General Provisions of Civil Law* also similarly replaces the comma with semicolon.

When compiling the rules for the undertaking of outward obligations by individually-owned business as provided in Article 29 of *General Principles of the Civil Law*, Paragraph 1 of Article 56 of the *General Provisions of Civil Law* uses semicolons in the positions corresponding to some newly-added rules: "If operated by individual, the obligations of an individually-owned business shall be undertaken with the properties of such individual; if operated by a family, the obligations shall be undertaken with the properties of such family; if it is impossible to distinguish between individual or family, the obligations shall be undertaken with the properties of such family." This is the conscious compliance with the requirements on formal article compilation in the course of essential compilation of articles.

11.2.3.2 Period Is Changed to Semicolon

A period indicates the end of a sentence, and has the higher discriminative power than semicolon. In some articles of the *General Provisions of Civil Law*, the periods are changed to semicolons,[12] which have generated good effect. For example, Article 137 of *General Principles of the Civil Law* is divided into three sentences: "The limitation of action shall be calculated from the date on which the infringement is known or should be known. However, in case more than twenty years have elapsed since the date on which the rights are infringed upon, the people's court will not grant protection. Under special circumstances, the people's court may extend the limitation of action." The effect of second period is not clear enough, so that it may be misunderstood as that the third sentence can be applied for the first sentence, and thus it may be misunderstood that the may be extended. In Paragraph 2 of Article 188 of the *General Provisions of Civil Law*, all periods corresponding to those in Paragraph 2 of Article 137 of *General Principles of the Civil Law* are changed to semicolons: "The limitation of action shall be calculated from the date on which the right holder knows or should know the damage to rights and the obligor. In case there are other provisions in other laws, such provisions shall apply. However, in case more than twenty years have elapsed since the date on which the rights are damaged, the people's court will not grant protection; under special

---

[12]The second semicolon of the item 2 of paragraph 1 of article 76 of the *Road Traffic Safety Law* is the typical example in which the period is misused as semicolon, see Yao and Wang (2008).

circumstances, the people's court may, on the basis of the request lodged by the right holder, decide to extend the limitation of action." In this way, the object which may be extended by the people's court is only limited to the maximum protection.

11.2.4 Compilation Technique Whereby an Article Is Reasonably Split

Reasonably splitting an article means to use several articles to refine an article, which involves the following types:

The first is that an article is reasonably split, but the expression remains unchanged. Article 36 of *General Principles of the Civil Law* contains two paragraphs about capacity of civil rights and capacity of civil conducts of legal persons. While retaining the contents of such article, the *General Provisions of Civil Law* has split it into Article 57 and Article 59.

The second is that an article is reasonably split and the expression is slightly adjusted. The provisions relating to agency in Article 63 of *General Principles of the Civil Law* are split into three paragraphs. Article 161 of the *General Provisions of Civil Law* is equivalent to Paragraphs 1 and 3 of such article, and Article 162 is equivalent to Paragraph 2 of such article. The form of articles is slightly adjusted, while the essential contents remain unchanged.

The third is that an article is reasonably split article and the expression is appropriately adjusted. The provisions relating to capacity of civil conducts of mentally-deranged persons in Article 13 of *General Principles of the Civil Law* are contained in two paragraphs, and the *General Provisions of Civil Law* split them into Article 21 and Article 22 and appropriately adjusts the contents on the basis of the situation that the mentally-deranged person is adult or minor. Article 11 and Article 12 of *General Principles of the Civil Law* are similarly treated in the *General Provisions of Civil Law*.

The fourth is that the provisions which have the same legal effect are split into articles. Article 58 of *General Principles of the Civil Law* is the enumeration of types of invalid juristic act, Article 52 of the *Contract Law* is the enumeration of types of invalid contracts, and the *General Provisions of Civil Law* splits the provisions about invalid juristic act into Articles 144, 146, 153 and 154. Similarly, Article 59 of *General Principles of the Civil Law* is the enumeration of types of juristic acts of which the validity is to be determined, Article 54 of the *Contract Law* is the enumeration of types of contracts of which the validity is to be determined, and while splitting the civil juristic act of which the validity is to be determined into Articles 147–151, the *General Provisions of Civil Law* further divides fraud into the situation that the other party carries out fraud and the situation that the other party knows that a third party carries out fraud. This is also the typical example for application together with essential article-compiling techniques.[13]

11.2.5 Compilation Technique Whereby Articles Are Reasonably Combined

The incorporation of articles of *General Principles of the Civil Law* into the *General Provisions of Civil Law* reveals that, the formal article-compiling technique frequently applied is to split an article into several articles, but there are also some articles which are combined. *General Principles of the Civil Law* provides the legal effect of force majeure in Article 107, and provides the definition of force majeure in Article 153. In the *General Provisions of Civil Law*, such two articles are combined into Article 180, and this combination is really reasonable.

However, not all combinations are the reasonable application of formal article-compiling technique. Article 135 of *General Principles of the Civil Law* is the provisions on general limitation of action, and Article 137 is the provisions on starting time of limitation of action and maximum protection period. The *General Provisions of Civil Law* deletes the one-year short special limitation of action system provided in Article 136 of *General Principles of the Civil Law*, and then combines these two rules into Article 188. The Writer believes that, the general limitation of action, the starting time of limitation of action and maximum protection period are different legal norms, so that it is appropriate not to combine these two articles.

11.3 Formal Article-Compiling Techniques Which Take Judicial Interpretation as Object of Compilation

The formal article-compiling techniques which take judicial interpretation as object of compilation mainly include the following types.

---

[13]About the application of the essential article-compiling techniques, see Wang (2016) and Chen (2016a).

11.3.1 Article-Compiling Techniques Whereby Law Absorbs the Corresponding Judicial Interpretation

11.3.1.1 Absorb the Article of the *Opinions on General Principles of Civil Law* on the Basis of *General Principles of the Civil Law*

On the basis of Article 25 of *General Principles of the Civil Law*, the *General Provisions of Civil Law* absorbs the provisions of Article 39 of the *Opinions on General Principles of Civil Law*, and combines them into Article 53: "A person for which the declaration of death has been revoked shall have the right to require any civil subject which has obtained his/her properties in accordance with the *Succession Law* to return such properties. In case such properties can't be returned, appropriate compensation shall be made. In case an interested party conceals the true situation, and thus any other person is declared as dead and his/her properties are obtained by such party, such party shall return the properties, and shall also be liable to make compensation for losses arising therefrom." The similar situations also include the provisions about legal effect of performance after expiration of limitation of action in Paragraph 2 of Article 192 of the *General Provisions of Civil Law*, which integrate the contents of Article 171 of the *Opinions on General Principles of Civil Law* on the basis of Article 138 of *General Principles of the Civil Law*.

11.3.1.2 Absorb the Articles of the *Provisions on Limitation of Action of Civil Cases* on the Basis of *General Principles of the Civil Law*

It is provided in Article 140 of *General Principles of the Civil Law* that: "In case the limitation of action is interrupted owing to the fact that the litigation is initiated or a party concerned requires the performance of or agrees to perform the obligation, the limitation of action shall be re-calculated from the date on which it is interrupted." Keeping enough restraint, Article 195 of the *General Provisions of Civil Law* only lists the three situations provided in Article 140 of *General Principles of the Civil Law*, and adds Item 4: "(4) other situations which have the same validity as initiation of litigation or application for arbitration." As a result, Articles 10, 12–16, 18 and 19 of the *Provisions on Limitation of Action of Civil Cases* are carried forward in a better manner, and the inclusion of excessively-detailed rules into the *General Provisions of Civil Law* is avoided.

It is provided in Article 139 of *General Principles of the Civil Law* that: "In the last six months of the limitation of action, in case the right of claim can't be exercised owing to force majeure or other obstacle, the limitation of action will be suspended. From the date on which the reason for suspension of limitation of action is eliminated, the limitation of action will continue." On this basis, in Article 194 of the *General Provisions of Civil Law*, the four interpretation contents given in

Paragraph 1 of Article 20 of the *Provisions on Limitation of Action of Civil Cases* for "other obstacles" provided in Article 139 of *General Principles of the Civil Law* are directly listed together with force majeure as five items under such paragraph, and it seems that this treatment is too simple.

11.3.2   Article Compilation Techniques Whereby "Judicial Interpretation Is Converted Into Legislation"

As a judicial interpretation, the wording of the *Opinions on General Principles of Civil Law* must consider the procedural provision and avoid making itself too legislative. For example, it is not appropriate to directly take the words "shall not be permitted generally" in Article 38 of the *Opinions on General Principles of Civil Law* as the legislative expression without amendment. The judicial interpretations issued by the Supreme People's Court over recent years generally use the words "shall be supported by the people's court" and "shall not be supported by the people's court", so as to avoid making the wording too legislative. In the future, if the relevant articles are incorporated into the *Civil Code*, it is necessary to carry out the treatment whereby the "judicial interpretation is converted into legislation".

When taking Article 38 of the *Opinions on General Principles of Civil Law* as the object of compilation, Article 52 of the *General Provisions of Civil Law* adjusts the legislative wording as follows: "In case the children of a person which is declared as dead are adopted by others legally within the period when such person is declared as dead, then, after the declaration of death is cancelled, such person may not claim the adoption relationship as invalid for the reason that such adoption is carried out without the consent from him/her." The similar treatments also include the compilation of the rule "declaration of death prevails over declaration of missing" provided in Article 29 of the *Opinions on General Principles of Civil Law* into Article 47 of the *General Provisions of Civil Law*, the compilation of implication rule provided in Article 66 of the *Opinions on General Principles of Civil Law* into Article 140 of the *General Provisions of Civil Law,* and the compilation of rule for change of property administrator for missing person provided in Article 35 of the *Opinions on General Principles of Civil Law* into Article 44 of the *General Provisions of Civil Law*.

Different from the special history standing of the *Opinions on General Principles of Civil Law*, most of the provisions of the *Provisions on Limitation of action of Civil Cases* are the detailed provisions issued for settlement of problems in actual practice, and some rules are even brand new rules relative to *General Principles of the Civil Law*. Therefore, it should be more prudent to take the articles of the *Provisions on Limitation of action of Civil Cases* as compilation object. The treatment of some articles in the *General Provisions of Civil Law* is not so reasonable:

Firstly, some articles are too much like "judicial interpretation". On the basis of Article 3 of the *Provisions on Limitation of action of Civil Cases*, Article 193 of the

General Provisions of Civil Law provides the adversary system for defense of limitation of action: "The people's court may not at its own initiative apply the provisions about limitation of action." The expression style makes such rule much like a "judicial interpretation", and should be so adjusted that it has the legislative nature.

Secondly, some articles are too specific. Article 189 of the *General Provisions of Civil Law* directly adopts the contents of Article 5 of the *Provisions on Limitation of action of Civil Cases*: "In case the parties concerned agree that an obligation may be performed in several instalments, the limitation of action shall be calculated as of the date on which the period for last instalment expires." It is really too specific to take such a special situation as an article of the *General Provisions of Civil Law*.

11.4 Requirements on Application of Formal Compilation Techniques in Compilation of *Civil Code*

In summary, the formal article-compiling techniques in the course of compilation of *Civil Code* are subject to restrictive application requirement, and should avoid formal omission, which are embodied in the following aspects:

Firstly, the number of articles involved in formal article compilation reveals that, the *General Provisions of Civil Law* only retains few contents of *General Principles of the Civil Law*, and amends a lot of contents. This is mainly because that, *General Principles of the Civil Law* was enacted earlier, and both the wording habit and social background have changed to a certain extent. The *Succession Law* which was enacted in the same period as *General Principles of the Civil Law* involves more situations of article formal compilation owing to the similar reason, Chapter 2 "Guaranty" of the *Guarantee Law* and the *Adoption Law* which were enacted later also involve such situations, and the *Contract Law*, the *Real Rights Law* and the *Tort Liability Law* which were enacted more later should comply with the restrictions, and take retention as primary mode and take amendment as auxiliary mode.

Secondly, in the future when the contents of every volume of the *Civil Code* are provided, the drafting organ should actively comply with the requirements of formal article-compiling techniques. In the course of final compilation of *Civil Code*, it is necessary to summarize the formal article-compiling techniques respectively used in compilation of the *General Provisions of Civil Law* and every volume, so as to realize the unified form of wording habit and punctuation mark.

Thirdly, in the course of compilation of *Civil Code* in the future, the legislative expression in essential article compilation should also actively comply with the formal compilation requirement. It is advised that, after the essential compilation is completed, the comprehensive examination should be carried out, so as to avoid the difference in expression of articles caused by essential compilation and ensure the unified effect of form of articles.

References

Chen Huabin, "The Construction of the System of Juristic Act", *Political Science and Law*, No. 7, 2016a.

Chen Huabin, "The Structure, Innovation and Improvement of the *General Provisions of Civil Law* of China", *Journal of Comparative Law*, No. 5, 2016b.

Jiang Ping, "Making an Open Style Civil Code", *Tribune of Political Science and Law*, No. 1, 2003. JIANG Ping, "Re-discussion on Drafting an Open Civil Code", *Jurist's Review*, No. 4, 2003.

Liang Huixing, "Incompact and Assembled Civil Code is Improper to the Situation of China", *Tribune of Political Science and Law*, No. 1, 2003.

Liang Huixing, "Interpretation, Comment and Suggestion of the *General Provisions of Civil Law (Draft)*", *Journal of East China University of Political Science and Law*, No. 5, 2016.

Wang Zhu, "The Legislative Procedure to Formulate Civil Code in the Mode of Codification of Nonbasic Law", Peking University Law Journal, No. 6, 2014.

Wang Yi, "Legislative Suggest of System of Validity of Juristic Act", *Journal of Comparative Law*, No. 2, 2016.

Yao Baohua, Wang Zhu, "Interpretation and Application of the item 2 of paragraph 1 of article 76 of the *Road Traffic Safety Law* (Newly Amended Version)", *People's Justice*, No. 15, 2008.

Chapter 12
Setting of Chapter "Obligation and Liabilities" in the *General Provisions Volume of Civil Code* for Providing the System "General Provisions of Obligation Law"

In order to complete the compilation of *Civil Code* as quickly as possible and avoid the abandon of such work before it is almost completed, the legislative mode of the system of "general provisions of obligation law" is a major issue which must be settled. Is it necessary to enact the general provisions of obligation law[1]? If necessary, which general provisions of obligation law will be incorporated into the *Civil Code*? Which legislative technique will be used to incorporate such rules into the *Civil Code*? In the opinion of the Writer, they are three interlinked but different questions, among which "Will it be written?" is a necessity question, "What will be written?" is a selection question, and "How will it be written?" is a technique question. Hereinafter, taking the legislative mode of "general provisions of obligation law" as an example, the "pragmatic thinking" for the compilation of *Civil Code* held by the Writer is shown for reference by the Legislature.

12.1 Will It Be Written?—Necessity for Providing the General Provisions of Obligation Law

12.1.1 Three Phases of Discussion on Legislative Mode of the General Provisions of Obligation Law

Taking the deliberation of the 2002 *Civil Law (draft)* and the adoption of the *Tort Liability Law* at the end of 2009 as indicators, the exploration into legislative mode of general provisions of obligation law in the course of fourth drafting of *Civil Code* can be divided into three main phases.

---

[1]The Writer uses the "general rules of obligation law" to refer to the essential general provisions of obligation law, so as to avoid the conclusion advancement. Meanwhile, this term is also different from "General Provisions" Chapter of "General Provisions of Obligation Law" Volume in the "Civil Code" draft submitted by the scholar.

© China University of Political Science and Law Press 2020
Z. Wang, *On the Constitutionality of Compiling a Civil Code of China*,
https://doi.org/10.1007/978-981-13-7900-0_12

12.1.1.1   *2002 Civil Law (Draft)* Phase (About 2003): Difference Between Legislative Ideal and Actuality of the General Provisions of Obligation Law

The *2002 Civil Law (draft)* does not provide the general provisions of obligation law, for which the interpretation given by the Legislature is that: "As for the basic concepts of obligation, there shall be the corresponding principles. If the *General Provisions of Obligation Law* is to be enacted, the largest problem is that many contents of the *General Provisions of Obligation Law* will duplicate the general provisions of the *Contract Law*. ... The most basic provisions of obligation, including the causes of obligation and the validity of obligation are firstly written in the Chapter 'Civil Rights' of the *General Provisions of Civil Law*."[2] With respect to this treatment, the opinion of the scholars holding negative attitude is especially outstanding. For example, some scholars regarded it as "a thoroughly loose and assembly mode whereby the current laws are incorporated without any change", and believed that the *Volume of General Provisions of Obligatory Right* should be set up so as to lead the *Contract Volume* and the *Tort Liability Volume* and further improve the system of obligatory right.[3] Some scholars participating in drafting of the *Contract Law* have stated that, the general provisions of the *Contract Law* are the products under particular historical conditions; since the *Civil Code* and the *Obligation Code* could not be enacted within several years at that time, it was decided that the general provisions of the *Contract Law* would temporarily play the role of the *General Provisions of Obligation Law* to a certain extent, and contain some systems and norms which are beyond its boundary and essentially belong to the *General Provisions of Obligation Law*; it was also decided that, once the *Civil Code* and *Obligation Code* are enacted, the systems and norms which belong to the *General Provisions of Obligation Law* should be returned. At the moment when the *Civil Code* is to be enacted, the above-mentioned commitment should be performed.[4] However, from the viewpoint that the *Tort Liability Law* is enacted separately, some other scholars accept this legislative mode whereby the *General Provisions of Obligation Law* will be cancelled.[5] The subsequent legislative practice reveals that, the foreshadowing about the separate enactment of the *Tort Liability Law* has been laid in the *2002 Civil Law (draft)*, and the legislature thus stated that "We should draft the general provisions of contract law and the general provisions of tort liability law, and then further improve the provisions of negotiorum gestio and unjustified enrichment. As a result, the issue about obligation will be basically settled.",[6] which reflects a pragmatic treatment under the circumstance

---

[2]Wang (2003a).
[3]Liang (2003).
[4]Cui (2003).
[5]Qin (2003).
[6]Wang (2003b).

that it is difficult for the Legislature to select the legislative mode of general provisions of obligation law.

12.1.1.2   Pre-*Tort Liability Law* Phase (Before 2009): Game Playing Between the *General Provisions of Obligation Law* and the *Tort Liability Law*

The "unconstitutional event" of the *Real Rights Law* has delayed the drafting of the *Tort Liability Law* for about two years.[7] This delay in legislative works has brought about a new round of debate over the issue whether the tort law should be enacted separately. Against this background, some scholars, taking the opinion that there is no sufficient reason to separate the tort law from obligation law system as one of the main grounds of argument, believe that the *General Provisions of Obligation Law* should be enacted.[8] Some other scholars also list the tort as one of the cause of obligation, and believe that the obligatory right law should adopt the three-volume legislative structure, including the general provisions of obligatory law, contract law and obligation arising from causes other than contract.[9] At present, the debate on the issue whether the *General Provisions of Obligation Law* should be separately enacted has essentially become the game playing with the issue whether the *Tort Liability Law* should be enacted separately, among which one has to be selected. The academic and theoretical demonstration has completed its historical mission, and then the Legislature has to make a political decision.

12.1.1.3   Post-*Tort Liability Law* Phase (After 2009): "Deformalization" and "Essentialization" of General Provisions of Obligation Law

Finally, the tort law of China is titled as "the *Tort Liability Law*", and no wording relating to "obligation" is contained in any article. This has brought forth a new challenge for the enactment of *General Provisions of Obligation Law*. Under the circumstance that both the *Contract Law* and the *Tort Liability Law* contain general provisions, if the *General Provisions of Obligation Law* is still provided in details, just like that of traditional continental law, a lot of norms will be inevitably duplicated.[10] The formal *General Provisions of Obligation Law* has become less important, and this phenomenon is called by the Writer as the deformalization of general provisions of obligation law. In addition, owing to the fact that the *Contract Law* and the *Tort Liability Law* have been separately enacted, the demands on

---

[7]About the main dispute and solution, see Wang (2006).

[8]Liu (2007a).

[9]Yang (2007).

[10]Wang (2009a).

general provisions of obligation law as well as provisions for relationship between them and negotiorum gestio/unjustified enrichment are becoming more and more outstanding. This phenomenon is called by the Writer as "essentialization" of general provisions of obligation law. The "deformalization" and "essentialization" of general provisions of obligation law are embodied in the trend that the legislative modes available for general provisions of obligation law have become less and less, and from the pragmatic viewpoint, the turn point that the aesthetics gives place to practicability has emerged.

12.1.2 Impossibility to Cancel the Concept of Obligation

With respect to the issue whether the concept of obligation should be cancelled form the civil law of China, fierce debate has occurred in the course of drafting of *General Principles of the Civil Law*[11] and in the course of drafting of *Civil Code*.[12] The Writer believes that, this debate can't be argued theoretically, because the theoretical divergence can't be settled by the theory itself. From the viewpoint of pragmatic thinking, whether the concept of obligation should be retained must be considered on the basis of legislative costs and social costs.

On the basis of the study carried out by the Writer, except for the terms such as "treasury bond", "bond" and "debt" which are not obligation within the meaning of civil law, in the currently valid laws of China,[13] the concept relating to obligation within the meaning of the civil law are widely used in 36 laws in the following fields: The first is that among the components of the future *Civil Code*, the *Real Rights Law*, the *Contract Law*, the *Marriage Law* and the *Succession Law* involve the relationship between obligatory right and obligation. The *Law of the Application of Law for Foreign-related Civil Relations* uses "obligatory right" as title of Chapter 6. The second is that, in the commercial law field, Article 16 of the *Law of China People's Bank* gives provisions on lawful currency in repayment of obligation; Chapter 7 "Takeover and Termination" of the *Commercial Bank Law* involves a lot of provisions relating to bank obligation; Paragraph 3 of Article 10 of the *Accounting Law* expressly provides that accounting formalities shall be gone through and final accounting should be carried out for "occurrence and settlement of obligatory rights and obligations"; the *Negotiable Instrument Law* and the *Securities Law* also involve a lot of provisions relating to obligatory right and obligation. The third is that in the civil procedure law field, the *Civil Procedure Law* provides the relationship between obligatory rights and obligations in the aspects of recovery of obligation, notarized instrument of obligatory right, payment order, repayment of heritage and execution of obligation. Article 37 of the

---

[11]Tong (1996).

[12]Liang (2003).

[13]About the scope of current valid law, see Wang (2011c).

Notarization Law gives specific provisions on compulsory execution of notarized instrument of obligatory right. The fourth is that the rules for undertaking of outward liabilities and apportionment of inward liabilities for entity-type civil subject and its members contain a lot of issues about relationship between obligatory rights and obligations, and involve the *Company Law*, the *Partnership Enterprise Law*, the *Sole Proprietorship Enterprise Law*, the *Law on Chinese-foreign Contractual Joint Ventures*, the *Securities Investment Fund Law*, the *Trust Law*, the *Certified Public Accountant Law*, the *Lawyer Law* and the *Law on Specialized Farmer Cooperatives*. The fifth is that the issue about tax priority in bankruptcy liquidation is mainly linked with the treatment of relationship between obligatory rights and obligations, which takes the *Law on the Administration of Tax Collection* as center, and involves the *Enterprise Bankruptcy Law*, the *Partnership Enterprise Law*, the *Sole Proprietorship Enterprise Law*, the *Insurance Law*, the *Trust Law* and the *Non-governmental Education Promotion Law*. The sixth is that the guaranty system is also mainly linked with treatment o f obligations, which takes the *Real rights law* and the *Guarantee Law* as center, and also involves the *Urban Real Estate Administration Law*, the *Civil Aviation Law* and the *Maritime Law* as well as relevant international conventions participated in by our country. The seventh is that, as another basic law within the meaning of the *Constitution*, Article 60 of the *Criminal Code* provides the priority between confiscation of properties and proper obligation, and the concept of obligation is also involved in specific crimes provided in Articles 162, 169 and 238. The eighth is that, the *Organic Law of Villagers Committee*, the *Law on State-owned Assets of Enterprise*, the *Law on Industrial Enterprises Owned by the Whole People*, the *Corporate Income Law* and the *Anti-Unfair Competition Law* also use the term of obligation in civil law meaning. It is thus clear that, the concepts "obligatory right", "obligation", "obligatory right holder" and "obligor" are widely used in the civil laws and regulations enacted after *General Principles of the Civil Law*.[14] From the viewpoint of pragmatic thinking, during the compilation of *Civil Code*, attention should be paid to the coordination with current legal system. Therefore, it is impossible to cancel the concept of obligation in the field of legislation.

Starting with the *Circular on Protection of Obligatory Rights of State-owned Banks* issued in 1951, the supreme judicial organ has always used the concepts "obligatory right" and "obligation" in various judicial documents. There are more than 100 judicial interpretations and other normative documents of which the title contains the term "obligation", and there are more than 600 judicial interpretation and other normative documents of which the text uses such term.[15] In addition,

---

[14]Liang (2003).

[15]According to the retrieval statistics of "pkulaw.cn", the retrieval time was December 31, 2011. The retrieval aims to explain the extensive use of "obligation", the invalid judicial interpretations and other normative documents are not excluded.

against the background that the general provisions of obligation law have not been improved for long time, the trend that the concepts "obligatory right" and "obligation" are taken as the core concepts of judicial interpretation has become more and more obvious, and the most obvious embodiment is the provisions in Article 1 of the *Provisions of Supreme People's Court on Several Issues Relating to Application of Limitation of action System In Trial of Civil Cases (F.SH. (2008) No. 11)*: "The party concerned may give the limitation of action-based defense for claim for obligatory right, but as for the limitation of action-based defense given for the following claim for obligatory right, the people's court shall not give support: ......" In the actual trial practice, let us take the cases published in the *Bulletin of Supreme People's Court* as an example. From the first issue in 1985 to Issue 12 in 2016, there are a total of 242 issues, which publish 1063 cases (including criminal cases and administrative cases) and use the concept "obligation" for 7,373 times, slightly less than 8,549 times for the concept "property", and 6.9 times for every case in average. Though such figures are not precise, they from one side prove the judgment made by scholars that "The concepts such as obligatory right and obligation are the basis for judges and lawyers to carry out legal thinking, analyze cases and judge cases".[16] From the viewpoint of pragmatic thinking, the drafting of *Civil Code* should make it convenient for laws to be applied, and pay attention to settlement of actual issues. Therefore, there is impossibility to cancel the concept "obligation" in actual practice.

12.1.3   Necessity to Provide General Provisions of Obligation Law

There is demand on the general provisions of obligation law at different legal levels:

Firstly, at the obligation law level, the general provisions of obligation law are required for settling the relationship among various obligations. As mentioned above, in the current legal system of China, there are a lot of provisions about obligation, the economic life to be dealt with by such provisions is more diversified and complicated, and its core is the general provisions for equality of properties in transfer and the priority of obligatory right in repayment. In addition, the general provisions of obligation law are also the necessary system for settlement of issues about non-typical obligation in actual practice.[17] Even if the Legislature has to avoid the use of concept "obligation", it also must create a term similar to "properties ownership and property rights relating to properties ownership" in *General Principles of the Civil Law*. Nowadays when there is no problem about whether a legal term is "socialist or capitalist", it is really easy to realize such creation.

---

[16]Chen (2003).

[17]About this issue, see Liu (2006, 2007b, 2008).

Secondly, at the level of civil code, the general provisions of obligation law are required by the abstract and generalized legislative techniques.[18] No matter whether the structure "general provisions—specific provisions" proposed by the realistic thinking or the structure "general provisions—specific provisions—liabilities" proposed by the pragmatic thinking is adopted, the future *Civil Code* of China will surely adopt the abstract and generalized legislative techniques. In addition to the legal terms used to express various systems of obligation law, the general provisions of obligation law are also required to settle the relationship between obligation law and real rights law, so as to jointly constitute the objects of property law, and accept the adjustment to systems in the *General Provisions of Civil Law* such as juristic act, agency and limitation of action.

Thirdly, in the field of civil and commercial laws, the general provisions of obligation law are required to promote the integration between the rules of civil law and the rules of commercial law.[19] In China, *General Principles of the Civil Law*, the *General Provisions of Civil Law*, the *Contract Law*, the *Real Rights Law* and the *Law of the Application of Law for Foreign-related Civil Relations* adopt the legislative style whereby civil and commercial rules are integrated. It can be expected that, the future *Civil Code* will also adopt the legislative style whereby civil and commercial rules are integrated. The rules of obligation law extensively exist in civil field and commercial field, and the guaranty system, bankruptcy system and obligation discharge system for entity-type civil subject are especially important in actual practice. The general provisions of obligation law will also be enacted by using the legislative style whereby civil and commercial rules are integrated, so as to drive the essential integration of civil rules and commercial rules in civil and commercial law field of China.

According to pragmatic thinking, from the obligation law level to the whole civil and commercial law level, the general provisions of obligation law are indispensable and irreplaceable. If it is compulsorily required not to provide the general provisions of obligation law, various obligation-related systems in legislation can't be easily applied, so that a lot of judicial interpretations have to be used to provide various general provisions of obligation law in actual practice, and finally the general provisions of obligation law will become "judicial interpretation" and the authoritativeness and unitary of legal rules will reduce. Frankly speaking, the general provisions of obligation law are indispensable, and it is advised to directly provide them in the *Civil Code* rather than force the supreme judicial organ to draft "judicial interpretation for obligation law".

---

[18]See Cui (2003).
[19]Wang (2009a).

12.2 What Should Be Written?—Contents Selectivity of the General Provisions of Obligation Law

12.2.1 Two Legislative Scope Mode for the General Provisions of Obligation Law

The existing legislative draft of general provisions of obligation law and the comments given by scholars reveal that, the academic circle has brought forth two legislative modes for the general provisions of obligation law, namely "large and comprehensive general provisions of obligation law" and "small and simple general provisions of obligation law".

The "large and comprehensive general provisions of obligation law" is represented by Professor Liang Huixing. In the *Volume of General Provisions of Obligation Law of Civil Code (draft)* presided over by him, 7 chapters including "General Provisions", "Cause of Obligation", "Type of Obligation", "Performance of Obligation", "Preservation of Obligation", "Modification and Transfer of Obligation" and "Elimination of Obligation" are designed,[20] covering all general provisions of obligation law in civil code in traditional continental legal system.

The "small and simple general provisions of obligation law" is represented by Professor Wang Liming. In the *Volume of General Provisions of Obligation Law of Civil Code (draft)* presided over by him, 6 chapters including "General Provisions of Obligation", "Generation of Obligation", "Type of Obligation", "Preservation of Obligation", "Transfer of Obligation" and "Elimination of Obligation" are designed.[21] For this scope mode, the main consideration is to simplify the contents of general provisions of obligatory right, only provide the common rules in obligation law field, incorporate the rules which are beyond the contract field and the rules which are generally applied to various types of obligations into the *General Provisions of Obligatory Law*, still keep those rules which are only applied to contract field in the general provisions of contract law, and in principle, retain the general provisions of the *Contract Law* of China.[22]

12.2.2 Actual Needs to Be Settled by the General Provisions of Obligation Law

The above-mentioned two legislative modes for general provisions of obligation law cover most of the rules which must be contained in the *General Provisions of Obligation Law*. However, in light of the actuality of civil legislation and the

---

[20]Liang (2004).

[21]See Wang (2005b).

[22]Wang (2009a).

demands on legal application in China, the Writer believes that, in addition to the common contents of general provisions of obligation law in continental legal system, the general provisions of obligation law in the future *Civil Code* of China should also settle the following legislative demands with Chinese characteristics:

First, the demands on generalization of the obligation of damage compensation or the liabilities of damage compensation. Though there is controversy on whether the obligation relationship is necessarily property relationship,[23] as the core concepts for protection on civil rights, the relationship between the obligation of damage and the liabilities of damage compensation is a general issue which must be settled by the future *Civil Code*. It is provided in Article 84 of *General Principles of the Civil Law* that "The obligation is the particular right and obligation relationship between parties concerned, which is generated in accordance with the provisions of contract or law", but the section "Obligatory Right" does not provide tort as a cause of obligation, but only provide contract, unjustified enrichment and negotiorum gestio as three causes of obligation. In the part "Civil Liabilities", the consequence of breach and consequence of tort are provided as civil liabilities. In the *Contract Law*, though the generation of contractual obligation and the liabilities for breach are provided together, just like the *Tort Liability Law* which was enacted later, the relationship between the obligation of damage compensation and liabilities of damage compensation has not been settled. This legislative actuality leads to the necessity to generalize the relationship between the obligation of damage compensation and the liabilities of damage compensation.

Second, the demands on generalization of the coopetition of liabilities of damage compensation or the coopetition of obligation of damage compensation. Though the "civil liabilities" are provided in centralized manner in Chapter 6 of *General Principles of the Civil Law,* the coopetition rule for liabilities is omitted. This heavy task was undertaken by Article 122 of the *Contract Law* later. This is really a transitional treatment, and can be proven by the legislative treatment that no similar provision is given in the *Tort Liability Law*. Frankly speaking, during the compilation of *Civil Code*, it is necessary to restore such rule into a general rule. However, the generalization of such rule was not completed in two main drafts of the *Civil Code*. In the *Draft of Civil Code* presided over by Professor Liang Huixing, the concurrence rules for liabilities take the tort liabilities as center, and are provided in Article 1563 of the *Tort Volume*, including the concurrence rules for tort liabilities, breach behavior, unjustified enrichment, negotiorum gestio and claim for real right.[24] In the *Draft of Civil Code* presided over by Professor Wang Liming, the legislative mode of the *Contract Law* is adopted, and the concurrence rules for liabilities are provided in Article 1351 of the *Contract Volume*.[25] In addition, Article 287 of the *General Provision Volume* also provides the concurrence rules for liabilities, but in light of the adjacent Article 285 "Generation of Civil

---

[23]Cui (2003).

[24]Liang (2004, p. 31).

[25]See Wang (2005b, p. 311).

Liabilities", such rules are the concurrence rules for liabilities which take the tort liabilities as center.[26] The above-mentioned two treatments for non-general rules are obviously different from the orientation that the four causes of obligation are taken as general provisions of obligation law, and the selection which must be made in legislation is to, on the basis of the orientation of relationship between the obligation of damage compensation and liabilities of damage compensation, provide the coopetition of liabilities of damage compensation or coopetition of obligation of damage compensation, but there is no legislative legitimacy to take them as rules of tort law or contract law and then incorporate them into other parts of obligation law. From the viewpoint of pragmatic thinking, it is necessary to generalize such concurrence rules.

Third, the demands on generalization of relationship between multi-party obligation and multi-party liabilities. What may be ignored is the issue about multi-party obligation and multi-party liabilities. With respect to this issue, Professor QIU Congzhi has specially pointed out that, it can't be said that there is no room for discussion over the issue whether the joint and several liabilities provided in the *Civil Code of Taiwan* are joint and several obligations or unreal joint and several obligations.[27] This issue is especially outstanding in the civil law of China.[28] Article 87 of *General Principles of the Civil Law* provides the joint and several obligations, but the general provisions for joint and several liabilities are not provided in the Chapter "Civil Liabilities". Article 13 and Article 14 of the *Tort Liability Law* give detailed provisions on rules for outward undertaking and inward apportionment of joint and several liabilities. Owing to the abstract legislative techniques of the *Civil Code*, it is impossible for the future *Civil Code* to provide that the case of joint and several liabilities apply the *Tort Liability Law*, therefore there will be the demands on generalization of relationship between multi-party obligation and multi-party liabilities in the part of general rules.

Fourth, the demands on generalization of non-damage compensation civil liabilities. Article 134 of *General Principles of the Civil Law* of China creates the legislative style whereby the civil liabilities are provided in a centralized manner, which has won unanimous applause from the academic circles at home and abroad. In the course of compilation of *Civil Code*, however, there is secret worry on retention or cancellation of this legislative style. The *Contract Law* and the *Real Rights Law* adopt the legislative strategy whereby this issue is evaded. While providing the damage compensation liabilities, they also provide other civil liabilities, but don't expressly enumerate the type of liabilities. Article 15 of the *Tort Liability Law* adopts the mode whereby the typical contract liabilities are excluded and other liabilities are expressly enumerated. With respect to the legislative mode of future *Civil Code*, it is necessary to generalize the non-damage compensation civil liabilities in the general provisions; otherwise, it will be very difficult to

---

[26]See Wang (2005b, pp. 505, 510).

[27]Qiu (2004, p. 394).

[28]See Wang (2011a).

understand that, as the civil liabilities extensively existing in various volumes of future *Civil Code*, why the damage compensation liabilities can be generalized, while other civil liabilities may not be generalized.

12.2.3 Selection of Contents of the General Provisions of Obligation Law

As for selection of contents of the general provisions of obligation law, the Writer believes that the contents may be divided into three parts, namely the main part of general provisions of obligation law, the answer to the above-mentioned demands of generalization as well as those which do not need to be provided as general provisions of obligation law. The latter is mainly the issue about priority rules for obligations.

In essence, the above-mentioned two scope modes of general provisions of obligation law are the issue about selection of main part of general provisions of obligation law. The difference between these two modes is mainly embodied in the situation that, as compared with the draft of *Volume of General Provisions of Obligation Law* presided over by Professor Liang Huixing, the draft presided over by Professor Wang Liming does not contain the chapter "Performance of Obligation" and the contents about "modification of obligation", which are accordingly retained in the *Contract Volume*. This difference reflects two thinkings on settlement of duplicated contents between the *General Provisions of Obligation Law* and the *Contract Law*. From the viewpoint of pragmatic thinking, in consideration of the "deformalization" and "essentialization" of general provisions of obligation law in China, the "small and simple general provisions of obligation law" always preserve to a relatively high extent the *Contract Law* which has been separately enacted, involve less change to current laws, and make the judicial application more convenient. As a result, the Writer is more inclined to adopt this mode.

With respect to the above-mentioned issue about demands of generalization which must be settled, the Writer believes that, in the future, the general provisions of obligation law should give the following answer: Firstly, the four main causes of obligation should be provided. It is necessary to take tort as a cause of obligation, determine the types of obligations which involve tort damage compensation, and provide the tort damage compensation liabilities as the general guaranty for tort damage compensation obligation,[29] so as to settle the issue about relationship between obligation of damage compensation and liabilities of damage compensation. From the viewpoint of pragmatic thinking, the position of unjustified enrichment and negotiorum gestio system is not the key issue, but these two systems must be provided. The Writer agrees with the causes of obligation as provided in the *General Provisions of Civil Law,* and disagrees with the advice proposed by some scholars to place the negotiorum gestio and unjustified enrichment in

---

[29]Cui (2003).

contract-related provisions as semi-contract,[30] so as to meet the independence requirement of such two special obligations,[31] increase the coverage of these two systems in the *Civil Code*, and thus fully realize the functions of these two systems.[32]

Secondly, the concurrence rules for civil liabilities should be provided. On the basis that four causes of obligation are provided in the general provisions of obligation law, and from the viewpoint of pragmatic thinking, it is necessary to clarify the concurrence rules for various civil liabilities, so as to get in line with the general thoughts for search and application of laws. With respect to rules, it is necessary to contain the application rules for liabilities corresponding to non-typical obligations, and maintain the openness of obligation and liability systems.

Thirdly, the joint and several obligations should be replaced by the joint and several liabilities, and the unified provisions on claim for apportionment and claim for recovery should be given. Though Article 87 of *General Principles of the Civil Law* of China gives provisions on joint and several obligatory rights and joint and several obligations, in actual practice, the joint and several obligatory rights seldom occurs, and the concept "joint and several obligatory rights" has never been used in any case published in the *Bulletin of Supreme People's Court*. This is because that, though the joint and several obligations do not have the name of guaranty, it has the essence of guaranty. Thus, the joint and several obligations have been commonly applied, becoming the core of multi-party obligation.[33] Then, is the "joint and several obligations" or the "joint and several liabilities" used in actual practice? By Issue 12 in 2016, in the cases published in the *Bulletin of Supreme People's Court*, the term "joint and several liabilities" has been used for 438 times, while the "joint and several obligations" has only been used for 8 times, involving five cases.[34] Through inspection by the Writer, the "joint and several obligations" in 8 uses can be replaced by "joint and several liabilities". Therefore, it can be said without exaggeration that, even if the concept "joint and several obligations" does not exist, no obstacle will emerge in judicial practice. In laws and relevant judicial

---

[30]Qin (2003).

[31]Wang (2009a).

[32]Xu (2010).

[33]Qiu (2004, p. 395).

[34]These five cases are as follows: "Appeal Case of Notes Cashing Dispute between Qingdao AUCMA Group Sales Company and Lijin Sub-branch of Bank of China", the *Bulletin of Supreme People's Court*, No. 4, 2000; "Dispute Case of Late Payment of Ocean Freight and Port Surcharges in the Lawsuit Lodged by COSCO against Hong Kong Meitong, Tianjin Meitong", the *Bulletin of Supreme People's Court*, No. 4, 2002; "Appeal Case of Bill of Lading Infringement Dispute in the Lawsuit Lodged by HYOSUNG (HK) LTD. against Fangchenggang Company of China Marine Shipping Agency Co., Ltd.", the *Bulletin of Supreme People's Court*, No. 2, 2003; "Construction Contract Dispute Case of Construction Engineering in the Lawsuit Lodged by ShenYANG Chemical Co., Ltd. against Benxi Thermal Power Plant", the *Bulletin of Supreme People's Court*, No. 3, 2005; "Dispute Case of Bankruptcy Creditor's Rights Confirmation between Shenzhen Peiqi Import and Export Trade Co., Ltd. and Yichang Nanhu Sub-branch of Hubei Bank Corporation Limited, and Huacheng Investment Management Co., Ltd.", the *Bulletin of Supreme People's Court*, No. 12, 2012.

interpretations, the provisions relating to relationship between joint and several obligatory rights and obligations are mainly concentrated in civil property relationship field and bankruptcy law field. In the civil property relationship field, Article 102 of the *Real Rights Law* provides the relationship between joint and several obligatory rights and obligation for co-ownership, Article 90 of the *Contract Law* provides the relationship between joint and several obligatory right and obligation involved in division and merger of entity-type civil subjects, Article 17 of the *Provisions of Supreme People's Court on Several Issues Relating to Application of Limitation of action System In Trial of Civil Cases* provides the interruption of limitation of action for joint and several right holder and obligor, and the *Reply on Issue about Legal Application in Case Chao Caifeng et al. vs Xu Li* ([1993] M.T.Z. No. 3) issued by the Supreme People's Court provides the joint and several obligors for joint obligations of couple. These provisions are rare, and are attached to other civil legal systems, so that it is totally unnecessary to be provided in the general provisions of obligation law in the future. In the bankruptcy law field, however, they may appear as special rules. It is thus clear that, in judicial practice and legislation of China, the term "joint and several obligatory right" has almost never been used, and few provisions about "joint and several obligations" are either special provisions or can be replaced by "joint and several liabilities". The term "joint and several liabilities" is the mainstream in judicial practice, laws and judicial interpretations. From the viewpoint of pragmatic thinking, the Writer is inclined to replace the joint and several obligations with joint and several liabilities, and on this basis, clarify the difference between claim for apportionment and claim for recovery.[35]

Fourthly, the non-damage compensation liabilities should be enumerated in a centralized manner. Since the mode of centralized enumeration of civil liabilities in Article 134 of *General Principles of the Civil Law* has achieved good effect in judicial practice, it is advised by the Writer to enumerate the non-damage compensation liabilities in a centralized manner in the future. The key points ate as follows: The first is that, since the elimination of effect and restoration of reputation can be distinguished, they should be divided into two forms of civil liabilities; the second is that, injunction can be applied for ceasing the infringement, removing the obstacles[36] and eliminating the dangers; the third is that the forms of liabilities should be arranged in the order of specific provisions of the future *Civil Code*: firstly provide the elimination of effect, restoration of reputation and apology for claim for personality rights, and then provide the return of properties and restoration of original state for claim for real rights, and finally provide repair, rework, replacement[37] and compensation for breach as contract liabilities.

---

[35]Wang (2010).

[36]See Wang and Li (2011b).

[37]Repair, rework, replacement are the typical liabilities for breach, article 36 of the *Real Rights Law* confuses them with restoration of original state, which should be corrected in the future *Civil Code*.

The equality is the general attribute of obligation. Therefore, the needs of actual practice are satisfied by providing priority rules for various obligations, mainly including various guaranty rights and legal priority, among which the treatment of priority of taxes is relatively difficult. With respect to the issue whether taxes should be embodied as an obligation in private laws, there has been controversy in tax law circle over recent years.[38] The civil law circle has also begun to think whether it is necessary to provide the tax obligation in the *General Provisions of Obligation Law*.[39] The civil law circle in China has not attached sufficient importance to the meaning of tax in private laws for long time, so that the positive answer should be given in the course of compilation of *Civil Code*. Paragraph 2 of Article 21 of *General Principles of the Civil Law* provides "The taxes, obligations and other expenses payable by the missing person shall be paid by the administrator of the properties of the missing person.", but does not provide the priority among taxes, obligations and other expenses. The provisions about limited succession in Article 33 of the *Succession Law* also fail to provide the priority between taxes and obligations, and it is only provided in Article 34 that they are prior to heritage. Thereafter, the *1992 Law on Administration of Tax Collection* also failed to give provisions on such issue, and till such law was amended in 2001, the provisions "In case the tax authority collects taxes, the tax shall be prior to unsecured obligatory right, unless otherwise provided by laws; where the taxes payable by tax payer accrued before the relevant properties are pledged or mortgaged, the taxes shall be executed prior to pledge right and mortgage right." were added into Paragraph 1 of Article 45. The Writer believes that, various guaranty rights and legal priority, including tax priority, are the breakthrough in equality of obligations and are special rules. From the viewpoint of pragmatic thinking, the Writer is inclined not to provide these special rules in the *General Provisions of Obligation Law*.

12.3   How Will It Be Written?—Technical Nature of the General Provisions of Obligation Law

12.3.1   Form and Essence: Relationship Between the General Provisions of Obligation Law and the General Provisions of Obligation Law

The Writer has always used the term "general provisions of obligation law" to indicate the essential general provisions of obligation law and carry out analysis, and the Writer agrees to establish the essential general provisions of obligation law. The Writer hereby hopes to answer the technique question about enactment of general provisions of obligation law. If those opinions which actually demonstrate

---

[38]About the controversy in tax law, see Zhai (2005) and Wang (2005a).
[39]See Wang (2012) and Liu (2008).

the necessity to enact the essential general provisions of obligation law are excluded, there are only two main arguments on enactment of formal *General Provisions of Obligation Law*: The first is that the establishment of *General Provisions of Obligation Law* is the common practice in civil code of most countries (regions)[40]; the second is that the *General Provisions of Obligation Law* should be accordingly established after the concept "obligatory right" is retained.[41]

The Writer believes that, these two arguments are not sufficient to support the necessity to enact the *General Provisions of Obligation Law*. As for the first argument, when discussing over the setting of *General Provisions of Obligation Law*, the scholars often use comparative method to demonstrate the necessity to adopt this legislative mode in China, but fail to see the background of such legislative mode. The special drafting mode for *Civil Code* in China whereby the wholesale is changed to retail has greatly reduced the significance of this international practice. Frankly speaking, as for the enactment of *General Provisions of Obligation Law*, the convincingness of comparative study is limited.[42] As for the second argument, though the general provisions of obligation law are linked with the concept "obligatory right", they are in mutually-dependent relationship, but respectively have meaning. What can lead the whole obligation law is the concept "obligatory right" rather than the *General Provisions of Obligation Law*.[43] Even if the *General Provisions of Obligation Law* is not established in the *Civil Code*, this does not mean that the concepts "obligatory right" and "obligation" are abolished, because the obligatory right and obligation are not only the products of legal system and legal thinking, but also the purpose and contents of transactions which are well known and indispensable in commodity economy society.[44] The causes of obligation are diversified, and the so-called *General Provisions of Obligation Law* are only the embodiment of common characteristics of complicated relationship among obligations.[45] Therefore, there is no wonder why some scholars believe that the *General Provisions of Obligation Law* are not an independent part, so that it is not appropriate to set up a separate volume.[46]

Therefore, the essential general provisions of obligation law will not be enacted only through formal *General Provisions of Obligation Law*, and it can also be embodied through coverage of other legislative process. From the viewpoint of pragmatic thinking, this embodiment mode at least includes two key points: the first is that essential general provisions of obligation law must be generally enacted

---

[40]Liu (2007a).

[41]Chen (2003).

[42]Similar to the Writer's opinion, see Xu (2010).

[43]Qin and Ma (2003).

[44]Ma and Cao 2003).

[45]Liu (2007c).

[46]Liu (2002).

rather than be lowered to the specific provisions of civil law; the second is that the legislative costs of essential general provisions of obligation law are acceptable by the Legislature.

12.3.2 No Legislative Possibility to the Mode "Three-Volume Obligation"

The integration of form and essence is always better. Let's first explore into the possibility to realize the essential general provisions of obligation law through formal *General Provisions of Obligation Law*. The academic circle proposed two legislative mode "three- volume obligation". The first mode is to, on the basis of the provisions of Section 2 "Obligatory Right" of Chapter 5 and Chapter 6 "Civil Liabilities" of *General Principles of the Civil Law*, design t*he Volume of General Provisions of Obligation Law*, the *Contract Volume* and the *Tort Volume* of the *Civil Code*, and let the *Volume of General Provisions of Obligation Law* lead the *Contract Volume* and the *Tort Volume*.[47] This mode places the *Contract Volume* and the *Tort Volume* at the same level, and places the unjustified enrichment and negotiorum gestio into the *Volume of General Provisions of Obligation Law*. The other mode divides the obligation law in civil code into three volumes: *Volume of General Provisions of Obligation Law*, the *Contract Volume*, and *Volume of Obligation arising from Causes other than Contract*. In Volume 3, the obligation of unilateral promise, the obligation of negotiorum gestio, the obligation of unjustified enrichment and the obligation of tort should be provided.[48] This mode comprehensively considers the logical, aesthetic and practicable factors, and highlights the leading nature of the *Contract Law* in the general provisions of obligation law.

Regretfully, under the pragmatic thinking, no "three- volume obligation" can be enacted, and the main reasons are as follows: Firstly, the problems which must be settled by the "three-volume obligation" are the problems about codification, and in consideration of the increasingly-reduced standing of civil code and the deliberation ability of Legislature of China, it is impossible to enact such volumes, and such attempt will lead to a more incomplete *General Principles of Civil Law*, which is not favorable for the final codification; secondly, in legal application, the *General Provisions of Obligation Law*, as a volume other than *General Provisions of the Civil Code*, other volumes are permitted to be referred to it rather than applied to it, which will increase the difficulty in application of laws; finally, only the combination of *Contract Law Volume* and *Tort Volume* will become the specific provisions of obligation law corresponding to the *Volume of General Provisions of*

---

[47]See Liang (2001).
[48]Yang (2007).

Obligation Law. This "general provisions–specific provisions" structure which is expressed by using three volumes will adversely affect the structure of the *Civil Code* as a whole.[49]

12.3.3   Inspiration from Establishment of Legislative Mode for Civil Liabilities in General Principles of the Civil Law

The civil liabilities in the first drafting of *Civil Code* in PRC were centered around the obligation of damage compensation. The relevant title in the *First Deliberation Draft 1 of Obligation Volume* is "obligation arising from tort", the relevant title in *First Deliberation Draft 2 of Obligation Volume* is "obligation arising from damage of other persons", the relevant title in *First Deliberation Draft 2A of Obligation Volume* is "obligation arising from tort", and the title in another draft *First Deliberation Draft 3 for Damage Compensation* is "damage compensation (obligation arising from tort) [third draft]".[50]

The second drafting of *Civil Code* in PRC did not involve the issue about civil liabilities, while the third drafting of *Civil Code* embodied the trend of integration between civil sanction and damage compensation.[51] It is provided in Article 67 of Chapter 7 "Civil Sanctions" of Volume 1 "General Provisions" of the *Third Deliberation Draft 1 of the Civil Law* that: "When the civil rights of a citizen or legal person are infringed upon, the people's court, arbitration institution or other state organ may provide protection by applying the civil sanction method provided in this Chapter." Article 68 enumerates six civil sanctions, namely fine, confiscation of illegal gains, compensation for loss, statement of repentance, apologizing and notice of criticism. The provisions in Article 69 "The civil sanction methods provided in preceding article may be applied separately, and also may be applied together" are the embryo of Paragraph 2 of Article 134 of *General Principles of the Civil Law*. The provisions in Article 70 "The application of civil sanction method will not preclude the administrative punishment or criminal liabilities imposed on law-breaker in accordance with laws" are the embryo of Paragraph 3 of Article 134 of *General Principles of the Civil Law*. In Chapter 4 "Scope and Method of Compensation" of Volume 5 "Damage Liabilities", the provisions in Article 466 "In case the socialist public properties or personal properties are infringed upon, the original properties shall be returned or the original state shall be restored; where it is impossible to return the original properties or restore the original state, the compensation may be made by providing the properties of equivalent quality, or be made on the basis of the actual value of properties" are the embryo of property

---

[49]Xue (2001).

[50]For the relevant draft, see He (2003).

[51]About the relating articles, see He et al. (2003).

damage compensation as provided in Article 117 of *General Principles of the Civil Law*. The provisions in Article 467 "In case the health of any other person is damaged or the death of any other person is caused, the following expenses and loss shall be compensated under different circumstances: ① Necessary medical expenses; ② Salary or workpoint for lost working time; ③ Cost-of-living supplement for disabled person; ④ Funeral expenses of deceased person and cost-of-living supplement of persons supported by the deceased person; ⑤ Other necessary expenses" are the embryo of personal damage compensation as provided in Article 199 of *General Principles of the Civil Law*. As for the provisions in Article 468 about determining the medical damage on the basis of medical diagnostic certificate and the provisions in Article 469 about independence of personal insurance liabilities, no corresponding articles can be found in *General Principles of the Civil Law*. It should be especially noted that, Paragraph 1 of Article 470 provides that: "The maximum amount of fine imposed on the liable person may not exceed six-month actual income of such person." It is provided in Paragraph 2 that: "The fine shall be owned by the state"; Article 471 provides that: "The compensation and fine may be paid in a lump sum or in installments; and may also be withheld and paid in installments by the working unit." These two articles are the specific provisions for the fine provided in Article 68 of Chapter 7 "Civil Sanctions" in Volume 1 "General Provisions" in damage compensation. The equitable rules for compensation liabilities as provided in Article 472 are the rules which were omitted in the legislative process of *General Principles of the Civil Law*.[52]

Chapter 8 "Civil Sanctions" in Volume 1 "General Provisions" of the *Third Deliberation Draft 2 of the Civil Law* cancels the similar general provisions for civil sanction as provided in Article 67 of the *Third Deliberation Draft 1 of the Civil Law*. Article 62 increases the civil sanction methods to 12 items, namely removing the obstacles, returning the original properties, restoring the original state, compensation for loss, confiscation of illegal gains, fine, apologizing, statement of repentance, admonition, deprivation of civil right, termination of business or relocation, closing down or revocation of registration and civil detention. Article 63 is similar to Paragraph 2 of Article 134 of *General Principles of the Civil Law*. It should be noted that, Paragraph 1 of Article 62 provides that: "The gains arising from Item 4 (namely confiscation of illegal gains) and Item 5 (namely fine) of Article 62 shall be paid into treasury." Paragraph 2 provides that: "The fine imposed on a citizen may not exceed his/her six-month income." Paragraph 3 provides that: "The maximum term of civil detention may not exceed 15 days." Through comparison, we find that, the contents of Article 62 of the *Third Deliberation Draft 2 of the Civil Law* are equivalent to Article 471 of the *Third Deliberation Draft 1 of the Civil Law*, and the specific rules for fine originally provided in damage compensation are moved into civil sanctions, so that the structure is more reasonable. The contents of Article 65 are similar to *Third Deliberation Draft 1 of the Civil Law* Article 70. The contents of Articles 362–364 and Article 366 of Chapter 3 "Scope

---

[52]Wang (2008).

and Method of Compensation" in Volume 4 "Liabilities of Tort Damage" are similar to the contents of Articles 466–468 and Article 472 of the *Third Deliberation Draft 2 of the Civil Law*, and Article 365 which is similar to Article 471 of the *Third Deliberation Draft 2 of the Civil Law* continues to provide that: "The compensation and fine may be paid in a lump sum or in installments; and may also be withheld and paid in installments by the working unit." Such articles are still retained in this chapter mainly on the basis of the provisions for compensation.

The major change occurred in the *Third Deliberation Draft 3 of the Civil Law*. In the *Third Deliberation Draft 1 of the Civil Law* and *Third Deliberation Draft 2 of the Civil Law*, there are Volume 1 "General Provisions", Volume 2 "Property Ownership", Volume 3 "Contract", Volume 4 "Tort Damage Liabilities", Volume 5 "Intellectual Property Right" and Volume 6 "Succession of Properties". Volume 1"General Provisions" contains Chapter 1 "Tasks and Basic Principles", Chapter 2 "Citizen", Chapter 3 "Legal Person", Chapter 4 "Juritic Act", Chapter 5 "Agency", Chapter 6 "Term and Calculation", Chapter 7 "Limitation of Action", Chapter 8 "Civil Sanctions" and Chapter 9 "Scope of Application", and the contents are relatively complicated. In the *Third Deliberation Draft 3 of the Civil Law*, there are Volume 1 "Tasks and Basic Principles", Volume 2 "Civil Subjects" (The civil subjects and agency were included, and the juristic act was cancelled on the basis of the advices given in discussion over the *Third Deliberation Draft 2 of the Civil Law*[53]), Volume 3 "Property Ownership", Volume 4 "Contract", Volume 5 "Intellectual Properties", Volume 6 "Relatives and Succession", Volume 7 "Civil Liabilities" and Volume 8 "Miscellaneous" (including term, limitation of action and scope of application). Through comparison, we can find that, Volume 7 "Civil Liabilities" of the *Third Deliberation Draft 3 of the Civil Law* is the result of combination of Chapter 8 "Civil Sanctions" of Volume 1 "General Provisions" and Volume 4 "Tort Damage Liabilities" of the *Third Deliberation Draft 2 of the Civil Law*, and this kind of combination is especially highlighted in Chapter 3 "Scope and Method of Liabilities Undertaken".

It is provided in Article 486 that: "The scope and method of liabilities undertaken include: ① Removing the obstacles, ceasing the infringement and eliminating the dangers; ② Returning the original properties; ③ Restoring the original state; ④ Making compensation for loss; ⑤ Confiscation of properties used in illegal activities and illegal gains; ⑥ Fine; ⑦ Compensation for breach; ⑧ Carrying out repair, replacement or rework; ⑨ Apologizing, eliminating the effect, and restoring the reputation; ⑩ Making a statement of repentance; ⑪ Admonition; ⑫ Termination of business or relocation." Such article determines almost all civil sanctions in the *Third Deliberation Draft 2 of the Civil Law* as civil liabilities. It is provided in Article 487 that: "The damage includes property damage and personal damage." The property damage and personal damage respectively provided in Article 488 and Article 489, the determination of medical damage on the basis of medical diagnostic certificate provided in Article 490, the payment method for

---

[53]See He (2003, p. 377).

compensation and fine provided in Article 491 and the balancing of damage compensation provided in Article 492 provisions are the contents in part of tort damage liabilities in the *Third Deliberation Draft 2 of the Civil Law*. It is provided in Paragraph 1 of Article 493 that: "The incomes arising from Items 5 and 6 of Article 486 shall be paid into treasury." The provisions in Paragraph 2 "In general, the fine imposed on a citizen may not exceed the six-month labor income of such citizen" is the contents about civil sanction in the *Third Deliberation Draft 2 of the Civil Law*. Article 494 is the new provisions on limitation of action. Except for deletion of provisions about limitation of action, this style is almost fully retained by Volume 7 "Civil Liabilities" of the *Third Deliberation Draft 4 of the Civil Law*, and has become the basis of Chapter 6 "Civil Liabilities" of *General Principles of the Civil Law*.

The above-mentioned review reveals that, Chapter 6 "Civil Liabilities" of *General Principles of the Civil Law* of China is the combination of the "civil sanctions" which represent the "punishment theory" for civil liabilities and the "tort damage compensation liabilities" (its predecessor is the tort damage compensation obligation in first deliberation draft of *Civil Code*) which represent the "guaranty theory" for civil liabilities.[54] Frankly speaking, the contents about civil liabilities in *General Principles of the Civil Law* of China originally have the dual nature of liabilities and damage compensation obligations.

12.3.4 Legislative Procedure and Structure of General Provisions of Obligation Law Under Pragmatic Thinking

Since it is impossible to realize the integration of form and essence, the aesthetics should give place to the practicability. As analyzed above, the Legislature can achieve the enactment of *Civil Code* only through one codification process by NPC. Therefore, the enactment of general provisions of obligation law should be completed by NPC Standing Committee through amendment of current law. In consideration of the fact that the *General Provisions of Civil Law* has been promulgated, the only and practical possibility is that, in the future when the *General Provisions Volume of Civil Code* is compiled, the general provisions of obligation law will be incorporated.

The discussion above reveals that, there is very strong implication between obligations and liabilities in civil law of China. If the Legislation of general provisions of obligation law is realized in the course of compilation of the *General Provisions Volume of Civil Code* in the future, it is necessary to clearly state the relationship between obligations and liabilities. It is not appropriate to place the provisions relating to such relationship in the general provisions of obligation law

---

[54]See Wang (2009b).

or the general provisions of liability law. After being stripped by the *Contract Law*, the *Real Rights Law* and the *Tort Liability Law*, Chapter 5 "Civil Rights" and Chapter 6 "Civil Liabilities" of *General Principles of the Civil Law* have been broken up, and can't constitute a system by themselves. Owing to the dual source of liabilities and obligation in Chapter 6 "Civil Liabilities" of *General Principles of the Civil Law* as mentioned above, it is advised by the Writer to combine the remaining contents of Chapter 5 and Chapter 6 of *General Principles of the Civil Law* into a chapter "Obligations and Liabilities", and incorporate such chapter into the *General Provisions Volume of Civil Code* compiled in future in light of the provisions of the *General Provisions of Civil Law*. Actually, this legislative idea which seems unique highlights the practicability of legislation, and is also achievable by legislative techniques. As a result, it is very likely that such idea will become the only choice of legislature.[55]

12.3.5 Design of Contents of Chapter "Obligations and Liabilities" in Future General Provisions Volume of Civil Code

It is advised by the Writer that, the structure of Chapter "Obligations and Liabilities" in the *General Provisions Volume of Civil Code* in the future should be as follows:

Section 1 "General Provisions", of which the main contents include: first, the concept of obligation and the concept of liabilities (With respect to the relationship between obligation and liability, the general guaranty theory whereby liability is obligation is adopted); second, the independence and priority of civil damage compensation; third, the types of civil liabilities other than damage compensation; fourth, the concept and legal effect of force majeure; fifth, the causation.[56]

Section 2 "Causes of Obligations and Concurrence of Civil Liabilities", of which main contents include: first, the main causes of obligation provided in the sequence of contract, tort, unjustified enrichment, negotiorum gestio and unilateral promise, and the occurrence of non-typical obligation is not excluded; second, the rules for concurrence of civil liabilities.

---

[55]Based on this conception, finally, as the *General Principles of Civil Law* includes the "general provisions of civil law" and "general provisions of obligation law" and other contents in the traditional continental legal system sense, it may be more suitable when it is continuously called the "general principles of civil law". However, whether it is re-named the "general provisions of civil law" finally is subject to the attitude of the legislative body, but this is not the core of the issue.

[56]The causal relationship is often mistaken for the requisite of tort liability. However, the Writer thinks that the causal relationship should be stipulated in the general provisions part of "Obligation and Liability" Chapter as the general requisite of obligation and liability.

Section 3 "General Provisions of Obligation Law", of which the contents are equivalent to the main contents of general provisions of obligation law in traditional continental legal system, excluding the contents about performance of obligation and modification of obligation (Those contents are still retained in the *Contract Law*). This section mainly includes: first, the type of obligations; second, the preservation of obligations; third, the transfer of obligations; fourth, the elimination of obligations.

Section 4 "Apportionment of Multi-party Liabilities", which are divided into two parts, namely the part for general apportionment of multi-party tort liabilities and the part for special apportionment of multi-party tort liabilities. The part for general apportionment of multi-party tort liabilities provides the proportional liability, joint and several liabilities, unreal supplementary liability, one-way joint and several liability and uniform claim for apportionment. The part for special apportionment of multi-party tort liabilities provides the double-way unreal joint and several liabilities, one-way unreal joint and several liabilities caused by third-party fault, prepayment liability, supplementary liability and uniform claim for recourse.

References

Chen Huabin, "Several Problems of the Formulation of the Civil Code of PRC", *Law Science*, No. 5, 2003.

Cui Jianyun, "General Rule of Obligation Law and Drafting Civil Code of P. R China", *Journal of Tsinghua University (Philosophy and Social Sciences)*, No. 4, 2003.

He Qinhua, Li Xiuqing, Chen Yi, *Overview of the Civil Code (Draft) of PRC (Volume 1)*, Law Press, 2003.

Liang Huixing, "Observations on Drafting a Civil Code", Modern *Law Science*, No. 2, 2001.

Liang Huixing, "Civil Code Assembled in a Loose Manner Does Not Suit For China's National Condition", *Tribune of Political Science and Law*, No. 1, 2003.

Liang Huixing, *Draft of Chinese Civil Code with Reasons(Volume of General Provisions of Obligation Law)*, Law Press, 2004.

Liu Shiguo, "On the Organizing Structure of Chinese Civil Code", *Law and Social Development*, No. 3, 2002.

Liu Jingwei, "The Nature of the Claim for Compensation in Apposition", *Law Science*, No. 12, 2006.

Liu Jingwei, "A Chronicle of Chinese Legal Science", China Legal Science, No. 4, 2007a.

Liu Jingwei, "On the enactment of the *General Provisions of Obligation Law* through the system of Non-Typical Obligation", *Law Review of Xiamen University*, Xiamen University Press, 2007b, pp. 48–65.

Liu Jingwei, "The Application of the *General Provisions of Obligation Law* to the Specific Obligation", *Journal of Henan Administrative Institute of Politics and Law*, No. 5, 2007c.

Liu Jiingwei, "Preliminary Exploration of Non-Typical Obligation", *Journal of China University of Political Science and Law*, No. 4, 2008.

Ma Junju, Cao Zhiguo, "Conservative and Innovation", *Science of Law*, No. 5, 2003.

Qin Youtu, MA Changhua, "Presence or Absence of General Principles of Obligation Law in China's Civil Code", *Law Science*, No. 5, 2003.

Qiu Congzhi, General Rules of Obligation Volume of Newly Revised Civil Law (Volume II), China Renmin University Press 2004.

Tong Rou, *Collection of TONG Rou*, China University of Politics Science and Law Press, 1996, p. 246.

Wang Shengming, "the Only Road to a Country under the Rule of Law-Several Issues in the Compilation of *the Civil Law (Draft) of the People's Republic of China"*, *Tribune of Political Science and Law*, No. 1, 2003a.

Wang Shenming, "The Route that a Country with Legality Must Go—Several Questions in Compiling the Civil Code of People' s Republic of China (Draft)", *Tribune of Political Science and Law*, No. 1, 2003b.

Wang Jialin, "Consult Dr. ZHAI Jiguang with the issue about Obligation of Tax", Law Science Magazine, No. 6, 2005a.

Wang Liming, *Scholar-proposed Draft of Civil Code of China with Reasons(Volume of General Provisions of Obligation Law and Contract Volume)*, Law Press, 2005b.

Wang Zhu, "The Constitutionality of *General principles of the Civil Law* and *the Real Rights Law (Draft)"*, Case Study, No. 3, 2006.

Wang Zhu, "An Investigation into the History of 'Fair Liability' of Chinese Tort Law", *Journal of Gansu Political and Legal College*, No. 2, 2008.

Wang Liming, "The Status of General Provisions of Obligation Law in *Civil Code* and its system", *Social Science Front*, No. 7, 2009a.

Wang Zhu, *Research on Apportionment of Tort Liability*, China Renmin University Press, 2009b, pp. 91–93.

Wang Zhu, "On the Right of Contribution in Joint and Several Liability—With Comment on the Mode of Redistribution of the Share of Insolvent Jointly and Severally Liable Tortfeasor", *Law Science*, No. 3, 2010.

Wang Zhu, "On the Establishment of the Concept of Vicarious Liability", *Northern Legal Science*, No. 2, 2011a.

Wang Zhu, Li Dongyue, "Research on the Litigation Techniques of 'Removal of Obstacle' and 'Abatement of Nuisance', *Arguments in Civil and Commercial Law*, Vol. 3, Law Press, 2011b.

Wang Zhu, "How many currently valid laws are there in our country?", *Social Science*, No. 10 2011c.

Wang Liming, "The Enactment of *Civil Code* after the Formation of Legal System", Guangdong Social Sciences, No. 1, 2012.

Xu Zhongyuan, "The keep or Abolishment of the Concept of Contract and General Provisions of Obligation Law", *Tsinghua Law Review*, No. 1, 2010.

Xue Jun, "On the Structure Design of the Obligation Section in Future China's Corpus of Civil Law", *Studies in Law and Business*, No. 2, 2001.

Yang Daixiong, "On Systematic Constitution Of The Credit Law In China's Civil Code", *Law Science Magazine*, No. 6, 2007.

Zhai Jiguang, "Several Basic Issues about Obligation of Tax", *Law Science Magazine*, No. 6, 2005.

Chapter 13
Compiling Background and Structural Adjustment of the *Tort Liabilities Volume of Civil Code*

13.1 Background for the Compilation of *Tort Liabilities Volume of Civil Code*

The background for the compilation of *Tort Liabilities Volume of Civil Code* mainly means the change in legislative planning for general provisions of obligation law and personality rights law. Actually, the legislative planning in these two aspects is also embodied by the *General Provisions of Civil Law*.

13.1.1 Discrete General Provisions of Obligation Law and Drifting-Away Tort

13.1.1.1 Discrete General Provisions of Obligation Law

In the future *Civil Code*, the system of general provisions of obligation law will embody the trend of discreteness. As Year 2020 which is the potential deadline for the compilation of *Civil Code* is approaching and the general provisions of obligation are not contained in the *2002 Civil Law (draft)*, it seems that the academic circle and the legislature have reached a tacit agreement that the *General Provisions of Obligation Laws* will not be enacted.[1] Against this background, the *General Provisions of Civil Law* tries to achieve the system supply for general provisions of obligation law to the lowest extent in Chapter 5 "Civil Rights". Specifically, it is provided in Paragraph 1 of Article 118 that: "All civil subjects legally enjoy obligatory rights." It is provided in Paragraph 2 that: "The obligatory right is the

---

[1]Based on the observation by the Writer, the call for "General Provisions of Obligation Law" gradually faded away after 2013. Literature thereafter is relatively prudent for the legislative suggestions on the "General Provisions of Obligation Law", like Cui (2013). Zhou 2003, Lu (2014) and Wang (2014).

© China University of Political Science and Law Press 2020
Z. Wang, *On the Constitutionality of Compiling a Civil Code of China*,
https://doi.org/10.1007/978-981-13-7900-0_13

right of right holder to request for any act or omission from particular obligor owing to contract, tort, negotiorum gestio, unjustified enrichment or other provisions of law." Then, in Articles 119–122, an article is respectively used to provide four typical causes of obligatory right, namely contract, tort, negotiorum gestio and unjustified enrichment. As the alternative legislative program for general provisions of obligation law, the obvious insufficiency of system supply is embodied.

When the *Contract Law* was enacted, since it was expected that the *Civil Code* would not be enacted in short time, the legislature decided that the general provisions of the *Contract Law* would temporarily play the role of general provisions of obligation law, and once the planning for the enactment of *Civil Code* is determined, the systems and norms of general provisions of obligation law in the *Contract Law* will be back into the *General Provisions of Obligation Law*.[2] However, since the legislative planning for the *General Provisions of Obligation Laws* is not achieved, in the future, most of the norms of the general provisions of obligation law, such as the systems of performance of obligation, preservation of obligation, modification and transfer of obligation and elimination of obligation, will have to be incorporated into the *Contract Volume of Civil Code* together with the *Contract Law*.

13.1.1.2 Drifting-Away Tort Liabilities

Careful observation reveals that, Article 120 of the *General Provisions of Civil Law* ("In case civil rights and interests are infringed upon, the infringed party shall have the right to require the infringing party to undertake the tort liabilities.") is not the provisions about obligation of tort, but the combination of Paragraph 1 of Article 2 of the *Tort Liability Law* ("In case civil rights and interests are infringed upon, the infringing party shall undertake the tort liabilities in accordance with this Law.") and Article 3 of the *Tort Liability Law* ("The infringed party shall have the right to require the infringing party to undertake the tort liabilities."). The largest pity is that, the expression of this rule has missed the best opportunity to clarify the relationship between liabilities of tort and obligation of tort. On the other hand, Article 118 of the *General Provisions of Civil Law* does not give the rules corresponding to the claim for obligatory right as provided in Paragraph 2 of Article 84 of *General Principles of the Civil Law*: "The obligatory right holder shall have the right to require the obligor to perform the obligation in accordance with the provisions of contract or law."[3] As a result, in actual practice in the future, maybe there is the trend that the obligations of tort will be fully replaced by liabilities of tort, and the torts will also only be theoretically taken as cause of obligation of tort.

---

[2]Cui (2003).

[3]This legislation loophole will case a great bewilderment to the bewilderment. Refer to *Big Data Analysis on Whether to Keep or Eliminate Several Law Norms of the General Principles of Civil Law (Draft)*, *Journal of Sichuan University (Social Science Edition)*, No. 1, 2017.

13.1.2 Personality Right a Law in Deadlock and System of Personality Rights Protection to be Integrated

13.1.2.1 Evaluation and Analysis on Articles of Chapter 5 "Civil Rights" of the *General Provisions of Civil Law* Relating to Personality Rights

It should be pointed out that, Article 109 of the *General Provisions of Civil Law* ("The personal freedom and personal dignity of natural persons are protected by laws.") is not the general provisions on personality rights, but the protection from civil law for personal freedom provided in Article 37 of the *Constitution* and personal dignity provided in Article 38 of the *Constitution*. In the future, the *Tort Liabilities Volume of Civil Code* should provide the tort liability norms for general personality rights which take "personal dignity" as core, and protect the personal freedom right as specific personality right.

With respect to the specific personality rights of natural persons, as compared with Paragraph 2 of Article 2 of the *Tort Liability Law*, Paragraph 1 of Article 110 of the *General Provisions of Civil Law* ("The natural persons enjoy right to life, right to body, right to health, right to name, right to portrait, right to reputation, right to honor, right to privacy, right to marital autonomy and other rights.") separately lists the "right to body", changes the relative sequence "right to life, right to health and right to body" used in the *Judicial Interpretation on Emotional Damage Compensation* and the *Judicial Interpretation on Personal Damage Compensation*, and uses the sequence which is more similar to "life, body and health" as provided in Paragraph 1 of Article 823 of the *Civil Code of Germany*. In the future, the provisions relating to tort liabilities in the *Tort Liabilities Volume of Civil Code* should embody this change.

It is provided in Paragraph 2 of Article 110 of the *General Provisions of Civil Law* that: "The legal persons and unincorporated organizations enjoy the name right, reputation right, honor right and other rights." Such provisions directly correspond to the provisions in Paragraph 2 of Article 99, Article 101 and Article 102 of *General Principles of the Civil Law* relating to personality rights of legal persons, continue to adopt the "positive theory" for personality rights of legal persons, and expand to "unincorporated organizations", so that they are noteworthy.

Article 111 of the *General Provisions of Civil Law* absorbs the experience in the amendment of *Law on Protection of Rights and Interests of Consumers* and the enactment of *Network Security Law*, and gives special protection on personal information. In the future in the *Tort Liabilities Volume of Civil Code*, this declarative article shall be further converted into a more normalized article for tort liabilities.

It should be pointed out that, the article for protection on personal information right is added in the *General Provisions of Civil Law (draft) (draft for solicitation of opinion in second deliberation)*, while the contents of Article 110 of the *General Provisions of Civil Law*, especially the provisions about personality rights of legal persons and unincorporated organizations in Paragraph 2, are established in the *General Provisions of Civil Law (draft) (draft for solicitation of opinion in first deliberation)*. The sequence of such two articles leads to the separate provisions in Article 111 of the *General Provisions of Civil Law*. If Article 110 of the *General Provisions of Civil Law* considered the protection on "personal information" at the first beginning, the more reasonable legislative treatment should be addition of "personal information right" in Paragraph 1 of Article 110, similar to the addition of "privacy right" in Paragraph 2 of Article 2 of the *Tort Liability Law*. The advantages of the treatment in this way is that the "personal information right" is provided as right and listed in parallel to "privacy right", and the difference between them is clarified. The disadvantage of failure to use this practice is that, the *General Provisions of Civil Law* missed the legislative opportunity to add the "organizational information right" into personality rights of legal persons in Paragraph 2 of Article 111 in parallel to "personal information right". In the information society, the personal information should be separated from personal privacy, and accordingly the organizational information should be separated from trade secret. In the future, both the personal information and organizational information should be protected as personality rights and interests. Item 5 of Paragraph 2 of Article 123 of the *General Provisions of Civil Law* protects it as an object of intellectual property rights: "The intellectual property rights are the exclusive rights legally enjoyed by right holder with respect to the following objects: (5) Trade secret". The relationship among these four right subjects is as follows:

Table of secret information objects of civil subject

Type of civil subject\object	Secret	Information
Natural person	Personal privacy	Personal information
Legal person, and unincorporated organization	Trade secret	Organization information

Since Paragraph 2 of Article 110 of the *General Provisions of Civil Law* uses the legislative technique "other rights" after enumerating the name right, reputation right and honor right, in interpretation theory, the words "other rights" can be deemed as including "organizational information rights and interests" of legal persons and unincorporated organizations, which can be confirmed through judicial interpretation in the future. The *Tort Liabilities Volume of Civil Code* shall provide the tort liabilities for infringement upon personal privacy right, personal information and organization information, and leave the tort liabilities for infringement upon trade secret to be provided in the *Anti-unfair Competition Law*.

13.1.2.2 Personality Rights and Interests Protection System to Be Integrated

The debate on the issue whether the personality right law should be separately enacted has occurred again in the course of drafting of the *General Provisions of Civil Law*, and it seems that the dream about separate enactment of personality right law has been drifting away.[4] With respect to the protection on personality rights and interests, the system of personality rights in the *General Provisions of Civil Law* can't substitute *General Principles of the Civil Law* and current judicial interpretation. In the future, it is also a second-best option to let the *Tort Liabilities Volume of Civil Code* undertake the heavy task for protecting personality rights and interests, so that it is necessary to fully integrate the current system of personality rights and interests protection.

General Principles of the Civil Law has established the complete personality rights law system which covers various rights and protection on rights. In Article 98 through Article 103 of Section 4 "Personal Rights" of Chapter 5 "Civil Rights", the life & health right, name right, portrait right, reputation right, honor right and marital autonomy of natural person, as well as the name right, reputation right and honor right of legal person are provided. As compared with Article 110 of the *General Provisions of Civil Law*, except for the privacy right which was not established at that time, all other rights are involved, and the contents about claim for personality rights are contained.[5] In Article 119 of Section 3 "Civil Liabilities for Tort" of Chapter 6 "Civil Liabilities", the personal damage compensation is provided; in Article Paragraph 1 of Article 120, the tort liabilities for infringement upon mental personality rights of natural person are provided; in Paragraph 2, the tort liabilities for infringement upon personality rights of legal persons are provided. As a result, a relatively complete tort liability system for infringement upon personality rights is formed.

In consideration of the importance of protection on personality rights and interests in actual practice, the Supreme People's Court published a lot of cases about infringement upon personality rights in the *Bulletin of Supreme People's Court* at the end of 1980s and beginning of 1990s, summarized the experience in judicial practice, and successively issued two judicial interpretations, namely the *Answer for Some Questions about Reputation Right Cases* (1993) and the *Interpretation for Reputation Right Cases* (1998). Since the beginning of the 21st century, the *Judicial Interpretation on Emotional Damage Compensation* (2001) and the *Judicial Interpretation on Personal Damage Compensation* (2003) issued by the Supreme People's Court have fully improved and systematically established

---

[4]Li (2016).
[5]Yang (2003).

the protection system for personality rights and interests in China. The *Provisions on Civil Disputes Arising from Information-network-based Infringement upon Personal Rights and Interests* issued in 2014 provides in details the tort liabilities for information-network-based infringement upon personality rights and interests of other persons such as name right, reputation right, honor right, portrait right and privacy right.

The interpretation objects of the above-mentioned judicial interpretations are the provisions about liabilities of network tort in the relevant articles of *General Principles of the Civil Law* and Article 36 of the *Tort Liability Law*. The provisions about type of personality rights and liabilities for infringement upon personality rights in *General Principles of the Civil Law* will be abolished together with *General Principles of the Civil Law* after the compilation of *Civil Code* is completed. The protection system for personality rights and interests in current laws of China should be integrated in the future *Tort Liabilities Volume of Civil Code*.

13.2 It Is Advised to Set up the Chapter "Damage Compensation of Tort Liabilities" Separately

13.2.1 Complicated Chapter 2 "Composition of Liabilities and Form of Liabilities" of the Tort Liability Law

There are 92 articles under 12 chapters in the *Tort Liability Law*. The last chapter "Supplementary Provisions" has only one article, and other chapters each have 8–9 articles in average. Chapter 8 "Liability for Environmental Pollution" has only 4 articles, while Chapter 2 "Constitution of Liability and the Forms to Bear Liability" has 20 articles. From the viewpoint of formal beauty, such chapter is too long. Though Articles 12–15 and Article 23 of such chapter have been generalized by Articles 177–179 and Article 183 of the *General Provisions of Civil Law*, the remaining articles still contain the constitution of tort liabilities (Articles 6 and 7), application scope of joint and several liabilities (Articles 8–11), liabilities of damage compensation (Articles 15–20, 22 and 25), preventive tort liabilities (Article 21)[6] and controversial equitable liabilities (Article 24),[7] so that they are slightly complicated. In the future *Tort Liabilities Volume of Civil Code*, such articles may be split into two chapters.

---

[6]Wang (2010a, p. 620).

[7]This chapter mainly discusses the structural adjustment of the *Civil Code · Tort Liability Volume*, but does not discuss the retention and elimination of equitable liabilities and style arrangement temporarily.

13.2.2   Legislative Orientation of Various Tort Liabilities Which Take "Damage Compensation" as Core

On the basis of the provisions of Article 179 of the *General Provisions of Civil Law*, in the future, the tort liabilities of the *Tort Liabilities Volume of Civil Code* involve four aspects, for which the legislative orientation is different:

Firstly, the filling-type tort liabilities are taken as primary liabilities. The restoration of original state and compensation for loss are filling-type tort liabilities, take the occurrence of damage as requisite and are the main part of tort liabilities, and the compensation of loss is taken as core.

Secondly, the preventive tort liabilities are taken as auxiliary liabilities. The liabilities such as "ceasing the infringement", "removing the obstacles" and "eliminating the dangers" are preventive tort liabilities, for which the occurrence of damage is not a requisite, and of which the purpose is to prevent the occurrence of damage and play the supporting role.

Thirdly, the mental tort liabilities are considered. The elimination of effect, restoration of reputation and apology are the special embodiments of "restoration of original state" in the field of infringement upon personality rights and interests,[8] and this also proves the necessity to provide the tort liabilities for infringement upon personality rights and interests in the *Tort Liabilities Volume of Civil Code* from the viewpoint of main means for undertaking tort liabilities.

Fourthly, the punitive compensation liabilities are legally determined. The punitive compensation liabilities are limited by express provisions of laws, and are subject to exceptional rules. It is necessary to set the conditions for extension of their application scope in the *Tort Liabilities Volume of Civil Code*.

13.2.3   It Is Advised to Set up Chapter "Damage Compensation of Tort Liabilities" as Chapter 2

In accordance with the above-mentioned legislative orientation, it is advised by the Writer to set up Chapter "Damage Compensation of Tort Liabilities" as Chapter 2, and provide the basic rules and type of damage compensation liabilities. The basic rules for damage compensation liabilities are absent from the *Tort Liability Law* and even the whole civil law in China, including the rules for restoration of original state and full compensation, the rules for determination of damage compensation liabilities, the benefit rules, the rules for maintenance of minimum living standard,[9]

---

[8]Zhang (2007).

[9]The traditional civil law generally retains three items, namely, maintain the minimum living guarantee, perform the statutory fosterage obligation and pay the fees required by the education of the raised minors. Considering the reality of deficiency of social medical care of China, it is

the priority rules[10] and the rules for payment method. As for types of damage compensation liabilities, the personal damage compensation liabilities, properties damage compensation liabilities and emotional damage compensation liabilities are provided on the basis of Articles 16–20 and Article 22 of the *Tort Liability Law*, and the general provisions for punitive compensation liabilities are under consideration.

The provisions on punitive compensation liabilities in current laws of China mainly include the provisions of Article 47 of the *Tort Liability Law*, Paragraph 2 of Article 55 of the *Law on Protection of Rights and Interests of Consumers* and Paragraph 2 of Article 148 of the *Food Safety Law*. It is noteworthy that, when the *Trademark Law* was amended in 2013, the second sentence of Paragraph 1 of Article 63 was added: "In case of malicious infringement upon trademark right, where the circumstance is serious, the amount of compensation may be determined as 1 to 3 times the amount calculated in accordance with the above-mentioned method." Such provisions are actually the provisions on punitive compensation. The latest draft amendment to the *Copyright Law*[11] and draft amendment to the *Patent Law*[12] also contain similar articles for punitive compensation liabilities. It is advised that, subjectively the punitive compensation liabilities should be limited to "malice" or "intentional conduct", and be limited to the situation that the death or serious health damage of other person is caused or the intellectual property rights are infringed upon.

suggested that the required expenses of "basic medical treatment and ongoing critical disease treatment" of the tort liability person and his raised minor should be retained.

[10]The *General Provisions of Civil Law* has stipulated the "civil property liability priority" rule. The *Civil Code · Tort Liability Volume* should stipulate the civil tort liability prior to the public welfare lawsuit, rescue expense and funeral expense priority, and punitive damages liability posteriority.

[11]Paragraph 2, Article 76, the *Copyright Law of the People's Republic of China* (Revised Draft for Comment): "for two or more purposeful infringements upon the copyright or related right, the people's court may determine the compensation based on two to three times of compensation amount calculated per debts." http://zqyj.chinalaw.gov.cn/readmore?listType=1&id=125, the latest access time: August 31, 2017.

[12]Sentence 3, Paragraph 1, Article 68, the *Revised Draft of the Patent Law of the People's Republic of China* (Draft for Comment): "for the purposeful infringement upon the patent right, based on the circumstance, scale and damage consequence and other factors of infringement act, the people's court may determine the compensation amount more than one time but less than three times of amount determined per the abovementioned method. The compensation amount should include the reasonable expenditures of the right holder for curbing the infringement act." http://zqyj.chinalaw.gov.cn/readmore?listType=1&id=905, the latest access time: August 31, 2017.

13.3   It Is Advised to Set up Chapter "Constitution of Liabilities and Apportionment of Liabilities"

After Chapter 2 "Damage Compensation of Tort Liabilities" is set up in the *Tort Liabilities Volume of Civil Code*, the remaining articles in Chapter 2 "Constitution of Liability and the Forms to Bear Liability" of the *Tort Liability Law* mainly include three groups of rules, namely constitution of tort liabilities (Articles 6 and 7), application scope of joint and several liabilities (Articles 8–11) and preventive tort liabilities (Article 21). It is advised by the Writer to slightly adjust the contents, rename such chapter as "Constitution of Liabilities and Apportionment of Liabilities", and take such chapter as Chapter 1 of the *Tort Liabilities Volume of Civil Code*. This chapter includes two parts of contents.

13.3.1   Rules for Constitution of General Tort Liabilities

It is provided in Paragraph 1 of Article 6 of the *Tort Liability Law* that: "An actor, who is at fault in infringing on another's civil rights or interests, shall bear tort liability." It is provided in Article 7 that: "If an actor damages another's civil rights or interests, no matter the actor is at fault or not, in case that a provision of law requires him to bear tort liability, then that provision shall govern." These two articles don't provide the requisites of "damage", so as to keep consistent with the requisites of preventive tort liabilities provided in Article 15 of the *Tort Liability Law*, which means that damage is not the requisite of preventive tort liabilities. Therefore, the requisites of "damage" are provided in the part about types of damage compensation.[13] If the constitution of tort liabilities is divided into damage compensation liabilities and preventive tort liabilities, then the requisites of "damage" may be added into the articles which contain the imputation principle for damage compensation of tort liabilities, and it is unnecessary to provide such requisite in the part about types of damage compensation of tort liabilities.

It is advised that in the future, the *Tort Liabilities Volume of Civil Code* should firstly provide the components of damage compensation of tort liabilities on the basis of Article6 and Article 7 of the *Tort Liability Law*, and then provide the components of preventive tort liabilities on the basis of Article 21 of the *Tort Liability Law*, so as to form the general tort liability system composed of "damage compensation of tort liabilities & preventive tort liabilities".

---

[13]However, Article 19, the *Tort Liability Law* does not stipulate the element of "cause the damage" subject to the legislation planning, which belongs to the legislation defect: "as for infringement upon properties of other persons properties, the loss of properties shall be calculated on the basis of the market price when such loss occurs or other method".

13.3.2 General Apportionment Rules for Damage Compensation of Tort Liabilities

The apportionment rules for general damage compensation of tort liabilities in the *Tort Liabilities Volume of Civil Code* shall at least include two parts, namely the apportionment rules for general multi-party tort liabilities and the rules for fault of infringed party.[14]

13.3.2.1 General Apportionment Rules for Multi-party Tort Liabilities

The general apportionment rules for multi-party tort liabilities mean the application rules for joint and several liabilities and proportional liabilities. Articles 8–11 of the *Tort Liability Law* provide the application scope for joint and several liabilities, corresponding to Article 130 of *General Principles of the Civil Law*. Adopting the legislative mode of traditional continental legal system, *General Principles of the Civil Law*, in the field of general apportionment for multi-party tort liabilities, only provide the application scope of joint and several liabilities, and apply the proportional liabilities for those multi-party torts beyond such scope. Article 12 of the *Tort Liability Law* gives provisions on the situations for application of proportional liabilities in case "the same damage is caused by tort respectively implemented by more than two persons". Those provisions are really redundant, and maybe they are affected by Paragraph 2 of Article 3 of the *Judicial Interpretation on Personal Damage Compensation*.[15] In the future, in the *Tort Liabilities Volume of Civil Code*, it is unnecessary to provide the application scope of proportional liabilities.

13.3.2.2 Rules for Fault of Infringed Party

With respect to style, Article 130 of *General Principles of the Civil Law* provides the application scope of joint and several liabilities, and Article 131 provides the fault of infringed party, and constitutes the complete rules for apportionment of general tort liabilities. The interpretation object of Article 2 of the *Judicial Interpretation on Personal Damage Compensation* is Article 131 of *General Principles of the Civil Law*, and the interpretation object of Articles 3–5 is Article

---

[14]The complete rules for apportionment of general tort liabilities should include the apportionment rules for general multi-party tort liabilities involving the fault of infringed party. Refer to Wang (2010c).

[15]Paragraph 2 of article 3 of the *Interpretation of the Supreme People's Court of Some Issues Concerning the Application of the Law on the Trial of Cases to Compensation for Personal Injury* provides that: "Where two or more persons have no joint intent or joint negligence, but separately commit several acts that are indirectly combined and result in the same injury consequence, they shall bear corresponding compensation liabilities respectively in appropriate proportions upon the extent of their faults or the reasons of such injury".

130 of *General Principles of the Civil Law*. Though the relative sequence is exchanged, the complete system for apportionment rules for general tort liabilities is still used.

The system of fault of infringed party is incorporated into the newly-added Chapter 3 "Defense Cause" from Volume 8 "Tort Liability Law" of the *Civil Law (draft)* (December 23, 2002), and such chapter also involves justifiable defense, act of rescue and self-help. In the subsequent drafts, Chapter 3 was renamed as "Situations for Exemption from and Reduction of Liabilities", and gradually absorbed the contents such as force majeure, intentional conduct of injured person and third-party reason. Finally, the system of fault of infringed party was provided in Article 26 of such chapter in the *Tort Liability Law*: "In case the infringed party has any fault in occurrence of damage, the liabilities of the infringing party may be reduced."

The Writer believes that, the method to apply the system of fault of infringed party is to compare the fault and causation of both parties, which is more similar to the comparison of rules for fault and reason of infringing party for apportionment of multi-party tort liabilities.[16] The effect of application of the system of fault of infringed party is reduction of liabilities rather than exemption of liabilities, while the effect of application of other defense is exemption of liabilities. In the future *Tort Liabilities Volume of Civil Code*, the system of fault of infringed party fault should, together with the apportionment system for multi-party tort liabilities, constitute the complete apportionment system for general tort liabilities.

13.4 It Is Advised to Delete the Chapter "Exculpatory or Extenuating Circumstances"

13.4.1 Generalization of "Intentional Conduct of Injured Person" and "Third-Party Reason" Is Denied

Article 27 of the *Tort Liability Law* provides the generalized defense for intentional conduct of injured person: "If the harm is [solely] due to the injured person's intentional [act], the actor shall not bear liability." With respect to such provisions, it is provided in the authoritative interpretation given by the drafting organ of the *Tort Liability Law* that: "The provisions of this article exempt the actor from liabilities on the basis of the precondition that the damage is fully caused by the intentional conduct of the injured person, which means that the intentional conduct of the injured person is the only cause of damage."[17] This interpretation on one hand emphasizes the subjective intention of the injured person, and on the other

---

[16]Yang Lixin, Wang Zhu, "On the System of Victim's Fault in Tort Law", *Private Law Review (Vol. 7)*.

[17]See Wang (2010b, p. 129).

hand emphasizes the "only cause". According to this logic, it seems that "negligence of injured person + only cause" can't exempt the liabilities. It should be pointed out that, in the general tort liabilities, if the behavior of the injured person is the only cause of damage, no matter whether any subjective fault is involved, and no matter how serious such fault is, the liabilities will be exempted for the reason that the behavior of infringing party has no causation with the damage. This is the situation that the liabilities are not constituted owing to insufficient requisites of tort liabilities, rather than defense. The Writer believes that, the use of intentional conduct of injured person as a defense is only limited to the field of dangerous liabilities, which means that, the situation that the injured person intentionally uses the dangerous nature of dangerous operation to get himself/herself damaged may not be taken as defense for general tort liabilities.

Article 28 of the *Tort Liability Law* provides the generalized defense "third-party's fault": "In case the damage is caused by a third party, such third party shall undertake the tort liabilities." According to the authoritative interpretation given by the drafting organ of the *Tort Liability Law*, it is necessary to distinguish between "third party fault which is the only cause of damage" and "third party fault which is the partial cause of damage". The situations that the third-party fault is the only cause of damage will be distinguished again in accordance with the imputation principle. In the field of fault liabilities and presumed-default liabilities, the third party reason is actually taken as ground for exemption; in the field of no-fault liabilities, there are different treatments, such as the treatment that the defendant undertakes the liabilities and the treatment that the infringed party select the liable person or the third party to undertake the liabilities, but the provisions of special law shall always be applied. As for the situation that the third party fault is the partial cause of damage, the provisions about application scope of joint and several liabilities in Articles 9–12 the *Tort Liability Law* shall be applied respectively on the basis of actual situation.[18] The careful analysis on the above-mentioned interpretation reveal that, Article 28 is only applied separately as grounds for exemption in fault liabilities and presumed-default liabilities; as for other types of liabilities, actually other articles are applied. Then, Article 28 is provided as defense for general tort, and its actual value is to give the provisions on taking third-party fault which is the only cause of damage as ground for exemption in the field of fault liabilities and presumed-default liabilities.[19]

According to such understanding, we should further think. It is appropriate to say that the behavior of defendant is not the cause of damage rather than take the third-party's fault in fault liabilities and presumed-default liabilities as the ground for exemption. From the viewpoint of composition of litigation, if the plaintiff brings an accusation against the defendant, and the defendant proves that the third-party's fault is the cause of damage, then the burden of proof is completed and the defendant shall be exempted from liabilities. The plaintiff should separately claim against the third party for tort liabilities, and then "the third-party reason is the only cause of damage"

---

[18]See Wang (2010b, pp. 132–135).
[19]Zhang and Zheng (2015).

proven by the defendant in the former case will be the causal element for the third party as defendant in the second case to undertake the tort liabilities. By this token, Article 28 is actually the embodiment of such causal element in the first case, which is the issue about casual element in composition of tort liabilities, and should not be provided as general defense. In the field of dangerous liabilities, such as the unreal joint and several liabilities for environmental pollution caused by third-party's fault as provided in Article 68 of the *Tort Liability Law* and the unreal joint and several liabilities for damage caused by domesticated animal owing to third-party's fault as provided in Article 83, the third-party's fault can't constitute the ground for exemption. If the infringed party selects to claim against the dangerous liable person for compensation, the dangerous liable person may recover such compensation from the third party as final liable person only after paying the compensation.

13.4.2   *"Generalized" Rather Than "General" Orientation of Rules for Dangerous Liabilities Not Caused by Infringing Party*

It should be noted that, the defense "gross negligence of injured person" provided in Chapter 8 "Liability for Environmental Pollution", Chapter 9 "Liability for Ultra-hazardous Activities" and Chapter 10 "Liability for Harm Caused by Domesticated Animals" of the *Tort Liability Law* has not been "generalized". It is provided in Paragraph 2 of Article 2 of the *Judicial Interpretation on Personal Damage Compensation* that: "When the provisions of Paragraph 3 of Article 106 of *General Principles of the Civil Law* are applied to determine the compensation liabilities of person liable to make compensation, in case the injured person has gross negligence, the compensation liabilities of liable person may be reduced." However, it is provided in Paragraph 3 of Article 106 of *General Principles of the Civil Law* that: "In case the person has no fault, but the law provides that the civil liabilities shall be undertaken, then such person shall undertake the civil liabilities." It is thus clear that, this is still specific no-fault liability which will refer to the "provisions of other law". The Writer believes that, as compared with the generalization made by the *Tort Liability Law* for intentional conduct of injured person and third-party reason, the more reasonable practice is to carry out generalization in the field of dangerous liabilities by reference to the legislative mode of "gross negligence of the injured person".[20] The deduction from such legislative mode is that, the provisions about unreal joint and several liabilities for "third-party reason" should be provided in Chapter 9 "Liability for Ultra-hazardous Activities" of the *Tort Liability Law*.

---

[20]The Writer uses the "dangerous liabilities" but not "no-fault liabilities" concept to exclude the "product liabilities". The defense cause system of product liabilities is relatively special, and it is relatively greatly different from the dangerous liabilities.

13.4.3 It Is Unnecessary to Retain the Chapter "Exculpatory or Extenuating Circumstances"

Chapter 3 "Exculpatory or Extenuating Circumstances" of the *Tort Liability Law* has only 6 articles. Among such article, the provisions about force majeure, justifiable defense and act of rescue in Articles 29–31 have been incorporated into Articles 180–182 of the *General Provisions of Civil Law*. The provisions about fault of infringed party in Article 26 are actually the apportionment rules for tort liabilities. The provisions about intentional conduct of injured person in Article 27 and the provisions about third-party's fault in Article 28 involve the situation that the "generalized" rules are wrongly provided by using the "generalized" approach. As a result, the contents of such chapter have been fully discomposed, and it is unnecessary to retain the chapter "Exculpatory or Extenuating Circumstances" in the future *Tort Liabilities Volume of Civil Code*. Therefore, it is advised to delete such chapter.

13.5 It Is Advised to Set up the Chapter "Tort Liabilities for Infringement Upon Personality Rights and Interests"

13.5.1 It Is Advised to Set up Chapter 3 "Tort Liabilities for Infringement Upon Personality Rights and Interests" in the Tort Liabilities Volume of Civil Code

The present situation reveals that, the *Personality Rights Volume* will not be set up in the future *Civil Code*, and the rules of personality right in the *General Provisions of Civil Law* are too simple to sufficiently protect the personality rights. In the future, the task to protect the personality rights will be allocated to the *Tort Liabilities Volume of Civil Code*, and the best legislative choice is to set up the chapter "Tort Liabilities for Infringement upon Personality Rights and Interests" in the *Tort Liabilities Volume of Civil Code*.

The setting of specific chapter and section should be coordinated with the structure of the *Tort Liability Law*. It is generally believed that, the first three chapters of the *Tort Liability Law* are the provisions on general tort liabilities, and Chapter 4 through Chapter 11 are the provisions on special tort liabilities. The chapter "Tort Liabilities for Infringement upon Personality Rights and Interests" would be the contents of the *Personality Rights Volume*, and its orientation is similar to that of Chapter 3 "Protection on Property Rights" of the *Real Rights Law*. Such chapter can be excluded from the *Tort Liabilities Volume of Civil Code* only because the Legislature has changed the legislative planning whereby the personality rights law in the *2002 Civil Law (draft)* will be enacted separately. In consideration of the general nature and special nature of contents of such chapter, the "tort liabilities for infringement upon personality rights and interests" are generally applied to fault liabilities, and should be classified into general tort liabilities. However, the rights and interests infringed have the special nature, namely "personality rights and interests". Therefore, the best setting is to place Chapter 3 as the transition between general tort liabilities and special tort liabilities.

With respect to design of rules, in order to carry forward the system of personality rights protection of *General Principles of the Civil Law*, it is advised that every article should provide the claim for personality rights and claim in tort, so as to provide the more comprehensive protection for personality rights and interests. With respect to design of style, since the personality right system is designed by taking natural person as typical subject, it is advised to firstly provide the protection on personality rights and interests of natural persons, and then provide the protection on personality rights and interests of special subjects. The special subjects above mentioned mainly mean fetus, deceased persons, minors, women, legal persons and unincorporated organizations.

13.5.2   Tort Liabilities for Infringement Upon Personality Rights and Interests of Natural Persons

Under "I. Disputes Over Personality Rights" in Part 1 "disputes over personality rights" of the *Provisions on Causes of Action for Civil Cases* (F. [2011] No. 42), 9 causes of action in three classes are listed: 1. Disputes over right to life, right to health or right to body; 2. Disputes over right to name; 3. Disputes over right to portrait; 4. Disputes over right to reputation; 5. Disputes over right to honor; 6. Disputes over right to privacy; 7. Disputes over marital autonomy; 8. Disputes over right to personal freedom; 9. Disputes over general personality rights. The above provisions are basically consistent with the contents of Article 109 and Paragraph 1 of Article 110 of the *General Provisions of Civil Law*. It should be pointed out that, the right to personal freedom is a specific personality right, and the core contents of "general personality rights" are "personal dignity", which is personality interest rather than personality right. At present, it is also more appropriate to protect the personal information provided by Article 111 of the *General Provisions of Civil Law* as personality interests.

By reference to the sequence and contents of articles of the *General Provisions of Civil Law*, the future *Tort Liabilities Volume of Civil Code* may use the articles in four aspects to provide the tort liabilities for infringement upon personality rights and interests of natural persons, which is detailed as follows:

Firstly, in order to provide the tort liabilities for infringement upon general personality rights, it is advised to adopt the article: "In case serious consequences are caused owing to infringement upon personal dignity of natural person, the tort liabilities shall be undertaken."

Secondly, in order to provide the tort liabilities for infringement upon specific personality rights, it is advised to set up 11 articles as follows: (1) Tort liabilities for infringement upon right to life; (2) Tort liabilities for infringement upon right to body[21]; (3) Tort liabilities for infringement upon right to health; (4) Tort liabilities for infringement upon right to name; (5) Tort liabilities for infringement upon right to portrait; (6) Tort liabilities for infringement upon right to reputation; (7) Tort liabilities for infringement upon right to honor; (8) Tort liabilities for infringement upon right to privacy; (9) Tort liabilities for infringement upon right to marital autonomy; (10) Tort liabilities for infringement upon right to sexual autonomy and reproductive autonomy[22]; (11) Tort liabilities for infringement upon right to personal freedom.

Thirdly, the provisions on tort liabilities for infringement upon personal information can be designed in light of the contents of Article 111 of the *General Provisions of Civil Law*.

Fourthly, the provisions on tort liabilities for infringement upon publicity right should be given. The right of natural person to commercially utilize his/her personality interests is generally recognized in the legal theory of tort and the actual practice in China, so that it is necessary to provide the publicity right of natural person and the tort liabilities for infringement upon publicity right in the last article relating to protection on personality rights and interests of natural person.

13.5.3 Special Norms on Infringement Upon Personality Rights and Interests of Special Subjects

The tort liabilities for infringement upon personality rights and interests of special subjects include:

First, the tort liabilities for infringement upon personality interests of fetus. It is provided in Article 16 of the *General Provisions of Civil Law* that: "With respect to protection on interests of fetus such as succession of estate, acceptance of gift and etc., a fetus shall be deemed as having the capacity for civil rights. However, if the fetus is a dead body at birth, its capacity for civil rights shall be deemed as nonexistent at first." The above provisions may be taken as the general provisions for protection on interests of fetus, but the tort liabilities for infringement upon personality interests of fetus should also consider the specific provisions in the *Tort Liabilities Volume of Civil Code*.

Second, the tort liabilities for infringement upon personality interests of deceased persons. Article 185 of the *General Provisions of Civil Law* actually provides the

---

[21]The remedy of body autonomy infringement should be highlighted. Refer to Wang (2012).

[22]Considering the article 191 of the *General Provisions of Civil Code* provides the special limitation of action for sexual abuse of minors, so it is advised to set up the tort liabilities for infringement upon right to sexual autonomy and reproductive autonomy in the *Tort Liability Law*.

special type of infringement upon personality interests of deceased persons, and against the background that the *Personality Right Law* will not be enacted as a separate volume, such article should be provided in the *Tort Liabilities Volume of Civil Code*. Owing to the absence of legislative planning, it is slightly inappropriate to give the corresponding provisions in the *General Provisions of Civil Law*. In the course of the compilation of *Civil Code* in the future, such article should be returned to the *Tort Liabilities Volume of Civil Code*, and the rules should be refined. Logically, it is necessary to firstly give general provisions on infringement upon personality interests of deceased persons, and then give the special provisions.

Third, the tort liabilities for infringement upon personality rights and interests of minors and women. It is provided in Article 128 of the *General Provisions of Civil Law* that: "In case there are special provisions on protection of civil rights of minors, elderly persons, disabled persons, women and consumers in other laws, such special provisions shall apply." As for the five disadvantaged populations listed in such article, there are the corresponding special protection laws. In consideration of the provisions about special limitation of action for infringement upon minors in Article 190 and Article 191 of the *General Provisions of Civil Law*, as well as the equal importance between protection on sexual autonomy of women and protection on sexual autonomy of minors, it is advised to give the special provisions about infringement upon personality rights and interests of minors and women (especially sexual autonomy) in the *Tort Liabilities Volume of Civil Code*.

Fourth, the tort liabilities for infringement upon personality rights and interests of legal persons or unincorporated organizations. The tort liabilities for infringement upon personality rights and interests of legal persons and unincorporated organizations are mainly provided by reference to the provisions on infringement upon personality rights and interests of natural persons, but the limit is the legally-determined personality rights and interests of legal persons. In addition, by reference to personal information, it is also necessary to normalize the tort liabilities for infringement upon organizational information.

13.6 It Is Advised to Set up Chapter "Liabilities of User" as a Separate Chapter

13.6.1 Evaluation and Analysis on Rules of Liabilities of User in Current Laws

13.6.1.1 Evaluation and Analysis on Rules of Liability of User in the *Tort Liability Law*

In Chapter 4 "Special Provisions on Liable Person", the *Tort Liability Law* uses two articles to establish the system of liability of user, including the rules in three aspects:

The first is the outward vicarious liabilities which are determined dependent on whether the employer is an entity. What Paragraph 1 of Article 34 provides are the vicarious liabilities of employer, and are applicable to entity employment relationship and entity service relationship. What the first sentence of Article 35 provides are the vicarious liabilities of individual service.[23]

The second is the inward liabilities of personal protection. It is provided in the second sentence of Article 35 that: "The party, which provides service, suffers harm to himself for the service, [the parties] shall bear corresponding liability according to each party's fault." Though the rule of comparative fault adopted by this article is criticized by scholars,[24] it has established the inward liabilities of personal protection in personal employment relationship in the *Tort Liability Law*.

The third is the unreal supplementary liabilities for labor dispatch.[25] It is provided in Paragraph 2 of Article 34 that: "In the course of labor dispatch, if the dispatched employee causes harm to another while performing a task, the employer entity, which receives labor dispatch, shall bear tort liability. If the labor dispatch entity is at fault, [it] shall bear corresponding secondary liability." These are the new provisions in the *Tort Liability Law* as compared with the liabilities of user established by the *Judicial Interpretation for Personal Injury Compensation*.

13.6.1.2 Evaluation and Analysis on Rules of Liability of User in the *Judicial Interpretation on Personal Damage Compensation*

The liabilities of user in the *Judicial Interpretation for Personal Injury Compensation* are provided in Articles 8–14, including the rules in the following three aspects:

First, the outward vicarious liabilities distinguished on the basis of "employment relationship—service relationship—unpaid help". Paragraph 1 of Article 8 gives the provisions on outward vicarious liabilities in employment relationship, the first portion of Paragraph 1 of Article 9 gives the provisions on outward vicarious liabilities in service relationship, and the first sentence of Article 13 gives the provisions on outward vicarious liabilities in the special service relationship, namely unpaid help.

Second, the inward liabilities of personal protection distinguished on the basis of Paragraph 1 of Article 11 gives the provisions on inward liabilities of personal protection in service relationship, the first sentence of Paragraph 1 of Article 14 gives the provisions on inward liabilities of personal protection in unpaid help

---

[23]Since the labor relation stipulated in the *Labor Law* of China only exists between the employer and the individual, no individual labor relation exists.

[24]Cheng (2015).

[25]There is controversy over the nature of the unreal supplementary liabilities for labor dispatch, see Wang and Zhang (2013).

relationship, and Paragraph 3 of Article 11 clarifies that the system of employment injury insurance shall be applied to the inward liabilities of personal protection in employment relationship.

Third, the rules for inward liabilities of personal protection and apportionment of tort liabilities of third-party distinguished on the basis of "employment relationship—service relationship—unpaid help". Paragraph 2 of Article 12 provides the rules for inward liabilities of personal protection and apportionment of tort liabilities of third-party in employment relationship as combined liabilities,[26] the second sentence of Paragraph 1 of Article 11 provides the rules for inward liabilities of personal protection and apportionment of tort liabilities of third-party in service relationship as one-way unreal joint and several liabilities, and Paragraph 2 of Article 14 provides the rules for inward liabilities of personal protection and apportionment of tort liabilities of third-party in unpaid help relationship as supplementary compensation liabilities.

It is thus clear that, the *Judicial Interpretation for Personal Injury Compensation* establishes the systems for outward vicarious liabilities, inward liabilities of personal protection as well as rules for inward liabilities of personal protection and apportionment of tort liabilities of third-party distinguished on the basis of "employment relationship—service relationship—unpaid help". Article 10 provides that, in contracting work relationship, the fault liabilities shall be applied for outward vicarious liabilities and inward liabilities of personal protection, but does not clarify the apportionment rules for such inward liabilities of personal protection and tort liabilities of third-party.

13.6.1.3 Comparison and Evaluation of Such Two Liabilities

Through the comparison between provisions of liabilities of user in the *Tort Liability Law* and the *Judicial Interpretation for Personal Injury Compensation*, the following conclusion can be obtained:

Firstly, the complete rules of liability of user include three contents, namely rules for outward vicarious liabilities, rules for inward liabilities of personal protection, as well as apportionment rules for inward liabilities of personal protection and tort liabilities of third-party. It is really a pity that the *Tort Liability Law* is not unfolded

---

[26]Paragraph 2 of article 12 of the *Interpretation of the Supreme People's Court of Some Issues Concerning the Application of the Law on the Trial of Cases to Compensation for Personal Injury* provides that: "Where a laborer suffers from a personal injury due to the tort of a third person other than the employing entity, and the obligee to compensation claims against the third person for bearing the civil compensation liabilities, the people's court shall support such claim." Article 42 of the *Social Insurance Law* provides that: "Where any work-related injury is caused by a third party, which refuses to pay the medical expenses for work-related injuries or cannot be determined, the medical expenses shall be prepaid from the employment injury insurance funds. The employment injury insurance funds shall be entitled to be reimbursed by the third party after prepayment".

in accordance with this system, and in the future, the *Tort Liabilities Volume of Civil Code* should be unfolded in accordance with this system.

Secondly, it is more scientific to unfold the vicarious liabilities system on the basis of the types of user relationship rather than the types of employer. The relationship between in vicarious liabilities of user in the *Tort Liability Law* and the *Judicial Interpretation for Personal Injury Compensation* may be shown in the table below[27]:

Table for comparison of system of liability of user in the *tort liability law* and the *judicial interpretation for personal injury compensation*

	Paragraph 1 of article 34 of the *tort liability law*	First sentence of article 35 of the *tort liability law*
Article 8 of the *interpretation*	Employment relationship	(Excluded by legislation)
Article 9 of the *interpretation*	Entity employment relationship \entity service relationship	Individual employment relationship \paid individual service relationship
Article 13 of the *interpretation*	(Not provided)	Unpaid help relationship

It is clear through comparison that, the disadvantage of legislative mode of the *Tort Liability Law* is that the same rules are applied to employment relationship and entity service relationship. Though it seems that there is no difference in the aspect of outward vicarious liabilities, such mode is not favorable for the unified establishment of the rules for inward liabilities of personal protection as well as the apportionment rules for such liabilities and tort liabilities of third party. The *Judicial Interpretation for Personal Injury Compensation* focuses on the basic difference among "employment relationship—service relationship—unpaid help", which is more favorable for the unified establishment of the rules for inward liabilities of personal protection as well as the apportionment rules for such liabilities and tort liabilities of third party. As a result, it is advised that in the future, the *Tort Liabilities Volume of Civil Code* should be unfolded on the basis of type of relationship.

Thirdly, it is necessary to provide the liabilities of labor dispatch and liabilities of contracting work. Since the implementation of the *Labor Contract Law* in 2008, the scale of labor dispatch has increased quickly, and the cases involving dispute over labor dispatch have also increased obviously. The contracting work relationship is not the user relationship in a narrow sense (namely employment relationship). However, in a lot of cases involving dispute over liabilities for damage caused by contractor without fault of ordering party in actual practice, the equitable liabilities have been wrongly applied. In order to clarify the application of law, it is advised to normalize such two special user relationship in *Tort Liabilities Volume of Civil Code* in the future.

---

[27]Wang and Zhang (2013).

13.6.2   Necessity to Set up Chapter "Liabilities of User" as a Separate Chapter

The necessity to set up Chapter "Liabilities of User" as a separate chapter mainly comes from the special rules and system orientation of liabilities of user, which is specifically embodied as follows:

Firstly, the outward vicarious liabilities are not special tort liabilities. Different from the guardian liabilities as provided in Article 32 of the *Tort Liability Law*, the object replaced by the user's outward vicarious liabilities is the person with full capacity for civil conduct. Such person with full capacity for civil conduct should firstly undertake the tort liabilities, and then such liabilities will be replaced. The guardian liabilities are more similar to liabilities for damage caused by domesticated animal or liabilities for damage of objects in structure, and are the own liabilities of guardian. The user's outward vicarious liabilities are relatively common in liabilities for traffic accident of motor vehicle and liabilities for medical damage. Article 54 of the *Tort Liability Law* actually takes vicarious liabilities as prototype of design.[28] Among other special tort liabilities, there are also the situations for application of vicarious liabilities. Therefore, the user's outward vicarious liabilities are not special tort liabilities, but the vicarious rules got tort liabilities.

Secondly, in essence, the inward liabilities of personal protection are not tort liabilities. As for inward liabilities of personal protection and non-tort liabilities, user is not the infringing party which has caused the damage. Since the labor law of China distinguishes between employment relationship and service relationship, and the employment injury insurance can't cover all user relationships, the remedy can be provided for damage of used person in service relationship and unpaid help relationship only through tort law.

Thirdly, the inward liabilities of personal protection and apportionment of tort liabilities of third-party is not the apportionment between tort liabilities. Since the inward liabilities of personal protection is not tort liabilities, the apportionment of tort liabilities of third-party and inward liabilities of personal protection is also not the apportionment between ordinary tort liabilities, and thus the basic rules for apportionment between tort liabilities are not applied.

On the basis of the above-mentioned consideration, it is advised by the Writer that, after the liabilities of user are systematically provided in the *Tort Liabilities Volume in Civil Code* in the future, they can be separated from the chapter "Special Provisions on Liable Person" and be provided as a separate chapter.

---

[28]See Wang (2001).

13.6.3 Design Thinking for Setting up Chapter "Liabilities of User" as a Separate Chapter

13.6.3.1 To Separately Set up Chapter "Liabilities of User" as Chapter 4

Though the three liabilities of user are not fully subordinated to tort liabilities, they can be systematically provided in the *Tort Liabilities Volume of Civil Code*, and have the advantage of unified legal application. Since the user's outward vicarious liabilities are not special tort liabilities but the replaced is the damage compensation liabilities, and the inward liabilities of personal protection and the rules for inward liabilities of personal protection and apportionment of tort liabilities of third-party are subordinated to outward vicarious liabilities, it is advised by the Writer to take the liabilities of user as a separate chapter, and place them in front of the original chapter "Special Provisions on Liable Person" as Chapter 4.

13.6.3.2 Taking "Control Force" as Foundation for Establishment of User Relationship Pedigree[29]

In the user pedigree "employment relationship—service relationship—unpaid help" as provided in the *Judicial Interpretation on Personal Damage Compensation*, by taking "subordinated—equal" and "paid—unpaid" as two distinguishing dimensions, the typical user relationships can be included into the table below:

Table of element of control force in user relationship

	Subordinated	Equal
Paid	① Employment relationship	② Service relationship
Unpaid	(Excluded by legislation)	③ Unpaid help relationship

The Writer believes that, the control force in subordinated user relationship is generally higher than that in equal user relationship, and the control force in paid user relationship is generally higher than that in unpaid user relationship. Therefore, the user relationship pedigree in the table above can be arranged in order of intensity of control force, and be taken as the foundation for establishment of liabilities of user system as a pedigree: ① employment relationship, ② service relationship, ③ unpaid help relationship.

Subsequently, on the basis of intensity of control force, the same imputation principle can be applied to outward vicarious liabilities and inward liabilities of personal protection in every user liability, and the corresponding rules for inward liabilities of personal protection and apportionment of third-party liabilities can be

---

[29]As to the thought of the pedigree construction, see Wang and Zhang (2013).

designed, so as to achieve the legislative purpose, namely providing the liabilities of user as a pedigree. The specific design is as follows:

Table of types of liabilities of user

Liabilities of user \relationship	Employment relationship	Service relationship	Unpaid help relationship
Vicarious liabilities	No-fault liabilities	Presumed-fault liability	Fault liabilities
Personal protection liabilities	No-fault liabilities	Presumed-fault liability	Fault liabilities
Apportionment of third-party liabilities	Combination liabilities	One-way unreal joint and several liabilities	Supplementary indemnity liability

13.6.3.3 To Provide the Liabilities of User for Labor Dispatch Relationship and Fault Liabilities for Contracting Work Relationship

With respect to the outward vicarious liabilities of labor dispatch relationship, the unreal supplementary liabilities provided in Paragraph 2 of Article 34 of the *Tort Liability Law* can be used. As for inward liabilities of personal protection, since the relationship between employer and laborer is employment relationship, the laborer should be brought under the coverage of employment injury insurance. The rules for inward liabilities of personal protection and apportionment of tort liabilities of third-party should also be applied by reference to the employment relationship.

As for the exceptional outward vicarious liabilities and inward liabilities of personal protection for contracting work relationship, the principles of fault liabilities can be applied by taking the provisions of Article 10 of the *Judicial Interpretation on Personal Damage Compensation* as basis. In case the contractor is damaged by third party and the ordering party is without fault, such third party shall undertake the tort liabilities; where the ordering party has any fault, the proportional liabilities shall be applied.

13.7 Advices on Structural Adjustment for *Tort Liabilities Volume of Civil Code*

The analysis above reveals that, the requirements on structural adjustment for the *Tort Liabilities Volume of Civil Code* arising from the promulgation of the *General Provisions of Civil Law* and the adjustment of legislative planning for the compilation of *Civil Code* by the legislature mainly focus on general tort liabilities. The specific advices on structure adjustment are as follows:

Firstly, Chapter 1 "General Provisions" of the *Tort Liability Law* should be deleted after it is absorbed by the *General Provisions of Civil Law*.

Secondly, except for those which have been generalized, the remaining articles in Chapter 2 "Constitution of Liability and the Forms to Bear Liability" of the *Tort Liability Law* should be taken as the first two chapters of the *Tort Liabilities Volume of Civil Code*, namely Chapter 1 "Composition of Liabilities and Apportionment of Liabilities" and Chapter 2 "Damage Compensation Liabilities".

Thirdly, since the articles are fully "generalized" or are not required, Chapter 3 "Exculpatory or Extenuating Circumstances" of the *Tort Liability Law* should be deleted.

Fourthly, the new Chapter 3 "Tort Liabilities for Infringement upon Personality Rights and Interests" should be added in the *Tort Liabilities Volume of Civil Code*.

Fifthly, the rules for liabilities of user in Chapter 4 "Special Provisions on Liable Person" of the *Tort Liability Law* and the rules of liability of user in the *Judicial Interpretation on Personal Damage Compensation* should be integrated as Chapter 4 "Liabilities of user".

Sixthly, the remaining articles of Chapter 4 "Special Provisions on Liable Person" of the *Tort Liability Law* are taken as Chapter 5 of the *Tort Liabilities Volume of Civil Code*.

Seventhly, the relative positions of Chapter 5 through Chapter 11 of the *Tort Liability Law* remain unchanged, and are renumbered as Chapter 6 through Chapter 12 of the *Tort Liabilities Volume of Civil Code*. Chapter 8 "Liabilities for Environmental Pollution" of the *Tort Liability Law* is enriched as Chapter 9 "Liabilities for Polluting Environment and Damaging Ecology" of the *Tort Liabilities Volume of Civil Code*.

Eighthly, Chapter 12 "Supplementary Provisions" of the *Tort Liability Law* should be deleted.

The comparison of structure between the adjusted *Tort Liabilities Volume of Civil Code (draft for advice on compilation)* and the *Tort Liability Law* is detailed as follows:

Table of comparison of structure between the tort liabilities volume of civil code (draft for advice on compilation) and the tort liability law

Tort liabilities volume of civil code (draft for solicitation of advices for compilation)	Tort liability law
(Deleted)	Chapter 1 General Provisions
Chapter 1 Composition of liabilities and apportionment of liabilities	Chapter 2 Constitution of liability and the forms to bear liability
Chapter 2 Damage compensation liabilities	(A separate chapter)
(Deleted)	Chapter 3 Exculpatory or extenuating circumstances
Chapter 3 Tort liabilities for infringement upon personality rights and interests	(Newly added)

(continued)

(continued)

Tort liabilities volume of civil code (draft for solicitation of advices for compilation)	Tort liability law
Chapter 4 Liabilities of user	(A separate chapter)
Chapter 5 Special provisions on liable person	Chapter 4 Special provisions on liable person
Chapter 6 Products liabilities	Chapter 5 Products liabilities
Chapter 7 Liability for motor vehicle traffic accidents	Chapter 6 Liability for motor vehicle traffic accidents
Chapter 8 Liability for injury in medical treatment	Chapter 7 Liability for injury in medical treatment
Chapter 9 Liabilities for polluting environment and damaging ecology	Chapter 8 Liabilities for environmental pollution
Chapter 10 Liability for ultra-hazardous activities	Chapter 9 Liability for ultra-hazardous activities
Chapter 11 Liability for harm caused by domesticated animals	Chapter 10 Liability for harm caused by domesticated animals
Chapter 12 Liability for harm caused by objects	Chapter 11 Liability for harm caused by objects
(Deleted)	Chapter 12 Supplementary provisions

References

Cheng Xiao, *Tort Law (The 2nd Edition)*, Law Press, 2015, pp. 431–432.

Cui Jianyun, "Generan Rule of Obligation Law and Drafting Civil Code of P. R. China", *Journal of Tsinghua University (Philosophy and Social Sciences)*, No. 4, 2003.

Cui Jianyuan, "Current Situation and Future of Obligation Law of China", *Science of Law*, No. 1, 2013.

Hasibagen, Zhou Wei, "Approaches to Establish the General Provisions of Obligation Law and Reality", *Ningxia Academy of Social Sciences*, No. 2, 2003.

Li Shishi: the *Explanation of the Daft of the General Provisions of Civil Law of the People's Republic of China*, at the 21st Session of the Standing Committee of the Twelfth National People's Congress, June 27, 2016.

Lu Qing, "Functional Evolution of General Provisions of Obligation Law-from Common Norm to System Integration", *Contemporary Law Review*, No. 4, 2014.

Wang Liming, *Research on Tort Liability Law*, China Renmin University Press, 2001, p. 377.

Wang Liming, *Research on Tort Liability Law (Volume 1)*, China Renmin University Press 2010a.

Wang Shengming, *The Interpretation of Tort Law of People's Republic of China*, China Legal Publishing House, 2010b.

Wang Zhu, "Apportionment of Multi-party Tort Liabilities Involving the Fault of Infringed Party", *Tsinghua Law Review*, No. 2, 2010c.

Wang Liming, "Relationship between General Provisions of Obligation Law and General Provisions of Contract Law", *Guangdong Social Sciences*, No. 5. 2014.

Wang Zhu, Fang Yan: *Independent Process Textual Research of Scientific Principle of Body Right, Journal of Guangzhou University*, No. 5, 2012.

Wang Zhu, Zhang Heng, "On the Construction of the Pedigree of Vicarious Liability of Hirer in Tort Law of China," *Journal of Sichuan Normal University (Social Sciences Edition)*, No. 5, 2013.

Wang Zhu, Zhang Heng, "Tort Liability of Dispatch Staff—with Determination and Expansion Appliance of Apparent Supplementary Liability", *Legal Science*, No. 2, 2013.

Yang Lixin, Yuan Xueshi, "On the Claim of the Personality Right", *Chinese Journal of Law*, No. 6, 2003.

Zhang Li, Zheng Zhifeng, "The Third Party's Tortious Act in Tort Liability of China", *Modern Law Science*, No. 1, 2015.

Zhang Xinbao, *Interpretation of General Provisions of Civil Law of People's Republic of China*, China Renmin University Press, 2007, p. 389.

Part IV
Extensive Discussion on the Compilation of *Civil Code*

Both the constitutionality consideration for compilation of Civil Code and the road map for compilation of *Civil Code* under "pragmatic thinking" are the codification process carried out against the background of whole legal system of China and are the systematic adjustment to the current legal system of China. Therefore, it is necessary to take all currently valid laws in China as legal system background for compilation of *Civil Code*. During the more than ten years when the fourth drafting of civil code was suspended, the achievements made by the civil law circle of China in participation in interregional legal integration are obvious to all; in face of the "missed 15 years" for survey on civil customs, the writer has brought forth the *Plan for Survey on Civil Customs in Judgment Instruments* and hopes to absorb more scholars by sharing the preliminary analysis results. In short, let's expand the scope of discussion and support the compilation of *Civil Code*!

Chapter 14 Legal Background for the Compilation of *Civil Code*—How Many Currently Valid Laws are there in China?.

Chapter 15 Supporting Works for the Compilation of *Civil Code*.

Attached: Statistical Table for Every Cause of Action in Civil Judgment Instruments Published on China Judgments Online (by December 31, 2016).

Chapter 14
Legal Background for the Compilation of *Civil Code*—How Many Currently Valid Laws Are There in China?

14.1 Raising, Unfolding and Conversion of the Question

14.1.1 Raising of Question: How Many Currently Valid Laws Are There in China?

For a long time, there has been no authoritative answer to the question "How many currently valid laws are there in China?"[1] According to Annex "Classified Catalog of Currently valid Laws of the People's Republic of China" (hereinafter referred to as "*White Book Catalog*") to the *White Book for Rule by Law in China* issued by the News Office of the State Council, by the beginning of 2008, there were 229 valid laws in China (including the *Constitution*). Thereafter, in the *Work Report of Standing Committee of National People's Congress* given by the chairman Wu Bangguo at the 1st Meeting of 11th National People's Congress, the number of valid laws in China at that time was stated as 229.[2]

On the basis of the *White Book Catalog* and in light of the actual situation of adoption, amendment and abolishment of laws in China, by the end of 2010, there were 237 valid laws (including the *Constitution*) in China. On January 24, 2011, the chairman Wu Bangguo pointed out in the *Speech at Symposium for Formation of Socialist Legal System with Chinese Characteristics* (hereinafter referred to as "*Symposium Speech*") that, "By the end of 2010, China has enacted 236 currently valid laws".[3] If we regard the figure given by the chairman Wu Bangguo as not having counted the *Constitution*, such two figures are identical. Therefore, this may

---

[1] According to the inquiry by the Writer, the stage authoritative statistic of decision quantity of laws and relevant legal issues passed by the National People's Congress is published once only: "the Directory of Decisions of Laws and Relevant Legal Issues passed by the Eighth National People's Congress and Its Standing Committee", *the Bulletin of the Standing Committee of the National People's Congress*, No. 1, 1998.

[2] Wu (2008).

[3] Wu (2011).

© China University of Political Science and Law Press 2020
Z. Wang, *On the Constitutionality of Compiling a Civil Code of China*,
https://doi.org/10.1007/978-981-13-7900-0_14

be deemed as the authoritative answer to the question "How many currently valid laws are there in China?"

14.1.2   Unfolding of Question 1: Is the Figure Given in White Book Catalog *Essentially Identical with the Figure Given by NPC Standing Committee?*

The Writer has noticed that, among the 8 "laws and decisions relating to legal issues" abolished by the *Decision of Standing Committee of National People's Congress on Abolishment of Some Laws* adopted by the NPC Standing Committee in 2009 (hereinafter referred to as *2009 Abolishment Decision*), only 4 laws and documents are covered by the *White Book Catalog*, namely the *Regulations on Organization of Police Posts*, the *Regulations on Organization of Urban Sub-district Office*, the *Regulations on Application by Overseas Chinese for Use of State-owned Barren Hills and Wastelands* and the *Resolution of Standing Committee of National People's Congress on Approval of the Measures of State Council for Establishment of Schools with Donation from Overseas Chinese*. Therefore, it can be deduced that the *2009 Abolishment Decision* has abolished only 4 "laws", and the other 4 laws should be regarded as "decisions relating to legal issues", namely the *Decision of Standing Committee of National People's Congress on Authorizing State Council to Reform System of Industrial and Commercial Taxes and Issue Relevant Draft Tax Regulations for Trial Application*, the *Supplementary Provisions of Standing Committee of National People's Congress on Imposition of Punishments in Respect of Offenses of Tax Evasion and Refusal to Pay Tax*, the *Several Provisions of Standing Committee of National People's Congress on Strengthening Inspection and Supervision over Implementation of Laws* and the *Supplementary Provisions of Standing Committee of National People's Congress on Severely Punishing Crimes of Organizing and Transporting Another Person to Secretly Cross National Boundary (Borderline)*.

However, the problem is that, the two legal documents, namely the *Supplementary Provisions of Standing Committee of National People's Congress on Imposition of Punishments in Respect of Offenses of Tax Evasion and Refusal to Pay Tax* and the *Supplementary Provisions of Standing Committee of National People's Congress on Severely Punishing Crimes of Organizing and Transporting Another Person to Secretly Cross National Boundary (Borderline)*, were issued with order of President of State, and the validity of administrative punishment and administrative measure therein are determined by Annex 2 to the *1997 Criminal Code*. So that it seems appropriate not to regard them as laws; in contrast, the *Resolution of Standing Committee of National People's Congress on Approval of the Measures of State Council for Establishment of Schools with Donation from Overseas Chinese* was approved by the NPC Standing Committee in 1957. However, according to the *1954 Constitution*, the NPC Standing Committee has no legislative right. Through search of all laws listed in the *White Book Catalog*, the Writer found that there are 10 laws issued without the order of President.[4] This has brought a doubt to me: Is there the likelihood that, the data given by the *White Book Catalog* and the authoritative data given by the NPC Standing Committee are identical in figure only, and their meanings are different from each other?

14.1.3 Unfolding of Question 2: Who Is Entitled to and Should Answer This Question?

According to the provisions of the *Constitution* and the *Legislation Law*, NPC and the NPC Standing Committee exercise the legislative right. Therefore, as the permanent body of NPC, the NPC Standing Committee is entitled to and should answer such question. The *White Book Catalog* is not issued in the name of the NPC Standing Committee, till now the NPC Standing Committee has not issued the catalog of currently valid laws of China.

14.1.4 Unfolding of Question 3: What on Earth Is the Nature of "Decisions Relating to Legal Issues" in the Constitution?

Some scholars prudently mentioned the "decisions relating to legal issues" as the "resolutions and decisions relating to the constitutional and legal issues".[5] Strictly speaking, this wording has not expressly appeared in the powers and duties of the NPC Standing Committee as provided in any *Constitution*. This wording appeared for the first time in two legal documents adopted by the NPC Standing Committee on November 24, 1987, namely the *Decision of Standing Committee of National People's Congress on Approving the Report of Legal Affairs Commission for Sorting-out of Laws Promulgated before End of 1978* (hereinafter referred to as "1987 Abolishment Decision") and the *Deliberation Rules of Standing Committee of National People's Congress*. It is mentioned in the *1987 Abolishment Decision* that: "…The Legal Affairs Commission sorted out the laws promulgated before the end of 1978 (including decisions relating to legal issues)." It is provided in Paragraph 2 of Article 15 of the *Deliberation Rules of Standing Committee of National People's Congress* that: "After deliberating the proposal for decisions relating to legal issues and the proposals for amendment to laws, the Legal Affairs Commission may submit the report on deliberation results to current meeting of the Standing Committee, and may also submit the report on deliberation results to the

---

[4]See later analysis.
[5]Shen (2009).

next or subsequent meeting of the Standing Committee." Then, the "decisions relating to legal issues" can only be regarded as a manner for exercise of powers and duties of the NPC Standing Committee as provided in the *Constitution*, which are given in the form of "decision", are related to laws and are not used to enact or amend any law. Frankly speaking, from the viewpoint of constitutionality, all "decisions relating to legal issues" should correspond to the powers and duties of the NPC Standing Committee as provided in the *Constitution*,[6] or be specially authorized by NPC.

14.1.5 Conversion of Question: What Is the Judgment Standard for Law?

It is thus clear that, the key to the doubt on number of currently valid laws in China is the situation that, some "decisions relating to legal issues" have the "semi-law" nature. In the legal practice in China, for a long time, these "decisions relating to legal issues" which have the nature of "semi-law" (hereinafter referred to as "Semi-law Decisions") have been regarded as laws, and have won certain trust in the whole society. Though these "semi-law decisions" are essentially the exercise of legislative right, they fail to meet the provisions on exercise of legislative right as provided in the *Constitutions*, so that the confusion indetermination occurs.

Laws are the legal documents of which the authority is only second to that of the *Constitution* in the legal system of China, and are the basic framework for rule by law. Our country has declared the establishment of socialist legal system with Chinese characteristics,[7] but left the above-mentioned doubts in determination of catalog of currently valid laws, which has to be regarded as a pity. Though the "semi-law decisions" are not laws within the meaning of the *Constitution*, since neither the *Constitution* nor the *Legislation Law* has expressly provided their law status, their legal validity in practice must be clarified. Therefore, the more important question is "What is the judgment standard for law?", and then the constitutional status of those "semi-law decisions" will be determined on this basis. Hereinafter, from the viewpoint of legal theory, this issue will be explored into, and the advices on issuance by the NPC Standing Committee of catalog of currently valid laws in future will be given.

---

[6]According to the preliminary observation by the Writer, some "decisions about relevant legal issues" of the National People's Congress cannot be directly brought into the powers and duties specified in Article 67, the *Constitution*, and they can only be brought by the extensive interpretation.

[7]Wu (2011).

14.2   Judgment Standard for Law Within Meaning of the *Constitution*

14.2.1   Types of Currently Valid Laws in China

14.2.1.1   The *Constitution* Is Not a Law

With respect to the question whether the *Constitution* is a law, there is still certain controversy in academic circle. For example, the *White Book Catalog* lists the *Constitution* under the category "Constitution and Constitution-related Laws". It is stated in the first sentence of last paragraph of preface of the *Constitution* that: "In the form of <u>law</u>, this *Constitution* confirms the achievements made by all people of China through struggle, provides the fundamental system and fundamental tasks of the state, is the <u>fundamental law</u> of the state, and has the <u>supreme legal authority</u>." Some scholars believe that, the word "law" here is actually used from the viewpoint of general characteristics of law, namely general nature, normative nature, abstract nature and compulsory nature.[8] However, more articles in main body of the *Constitution* distinguish between "the constitution" and "laws". For example, it is provided in Paragraph 3 of Article 5 that: "All <u>laws</u>, administrative regulations and local regulations may not conflict with <u>the Constitution</u>." The Writer believes that, though the *Constitution* has its title ended with "law", it really has the status higher than laws, and may not be regarded as laws.[9]

14.2.1.2   All Legal Documents of Which the Title Is Ended with "Law" Are Laws

Generally, the currently valid laws in China can be divided into the laws of which the title is ended with "law" and the laws of which the title is not ended with "law". By 31th January 2018, excluding the *Constitution*, there are 241 valid legal documents of which the title is ended with "law" in the current legal system of China, among which the earliest one was the *1979 Criminal Code*. The *1987 Abolishment Decision* has abolished all the 11 laws[10] which were enacted before 1978 and of which the title is ended with "law". Since there is no controversy on these legal

---

[8]Han and Wang (2005a).

[9]As previously mentioned, if it is presumed that the "*White Book Catalog*" matches the authoritative data published by the National People's Congress, the *Constitution* should not be brought into the law, though this judgment does not leave material effects on the probe into the legal judgment standard in the following text.

[10]These laws includes: the *1949 Organization Law of Chinese People's Political Consultative Conference*, the *1949 Organization Law of Central People's Government*, the *1950 Marriage Law*, the 1950 *Agrarian Reform Act*, the *1953 Electoral Law of the National People's Congress and Local People's Congresses*, the *1954 Electoral Law of the National People's Congress*, the *1954 Organization Law of Local People's Congresses and Local People's Commission*, the *1954*

documents as laws on theoretic basis, it can be concluded that all legal documents of which the title is ended with "law" are laws. Hereinafter, the study will be focus on the judgment standard for laws of which the title is not ended with "law".

14.2.1.3 Types of Legal Documents of Which the Title Is Not Ended with "Law"

Among the currently valid laws in China, the legal documents of which the title is not ended with "law" are diversified, mainly including general principles, regulations, deliberation rules, election measures, decisions, provisions as well as decisions or resolutions of NPC Standing Committee for approving norm documents enacted by other organs. It should be specially pointed out that, among the legal documents of which the title is not ended with "law" as listed in the *White Book Catalog*, some have great impact on our life,[11] and some even involve the fundamental political systems of China.[12] Therefore, it is very urgent to determine whether such legal documents are laws.

14.2.2 Judgment Standard for Laws Within the Meaning of the Constitution

With respect to judgment standard for laws, some scholars have brought forth the formal rationality standard and essential rationality standard, believing that a law within the strict meaning must be a norm document with formal rationality and essential rationality adopted by the Legislature in accordance with the legislative procedure.[13] The Writer agrees to the judgment standard which distinguishes between formal rationality and essential rationality, but believes that, this dual standard is more suitable for increasing-normalized legislative activities carried out after the *1982 Constitution* was promulgated, especially after the *Legislation Law*

Organization Law of State Council, the *1954 Organization Law of People's Court*, the *1954 Organization Law of People's Procuratorates* and the *1954 Military Service Law*.

[11]The *General Principles of Civil Law*, the *Regulations on Household Registration*, the *Regulations on Academic Degrees*, the *Interim Measures of the State Council for Retirement and Resignation of Workers*, the *Resolution of Standing Committee of National People's Congress on Approval of the Provisions of State Council on Treatment of Family Visits of Workers and Staff Members*, etc.

[12]The *Measures for Election of Deputies from Chinese People's Liberation Army to National People's Congress and Local People's Congresses at or Above County Level*, the *Several Provisions of Standing Committee of National People's Congress on Direct Election of Delegates of People's Congress below County Level*, the *Rules of Procedure of Standing Committee of National People's Congress*, the *Rules of Procedure for the NPC*, etc.

[13]Therefore, some scholars determine the normative documents as the laws without exception, but the Writer does not approve of it. Refer to Han and Wang (2005b).

came into effect. As for the laws enacted before the *1982 Constitution*, the articles of the *Constitution* and the special characteristics at that time should be considered. Therefore, different times should be determined for judgment standard for currently valid laws in China on the basis of four constitutions. The legal documents in different times should be judged on the basis of the "formal rationality standard" of such times and in light of the "essential rationality standard".

14.2.2.1 Formal Rationality Standard for Different Times

The so-called formal rationality of law means that, a law must be the legal document adopted by the Legislature in accordance with the relevant procedure, and the enactment of law must meet the procedural requisites of law, including the lawfulness of legislative subject.[14] Therefore, not all the "decisions" and "resolutions" given by the NPC Standing Committee can be regarded as laws.[15] The Writer believes that, the most important is that the enacting organ, enactment procedure and issuing organ must meet the provisions of the *Constitution* at time of legislation. From the viewpoint of presumption of constitutionality, it is not appropriate to carry out excessively strict inspection on constitutionality of enactment procedure for those laws which have been implemented. Therefore, the constitutionality standard for enactment organ and the constitutionality standard for issuing organ are studied hereinafter.

First, the constitutionality standard for enacting organ. It is provided in Article 22 of the *1954 Constitution* that: "The National People's Congress is the only organ which exercises the legislative right of the state." According to the provisions of Items 3 and 4 of Article 31 of such *Constitution,* the Standing Committee of NPC can only "interpret laws" and "enact decrees". Article 17 and Article 18 of the *1975 Constitution* as well as Item 2 of Article 22 and Item 3 of Article 25 of the *1978 Constitution* also give the similar provisions. It is provided in Article 58 of the *1982 Constitution* that: "The National People's Congress and the Standing Committee of National People's Congress exercise the legislative right of the state." It is provided in Item 3 of Article 67 that: "The Standing Committee of National People's Congress shall exercise the following powers and duties: ...③ During the period when the National People's Congress is not in session, partially supplement and amend the laws enacted by the National People's Congress, provided that the basic principles of such law may not be violated; ..." Therefore, it should be determined that, all the legal documents formulated by the NPC Standing Committee before December 3, 1982 are not laws.

---

[14]Li and Zheng (2004).

[15]Therefore, some scholars affirm the normative documents promulgated by the National People's Congress and its Standing Committee as the laws without exception, the Writer does not approve of it. Refer to Han and Wang (2005b).

Second, the constitutionality standard for issuing organ. It is provided in Article 40 of the 1954 Constitution: "The President of the People's Republic of China shall, on the basis of the decision of the National People's Congress and the decision of the Standing Committee of the National People's Congress, issue the laws and decrees, …, and issue the mobilization order." It is provided in Article 80 of the *1982 Constitution* that: "The President of the People's Republic of China shall, on the basis of the decision of the National People's Congress and the decision of the Standing Committee of the National People's Congress, issue the laws, …, and issue the mobilization order." Both the *1975 Constitution* and the *1978 Constitution* fail to provide the President of State as state organ. Since the articles of the *1954 Constitution* and the *1982 Constitution* fail to expansively provide the powers and duties of President of State with the word "etc.", a legal document enacted by the legislature before January 16, 1975 or after December 4, 1982 may be regarded as law only if it was issued with the order of President.[16] The legal documents enacted by the Legislature but issued without order of President during the period from January 17, 1975 to December 3, 1982 may also be regarded as laws.[17]

14.2.2.2 Essential Rationality Standard

The so-called essential rationality of law means that a law enacted by the Legislature in accordance with the procedure must meet the general requisites of law. For example, a law must is abstract, generally applicable, public, clear, stable and non-retroactive. The laws enacted by legislatures may not aim at specific case, and also may not become the measure for handling any specific event.[18] The Writer believes that, in the judgment standard for essential rationality of law, the most important is abstract nature standard and normative nature standard. The so-called abstract nature means that a law is the provisions given for abstract social relationship rather than specific event. The so-called normative nature means that a law must to a certain extent contain behavior norm or judgment norm. It is thus clear that, why the "semi-law decisions" could be misunderstood as laws is because that they meet the essential rationality standard of law, but fail to meet the formal rationality standard.

---

[16]In the constitutional practice of China, the form of exercising the powers and duties of "law publishing" by the order of President also includes the publishing of law amendment and abolishment.

[17]Due to the historical causes, in fact, no state President existed from 1966 to 1975 in China. However, the legislative body during this period did not pass any legal document either. Therefore, the discussed content and conclusion in this paper are not affected.

[18]Li and Zheng (2004).

14.3   Number of Currently Valid Laws in China

The above analysis on judgment standard for law reveals that, in the aspect of formal rationality standard, the *1982 Constitution* greatly changes the law enacting organ and law issuing organ. Therefore, by taking December 4, 1982 (namely the time when such Constitution was adopted) as dividing line and on the basis of the time when the legislature adopted or amended legal documents, the number of laws of which the title is not ended with "law" before and after the *1982 Constitution* is respectively explored into hereinafter. Since it is relatively easy to judge whether most of the "decisions relating to legal issues" are laws, the Writer, on the basis of the *White Book Catalog*, only include those "semi-law decisions" which may be easily misunderstood as laws into the study.

14.3.1   Number of Laws of Which the Title Is Ended with "Law" After the Implementation of the 1982 Constitution

As for the legal documents issued after the implementation of the *1982 Constitution* of which the title is not ended with "law", on the basis of the ending words and contents, their legal status is confirmed category by category as follows:

First category: "general principles". As a transitional civil code, the title of *General Principles of the Civil Law* is ended with "general principles"[19] owing to their special legislative background, and its legal status is undoubtable.

Second category: "deliberation rules". It is provided in Article 78 of the *Constitution* that: "The organization and work procedures of the National People's Congress and its standing committee shall be provided by laws." The "work procedure" laws corresponding to such provisions are two "deliberation rules", namely the *Deliberation Rules of National People's Congress* and the *Deliberation Rules of Standing Committee of National People's Congress*. They were issued with order of President, and should be regarded as laws.

Third category: "regulations". Though most of the "regulations" are administrative regulations,[20] a few "regulations" are laws. Since the implementation of the *1982 Constitution*, there are 6 currently valid laws of which the title is ended with "regulations", including the *Regulations on Academic Degrees*, the *Regulations on*

---

[19]See Wang (2010).

[20]Subject to Paragraph 1, Article 4, the *Regulations on Formulation Procedures of Administrative Laws and Regulations*: "generally, the name of administrative laws and regulations is called "regulation", and it may also be called 'provision', 'measure' and the like. The administrative laws and regulations formulated by the State Council based on the authorization decision of the National People's Congress and its Standing Committee are called 'interim regulations' or 'interim provisions'.

Diplomatic Privileges and Immunities, the *Regulations on Consular Privileges and Immunities*, the *Regulations on Police Ranks of the People's Police*, the *Regulations on Military Ranks of Officers of Chinese People's Liberation Army* and the *Regulations on Customs Ranks*. Among them, the process for determination of legal status of the *Regulations on Academic Degrees* is relatively special. Such regulations were originally adopted by the NPC Standing Committee in 1980, and according to the *1978 Constitution*, such regulations could only be determined as a decree at that time. In 2004, the amendment to such regulations was adopted by the NPC Standing Committee and was issued with order of President. Since such date, such regulations have been converted into a law.

Fourth category: election systems. The *Measures for Election of Deputies from Chinese People's Liberation Army to National People's Congress and Local People's Congresses at or Above County Level* was adopted by the NPC Standing Committee in 1981, and was issued by the NPC Standing Committee by itself. In accordance with the *1978 Constitution*, such "measures" can only be regarded as decrees. In 1996, such measures were amended by the NPC Standing Committee, and issued with order of President. Since such date, the nature of such measures has been changed to law. The *Several Provisions of Standing Committee of National People's Congress on Direct Election of Delegates of People's Congress below County Level* adopted by the NPC Standing Committee in 1983 was issued without order of President, and should be regarded as "semi-law decision".

Fifth category: decisions of the NPC Standing Committee, which is the difficult point for judgment. For the purpose of judgment, the Writer divides this category into the following sub-categories:

First sub-category: Wholly-valid decisions. The *Decision of Standing Committee of National People's Congress on Application of Provisional Regulations on Such Taxes as Value-added Tax, Consumption Tax and Business Tax to Enterprises with Foreign Investment and Foreign Enterprises* was adopted by the NPC Standing Committee and issued with order of President in 1993, and should be regarded as law.

Second sub-category: partially-valid decisions. It is provided in Annex 2 to the *1997 Criminal Code* that: "The following supplementary provisions and decisions enacted by the Standing Committee of the National People's Congress are retained, and the provisions relating to administrative punishment and administrative measures shall be continuously valid; the provisions relating to criminal liabilities have been incorporated into this Law, and as of the date on which this Law is implemented, the provisions of this Law shall apply." Among the items enumerated in such annex, Item 1 "*Anti-drug Decision*" has been abolished by the *Anti-drug Law*, Item 5 "the *Supplementary Provisions on Imposition of Punishments in Respect of Offenses of Tax Evasion and Refusal to Pay Tax*" and Item 6 "*Supplementary Provisions on Severely Punishing Crimes of Organizing and Transporting Another Person to Secretly Cross National Boundary (Borderline)*" have been abolished by the 2009 Abolishment Decision, and the remaining 5 items are still partially valid and should be regarded as laws.[21]

Third sub-category: decisions established by judicial organs. The *Decision of Standing Committee of National People's Congress on Establishment of Maritime Courts in Coastal Port Cities* was adopted by the NPC Standing Committee and issued with order of President on November 14, 1984, and should be regarded as law.[22]

Fourth sub-category: partial supplementation of law. The *Decision of Standing Committee of National People's Congress on Punishing Crimes of Fraudulently Purchasing, Evading and Illegally Trading in Foreign Exchange* was adopted by the NPC Standing Committee and issued with order of President in 1998. Such decision is the exercise of power and duty of the NPC Standing Committee to "partially supplement" laws as provided in Paragraph 3 of Article 67 of the *Constitution*. Since such decision is contained in the subsequent amendment to the *Criminal Code*, has not been incorporated into the *Criminal Code*, and meets the dual standard (formal rationality and essential rationality) for law, it should also be regarded as law.

Fifth sub-category: other decisions relating to legal issues. The decision listed in the *White Book Catalog*, namely the *Decision of Standing Committee of National People's Congress on Exercise of Criminal Jurisdiction on Crimes Provided in International Treaties Concluded or Participated in by the People's Republic of China* (1987), and the decisions which are not listed in the *White Book Catalog*, namely the *Decision of Standing Committee of National People's Congress on Maintenance of Security of Internet* (2000), the *Decision of Standing Committee of National People's Congress on Improvement of People's Jury System* (2004), and the *Decision of Standing Committee of National People's Congress on Issue about Administration of Judicial Authentication* (2005), have the relatively strong abstract nature and normal nature, were issued without order of President, and should be regarded as "semi-law decisions". However, it is provided in Article 5 of the *Decision of Standing Committee of National People's Congress on Amendment of Five Laws Including the Compulsory Education Law of People's Republic of China* adopted at the 14th Meeting of Standing Committee of 12th NPC on April 24, 2015 that: "The amendment is hereby made to the *Decision of Standing Committee of*

---

[21]Five partially valid laws are as follows: the *Decision of the Standing Committee of the National People's Congress on Punishing the Criminal Offenders Who Are Engaged in the Smuggling, Production, Sales and Spread of Obscene Goods*, the *Decision of the Standing Committee of the National People's Congress on Severely Punishing the Criminal Offenders Who Are Engaged in the Abduction and Kidnapping of Women and Children*, the *Decision of the Standing Committee of the National People's Congress on Prohibiting the Prostitution and Whoring*, the *Decision of the Standing Committee of the National People's Congress on Punishing the Crime of Destroying the Financial Order*, and the *Decision of the Standing Committee of the National People's Congress on Punishing the Crime of False Issuance, Fabrication and Illegal Sales of Special Invoice for Value-added Tax*.

[22]Professor Cai Dingjian thinks that such decision belongs to the decision of interpretation, modification and supplement of law. Refer to Cai (2003, p. 320).

National People's Congress on Issue about Administration of Judicial Authentication, and Article 15 thereof is amended as: 'The charging standard for judicial authentication shall be formulated by the price administration authority of the people government of province, autonomous region or municipality directly under the central government in conjunction with the judicial administrative authority at the same level.'" Such decision was issued with the *Order No. 25 of the President of the People's Republic of China*, and thus the amended *Decision of Standing Committee of National People's Congress on Issue about Administration of Judicial Authentication* was converted into law.

Sixthly category: approval decision. The *Decision of Standing Committee of National People's Congress on Approving the Provisions of Central Military Commission on Granting Meritorious Service Medal of Chinese People's Liberation Army to Retired Military Officers* as enumerated in the *White Book Catalog* was adopted by the NPC Standing Committee and issued without order of President in 1988, and thus should be regarded as "semi-law decision".

In summary, among the above-mentioned six categories of legal documents of which the title is not ended with "law", there are 19 laws.

14.3.2 Number of Laws of Which the Title Is Not Ended with "Law" Before the 1982 Constitution

As for determination of number of laws of which the title is not ended with "law" before the enactment of the *1982 Constitution*, the first problem encountered is the remote past. Therefore, the Writer firstly determined the total number of legal documents which are still valid, and then determined the law status of such legal documents one by one.

14.3.2.1   Total Number of Valid Legal Documents of Which the Title Is Not Ended with "Law" Before the *1982 Constitution*

It is pointed out in the *1987 Abolishment Decision* that: "During the period from September 1949 to the end of 1978, 134 laws were enacted or approved by the 1st Meeting of Chinese People's Political Consultative Conference, the Central People's Government Commission, the National People's Congress and its Standing Committee, among which 111 laws are invalidated (See Annex 1), and 23 laws are still valid, and 23 are amended." It should be noted that, the *Resolution of 2nd Meeting of 1st National People's Congress on Authorizing Standing Committee to Enact Specific Regulations* issued in 1955 was invalidated when the *1982 Constitution* was adopted. According to the search carried out by the Writer, all separate regulations enacted by the NPC Standing Committee before the adoption of the *1982 Constitution* have been abolished by the *1987 Abolishment Decision*.

Therefore, when we explore into the number of currently valid laws in China, no separate regulation is involved.

Through the search and study carried out one by one, the Writer has found that, among the 23 documents not abolished by the *1987 Abolishment Decision*, 10 have been expressly abolished for various reasons.[23] Though the *Resolution of Standing Committee of National People's Congress on Adjustment to Organizations and Institutions under the State Council* issued in 1956 is not expressly abolished, it has no abstract nature, and as its adjustment object changes, it should be regarded as having been invalidated. Therefore, there are 12 legal documents which were promulgated before 1978 and were not expressly abolished by the *1987 Abolishment Decision*. Among them, the *Resolution of NPC on Chinese Phonetic Alphabet Program* was adopted by NPC in 1958, but was issued without the order of President, so that it is also not a law. In addition, from 1979 to 1982 when the *Constitution* was promulgated, the NPC Standing Committee approved 4 normative documents submitted by the State Council. These 15 legal documents are all laws and "semi-law decisions" issued before the implementation of the *1982 Constitution*.

14.3.2.2   Legal Documents Adopted by NPC Standing Committee

The legal documents adopted by the NPC Standing Committee may be divided into the following categories:

First category: regulations. The *Regulations on Household Registration* were adopted by the NPC Standing Committee and issued with the order of President in 1958, so that they should be regarded as a law.

Second category: decisions made by the NPC Standing Committee. Though the *Decision on Disposal of Illegal Books and Magazines* (1955), the *Decision on Acceptance of Foreign Envoys by Chairman of Standing Committee of National People's Congress during Period When President and Vice President of the People's Republic of China are on Vocation or Travel* (1955) and the *Decision on Issue Whether Persons Deprived of Political Rights can Serve as Defenders* (1956)

---

[23]Per the promulgation time sequence: the *Trade Union Law* (1950), the *Regulations on Organization of Urban Sub-district Office* (1954), the *Regulations on Organization of Police Posts* (1954), the *Regulations on Organization of Urban Neighborhood Committee* (1954), the *Regulations on Application by Overseas Chinese for Use of State-owned Barren Hills and Wastelands* (1955), the *Regulations on People's Police* (1957), the *Resolution of Standing Committee of National People's Congress on Approval of the Interim Provisions of the State Council for Reward and Punishment of Workers of State Administrative Organs* (1957), the *Regulations on Agricultural Tax* (1958), the *Resolution of Standing Committee of National People's Congress on Approval of the Draft of the Regulations on Industrial and Commercial Consolidated Tax of the People's Republic of China* (1958), the *Resolution of Standing Committee of National People's Congress on Approval of the Regulations on Service of Cadres of the Chinese People's Liberation Army* (1978).

have abstract nature and normative nature, on the basis of the legislative authority as provided in the *1954 Constitution*, they can only be regarded as "decrees".

Third category: approval resolutions made by the NPC Standing Committee. The *White Book Catalog* enumerates seven special resolutions made by the NPC Standing Committee for approving the proposals of the State Council,[24] with the time span from August 1, 1957 to March 6, 1981. As mentioned above, since the 1954, 1975 and *1978 Constitutions* don't provide that the NPC Standing Committee may enact laws, these approval legal document are not the laws within the meaning of the *Constitution*, and can only be regarded as "semi-law decisions".

In summary, among the above-mentioned three categories of legal documents of which the title is not ended with "law", there is only one law.

14.3.2.3   Legal Documents Formulated and Adopted by Other Organs

The nature of remaining four legal documents adopted by other organs has to be determined on the basis of the analysis on Annex 3 *"National Laws Implemented in Kong Special Administrative Region"* to the *Basic Law of Hong Kong Special Administrative Region*. When the *Basic Law of Hong Kong Special Administrative Region* was adopted in 1990, six laws were listed in Annex 3 thereto: the *Resolution on National Capital, Annals, National Anthem, National Flag of the People's Republic of China* (adopted at 1st Plenary Session of Chinese People's Political Consultative Conference on September 27, 1949), the *Resolution on National Day of the People's Republic of China* (adopted at 4th Meeting of Central People's Government Commission on December 2, 1949), the *Order of Central People's Government for Issuance of National Emblem of the People's Republic of China (attached: pattern, instruction and using method of national emblem)* (September 20, 1950), the *Declaration of Government of the People's Republic of China on Territorial Sea* (approved at 100th Meeting of NPC Standing Committee on September 4, 1958), the *Nationality Law* and the *Regulations on Diplomatic Privileges and Immunities*.

---

[24]Seven special resolutions are as follows: the *Resolution of Standing Committee of National People's Congress on Approval of Labor Education Issue of the State Council* (August 1, 1957), the *Resolution of Standing Committee of National People's Congress on Approval of the Interim Measures of State Council on Resettlement of Sick and Elderly Cadres* (May 24, 1978), the *Resolution of Standing Committee of National People's Congress on Approval of the Interim Measures of the State Council for Retirement and Resignation of Workers* (May 24, 1978), the *Resolution of Standing Committee of National People's Congress on Approval of Supplemental Provisions for Labor Education of the State Council* (November 29, 1979), the *Resolution of Standing Committee of National People's Congress on Approval of the Regulations on Guangdong Special Economic Zone* (August 26, 1980), the *Resolution of Standing Committee of National People's Congress on Approval of* the Interim Provisions of State Council on Discharge and Recuperation of Veteran Cadres (September 29, 1980), the *Resolution of Standing Committee of National People's Congress on Approval of the Provisions of State Council on Treatment of Family Visits of Workers and Staff Members* (March 6, 1981).

It is proposed in the *Proposal of Preparatory Committee for Hong Kong Special Administrative Region under National People's Congress on Addition and Deletion of Some National Laws listed in Annex 3 to the Basic Law of Hong Kong Special Administrative Region of the People's Republic of China* issued on May 23, 1997 that: "2. To delete the following national law in Annex 3 to the *Basic Law*: the *Order of Central People's Government for Issuance of National Emblem of the People's Republic of China (attached: pattern, instruction and using method of national emblem).*" The *Decision of Standing Committee of National People's Congress on Addition and Deletion of Some National Laws listed in Annex 3 to the Basic Law of Hong Kong Special Administrative Region of the People's Republic of China* issued on July 1, 1997 approved the above-mentioned proposal, but did not declare the abolishment of the *Order of Central People's Government for Issuance of National Emblem of the People's Republic of China (attached: pattern, instruction and using method of national emblem).* Therefore, the above-mentioned four legal documents listed in Annex 3 of the *Basic Law of Hong Kong Special Administrative Region* should be regarded as laws.[25]

14.3.3   Determination of Number of Currently Valid Laws in Our Country

On the basis of the above analysis, there are currently valid 22 laws of which the title is not ended with "law" in China. Plus the 241 laws of which the title is ended with "law" by 31th January 2018, excluding the *Constitution*, the total number of currently valid laws in China is 263. It should be specially pointed out that, among the above-mentioned laws of which the title is not ended with "law", when the *White Book Catalog* was issued, 10 were not listed in the *White Book Catalog*,[26]

---

[25]According to the analysis above, the *Declaration of Government of the People's Republic of China on Territorial Sea* should be affirmed as a decree. However, it is listed by the *Basic Law of Hong Kong Special Administrative Region* as the "national law". Besides, it is published through the order of President of China. Therefore, from the effective date of the *Basic Law of Hong Kong Special Administrative Region*, namely, July 1, 1990, it is converted into the law.

[26]Per the initial promulgation time sequence: the *Resolution on National Capital, Annals, National Anthem, National Flag of the People's Republic of China* (1949), the *Resolution on National Day of the People's Republic of China* (1949), the *Order of Central People's Government for Issuance of National Emblem of the People's Republic of China* (attached: pattern, instruction and using method of national emblem) (1950), the *Resolution of Standing Committee of National People's Congress on Approval of the Declaration of Government of the People's Republic of China on Territorial Sea* (1958), the *Decision of the Standing Committee of the National People's Congress on Punishing the Criminal Offenders Who Are Engaged in the Smuggling, Production, Sales and Spread of Obscene Goods* (1990), the *Decision of the Standing Committee of the National People's Congress on Severely Punishing the Criminal Offenders Who Are Engaged in the Abduction and Kidnapping of Women and Children* (1991), the *Decision of the Standing Committee of the National People's Congress on Prohibiting the Prostitution and Whoring* (1991), the *Decision of the Standing Committee of the National People's Congress on Punishing the*

and 10 legal documents listed in the *White Book Catalog* of which the title is not ended with "law" are not laws but "semi-law decisions".[27] Therefore, though apparently the number of currently valid laws given by the NPC Standing Committee is identical with the updated statistics given in the *White Book Catalog*, they can't correspond to each other essentially. As a result, it is advised by the Writer that, the NPC Standing Committee should, on the basis of the provisions of every *Constitution*, formally issue the catalog of currently valid laws of China.

14.4   Improvement of Constitutionality of "Semi-Law Decisions"

14.4.1   Embarrassed Constitutional Status of "Semi-Law Decisions"

In addition to determining the number of current laws in China, the above analysis has a byproduct, namely determining 12 "semi-law decisions" in the following three categories:

First category: decrees. Since the NPC Standing Committee had no legislative right before the *1982 Constitution* was enacted, 7 approval decisions for proposals

---

Crime of Destroying the Financial Order (1995), the *Decision of the Standing Committee of the National People's Congress on Punishing the Crime of False Issuance, Fabrication and Illegal Sales of Special Invoice for Value-added Tax* (1995) and the *Decision of Standing Committee of National People's Congress on Punishing Crimes of Fraudulently Purchasing, Evading and Illegally Trading in Foreign Exchange* (1998).

[27]Per the initial promulgation time sequence: the *Resolution of Standing Committee of National People's Congress on Approval of Labor Education Issue of the State Council* (1957), the *Resolution of Standing Committee of National People's Congress on Approval of the Interim Measures of the State Council for Retirement and Resignation of Workers* (1978), the *Resolution of Standing Committee of National People's Congress on Approval of the Interim Measures of State Council on Resettlement of Sick and Elderly Cadres* (1978), the *Resolution of Standing Committee of National People's Congress on Approval of Supplemental Provisions for Labor Education of the State Council* (1979), the *Resolution of Standing Committee of National People's Congress on Approval of* the Interim Provisions of State Council on Discharge and Recuperation of Veteran Cadres (1980), the *Resolution of Standing Committee of National People's Congress on Approval of the Regulations on Guangdong Special Economic Zone* (1980), the *Resolution of Standing Committee of National People's Congress on Approval of the Provisions of State Council on Treatment of Family Visits of Workers and Staff Members* (1981), the *Several Provisions of Standing Committee of National People's Congress on Direct Election of Delegates of People's Congress below County Level* (1983), the *Decision of Standing Committee of National People's Congress on Exercise of Criminal Jurisdiction on Crimes Provided in International Treaties Concluded or Participated in by the People's Republic of China* (1987), the *Decision of Standing Committee of National People's Congress on Approving the Provisions of Central Military Commission on Granting Meritorious Service Medal of Chinese People's Liberation Army to Retired Military Officers* (1988).

of the State Council were made during such period,[28] and their nature should be determined as "decrees". After the *1982 Constitution* was enacted, however, the category "decree" has no longer existed in legal system of China. Though their legal validity is undoubtable, but the constitutional status of such 5 "decrees" is questionable.[29]

Second category: "semi-law decisions" which have significance of legal interpretation. It is provided in Article 1 of the *Resolution of Standing Committee of National People's Congress on Strengthening Legal Interpretation Works* issued in 1981 that: "In case it is necessary to further define the boundary or give supplementary provisions for any article in laws and decrees, the Standing Committee of National People's Congress shall give interpretation or give provisions in the form of decrees." According to such resolution, the two "semi-law decisions", namely the *Several Provisions of Standing Committee of National People's Congress on Direct Election of Delegates of People's Congress below County Level* and the *Decision of Standing Committee of National People's Congress on Exercise of Criminal Jurisdiction on Crimes Provided in International Treaties Concluded or Participated in by the People's Republic of China*, have no power or duty as provided in Article 67 of the *Constitution*, and can only be narrowly regarded as having certain significance of legal interpretation, but their constitutional status is still questionable.

Third category: other normative "semi-law decisions". It is provided in Paragraph 2 of Article 45 of the *Legislation Law* that: "In case a law is involved in any of the following circumstances, the Standing Committee of National People's Congress shall give interpretation: ① The meaning of provisions of such law must be further clarified; ② As for any new situation occurring after the enactment of law, it is necessary to clarify the basis for legal application." This provision essentially cancels the practice that NPC may make legal interpretation by giving supplementary provisions to law after the *Legislation Law* comes into effect.[30] Therefore, the following three legal documents adopted by the NPC Standing Committee after the *Legislation Law* came into effect may not exist as legal interpretation any longer: the *Decision of Standing Committee of National People's Congress on Maintenance of Security of Internet*, the *Decision of Standing Committee of National People's Congress on Issue about Administration of Judicial Authentication* and the *Decision of Standing Committee of National People's Congress on Improvement of People's Jury System*. In addition, their constitutional status is also questionable.

---

[28]See Cai (2003, p. 324).

[29]Subject to the *Decision of Standing Committee of National People's Congress on Abolishment of Relevant Legal Provisions for Labor Education* passed at the sixth meeting of the Standing Committee of the 12th National People's Congress on December 28, 2013, the *Resolution of Standing Committee of National People's Congress on Approval of Labor Education Issue of the State Council* and the *Resolution of Standing Committee of National People's Congress on Approval of Supplemental Provisions for Labor Education of the State Council* were abolished.

[30]Cai (2006, p. 334).

14.4.2   *Concept and Essence of "Semi-Law Decisions"*

The "semi-law decisions" are adopted by the NPC Standing Committee, but are different from the "decisions relating to legal issues" within general meaning. In other words, the "semi-law decisions" have the essentially rational features of law, but fail to meet the formally rational standards of law, and can't find the express basis in the powers and duties of the NPC Standing Committee as provided in the *Constitution*. Therefore, Paragraph 2 of Article 16 of the *Deliberation Rules for Standing Committee of National People's Congress* lists them together with the "proposals for amendment to laws", and distinguishes between them and "draft of law" in Paragraph 1 of such article. It is thus clear that, the so-called "semi-law decisions" mean the special decisions which are closely related to implementation of laws, other than those which are covered by the powers and duties of the NPC Standing Committee as expressly provided in the *Constitution*.

Formally, the "semi-law decisions" are the exercise of "decision right". The so-called decision right is the right to make decision for major matters of the state or locality.[31] When the legislation is a certain aspect is not mature, the decisions may be used to fill the gap, and decisions may be extensively used to amend, supplement and interpret laws.[32] Essentially, this is the exercise of legislative right in the form of "semi-law decisions" and in the name of "decision right".

14.4.3   *Constitutionality and Reasonableness of "Semi-Law Decisions"*

It should be pointed out that, though the *Constitution* of China has never expressly provided that the NPC Standing Committee has the power or duty to enact "semi-law decisions", such power or duty may be deduced from the provisions in Article 58 of the *1982 Constitution* "The National People's Congress and the Standing Committee of National People's Congress exercise the legislative right of the state" and the provisions in Item 11 of Article 62 "The National People's Congress shall exercise the following powers and duties: …⑪ Change or cancel the inappropriate decisions made by the Standing Committee of National People's Congress; …".

The review on the fact that the NPC Standing Committee obtains the legislative right from the *1982 Constitution* reveals the realistic needs of this legislative activity. As mentioned above, the NPC adopted the *Resolution of 2nd Meeting of 1st National People's Congress on Authorizing Standing Committee to Enact Specific Regulations* in 1955. In the course of drafting of the *Constitution* in 1982,

---

[31]Cai (2003, p. 314).
[32]Cai (2003, p. 315).

the expression about obtainment of legislative right by the NPC Standing Committee appeared for the first time in the Amendment to *Constitution* (draft for discussion) on February 27, 1982. The review on authoritative literatures reveals that, at that time, the consensus on expanding the legislative powers and duties of the NPC Standing Committee had been reached.[33] On April 22, 1982, the chairman PENG Zhen stated in the *Explanation on Draft of Constitution of the People's Republic of China* that, it is provided in the draft that NPC and the NPC Standing Committee "exercise the legislative right of the state and enact laws and decrees".[34] On November 26, 1982, the chairman PENG Zhen also stated in the *Report on Draft Revision of the Constitution of the People's Republic of China*: "We should strengthen the people's congress system. We should delegate some powers and duties originally exercised by NPC to its Standing Committee, so as to expand the powers and duties of the NPC Standing Committee and strengthen its organization. NPC and its Standing Committee exercise the legislative right of the state; except for the basic laws which shall be enacted by NPC, all other laws shall be enacted by the NPC Standing Committee enact." [35] Therefore, some scholars pointed out that, the new provisions relating to legislative right in the *1982 Constitution* have obviously expanded the powers and duties of the NPC Standing Committee.[36] The above-mentioned historical review reveals that, the occurrence of "semi-law decisions" is the embodiment of the legislative needs brought about by the fact that the meeting system of NPC and its Standing Committee fails to meet the rapidly-changing social actuality.

14.4.4   Method for Constitutional Improvement of "Semi-Law Decisions"

The NPC Standing Committee has adopted a lot of "semi-law decisions". Though the "semi-law decisions" are constitutional and reasonable to a certain extent, there comes the confusion on constitutional status of such "semi-law decisions". In consideration of the fact that the trust on legal validity of such "semi-law decisions" has been established in judicial practice, and in light of the constitutional practices since the establishment of China, it is advised by the Writer to realize the improvement of constitutionality of "semi-law decisions" by taking the legislative measures in the following three respects:

---

[33]Xu Chongde, *The History of Constitution of People's Republic of China (Vol. 2)*, Fujian Renmin Press, pp. 392, 395.

[34]Peng (1982a).

[35]Peng (1982b).

[36]Xu Chongde, *The History of Constitution of People's Republic of China (Vol. 2)*, Fujian Renmin Press, p. 512.

Firstly, to transform the decrees adopted before the *1982 Constitution* into laws through legislative procedure. It is advised by the Writer to realize the transformation by means of incorporation into law or conversion into law. Concretely speaking, it is advised to incorporate the *Resolution of Standing Committee of National People's Congress on Approval of the Interim Measures of the State Council for Retirement and Resignation of Workers* and the *Resolution of Standing Committee of National People's Congress on Approval of the Provisions of State Council on Treatment of Family Visits of Workers and Staff Members* into the *Labor Law*; it is advised to, by reference to the mode whereby the *Regulations on Academic Degrees* is converted into law, get the *Regulations on Guangdong Special Economic Zone*, the *Interim Measures of State Council on Resettlement of Sick and Elderly Cadres* and the *Interim Provisions of State Council on Discharge and Recuperation of Veteran Cadres* amended by the NPC Standing Committee in accordance with the legislative procedure.

Secondly, to recognize the "semi-law decisions" issued after the 1982 Constitution as laws by a special decision of NPC. It is advised by the Writer that, by reference to the *Resolution of 1st Meeting of 1st National People's Congress on the People's Republic of China on Continuous Validity of Current Laws and Decrees* issued in 1954, the NPC should adopt a special resolution to determine that all "semi-law decisions" issued since the promulgation of the *1982 Constitution* are laws, and issue such resolution with the order of President.

Thirdly, if necessary, it is advised by the Writer that NPC should authorize the NPC Standing Committee to issue the "special legal decision". In accordance with the provisions of Paragraph 21 of Article 67 of the *Constitution*, NPC should authorize the NPC Standing Committee to issue the "special legal decision" so as to settle the constitutionality problem, and name such resolution as "the Special Legal Decision of Standing Committee of National People's Congress on Issue Relating to …" so as to distinguish between such resolution and other decisions relating to legal issues. As for the wording of authorization, the mode used in the *Resolution of 2nd Meeting of 1st National People's Congress on Authorizing the Standing Committee to Enact Separate Regulations* issued in 1955 can be used. Different form the authorization in 1955 which may be deemed as having amended the *Constitution*,[37] the Writer believes that, on the basis of the provisions in Article 58 of the *1982 Constitution* "the National People's Congress and the Standing Committee of National People's Congress exercise the legislative right of the state", if NPC authorizes the NPC Standing Committee to make the "special legal decisions", such authorization can be deemed as embodiment of provisions of the *Constitution*. However, it should be pointed out that, for the sake of seriousness of legislative activities, the enactment of such "special legal decisions" should be minimized, and such authorization should be cancelled by NPC at an appropriate time point.

---

[37]Cai (2006, p. 344).

References

Cai Dingjian, *The Chinese People's Congress System(the 4th Edition)*, Law Press, 2003

Cai Dingjian, *Constitution: A Intensive Reading*, Law Press, 2006.

Han Dayuan, Wang Guisong, "The Meaning of Law in China's Constitution", *Law Science*, No. 2, 2005a.

Han Dayuan, Wang Guisong: "Connotation of 'Law' in the Constitutional Text of China", *Law Science*, No. 2, 2005b.

Li Enci, Zheng Xianjun, "Review on the Limitation of the Constitutional Basic Rights from the Sun Zhigang's Case", *Jurists Review*, No. 2, 2004.

Peng Zhen: the *Explanation on Draft of Constitution of the People's Republic of China*, the 23rd Meeting of the Standing Committee of the Fifth National People's Congress on April 22, 1982a.

Peng Zhen: the *Report on Draft Revision of the Constitution of the People's Republic of China*, the fifth Meeting of the Fifth National People's Congress on November 26, 1982b.

Shen Zongling, *Jurisprudence(the 3rd Edition)*, Peking University Press, 2009, p. 240.

Wang Zhu, "Interpretation of Constitutionality of the Legislative Procedure of Tort Liability Law", *Legal Science Monthly*, No. 5, 2010.

Wu Bangguo: "The Work Report of Standing Committee of National People's Congress" (at the 1st Meeting of 11th National People's Congress on March 8, 2008), *People's Daily*, March 22, 2008, Version 2.

Wu Bangguo: "The Speech at Symposium for Formation of Socialist Legal System with Chinese Characteristics", *People's Daily*, January 27, 2011, Version 2.

Chapter 15
Supporting Works for the Compilation of *Civil Code*

The Writer believes that, during the compilation of *Civil Code*, in addition to the works relating to subject for drafting of articles, the civil law circle in China may also support the decision for the compilation of *Civil Code* through the supporting works in the following two aspects.

15.1 Interregional Legal Integration for Civil Law—Taking the *Exemplary Law of Civil Laws in Four Regions Across Taiwan Strait* as an Example

In contrast to the stagnation of the drafting of civil code, recently, Chinese scholars have initiated a series of academic activities by following the example of Europe, where private laws are in the process of unification. The Chinese scholars began with efforts to unify laws in East Asia, such as the *Principles of Contract Law of Asia* launched in 2009,[1] and *Exemplary Tort Law of East Asia* in 2010.[2] In 2013, a group of research institutes from Mainland China, Taiwan, Hong Kong, and Macau jointly initiated the program of *Exemplary Civil Law of Four Regions across the Strait*,[3] which was a significant attempt to answer the question of the applicability of *Civil Code* in Hong Kong, Macau, and Taiwan.[4]

At the 11th Symposium on *Civil Code* in Both Sides of Taiwan Strait held on June 21, 2013, Professor Wang Liming proposed to draft an *Exemplary Law of Contract Law in Four Regions across Taiwan Strait* with the efforts from civil law scholars in four regions across the Taiwan Strait. Such proposal got the unanimous approval from the attending scholars from both sides of Taiwan Strait including

---

[1]Han (2013).
[2]Zhang (2010).
[3]Zhang and Wang (2013).
[4]Chen (2003).

© China University of Political Science and Law Press 2020
Z. Wang, *On the Constitutionality of Compiling a Civil Code of China*,
https://doi.org/10.1007/978-981-13-7900-0_15

Professor Wang Zejian, and Professor Yang Lixin was appointed to organize the implementation of such proposal. On July 5, 2013, the secretariat (under establishment) began to draft the *Exemplary Law of Contract Law in Four Regions across Taiwan Strait · Outline* (draft with brief explanation for solicitation of advices). Thereafter, such document was submitted to the originating scholars for deliberation, and then the secretariat (under establishment) amended it into the *Exemplary Law of Contract Law in Four Regions across Taiwan Strait · Outline (draft for discussion)* on the basis of the opinions given by originating scholars. Meanwhile, the main originating scholars prepared the *Work Plan of Working Team for Exemplary Law of Civil Laws in Four Regions across Taiwan Strait (draft)*.

On May 2, 2014, the Working Team for Exemplary Law of Civil Laws in Four Regions across Taiwan Strait (hereinafter referred to as "Working Team") was formally established. The originating institutions of the working team include: Renmin University of China, Tsinghua University, Peking University, Fu Jen Catholic University, National Taiwan University, Soochow University, City University Hong Kong and University of Macau. The structure of Working Team is divided into three layers, namely working team, advisory body and secretariat. The first layer is working team, wherein Professor Wang Liming acts as director, Professor Pan Weida, Professor Chen Rongyu, Professor Zhan Shenlin, Professor Wang Guiguo, Professor Tang Xiaoqing and Professor Yang Lixin act as deputy directors, and Professor Yang Lixin also acts as chief secretary. The members of working team include several experts from four regions. The second layer is advisory body, composed of senior civil law experts such as Jiang Ping, Wang Jiafu, Wei Zhenying, Wang Zhejian, Sun Senmiao, Xie Zaiquan, Qiu Congzhi and Lin Chenger. The third layer is secretariat, composed of young civil law scholars from four regions and responsible for implementing the plans formulated by the Working Team. The secretariat is set up in the Civil and Commercial Law Research Center under the Renmin University of China, and is headed by Wang Zhu with the assistance from Tao Ying. A contact person is appointed by every place. The contact person for Mainland China is Wang Zhu, the contact person for Taiwan is You Jinfa, the contact person for Hong Kong is Yang Fan, and the contact person for Macau is Chen Jiamin.

According to the Working Plan of the Group on Cross-Strait-Quad-Regions Model Civil Law,[5] the first project is devoted to contract law, which is made up three parts: the General Rules of Contract, Specific Rules of Contract, and Exemplary Texts of Contract. The major task of this phase of the project is to draft the *Group on Cross-Strait-Quad-Regions Model Civil Law—General Rules of Contract*. The drafting work proceeded through four stages—"Outline," "Comparative Report and the Principles of Drafting," "Articles," and "Interpretation of Articles." Structurally, "Outline" is made up of different chapters: the Comparative Report and the Principles of Drafting elaborates the comparative

---

[5]*Working Plan of the Group on Cross-Strait-Quad-Regions Model Civil Law*, available at http://old.civillaw.com.cn/mfsff/, the latest access time: August 31, 2017.

studies and theoretical evidence upon which those chapters are drafted; "Articles" is the specific presentation of provisions; "Interpretation of Articles" explains the specific expressions in "Model Contract Law."

The secretariat of the working group, consisting of young scholars from four regions across the Strait, has completed *Cross-Strait-Quad-Regions Model Civil Law—General Rules of Contract (Comparative Report and Principles of Drafting with Articles)*. With nearly 800,000 words, this document is composed of four parts —"Comparative Report," "Analysis and Explanation on Four Regions across the Strait and Comparative Law," "Principles of Drafting" and "Proposed Articles."

The *Exemplary Law of Civil Laws in Four Regions across Taiwan Strait · General Principles for Contract (draft ·draft 2)* amended by Yang Lixin Professor, Professor Cui Jianyuan, Professor Cheng Yongyu and Professor Zhu Yan and finally determined by Professor Yang Lixin was completed on March 23, 2015, containing a total of 381 articles. After soliciting the comments from the members of Working Team and the drafters of draft 1, the draft 2 was submitted to the 13th Symposium on Civil Code in Both Sides of Taiwan Strait for discussion on June 20–21, 2015.

15.2 Plan for Survey on Civil Customs in Judgment Instruments

Since the fourth attempts to draft the *Civil Code*, some scholars have been calling for a nation-wide investigation on civil customs of the people.[6] They also suggest that civil customs and legal precedents serve as the authorities of civil law.[7] It is regretful to point out that the past 15 years has been something of a "lost 15 years," in which no institution or individual has ever tried to make a substantial nation-wide investigation on civil customs.

In contrast, before drafting the *Civil Code*, Japan launched a large scale of investigation on the civil customs of its people.[8] Even during its invasion of China, in order to rule effectively, Japan undertook organized and quality investigations into the civil customs of the Chinese people in the villages of Northeast China,[9] systematically collecting economic and social data.[10]

---

[6]Yang (2003) and Fang and Zhang (2003).

[7]Hasibagen (2013).

[8]Dai (2013).

[9]Ji (2003).

[10]Due to the historical causes, the contents of *Relatives Inheritance Law of State of Manchuria* have been lost, and it is a pity in the educational circles. The *Civil Code of State of Manchuria* includes three volumes, namely, general provisions, property right and creditor's right. Refer to Yang (2011).

Prior to the draft of the *Civil Code of the Republic of China*, special institutions were also set up for civil customs investigation. The author believes that the investigation into civil customs is important not only to the compilation of *Civil Code* itself, but also to serve as a valuable historical opportunity to foster and disseminate civil law culture. Technically, it is possible to embark on a nation-wide investigation on civil customs at a low social cost by taking advantage of the National Economic Census (once every five years, with the fourth one starting in 2018), and the National Population Census (once every ten years, with the seventh one starting in 2020).

Even if a government-sponsored investigation is not a possibility, highly advanced internet technology has also indirectly provided us with the possibility to do so. The specific methods include:

1. Since the establishment of the website of China Judgments Online (wenshu.-court.gov.cn), the official site of the Supreme People's Court, in 2014, this website has published over 40 millions of judgment documents of all the courts throughout the country, and the judgment documents is still increasing. Therefore, just use the big data analytics technology to seriously poll millions of civil cases each year, a magnitude of data on civil customs can be collected if these documents are sorted and analyzed;
2. Data on civil customs can also be obtained by firstly analyzing news websites through big data technology, then further adjusted by hand.

In order to achieve the above-mentioned academic plan, the Writer presided over the establishment of Legal Big Data Laboratory in Law School of Sichuan University at the beginning of 2016, and in cooperation with www.lawsum.com, analyzed the 40 million judgments published in the website of China Judgement Online and extracted the judgment documents of 2016 (i.e., the case number is "2016")[11] on the basis of the class-1 through class-4 causes of action as listed in the *Provisions on Causes of Action for Civil Cases* (F. [2011] No. 42), and took the result of such classification as the basis for sorting-out of text for litigation-related civil customs. On this basis, the Writer tries to further typify the causes of action which are involved in too many cases, so as to reduce the number of cases involved in every sub-type to the magnitude at which the manual analysis is possible, and take them as the basis data for sorting-out of civil customs. The Writer hereby shares the this preliminary analysis results with the academic circle, and hopes that more scholars will join in the Plan for Survey on Civil Customs in Judgment

---

[11]The reason why the judgment instruments registered in 2016 (namely, case number is "2016") are extracted is that the published quantity of judgment instruments whose case number is "2015" and before is obviously fewer than that of judgment instruments whose case number is "2016", according to the analysis of 40,000,000 judgment instruments, though China Judgments Online started publishing the judgment instruments in 2014. Therefore, the incomplete publishing may exist. As of January 31, 2018, the judgment instruments whose case number is "2017" were not completely published. Therefore, relatively complete judgment instruments whose case number is "2016" are published for statistics.

Instruments proposed by the Writer, so as to provide the sufficient survey data about civil customs and thus support the compilation of *Civil Code*.

At the end of 2016, the Law School of Sichuan University, the Mathematics School of Sichuan University, the Research Center of Civil and Commercial Jurisprudence of Renmin University of China and the Statistics School of Renmin University of China jointly promoted the Center for Big Data and Statistics on Rule of Law, and, in cooperation with Beijing University Press, published the *Books for Articles Relating to Cause of Action under Legal Big Data*. The first batch includes 4 books, namely the *Disputes over Tort Liabilities and Disputes over Personality Rights*, the *Disputes over Marriage, Family and Succession*, the *Disputes over Property Rights* and the *Disputes over Contract, negotiorum gestio and Unjustified Enrichment*. The subsequently-published books will cover all the 844 civil causes of action and as listed in the *Provisions on Causes of Action for Civil Cases* and all the 469 crimes in criminal field, and, through the clarification of judgment basis in more than 40 million judgment instruments, disclose three groups of data: First, the laws, administrative regulations and judicial interpretation frequently used in every cause of action or crime, as well as the relevancy between such laws and cause of action or crime; Second, the cause of action mainly used in articles of every basic civil or criminal law, and the relevancy thereof; Third, the articles of other laws, administrative regulations or judicial interpretations which are also applied when the articles of every basic civil or criminal law are applied by court, and the relevancy thereof. The intensity of the above-mentioned relevancy is indicated by 1–5 stars (★).

References

Chen Huabin, "Several Problems of the Formulation of the Civil Code of PRC", *Law Science*, No. 5, 2003.

Dai Shuangxi, "On Civil Habits and Methodology of Civil Law—Taking Japanese Civil Law as an Example", *Journal of CUPL*, No. 4, 2013.

Fang Shaokun, Zhang Pinghua, "Three Ground Works for Legislating Civil Code", *Seeker*, No. 1, 2003.

Han Shiyuan, "Principles of Contract Law of Asia: A Voice from Asia in the Field of Contract Law", *Tsinghua Law Review*, No. 3, 2013.

Hasibagen Ma Changhua, "Nationality of Law and Legislation of Civil Code", *Guizhou Ethnic Study*, No. 5, 2013.

Ji Weidong, "The Complicated Process of the Compilation of *Civil Code*", *Read*, No. 2, 2003.

Yang Lixin, Editor-in-chief: Collection of Civil Code for a Century of China, China Legal Publishing House 2011, pp. 524–609.

Yang Zhenshan, "Several Major Issues in Drafting Civil Code", Tribune of Political Science and Law, No. 1, 2003.

Zhang Jinhai, Wang Zhu, "Comparative Study on General Principles of Contract Law of Four Regions Across the Strait", Case Study, Vol. 4, 2013.

Zhang Tiewei, Wang Zhu, "Ideas and Practices of Making Exemplary Tort Law in East Asia", Northern Legal Science, No. 6, 2010.

Appendix
Statistical Table for Every Cause of Action in Civil Judgment Instruments Published on China Judgments Online (Cases Registered in 2016)

Serial number	Identifier	Cause of action	Number of cases
1	M1	Disputes over personality rights	0
2	M1.1	Disputes over personality rights	2297
3	M1.1.1	Disputes over the right to life, the right to health and the right to body	97,221
4	M1.1.2	Disputes over the right to name	349
5	M1.1.3	Disputes over the right to portrait	560
6	M1.1.4	Disputes over the right to reputation	4185
7	M1.1.5	Disputes over the right to honor	26
8	M1.1.6	Disputes over the right of privacy	100
9	M1.1.7	Disputes over the right of marital autonomy	10
10	M1.1.8	Disputes over the right of personal freedom	28
11	M1.1.9	Disputes over the general right to personality	1771
12	M2	Disputes over marriage, family and succession	1472
13	M2.2	Disputes over marriage and family	6307
14	M2.2.10	Disputes over betrothal property	13,442
15	M2.2.11	Disputes over divorce	415,144
16	M2.2.12	Disputes over property issues after divorce	12,982
17	M2.2.13	Disputes over compensation for damages after divorce	182
18	M2.2.14	Disputes over void marriage	621
19	M2.2.15	Disputes over voidable marriage	15
20	M2.2.16	Disputes over marriage agreement with respect to property	248
21	M2.2.17	Disputes over cohabitation relationship	2752
22	M2.2.17.1	Disputes over severance of property of cohabitation relationship	2953

(continued)

© China University of Political Science and Law Press 2020
Z. Wang, *On the Constitutionality of Compiling a Civil Code of China*,
https://doi.org/10.1007/978-981-13-7900-0

(continued)

Serial number	Identifier	Cause of action	Number of cases
23	M2.2.17.2	Disputes over child support for cohabitation relationship	6631
24	M2.2.18	Disputes over child upbringing	3315
25	M2.2.18.1	Disputes over the cost of upbringing	57,224
26	M2.2.18.2	Disputes over change of foster relations	6816
27	M2.2.19	Disputes over support	467
28	M2.2.19.1	Disputes over cost of maintenance	724
29	M2.2.19.2	Disputes over change of support relations	25
30	M2.2.20	Disputes over aliment	10,396
31	M2.2.20.1	Disputes over alimony	4802
32	M2.2.20.2	Disputes over change of aliment relations	4
33	M2.2.21	Disputes over adoptive relations	106
34	M2.2.21.1	Disputes over acknowledgment of adoptive relations	77
35	M2.2.21.2	Disputes over dissolution of adoptive relations	488
36	M2.2.22	Disputes over right of custody	303
37	M2.2.23	Disputes over visitation right	1364
38	M2.2.24	Disputes over severance of family property	3742
39	M2.3	Disputes over succession	13,777
40	M2.3.25	Disputes over statutory succession	7206
41	M2.3.25.1	Disputes over sub-succession	27
42	M2.3.25.2	Disputes over succession by subrogation	74
43	M2.3.26	Disputes over testamentary succession	1668
44	M2.3.27	Disputes over repayment of debts of the decedent	2444
45	M2.3.28	Disputes over bequest	228
46	M2.3.29	Disputes over legacy-support agreement	270
47	M3	Disputes over property rights	2840
48	M3.4	Disputes over registration of real property	219
49	M3.4.30	Disputes over compensation for damage caused by undue objection to the registration of real property	4
50	M3.4.31	Disputes over compensation for damage caused by false registration	27
51	M3.5	Disputes over the protection of property right	10,028
52	M3.5.32	Disputes over confirmation of property right	2325
53	M3.5.32.1	Disputes over confirmation of ownership	8595
54	M3.5.32.2	Disputes over confirmation of usufructuary right	226
55	M3.5.32.3	Disputes over confirmation of security interest	94
56	M3.5.33	Disputes over specific return of the thing	23,635
57	M3.5.34	Disputes over removal of interference or/and harm	25,968
58	M3.5.35	Disputes over elimination of danger	152
59	M3.5.36	Disputes over repair, reworking and replacement	209

(continued)

(continued)

Serial number	Identifier	Cause of action	Number of cases
60	M3.5.37	Disputes over restoration to the status quo ante	4521
61	M3.5.38	Disputes over compensation for damages to property	36,602
62	M3.6	Disputes over ownership	2527
63	M3.6.39	Disputes over infringement on the rights and interests of a member of a collective economic organization	14,415
64	M3.6.40	Disputes over unit ownership of condominiums	209
65	M3.6.40.1	Disputes over unit owner's rights to exclusive parts	42
66	M3.6.40.2	Disputes over unit owner's rights to shared parts	190
67	M3.6.40.3	Disputes over rights to parking lots	137
68	M3.6.40.4	Disputes over rights to parking garages	17
69	M3.6.41	Disputes over unit owner's power to rescind	323
70	M3.6.42	Disputes over unit owner's right to information	135
71	M3.6.43	Disputes over specific return of lost property	32
72	M3.6.44	Disputes over specific return of drifting property	0
73	M3.6.45	Disputes over specific return of buried property	0
74	M3.6.46	Disputes over specific return of hidden property	1
75	M3.6.47	Disputes over adjacent relations	7392
76	M3.6.47.1	Disputes over the use of water and drainage within neighbourhood	401
77	M3.6.47.2	Disputes over the right of way within neighborhood	1490
78	M3.6.47.3	Disputes over the use of immovable within neighborhood	141
79	M3.6.47.4	Disputes over ventilation within neighborhood	22
80	M3.6.47.5	Disputes over right of light within neighborhood	483
81	M3.6.47.6	Disputes over damage caused by pollution within neighborhood	110
82	M3.6.47.7	Disputes over prevention of damage within neighborhood	486
83	M3.6.48	Disputes over co-ownership	3362
84	M3.6.48.1	Disputes over confirmation of co-ownership	531
85	M3.6.48.2	Disputes over severance of co-ownership	2894
86	M3.6.48.3	Disputes over co-owner's right of pre-emption	8
87	M3.7	Disputes over usufructuary rights	615
88	M3.7.49	Disputes over the right to use maritime space	27
89	M3.7.50	Disputes over exploration right	24
90	M3.7.51	Disputes over mining right	85
91	M3.7.52	Disputes over water-intake right	15
92	M3.7.53	Disputes over right of aquaculture and poultry	18
93	M3.7.54	Disputes over fishing right	1
94	M3.7.55	Disputes over the right to land contractual management	14,355
95	M3.7.55.1	Disputes over confirmation of the right to land contractual management	840

(continued)

(continued)

Serial number	Identifier	Cause of action	Number of cases
96	M3.7.55.2	Disputes over allocation of compensation for expropriation of contracted land	8308
97	M3.7.55.3	Disputes over succession of the right to land contractual management	51
98	M3.7.56	Disputes over the right to the use of land for construction	814
99	M3.7.57	Disputes over the right to the use of rural house sites	1733
100	M3.7.58	Disputes over real servitude	34
101	M3.8	Disputes over security interest	6371
102	M3.8.59	Disputes over the right of charge	475
103	M3.8.59.1	Disputes over the right of charge to buildings and other attachments to land	107
104	M3.8.59.2	Disputes over the right of charge to buildings under construction	2
105	M3.8.59.3	Disputes over the right of charge to the right to the use of construction land	8
106	M3.8.59.4	Disputes over the right of charge to the right of land contractual management	2
107	M3.8.59.5	Disputes over the right of charge to movables	23
108	M3.8.59.6	Disputes over the right of charge to vessels and aircrafts under manufacture	0
109	M3.8.59.7	Disputes over floating charge of movables	0
110	M3.8.59.8	Disputes over right of charge of a ceiling amount	15
111	M3.8.60	Disputes over the right of pledge	16
112	M3.8.60.1	Disputes over the right of pledge to movables	21
113	M3.8.60.2	Disputes over the right of sub-pledge	5
114	M3.8.60.3	Disputes over the right of pledge to secure debts of a maximum amount	4
115	M3.8.60.4	Disputes over the right of pledge to negotiable instruments	5
116	M3.8.60.5	Disputes over the right of pledge to bonds	0
117	M3.8.60.6	Disputes over the right of pledge to deposit receipts	5
118	M3.8.60.7	Disputes over the right of pledge to warehouse receipts	0
119	M3.8.60.8	Disputes over the right of pledge to bills of lading	2
120	M3.8.60.9	Disputes over the right of pledge to company shares	34
121	M3.8.60.10	Disputes over the right of pledge to shares in funds	0
122	M3.8.60.11	Disputes over the right of pledge to intellectual property rights	0
123	M3.8.60.12	Disputes over the right of pledge to receivables	7
124	M3.8.61	Disputes over the right of lien	20
125	M3.9	Disputes over the protection of possession	148
126	M3.9.62	Disputes over specific return of the property in possession	2032

(continued)

(continued)

Serial number	Identifier	Cause of action	Number of cases
127	M3.9.63	Disputes over removal of interference or/and harm to property in possession	278
128	M3.9.64	Disputes over elimination of danger to property in possession	12
129	M3.9.65	Disputes over compensation for damage to property in possession	144
130	M4	Disputes over Contract, Negotiorum Gestio, and Unjust Enrichment	37,629
131	M4.10	Disputes over contracts	141,268
132	M4.10.66	Disputes over culpa in contrahendo	605
133	M4.10.67	Disputes over confirmation of the validity of contract	6534
134	M4.10.67.1	Disputes over confirmation of a valid contract	3429
135	M4.10.67.2	Disputes over confirmation of a void contract	12,867
136	M4.10.68	Disputes over the creditor's power of personal subrogation	1874
137	M4.10.69	Disputes over the creditor's power to rescind	2548
138	M4.10.70	Disputes over contract of assignment of obligatory rights	9734
139	M4.10.71	Disputes over contract of assignment of debts	2360
140	M4.10.72	Disputes over contract of an overall assignment of obligatory rights and debts	235
141	M4.10.73	Disputes over advertisements offering rewards	59
142	M4.10.74	Disputes over contract of sale	500,014
143	M4.10.74.1	Disputes over contract of sale involving instalment	6906
144	M4.10.74.2	Disputes over contract of sale involving sample products	1064
145	M4.10.74.3	Disputes over contract of sale involving trial products	14
146	M4.10.74.4	Disputes over contract of barter	118
147	M4.10.74.5	Disputes over contract of international sale of goods	77
148	M4,10.74.6	Disputes over online shopping contracts	4517
149	M4.10.74.7	Disputes over TV shopping contracts	19
150	M4.10.75	Disputes over contracts for sales by bidding and bids	407
151	M4.10.76	Disputes over auction contracts	556
152	M4.10.77	Disputes over contract of the right to the use of land for construction	260
153	M4.10.77.1	Disputes over contract for the creation of the right to the use of land for construction	736
154	M4.10.77.2	Disputes over contract for the transfer of the right to the use of land for construction	938
155	M4.10.78	Disputes over contracts for temporary use of land	92
156	M4.10.79	Disputes over contract for the transfer of exploration rights	40

(continued)

(continued)

Serial number	Identifier	Cause of action	Number of cases
157	M4.10.80	Disputes over contract for the transfer of exploitation rights	219
158	M4.10.81	Disputes over contracts for real estate development and management	252
159	M4.10.81.1	Disputes over contracts for entrusted construction	169
160	M4.10.81.2	Disputes over contracts for real estate development by equity joint venture or cooperative joint venture	1295
161	M4.10.81.3	Disputes over contracts for transfer of projects	128
162	M4.10.82	Disputes over contracts for sales of housing	97,820
163	M4.10.82.1	Disputes over contract for appointment of sale of commercial residential housing	3610
164	M4.10.82.2	Disputes over contracts for pre-sale of commercial residential housing	48,650
165	M4.10.82.3	Disputes over contracts for sales of commercial residential housing	50,927
166	M4.10.82.4	Disputes over contracts for entrusted agency for sales of commercial residential housing	465
167	M4.10.82.5	Disputes over contracts on the transfer of economically affordable residential housing	50
168	M4.10.82.6	Disputes over contracts on sale of housing in rural areas	1173
169	M4.10.83	Disputes over contracts on the monetary relief for compulsory purchase and settlement of housing	16,273
170	M4.10.84	Disputes over contracts for supply of electricity	2284
171	M4.10.85	Disputes over contracts for supply of water	2738
172	M4.10.86	Disputes over contracts for supply of gas	390
173	M4.10.87	Disputes over contracts for supply of heating	14,074
174	M4.10.88	Dispute over contracts of gifts	1628
175	M4.10.88.1	Disputes over contracts for donations to public welfare undertakings	8
176	M4.10.88.2	Disputes over contract of conditional gifts	96
177	M4.10.89	Disputes over loan contracts	189,120
178	M4.10.89.1	Disputes over financial loan contracts	412,350
179	M4.10.89.2	Disputes over contracts for inter-bank loan	5
180	M4.10.89.3	Disputes over contracts for inter-enterprises loan	9347
181	M4.10.89.4	Disputes over contracts for private loan	1,136,025
182	M4.10.89.5	Disputes over contract of loan with a small sum	18,241
183	M4.10.89.6	Disputes over contracts on the transfer of non-performing financial debts	100
184	M4.10.89.7	Disputes over recovery of non-performing financial debts	910
185	M4.10.90	Disputes over contracts of guarantee	25,280
186	M4.10.91	Disputes over contract of charge	1911

(continued)

(continued)

Serial number	Identifier	Cause of action	Number of cases
187	M4.10.92	Disputes over contract of pledge	276
188	M4.10.93	Disputes over contract of deposit	1887
189	M4.10.94	Disputes over bill of exchange for import and export	28
190	M4.10.95	Disputes over contracts for savings deposit	3725
191	M4.10.96	Disputes over bank cards	2074
192	M4.10.96.1	Disputes over debit cards	492
193	M4.10.96.2	Disputes over credit cards	116,826
194	M4.10.97	Disputes over contract of lease	62,850
195	M4.10.97.1	Disputes over contract of lease to land use rights	6591
196	M4.10.97.2	Disputes over contract of lease to housing	71,753
197	M4.10.97.3	Disputes over contract of lease to motor vehicles	5438
198	M4.10.97.4	Disputes over contract of lease to construction equipments	9369
199	M4.10.98	Disputes over contracts for financial leasing	11,982
200	M4.10.99	Disputes over contracts for contracting work	37,693
201	M4.10.99.1	Disputes over processing contracts	13,009
202	M4.10.99.2	Disputes over contract of manufacturing on order	8393
203	M4.10.99.3	Dispute over contract of repairment	4218
204	M4.10.99.4	Disputes over contract of duplication	20
205	M4.10.99.5	Disputes over testing contracts	27
206	M4.10.99.6	Disputes over inspection contracts	49
207	M4.10.99.7	Disputes over contract for the manufacture of railway locomotives and vehicles	0
208	M4.10.100	Disputes over contracts for construction projects	19,886
209	M4.10.100.1	Disputes over contracts for survey of construction projects	164
210	M4.10.100.2	Disputes over contracts for design of construction projects	787
211	M4.10.100.3	Disputes over contracts for carrying out of construction projects	64,389
212	M4.10.100.4	Disputes over priority of claims for construction project price	63
213	M4.10.100.5	Disputes over contracts for subcontracting of construction projects	7413
214	M4.10.100.6	Disputes over contracts for supervision of construction projects	318
215	M4.10.100.7	Disputes over contracts for decoration	12,328
216	M4.10.100.8	Disputes over railway construction contracts	56
217	M4.10.100.9	Disputes over contracts for housing construction in rural areas	3371
218	M4.10.101	Disputes over contracts of carriage	13339
219	M4.10.101.1	Disputes over contracts of carriage of passengers by highway	1448

(continued)

(continued)

Serial number	Identifier	Cause of action	Number of cases
220	M4.10.101.2	Disputes over contracts of carriage of goods by highway	4686
221	M4.10.101.3	Disputes over contracts of carriage of passengers by waterway	5
222	M4.10.101.4	Disputes over contracts of carriage of goods by waterway	86
223	M4.10.101.5	Disputes over contracts of carriage of passengers by air	60
224	M4.10.101.6	Disputes over contracts of carriage of goods by air	142
225	M4.10.101.7	Disputes over contracts of taxi transport	301
226	M4.10.101.8	Disputes over contracts of transport by pipeline	0
227	M4.10.101.9	Disputes over contracts for urban public transport	485
228	M4.10.101.10	Disputes over contracts for combined transport	5
229	M4.10.101.11	Disputes over contract of multimodal transport	7
230	M4.10.101.12	Disputes over contracts of carriage of cargo by railway	45
231	M4.10.101.13	Disputes over contracts of carriage of passenger by railway	74
232	M4.10.101.14	Disputes over contracts of carriage of baggage by railway	0
233	M4.10.101.15	Disputes over contracts of carriage of parcel by railway	0
234	M4.10.101.16	Disputes over contracts for international railway transport	0
235	M4.10.102	Disputes over contract of bailment	1129
236	M4.10.103	Disputes over warehousing contracts	588
237	M4.10.104	Disputes over entrustment contracts	17,252
238	M4.10.104.1	Disputes over agency contracts for import and export	329
239	M4.10.104.2	Disputes over freight forwarding contracts	431
240	M4.10.104.3	Disputes over agency contracts for carriage by civil aviation	17
241	M4.10.104.4	Disputes over agency contracts for litigation, arbitration and people's meditation	1602
242	M4.10.105	Disputes over agency contracts for wealth management	982
243	M4.10.105.1	Disputes over financial management contracts entrusted by financial institutions	54
244	M4.10.105.2	Disputes over private agency contracts for wealth management	506
245	M4.10.106	Disputes over commission agency contracts	249
246	M4.10.107	Disputes over brokerage contracts	7607
247	M4.10.108	Disputes over compensation trade	0
248	M4.10.109	Disputes over contracts for borrowings	565
249	M4.10.110	Disputes over mortgage to chattels	1847
250	M4.10.111	Disputes over partnership agreements	21,746
251	M4.10.112	Disputes over contracts for repurchase of planted and bred products	3148

(continued)

(continued)

Serial number	Identifier	Cause of action	Number of cases
252	M4.10.113	Disputes over lotteries or lottery-linked deposits	143
253	M4.10.114	Disputes over contracts for Sino-foreign joint exploration and exploitation of natural resources	2
254	M4.10.115	Disputes over contracts for agricultural contracting	3357
255	M4.10.116	Disputes over contracts for forestry contracting	1787
256	M4.10.117	Disputes over contracts for fishery contracting	781
257	M4.10.118	Disputes over contracts for livestock husbandry contracting	209
258	M4.10.119	Disputes over contract of the right to land contractual management	14,497
259	M4.10.119.1	Disputes over contract for sub-contracting the right to land contractual management	3173
260	M4.10.119.2	Disputes over contract for transferring the right to land contractual management	1029
261	M4.10.119.3	Disputes over contract for exchanging the right to land contractual management	402
262	M4.10.119.4	Disputes over contract for subscribing for shares by transferring the right to land contractual management	12
263	M4.10.119.5	Disputes over contract of charge to the right to land contractual management	3
264	M4.10.119.6	Disputes over contract of lease to the right to land contractual management	3912
265	M4.10.120	Disputes over service contracts	13,897
266	M4.10.120.1	Disputes over contracts for telecom services	8820
267	M4.10.120.2	Disputes over contracts for postal services	136
268	M4.10.120.3	Disputes over contracts for medical services	2341
269	M4.10.120.4	Disputes over contracts for legal services	1610
270	M4.10.120.5	Disputes over contracts for travelling	1711
271	M4.10.120.6	Disputes over contracts for real estate consultancy	76
272	M4.10.120.7	Disputes over contracts for appraisal of real estate prices	43
273	M4.10.120.8	Disputes over contracts for contracts for hotel services	500
274	M4.10.120.9	Disputes over contracts for finance and accounting services	70
275	M4.10.120.10	Disputes over contracts for catering services	3445
276	M4.10.120.11	Disputes over contracts for entertainment services	518
277	M4.10.120.12	Disputes over contracts for cable television services	19
278	M4.10.120.13	Disputes over contracts for Internet services	415
279	M4.10.120.14	Disputes over contracts for education and training	1393
280	M4.10.120.15	Disputes over contracts for property management services	240,504
281	M4.10.120.16	Disputes over contracts for domestic service	138
282	M4.10.120.17	Disputes over contracts for celebration service	116

(continued)

(continued)

Serial number	Identifier	Cause of action	Number of cases
283	M4.10.120.18	Disputes over contracts for funeral service	51
284	M4.10.120.19	Disputes over contracts for agricultural technology service	76
285	M4.10.120.20	Disputes over contracts for service contracts for the operation of agricultural machinery	224
286	M4.10.120.21	Disputes over contracts for security service	533
287	M4.10.120.22	Disputes over contracts for bank settlement	27
288	M4.10.121	Disputes over performance contracts	146
289	M4.10.122	Disputes over labor services contracts	106,235
290	M4.10.123	Disputes over contracts for re-employment of retired persons	104
291	M4.10.124	Disputes over advertising contracts	3159
292	M4.10.125	Disputes over exhibition contracts	58
293	M4.10.126	Disputes over the right of recourse	64,115
294	M4.10.127	Petition for confirmation of the validity of people's mediation agreement	25,605
295	M4.11	Disputes over unjust enrichment	0
296	M4.11.128	Disputes over unjust enrichment	35,352
297	M4.12	Disputes over negotiorum gestio	0
298	M4.12.129	Disputes over negotiorum gestio	10,247
299	M5	Disputes over intellectual property rights and competition	2031
300	M5.13	Disputes over the contracts with respect to intellectual property rights	98
301	M5.13.130	Disputes over copyright contracts	58
302	M5.13.130.1	Disputes over contracts of entrusted creation	71
303	M5.13.130.2	Disputes over contracts of co-creation	6
304	M5.13.130.3	Disputes over contracts of assignment of copyright	18
305	M5.13.130.4	Disputes over contracts for licensing of copyright	75
306	M5.13.130.5	Disputes over publication contracts	19
307	M5.13.130.6	Disputes over performance contracts	0
308	M5.13.130.7	Disputes over contracts for production of audio or visual products	6
309	M5.13.130.8	Disputes over contracts for radio or television broadcast	5
310	M5.13.130.9	Disputes over contracts for assignment of neighboring rights	0
311	M5.13.130.10	Disputes over contracts for licensing of neighboring rights	0
312	M5.13.130.11	Disputes over contracts for computer software development	168
313	M5.13.130.12	Disputes over contracts for assignment of copyright to computer software	3

(continued)

(continued)

Serial number	Identifier	Cause of action	Number of cases
314	M5.13.130.13	Disputes over contracts for licensing of copyright to computer software	11
315	M5.13.131	Disputes over trademark contracts	14
316	M5.13.131.1	Disputes over contracts for transfer of trademarks	34
317	M5.13.131.2	Disputes over contracts for trademark licensing	62
318	M5.13.131.3	Disputes over contracts for trademark agency	39
319	M5.13.132	Disputes over patent contracts	26
320	M5.13.132.1	Disputes over contracts for transfer of the right to apply for patents	5
321	M5.13.132.2	Disputes over contracts for transfer of patent right	27
322	M5.13.132.3	Disputes over licensing contracts for exploitation of invention patents	15
323	M5.13.132.4	Disputes over licensing contracts for exploitation of utility model patents	9
324	M5.13.132.5	Disputes over licensing contracts for exploitation of design patents	0
325	M5.13.132.6	Disputes over patent agency contracts	22
326	M5.13.133	Disputes over contracts for new plant varieties	5
327	M5.13.133.1	Disputes over contracts for seed breeding of new plant varieties	0
328	M5.13.133.2	Disputes over contracts for transfer of the right to apply for new plant varieties	0
329	M5.13.133.3	Disputes over contracts for transfer of rights in new plant varieties	2
330	M5.13.133.4	Disputes over licensing contracts for exploitation of new plant varieties	3
331	M5.13.134	Disputes over contracts for layout-design of integrated circuits	0
332	M5.13.134.1	Disputes over contracts for creation of layout-design of integrated circuits	0
333	M5.13.134.2	Disputes over contracts for transfer of exclusive rights in layout-design of integrated circuits	0
334	M5.13.134.3	Disputes over licensing contracts for exploitation of layout-design of integrated circuits	0
335	M5.13.135	Disputes over contracts for trade secrets	3
336	M5.13.135.1	Disputes over contracts for assignment of technical secrets	1
337	M5.13.135.2	Disputes over licensing contracts for exploitation of technical secrets	2
338	M5.13.135.3	Disputes over contract for the transfer of business management secrets	0
339	M5.13.135.4	Disputes over contract for the licensing of business management secrets	0

(continued)

(continued)

Serial number	Identifier	Cause of action	Number of cases
340	M5.13.136	Disputes over technology contracts	211
341	M5.13.136.1	Disputes over contracts for entrusted development of technologies	111
342	M5.13.136.2	Disputes over contracts for co-development of technologies	46
343	M5.13.136.3	Disputes over contracts for transformation of technologies	0
344	M5.13.136.4	Disputes over contracts for transfer of technologies	70
345	M5.13.136.5	Disputes over contracts for technical consultancy	89
346	M5.13.136.6	Disputes over contracts for technical services	405
347	M5.13.136.7	Disputes over contracts for technical training	30
348	M5.13.136.8	Disputes over contracts for intermediary of technologies	0
349	M5.13.136.9	Disputes over contracts for import of technologies	0
350	M5.13.136.10	Disputes over contracts for export of technologies	0
351	M5.13.136.11	Disputes over awards and remuneration for persons who have made duty-related technological achievements	3
352	M5.13.136.12	Disputes over the right of authorship, right of honor and right to rewards of persons who have made technological achievements	2
353	M5.13.137	Disputes over concession contracts	1013
354	M5.13.138	Disputes over contracts for corporate names (trade names)	0
355	M5.13.138.1	Disputes over contracts for transfer of corporate names (trade names)	0
356	M5.13.138.2	Disputes over contracts for use of corporate names (trade names)	0
357	M5.13.139	Disputes over contracts for special marks	0
358	M5.13.140	Disputes over contracts for domain names	7
359	M5.13.140.1	Disputes over contracts for registration of domain names	4
360	M5.13.140.2	Disputes over contracts for transfer of domain names	3
361	M5.13.140.3	Disputes over licensing contracts for exploitation of domain names	2
362	M5.13.141	Contractual disputes over pledge of intellectual property rights	0
363	M5.14	Disputes over confirmation or infringement on intellectual property rights	299
364	M5.14.142	Disputes over confirmation or infringement on copyrights	24,904
365	M5.14.142.1	Disputes over confirmation of copyrights	1879
366	M5.14.142.2	Disputes over the right to publish works	34
367	M5.14.142.3	Disputes over infringement on the right of authorship of the work	20

(continued)

(continued)

Serial number	Identifier	Cause of action	Number of cases
368	M5.14.142.4	Disputes over infringement on the right to modify the work	1
369	M5.14.142.5	Disputes over infringement on the right to the integrity of the work	3
370	M5.14.142.6	Disputes over infringement on the right to duplicate the work	433
371	M5.14.142.7	Disputes over infringement on the distribution rights to the work	416
372	M5.14.142.8	Disputes over infringement on the rental rights to the work	0
373	M5.14.142.9	Disputes over infringement on the exhibition rights to the work	8
374	M5.14.142.10	Disputes over infringement on the performance rights to the work	60
375	M5.14.142.11	Disputes over infringement on the rights to screen the work	5625
376	M5.14.142.12	Disputes over infringement on the broadcasting rights to the work	83
377	M5.14.142.13	Disputes over infringement on right to communication through information network	7586
378	M5.14.142.14	Disputes over infringement on the rights to shoot film over the work	0
379	M5.14.142.15	Disputes over infringement on the rights of adaptation to the work	7
380	M5.14.142.16	Disputes over infringement on the rights to translation of the work	2
381	M5.14.142.17	Disputes over infringement on the rights to compilation of the work	0
382	M5.14.142.18	Disputes over infringement on other economic rights to copyrights	2433
383	M5.14.142.19	Disputes over confirmation of the rights of the publishers	4
384	M5.14.142.20	Disputes over confirmation of the rights of the performers	0
385	M5.14.142.21	Disputes over confirmation of the rights of the audio/video producers	34
386	M5.14.142.22	Disputes over confirmation of the rights of broadcasting organisations	1
387	M5.14.142.23	Disputes over infringement on rights of a publisher	28
388	M5.14.142.24	Disputes over infringement on rights of a performer	1
389	M5.14.142.25	Disputes over infringement on rights of an audio/visual producer	538
390	M5.14.142.26	Disputes over infringement on the rights of broadcasting organizations	1

(continued)

(continued)

Serial number	Identifier	Cause of action	Number of cases
391	M5.14.142.27	Disputes over the copyright to computer software	5
392	M5.14.142.28	Disputes over infringement on copyright to computer software	249
393	M5.14.143	Disputes over confirmation or infringement on the right to trademark	344
394	M5.14.143.1	Disputes over confirmation of the right to exclusive use of a trademark	152
395	M5.14.143.2	Disputes over infringement on the right to the exclusive use of a trademark	12,086
396	M5.14.144	Disputes over confirmation or infringement on the right to patents	122
397	M5.14.144.1	Disputes over confirmation of the right to apply for a patent	86
398	M5.14.144.2	Disputes over confirmation of the right to patent	146
399	M5.14.144.3	Disputes over infringement on invention patents	647
400	M5.14.144.4	Disputes over infringement on utility model patents	1457
401	M5.14.144.5	Disputes over infringement on design patents	3381
402	M5.14.144.6	Disputes over passing off the patent of another person	3
403	M5.14.144.7	Disputes over royalties charged during interim protection period of an invention patent	1
404	M5.14.144.8	Disputes over awards and remuneration for inventors and/or designers of duty-related invention and creation	39
405	M5.14.144.9	Disputes over the right of authorship of inventors or/and designers of inventions and creations	7
406	M5.14.145	Disputes over confirmation or infringement on the right to new plant varieties	4
407	M5.14.145.1	Disputes over confirmation of the right to apply for new plant varieties	0
408	M5.14.145.2	Disputes over confirmation of the right to new plant varieties	2
409	M5.14.145.3	Disputes over infringement on the right to new plant varieties	27
410	M5.14.146	Disputes over confirmation or infringement on the exclusive rights to layout-design of integrated circuits	0
411	M5.14.146.1	Disputes over confirmation of the exclusive rights to layout-design of integrated circuits	0
412	M5.14.146.2	Disputes over infringement on exclusive rights in layout-design of integrated circuits	1
413	M5.14.147	Disputes over infringement on the rights to corporate names (trade names)	21
414	M5.14.148	Disputes over infringement on exclusive rights in special marks	0
415	M5.14.149	Disputes over confirmation or infringement on the right to domain names	11

(continued)

(continued)

Serial number	Identifier	Cause of action	Number of cases
416	M5.14.149.1	Disputes over confirmation of the right to domain names	72
417	M5.14.149.2	Disputes over infringement on domain names	7
418	M5.14.150	Disputes over right of discovery	0
419	M5.14.151	Disputes over right of invention	1
420	M5.14.152	Disputes over rights in other scientific and technological achievements	3
421	M5.14.153	Disputes over confirmation of non-infringement on intellectual property rights	0
422	M5.14.153.1	Disputes over confirmation of non-infringement on patent rights	14
423	M5.14.153.2	Disputes over confirmation of non-infringement on the right to trademarks	12
424	M5.14.153.3	Disputes over confirmation of non-infringement on copyright	1
425	M5.14.154	Disputes over liability for losses arising from interim measures for intellectual property rights	0
426	M5.14.154.1	Disputes over liability for losses arising from pre-trial injunctive relief against infringement on patent rights	0
427	M5.14.154.2	Disputes over liability for losses arising from pre-trial injunctive relief against infringement on right to exclusive use of registered trademarks	0
428	M5.14.154.3	Disputes over liability for losses arising from pre-trial injunctive relief against infringement on copyrights	0
429	M5.14.154.4	Disputes over liability for losses arising from pre-trial injunctive relief against infringement on rights to new varieties of plants	0
430	M5.14.154.5	Disputes over liability for losses arising from the seeking of protective measures imposed by the Customs for the protection of intellectual property rights	2
431	M5.14.155	Disputes over the liability for losses arising from malicious claims of alleged intellectual property rights	10
432	M5.14.156	Disputes over the refund of expenses after patent rights are declared to be void	0
433	M5.15	Dispute over unfair competition	341
434	M5.15.157	Disputes over passing-off	16
435	M5.15.157.1	Disputes over unauthorized use of names, packaging and/or decoration unique to well-known commodities	44
436	M5.15.157.2	Disputes over unauthorized use of other corporate or personal names	35
437	M5.15.157.3	Disputes over counterfeiting or/and passing off of product quality marks	4
438	M5.15.157.4	Disputes over forging the proof of origin of a product	0
439	M5.15.158	Disputes over unfair competition by commercial bribery	195

(continued)

(continued)

Serial number	Identifier	Cause of action	Number of cases
440	M5.15.159	Disputes over false publicity	95
441	M5.15.160	Disputes over infringement on trade secrets	123
442	M5.15.160.1	Disputes over infringement on technical secrets	18
443	M5.15.160.2	Dispute over infringement on business management secrets	29
444	M5.15.161	Disputes over unfair competition by low-price dumping	0
445	M5.15.162	Disputes over unfair competition by bundled sales	0
446	M5.15.163	Disputes over prize-giving sales	8
447	M5.15.164	Dispute over commercial defamation	30
448	M5.15.165	Disputes over collusive bidding	12
449	M5.16	Disputes over monopolization	5
450	M5.16.166	Disputes over monopoly agreements	4
451	M5.16.166.1	Disputes over horizontal monopoly agreements	0
452	M5.16.166.2	Disputes over vertical monopoly agreements	1
453	M5.16.167	Disputes over the abuse of market dominant position	5
454	M5.16.167.1	Disputes over monopoly pricing	0
455	M5.16.167.2	Disputes over predatory pricing	0
456	M5.16.167.3	Disputes over refusal of trade	2
457	M5.16.167.4	Disputes over restriction of trade	1
458	M5.16.167.5	Disputes over bundled trade	2
459	M5.16.167.6	Disputes over discriminating treatment	0
460	M5.16.168	Disputes over concentration of business operators	1
461	M6	Labor disputes and personnel disputes	3451
462	M6.17	Labor disputes	193,222
463	M6.17.169	Disputes over labor contracts	29,883
464	M6.17.169.1	Disputes over confirmation of labor relations	5748
465	M6.17.169.2	Disputes over collective labor contracts	0
466	M6.17.169.3	Disputes over labor dispatching contracts	340
467	M6.17.169.4	Disputes over part-time employment	0
468	M6.17.169.5	Disputes over claims for labor remuneration in arrear	64,660
469	M6.17.169.6	Disputes over economic compensation	7406
470	M6.17.169.7	Disputes over restraint of competition	136
471	M6.17.170	Disputes over social insurance	1538
472	M6.17.170.1	Disputes over pension insurance benefits	1189
473	M6.17.170.2	Disputes over insurance benefits for work-related injuries	9662
474	M6.17.170.3	Disputes over insurance benefits for medical expenses	245
475	M6.17.170.4	Disputes over maternity insurance benefits	35
476	M6.17.170.5	Disputes over unemployment insurance benefits	397
477	M6.17.171	Disputes over welfare benefits	611

(continued)

(continued)

Serial number	Identifier	Cause of action	Number of cases
478	M6.18	Personnel disputes	0
479	M6.18.172	Personnel disputes	8315
480	M6.18.172.1	Resignation disputes	23
481	M6.18.172.2	Dismissal disputes	30
482	M6.18.172.3	Disputes over employment contracts	75
483	M7	Marine and maritime disputes	0
484	M7.19	Marine and maritime disputes	32
485	M7.19.173	Disputes over compensation for damage caused by vessel collision	66
486	M7.19.174	Disputes over compensation for damage caused by vessel contact	11
487	M7.19.175	Disputes over compensation for damage to facilities above or under water by vessels	0
488	M7.19.176	Disputes over compensation for damage by pollution from vessel	2
489	M7.19.177	Disputes over compensation for damage by pollution on the sea or sea-linked waters	12
490	M7.19.178	Disputes over compensation for damage to aquaculture on the sea or sea-linked waters	22
491	M7.19.179	Disputes over compensation for damage to property on the sea or sea-linked waters	18
492	M7.19.180	Disputes over compensation for personal injuries on the sea or sea-linked waters	241
493	M7.19.181	Disputes over compensation for damage for illegal detention against vessels, vessel cargos, bunker oil or ship's stores	2
494	M7.19.182	Disputes over contracts for carriage of goods by sea or on sea-linked waters	1070
495	M7.19.183	Disputes over contracts for carriage of passengers by sea or on sea-linked waters	8
496	M7.19.184	Disputes over contracts for carriage of luggage by sea or on sea-linked waters	0
497	M7.19.185	Disputes over contracts for vessel operation and management	34
498	M7.19.186	Disputes over contracts for sale of vessels	130
499	M7.19.187	Disputes over contracts for construction of vessels	137
500	M7.19.188	Disputes over contracts for repairment of vessels	93
501	M7.19.189	Disputes over contracts for reconstruction of vessels	2
502	M7.19.190	Disputes over contracts for dismantling of vessels	0
503	M7.19.191	Disputes over contracts for charge to vessels	141
504	M7.19.192	Disputes over voyage charter	122
505	M7.19.193	Disputes over contracts vessel leasing	59
506	M7.19.193.1	Disputes over time charter	35

(continued)

(continued)

Serial number	Identifier	Cause of action	Number of cases
507	M7.19.193.2	Disputes over bareboat charter contracts	25
508	M7.19.194	Disputes over contracts for financial leasing of vessels	19
509	M7.19.195	Disputes over contracts for contracting commercial vessels along coastal areas or sea-linked waters	0
510	M7.19.196	Disputes over contracts for fishing vessel contracting	0
511	M7.19.197	Disputes over contracts for lease of appurtenance of vessels	0
512	M7.19.198	Disputes over contracts for safekeeping of appurtenance of vessels	0
513	M7.19.199	Disputes over contracts for lease of marine containers	13
514	M7.19.200	Disputes over contracts for safekeeping of marine containers	2
515	M7.19.201	Disputes over contracts for safekeeping of port cargos	43
516	M7.19.202	Disputes over vessel agency contracts	17
517	M7.19.203	Disputes over freight forwarding contract at sea or on sea-linked waters	1662
518	M7.19.204	Disputes over tally service contracts	1
519	M7.19.205	Disputes over contracts for supply of ship stores and spares	311
520	M7.19.206	Disputes over labor contracts for ship crew	1988
521	M7.19.207	Disputes over contracts for assistance at sea	3
522	M7.19.208	Disputes over contracts for salvage at sea or on sea-linked waters	20
523	M7.19.209	Disputes over towage contracts at sea or on sea-linked waters	3
524	M7.19.210	Disputes over marine insurance contracts at sea or on sea-linked waters	193
525	M7.19.211	Disputes over protection and indemnity contracts at sea or on sea-linked waters	0
526	M7.19.212	Disputes over contracts for economic association of carriage by sea or sea-linked waters	0
527	M7.19.213	Disputes over loan contracts related to vessel operation	215
528	M7.19.214	Disputes over maritime guarantee contracts	8
529	M7.19.215	Disputes over contracts for dredging voyage channels and ports	21
530	M7.19.216	Disputes over shipyard and dock construction contracts	68
531	M7.19.217	Disputes over vessel inspection contracts	1
532	M7.19.218	Disputes over guarantee for maritime claims	5
533	M7.19.219	Disputes over compensation related to accountable serious transport accidents at sea or on sea-linked waters	0
534	M7.19.220	Disputes over compensation related to accountable serious accidents occurred in port operations	1

(continued)

(continued)

Serial number	Identifier	Cause of action	Number of cases
535	M7.19.221	Disputes over port operations	57
536	M7.19.222	Disputes over general average	2
537	M7.19.223	Disputes over the development and exploitation of marine resources	12
538	M7.19.224	Disputes over co-ownership of vessels	68
539	M7.19.225	Disputes over ownership of vessels	64
540	M7.19.226	Disputes over frauds in marine transport	1
541	M7.19.227	Disputes over the confirmation of maritime creditors' rights	54
542	M8	Civil disputes related to companies, securities, insurance, negotiable instruments, etc.	387
543	M8.20	Disputes related to enterprises	331
544	M8.20.228	Disputes over confirmation of equity of contributors of enterprises	106
545	M8.20.229	Disputes over infringement on equity of contributors of enterprises	117
546	M8.20.230	Disputes over contracts for transformation of enterprises into companies	59
547	M8.20.231	Disputes over contracts for transformation of enterprises into joint stock cooperatives	20
548	M8.20.232	Disputes over debt-for-equity swap of enterprises	7
549	M8.20.233	Disputes over division of enterprises	6
550	M8.20.234	Disputes over contracts for business operation under lease of enterprises	167
551	M8.20.235	Disputes over contracts for sale of enterprises	212
552	M8.20.236	Disputes over contracts for affiliated operation	7429
553	M8.20.237	Disputes over merge of enterprises	25
554	M8.20.238	Disputes over contracts for joint operation	1107
555	M8.20.239	Disputes over contract for undertaking business operation of enterprise	729
556	M8.20.239.1	Disputes over contract for undertaking business operation of Sino-foreign joint ventures	0
557	M8.20.239.2	Disputes over contract for undertaking business operation of Sino-foreign cooperative enterprises	1
558	M8.20.239.3	Disputes over contract for undertaking business operation of wholly foreign-owned enterprises	0
559	M8.20.239.4	Disputes over contract for undertaking business operation of enterprises in rural and town areas	25
560	M8.20.240	Disputes over contracts of Sino-foreign equity joint ventures	3
561	M8.20.241	Disputes over contracts of Sino-foreign contractual joint ventures	14
562	M8.21	Disputes related to companies	1276

(continued)

(continued)

Serial number	Identifier	Cause of action	Number of cases
563	M8.21.242	Disputes over confirmation of the shareholder's rights	3071
564	M8.21.243	Disputes over the records of registrar of shareholders	204
565	M8.21.244	Disputes over the claim of alteration of the company's registration	299
566	M8.21.245	Disputes over capital contribution of shareholders	839
567	M8.21.246	Disputes over the subscription to additional capital	66
568	M8.21.247	Disputes over shareholder's right to information	1371
569	M8.21.248	Disputes over the request for the company to acquire shares	71
570	M8.21.249	Disputes over equity transfer	9966
571	M8.21.250	Disputes over company resolution	256
572	M8.21.250.1	Disputes over confirmation of the validity of the company resolution	425
573	M8.21.250.2	Disputes over rescission of company resolutions	288
574	M8.21.251	Disputes over the establishment of company	70
575	M8.21.252	Disputes over the return of company's license and certificate	320
576	M8.21.253	Disputes over responsibilities of promoters	41
577	M8.21.254	Disputes over distribution of surplus of companies	536
578	M8.21.255	Disputes over the liability for damaging the shareholders' interests	296
579	M8.21.256	Disputes over the liability for damaging the company's interests	818
580	M8.21.257	Disputes over the liability of the shareholders for damaging the interests of the company's creditors	812
581	M8.21.258	Disputes over liability for damages due to connected party transactions	10
582	M8.21.259	Disputes over merger of companies	36
583	M8.21.260	Disputes over division of companies	5
584	M8.21.261	Disputes over capital reduction of companies	21
585	M8.21.262	Disputes over capital increase of companies	94
586	M8.21.263	Disputes over dissolution of companies	750
587	M8.21.264	Application for liquidation of the company	159
588	M8.21.265	Disputes over the liability of liquidation	272
589	M8.21.266	Disputes over acquisition of listed companies	0
590	M8.22	Disputes over partnership enterprises	125
591	M8.22.267	Disputes over the joining of the partnership	20
592	M8.22.268	Disputes over the withdrawal from the partnership	742
593	M8.22.269	Disputes over the transfer of the share of partnership's property	75
594	M8.23	Disputes over bankruptcy	68
595	M8.23.270	Applications for bankruptcy liquidation	301

(continued)

(continued)

Serial number	Identifier	Cause of action	Number of cases
596	M8.23.271	Applications for bankruptcy reorganization	69
597	M8.23.272	Applications for bankruptcy voluntary arrangement	1
598	M8.23.273	Disputes over the request to rescind the act of individual settlement	259
599	M8.23.274	Disputes on the request for confirming the act of the debtor as being invalid	103
600	M8.23.275	Disputes on external recovery of debt	984
601	M8.23.276	Disputes on recovery of unpaid capital contribution	27
602	M8.23.277	Disputes on recovery of the illegally withdrawn capitals	26
603	M8.23.278	Disputes on recovery of abnormal incomes	24
604	M8.23.279	Disputes over confirmation of creditor's rights in bankruptcy	822
605	M8.23.279.1	Disputes over confirmation of the rights of the employees in bankruptcy	367
606	M8.23.279.2	Disputes over confirmation of the rights of unsecured creditors in bankruptcy	215
607	M8.23.280	Disputes over right of vindication	57
608	M8.23.280.1	Disputes over general right of vindication	9
609	M8.23.280.2	Disputes over seller's right of vindication	0
610	M8.23.281	Disputes over right of set-off	13
611	M8.23.282	Disputes over the right of receivership	6
612	M8.23.283	Disputes over bankruptcy-related right of rescission	1012
613	M8.23.284	Disputes over the compensation for damage to the interests of the debtor	6
614	M8.23.285	Disputes over the liability of bankruptcy administrator	36
615	M8.24	Disputes over Securities	60
616	M8.24.286	Disputes over the confirmation of the rights of securities	0
617	M8.24.286.1	Disputes over the confirmation of the stock rights	105
618	M8.24.286.2	Disputes over the confirmation of the rights of corporate bonds	1
619	M8.24.286.3	Disputes over the confirmation of the rights of treasury bonds	1
620	M8.24.286.4	Disputes over the confirmation of the rights of securities investment funds	1
621	M8.24.287	Disputes over securities transaction contracts	13
622	M8.24.287.1	Disputes over stock transactions	13
623	M8.24.287.2	Disputes over corporate bond transactions	15
624	M8.24.287.3	Disputes over treasury bond transactions	0
625	M8.24.287.4	Disputes over securities investment fund transactions	2
626	M8.24.288	Disputes over derivative transactions	15
627	M8.24.289	Disputes over securities underwriting contracts	3
628	M8.24.289.1	Disputes over securities proxy sale contracts	0

(continued)

(continued)

Serial number	Identifier	Cause of action	Number of cases
629	M8.24.289.2	Disputes over securities exclusive sale contracts	0
630	M8.24.290	Disputes over securities investment consultancy	3
631	M8.24.291	Disputes over contracts for securities credit rating services	0
632	M8.24.292	Disputes over securities repurchase contracts	3
633	M8.24.292.1	Disputes over stock repurchase contracts	9
634	M8.24.292.2	Disputes over treasury bond repurchase contracts	0
635	M8.24.292.3	Disputes over corporate bond repurchase contracts	8
636	M8.24.292.4	Disputes over repurchase contracts for securities investment funds	0
637	M8.24.292.5	Disputes over repurchase of collateralized securities	2
638	M8.24.293	Disputes over contracts for listing of securities	0
639	M8.24.294	Disputes over agency contracts for securities transaction	8
640	M8.24.295	Disputes over contracts for sponsorship of listing of securities	0
641	M8.24.296	Disputes over securities offering	6
642	M8.24.296.1	Disputes over securities subscription	1
643	M8.24.296.2	Disputes over failure of securities offering	0
644	M8.24.297	Disputes over securities return	69
645	M8.24.298	Dispute over liabilities for securities fraud	10
646	M8.24.298.1	Dispute over liabilities for securities insider trading	24
647	M8.24.298.2	Dispute over liabilities for manipulation of the securities market	0
648	M8.24.298.3	Dispute over liabilities for misrepresentation on securities	1625
649	M8.24.298.4	Dispute over liabilities for cheating clients	2
650	M8.24.299	Disputes over securities custody	2
651	M8.24.300	Disputes over securities registration, depository and clearing	69
652	M8.24.301	Disputes over margin trading	28
653	M8.24.302	Disputes over trading and settlement funds of clients	2
654	M8.25	Disputes over futures transactions	99
655	M8.25.303	Disputes over futures brokerage contracts	4
656	M8.25.304	Disputes over futures overdraft transactions	0
657	M8.25.305	Disputes over forced liquidation of futures	6
658	M8.25.306	Disputes over physical delivery of futures	0
659	M8.25.307	Disputes over futures guarantee contracts	0
660	M8.25.308	Disputes over agency contracts for futures transactions	1
661	M8.25.309	Disputes over misappropriation of futures margin	0
662	M8.25.310	Dispute over liabilities for futures fraud	6
663	M8.25.311	Dispute over liabilities for manipulation of the futures market	0

(continued)

(continued)

Serial number	Identifier	Cause of action	Number of cases
664	M8.25.312	Dispute over liabilities for futures insider trading	28
665	M8.25.313	Dispute over liabilities for false information on futures	0
666	M8.26	Disputes over trusts	29
667	M8.26.314	Disputes over non-commercial private trusts	8
668	M8.26.315	Disputes over commercial trusts	14
669	M8.26.316	Disputes over charitable purpose trusts	0
670	M8.27	Disputes over insurance	13,640
671	M8.27.317	Disputes over property insurance contracts	17,246
672	M8.27.317.1	Disputes over insurance contracts regarding property losses	3475
673	M8.27.317.2	Disputes over liability insurance contracts	2694
674	M8.27.317.3	Disputes over credit insurance contracts	17
675	M8.27.317.4	Disputes over guarantee insurance contracts	185
676	M8.27.317.5	Disputes over underwriter's subrogation	3383
677	M8.27.318	Disputes over personal insurance contracts	4342
678	M8.27.318.1	Disputes over life insurance contracts	521
679	M8.27.318.2	Disputes over personal accident insurance contracts	1463
680	M8.27.318.3	Disputes over health insurance contracts	128
681	M8.27.319	Disputes over reinsurance contracts	5
682	M8.27.320	Disputes over insurance brokerage contracts	13
683	M8.27.321	Disputes over insurance agency contracts	129
684	M8.27.322	Disputes over import and export credit insurance contracts	1
685	M8.27.323	Disputes over insurance premium	73
686	M8.28	Disputes over negotiable instruments	1079
687	M8.28.324	Disputes over the right of claim for payment in negotiable instruments	444
688	M8.28.325	Disputes over the right of recourse in negotiable instruments	888
689	M8.28.326	Disputes over the right of claim for delivery of negotiable instruments	18
690	M8.28.327	Disputes over the right of claim for return of negotiable instruments	190
691	M8.28.328	Disputes over compensation for damage in connection with negotiable instruments	131
692	M8.28.329	Disputes over the right of claim for return of interests in negotiable instruments	275
693	M8.28.330	Disputes over the right of claim for issuance of bill of exchange receipts	0
694	M8.28.331	Disputes over guarantee of negotiable instruments	7
695	M8.28.332	Disputes over confirmation of the voidness of negotiable instruments	270

(continued)

(continued)

Serial number	Identifier	Cause of action	Number of cases
696	M8.28.333	Disputes over negotiable instrument agency	0
697	M8.28.334	Disputes over repurchase of negotiable instruments	0
698	M8.29	Disputes over letters of credit	82
699	M8.29.335	Disputes over entrusted issuance of letters of credit	7
700	M8.29.336	Disputes over issuance of letters of credit	79
701	M8.29.337	Disputes over negotiation of letters of credit	8
702	M8.29.338	Disputes over fraud in the use of letters of credit	11
703	M8.29.339	Disputes over financing by letters of credit	54
704	M8.29.340	Disputes over transfer of letters of credit	0
705	M9	Disputes over tort liabilities	0
706	M9.30	Dispute over tort liabilities	21,193
707	M9.30.341	Disputes over the liability of guardian	177
708	M9.30.342	Disputes over the liability of an employing entity	304
709	M9.30.343	Disputes over the tort liability of a dispatched employee	4
710	M9.30.344	Disputes over the liability of harm caused by a person providing labor service	1259
711	M9.30.345	Dispute over liabilities for injury suffered by service provider	35,139
712	M9.30.346	Disputes over tort liability on internet	259
713	M9.30.347	Disputes over liability for breach of duty of safety protection	1350
714	M9.30.347.1	Disputes over the liability of the administrators for public places	563
715	M9.30.347.2	Disputes over the liability of the organizers of public activities	10
716	M9.30.348	Disputes over liability of educational institutions	1592
717	M9.30.349	Disputes over products liability	10,429
718	M9.30.349.1	Disputes over the products liability of producers	403
719	M9.30.349.2	Disputes over the products liability of sellers	6090
720	M9.30.349.3	Disputes over the products liability of transporters	1
721	M9.30.349.4	Disputes over the products liability of warehousemen	1
722	M9.30.350	Disputes over liability of motor vehicles traffic accidents	415,400
723	M9.30.351	Disputes over liability for injury in medical treatments	7737
724	M9.30.351.1	Disputes over the liability for infringement on the patients' right of informed consent	36
725	M9.30.351.2	Disputes over the liability of medical products	26
726	M9.30.352	Disputes over liability for environmental pollution	1512
727	M9.30.352.1	Disputes over the liability for air pollution	73
728	M9.30.352.2	Disputes over the liability for water pollution	96
729	M9.30.352.3	Disputes over the liability for noise pollution	177

(continued)

(continued)

Serial number	Identifier	Cause of action	Number of cases
730	M9.30.352.4	Disputes over the liability for radioactivity pollution	3
731	M9.30.352.5	Disputes over the liability for soil pollution	62
732	M9.30.352.6	Disputes over the liability for pollution by electronic waste	0
733	M9.30.352.7	Disputes over the liability for pollution by solid waste	2
734	M9.30.353	Disputes over liability for ultra-hazardous activities	86
735	M9.30.353.1	Disputes over the liability for damage caused by civil nuclear facilities	0
736	M9.30.353.2	Disputes over the liability for damage caused by civil aircrafts	1
737	M9.30.353.3	Disputes over the liability for damage caused by the possession or the use of highly hazardous substances	23
738	M9.30.353.4	Disputes over the liability for damage caused by ultra-hazardous activities	56
739	M9.30.353.5	Disputes over the liability for damage caused by the loss or discarding of ultra-hazardous substances	6
740	M9.30.353.6	Disputes over the liability for damage caused by illegal possession of ultra-hazardous substances	0
741	M9.30.354	Disputes over liability for harm caused by domesticated animals	1403
742	M9.30.355	Disputes over liability for damage on objects	522
743	M9.30.355.1	Disputes over the liability for damage caused by objects falling off or falling down	403
744	M9.30.355.2	Disputes over the liability for damage caused by collapse of building or structure	160
745	M9.30.355.3	Disputes over the liability for damage caused by unidentified thrown object or falling object	24
746	M9.30.355.4	Disputes over the liability for damage caused by collapse of stacked objects	33
747	M9.30.355.5	Disputes over the liability for damage caused by obstructing passage at public roads	527
748	M9.30.355.6	Disputes over the liability for damage caused by broken trees or branches	98
749	M9.30.355.7	Disputes over the liability for damage caused by construction work on ground surface or underground facilities	641
750	M9.30.356	Disputes over the liability for personal injury by electric shock	1066
751	M9.30.357	Disputes over the liability for voluntary helpers' damage	1231
752	M9.30.358	Disputes over the liability for damage of the rescuer in emergency	19
753	M9.30.359	Disputes over the liability for damage caused by notarization	215

(continued)

(continued)

Serial number	Identifier	Cause of action	Number of cases
754	M9.30.360	Disputes over the liability for damage caused by excessive defense	1
755	M9.30.361	Disputes over the liability for damage caused by necessity	15
756	M9.30.362	Disputes over the liability for damage caused by the soldiers performing duties in Hong Kong or Macao Special Administrative Regions	0
757	M9.30.363	Disputes over the liability for damage caused by railway transport	3
758	M9.30.363.1	Disputes over the liability for personal injury caused by railway transport	137
759	M9.30.363.2	Disputes over the liability for property damage caused by railway transport	2
760	M9.30.364	Disputes over the liability for damage caused by water transport	3
761	M9.30.364.1	Disputes over compensation for personal injury resulting from water transport	3
762	M9.30.364.2	Disputes over compensation for property damage resulting from water transport	1
763	M9.30.365	Disputes over the liability for damage caused by air transport	3
764	M9.30.365.1	Disputes over compensation for personal injury resulting from air transport	0
765	M9.30.365.2	Disputes over compensation for property damage resulting from air transport	2
766	M9.30.366	Disputes over liability for losses arising from the application of pre-trial orders for the preservation of assets	2146
767	M9.30.367	Disputes over liability for losses arising from the application of pre-trial orders for the preservation of evidence	14
768	M9.30.368	Disputes over liability for losses arising from the application of orders for the preservation of assets in the course of trial	524
769	M9.30.369	Disputes over liability for losses arising from the application of orders for the preservation of evidence in the course of trial	0
770	M9.30.370	Disputes over liability for losses arising from the application of orders for pre-judgment enforcement of claim	3
771	M10	Causes of action for cases applying special procedures	386
772	M10.31	Cases concerning the eligibility of voters	6
773	M10.31.371	Applications for the confirmation of the eligibility of voters	8

(continued)

(continued)

Serial number	Identifier	Cause of action	Number of cases
774	M10.32	Cases concerning the declaration of missing status or presumed death of citizens	36
775	M10.32.372	Applications for the declaration of the missing status of citizens	2228
776	M10.32.373	Applications for the revocation of declarations of the missing status of citizens	19
777	M10.32.374	Applications for the appointment or change of the administrator for property of the missing persons	9
778	M10.32.375	Disputes over the payment of debts of the missing persons	0
779	M10.32.376	Applications for the declaration of presumed death of citizens	747
780	M10.32.377	Applications for the revocation of declarations of presumed death of citizens	37
781	M10.32.378	Disputes over petitions for the return of property upon the revocation of the declaration of presumed death	0
782	M10.33	Applications for the declaration of citizens as lacking civil legal capacity, or having limited civil legal capacity	296
783	M10.33.379	Applications for the declaration of the lack of civil legal capacity of citizens	4706
784	M10.33.380	Applications for the declaration of limited civil legal capacity of citizens	927
785	M10.33.381	Applications for the declaration of the restoration of limited civil legal capacity of citizens	0
786	M10.33.382	Applications for the declaration of the restoration of full civil legal capacity of citizens	9
787	M10.34	Cases concerning the declaration of property as *bona vacantia*	0
788	M10.34.383	Applications for the declaration of property as *bona vacantia*	7
789	M10.34.384	Applications for the revocation of the declaration of property as *bona vacantia*	0
790	M10.35	Cases concerning special procedures for guardianship	7
791	M10.35.385	Applications for the appointment of guardians	205
792	M10.35.386	Applications for the change of guardians	275
793	M10.35.387	Applications for the revocation of guardianship	75
794	M10.36	Cases concerning the debt enforcement procedure	56
795	M10.36.388	Applications for orders for payment	6114
796	M10.37	Cases concerning procedure for nullifying the negotiable instrument	29
797	M10.37.389	Applications for the nullifying the negotiable instrument	4742

(continued)

(continued)

Serial number	Identifier	Cause of action	Number of cases
798	M10.38	Cases concerning applications for pre-trial injunctive relief against infringement on intellectual property rights	3
799	M10.38.390	Applications for pre-trial injunctive relief against infringement on patent rights	0
800	M10.38.391	Applications for pre-trial injunctive relief against infringement on the exclusive right to use of trademarks	0
801	M10.38.392	Applications for pre-trial injunctive relief against infringement on copyrights	4
802	M10.38.393	Applications for pre-trial injunctive relief against infringement on rights to new varieties of plants	0
803	M10.39	Cases concerning applications for preservation orders	17,397
804	M10.39.394	Applications for pre-trial orders for preservation of assets	19,658
805	M10.39.395	Applications for orders for preservation of assets in the course of trial	1316
806	M10.39.396	Applications for pre-trial orders for preservation of evidence	95
807	M10.39.397	Applications for orders for preservation of evidence in the course of trial	1
808	M10.39.398	Orders for preservation of assets in arbitration proceedings	1000
809	M10.39.399	Orders for preservation of evidence in arbitration proceedings	1
810	M10.39.400	Applications for suspension of payment under a letter of credit	0
811	M10.39.401	Applications for suspension of payment under a letter of guarantee	0
812	M10.40	Cases concerning arbitration procedure	1986
813	M10.40.402	Applications for the confirmation of validity of arbitration agreements	1021
814	M10.40.403	Applications for the revocation of arbitral awards	9806
815	M10.41	Cases concerning special procedures for maritime claims	173
816	M10.41.404	Applications for preservation orders for maritime claims	21
817	M10.41.404.1	Applications for detention of vessels	766
818	M10.41.404.2	Applications for auction of detained vessels	77
819	M10.41.404.3	Applications for detention of vessel cargos	0
820	M10.41.404.4	Applications for auction of detained vessel cargos	0
821	M10.41.404.5	Applications for detention of bunker oil and ship's stores	0
822	M10.41.404.6	Applications for auction of detained bunker oil and ship's stores	0

(continued)

(continued)

Serial number	Identifier	Cause of action	Number of cases
823	M10.41.405	Applications for orders for payment in maritime claims	0
824	M10.41.406	Applications for maritime injunctions	10
825	M10.41.407	Applications for maritime evidence preservation	13
826	M10.41.408	Applications for the establishment of a limited liability fund for maritime claims	16
827	M10.41.409	Applications for procedure of public notice of maritime priority rights	23
828	M10.41.410	Applications for registration and enforcement of maritime claims	437
829	M10.42	Cases concerning recognition and enforcement of civil judgments and arbitral awards	10,657
830	M10.42.411	Applications for enforcement of maritime arbitral awards	0
831	M10.42.412	Applications for enforcement of arbitral awards for intellectual property rights	0
832	M10.42.413	Applications for enforcement of arbitral awards involving a foreign element	3
833	M10.42.414	Applications for recognition and enforcement of civil judgments of the courts of the Hong Kong Special Administrative Region	3
834	M10.42.415	Applications for recognition and enforcement of arbitral awards of the Hong Kong Special Administrative Region	3
835	M10.42.416	Applications for recognition and enforcement of civil judgments of the courts of the Macao Special Administrative Region	0
836	M10.42.417	Applications for recognition and enforcement of arbitral awards of the Macao Special Administrative Region	0
837	M10.42.418	Applications for recognition and enforcement of civil judgments of the courts of the Taiwan region	8
838	M10.42.419	Applications for recognition and enforcement of arbitral awards of the Taiwan region	0
839	M10.42.420	Applications for recognition and enforcement of civil judgments and orders by foreign courts	790
840	M10.42.421	Applications for recognition and enforcement of foreign arbitral awards	8
841	M10.43	Actions of objection to the enforcement of judgment	11,545
842	M10.43.422	Actions by a non-party of Objection to the enforcement of judgment	8069
843	M10.43.423	Actions by the applicant of the enforcement of Objection to the enforcement of judgment	1424
844	M10.43.424	Actions of objection to the plan of distribution to be enforced	298
	Sum	–	5,853,591

Postscript

How Will the Rice Dumpling Gift Box of *Civil Code* Be Packed as the Process of Compilation

This is a postscript of which the first draft was written hastily during the Dragon Boat Festival in 2017. Actually, the postscript of the first edition of this book was also simmered during the Dragon Boat Festival of 2015. It seems that in my mind, the rice dumpling is the embodiment of each civil single law; and the compilation of *Civil Code* is the packing process of a rice dumpling gift box.

1. New Rice Wrapped in Old Leaves: How was the Rice Dumpling of *General Provisions of the Civil Law* Wrapped Up?

Structurally, except for the technical difference in arrangement, the *2017 General Provisions of the Civil Law* actually inherits the chapters and sections of *1986 General Principles of the Civil Law*; moreover, the *General Provisions of the Civil Law* has almost fully updated every corresponding article of *General Principles of the Civil Law*, not to mention the law norms of the general provisions as the core of their respective contents. Different from "new wine in old bottle" which is a compromise, the *General Provisions of the Civil Law* is "new rice wrapped in old leaves", with its chapters and sections as the rice dumpling leaves, and its articles the sticky rice.

(1) Chapters and Sections as Rice Dumpling Leaves: Old Leaves Dominate While the New Ones Decorate

In *General Provisions of the Civil Law*, though the title of Chapter 1 is changed to "Basic Provisions", the tradition to provide the "basic principles" in details stays unchanged. In Chapter 2, the concept "natural person" is directly used, the section "Individual Partnership" is deleted, and other sections including "Guardianship", "Individually-Owned Business" and "Leaseholding Farm Household" are kept. Chapter 3 "Legal Persons" does not adopt the traditional classification of

© China University of Political Science and Law Press 2020
Z. Wang, *On the Constitutionality of Compiling a Civil Code of China*,
https://doi.org/10.1007/978-981-13-7900-0

"Foundation Legal Persons-Association Legal Persons". As compared with the classification of "Enterprise Legal Person-Non-enterprise Legal Person" in *General Principles of the Civil Law*, the classification of "Profit legal person-Non-profit Unincorporated organization" is not so essentially different, except for the fact that the section "Joint Operation" is deleted and the section "Special Legal Persons" is added. Following the legislative tradition, Chapter 5 still provides "Civil Rights" rather than "Object of Civil Rights"; Chapter 6 "Civil Juristic Act" and Chapter 7 "Agency" correspond respectively to two sections in Chapter 4 "Civil Juristic Act and Agency" of *General Principles of the Civil Law*; Chapter 8 "Civil Liabilities" and Chapter 9 "Limitation of Action" also still use the titles used in *General Principles of the Civil Law*. Chapter 9 "Supplementary Provisions" of *General Principles of the Civil Law* is divided into Chapter 10 "Calculation of Time Period" and Chapter 11 "Supplementary Provisions" in the *General Provisions of the Civil Law*. The contents of Chapter 8 of *General Principles of the Civil Law* are not provided due to the enactment of *Law of the Application of Law for Foreign-related Civil Relations in 2010* and the Chapter 4 "Unincorporated Organizations" of the *General Provisions of Civil Law* is newly set up. These two changes should be deemed as the main embodiment of this "retrofitting of old leaves". If the chapters and sections are deemed as rice dumpling leaves, through the above adjustments, the old leaves play a main role and the new ones are sparsely distributed.

(2) **Articles as Sticky Rice: 90% are Updated and 10% Newly Added**

There are 206 articles in the *General Provisions of the Civil Law*, which out-numbers *General Principles of the Civil Law*, which has 156 articles, by 50 articles. After comparing article by article, I found that in the *General Provisions of the Civil Law*, there are only 81 articles which take the articles of *General Principles of the Civil Law* as compilation subject, and 9 articles which take the *Opinions on General Principles of the Civil Law* as compilation subject, namely 90 articles in total. Among the remaining 116 articles, 90 articles take other laws and judicial inter-pretations as compilation subject, and only 26 articles are newly-added articles, namely: Article 29 [Custodian by Testament], Article 38 [Restoration of Qualification of Custodian], Article 65 [Wrong Registration of Legal Person May not Antagonize Against bona fides third party], Article 89 [Mechanism of Legal Person as Public Institution], Article 96 [Types of Special Legal Persons], Article 99 [Legal Person as Rural Collective Economic Organization], Article 103 [Principles for Establishment of Unincorporated organization], Article 108 [Referral Application for Unincorporated organization], Article 126 [Other Civil Rights and Interests], Article 127 [Protection on Data and Online Virtual Properties], Article 129 [Methods for Acquisition of Civil Rights], Article 130 [Voluntarily Exercise Civil Rights According to Laws], Article 131 [Obligations Shall be Performed When Exercising Rights], Article 132 [Prohibition on Abuse of Rights], Article 134 [Methods for Constitution of Civil Juristic Act], Article 138 [Effective Time for Intent Expressed without Counterpart], Article 139 [Effective Time for Intent Expressed by Public Notice], Article 149 [Validity of Civil Juristic Act Cheated by Third Party], Article 166 [Joint Agency], Article 168 [Prohibition on Self Agency and Bilateral Agency], Article 184 [Undertaking of Liabilities for Damage Caused by Voluntary Act of Rescue], Article 190 [Calculation of Limitation of Action for Claim of Principal against Legal Agent], Article 191 [Calculation of Limitation of Action for Claim of Compensation of Minors for Sexual Abuse], Article 196 [Claim Not Subject to Limitation of Action], Article 202 [Determination of Last Day of Time Period] and Article 204 [Determination of Calculation Method for Time Period].[1] The actual legislative effect of these newly-added articles will be verified in the following three years, and will serve as the important basis for deciding whether and how such articles will be compiled into the *Civil Code*. In this sense, among the articles as sticky rice, 90% are updated and 10% are newly added.

2. Mashup: Style of the Quality of the Rice Dumpling Gift Box of *Civil Code*

The wine will improve bouquet with age. However, the rice dumpling of *Civil Code* should be fresh. According to the officially-issued deadline for the compilation of *Civil Code* in 2020, the rice dumpling gift box of *Civil Code*, which is compiled on the basis of the current civil single laws, will have the "mashup" style in its quality. In chronological order, the rice dumplings can be divided into three-year fresh rice dumplings, ten-year shelf life rice dumplings, twenty-year expiration rice dumplings and thirty-year aged rice dumplings.[2] Let's start with aged rice dumplings.

(1) Thirty-Year Aged Rice Dumplings: The *Succession Law* and the *Adoption Law*

Among the aged rice dumplings, the *Succession Law* is the oldest, and it was enacted even one year earlier than the 1986 *General Principles of the Civil Law*. In fact, the proposal for amending the *Succession Law* was brought forth at the meeting of the 11th NPC, and the scholars also submitted several amendment drafts. However, such proposal was suspended by the *Legislative Planning of 12th NPC standing Committee* issued for the first time on October 30, 2013. Thereafter, the *Legislative Planning of the 12th NPC standing Committee* revised on June 1, 2015 re-initiated the legislative planning for the compilation of *Civil Code*, which lead to the amendment of such law was further postponed. Without major change, the *Succession Law* will become invalid together with *General Principles of the Civil Law* at the age of 35.

The *Adoption Law* was enacted in 1991, and the amendment in 1998 did not essentially change its main contents. However, with the amendment to the *Population and Family Planning Law* made by the NPC standing Committee in 2015, the two-kid policy has brought forth the needs to amend the core framework of the *Adoption Law*. Similarly, owing to the legislative planning that it will be

---

[1]See the *Check List for Regulations for Compilation Subjects such as he General Provisions of Civil Code and the General Principles of Civil Code*, compiled by Wang (2017).

[2]The so-called shelf life is the optimal period for eating of food. The expiry date means the last date on which the food can be eaten.

compiled into the *Civil Code*, the *Adoption Law* will also be on active service until it is 30 years old.

(2) **Twenty-Year Expiration Rice Dumplings: The *Marriage Law*, the *Guarantee Law* and the *Contract Law***

Though the *Marriage Law* was enacted in 1980, the comprehensive amendment in 2001 has converted it into a fully-updated law, and the issuance of the *Interpretation for Marriage Law* (I), (II) and (III) in 2001, 2003 and 2011, the *Supplementary Provisions for Interpretations for Marriage Law (II)* in 2017 and the *Interpretation for Disputes over Debt between Husband and Wife* in 2018 further emphasize the demand on updating of laws in this field. The *Guarantee Law* was enacted in 1995 in response to the guarantee demands arising from economic development, and was amended and improved in 2000 by the *Interpretation for Guarantee Law*. With the enactment of the *2007 Real Rights Law*, only Chapter 1 "General Provisions", Chapter 2 "Guaranty", Chapter 6 "Deposit" and Chapter 7 "Supplementary Provisions" in the *Guarantee Law* are still applicable, so that it is a law which is ready for reform among the civil single laws. The *Economic Contract Law* was enacted in 1981 and amended in 1993; the *Foreign Economic Contract Law* was enacted in 1985; the *Technical Contract Law* was enacted in 1987. In 1999, these three laws were integrated into the new *Contract Law*, which represents the relatively high legislative level at that time. In 1999 and 2009, the Supreme People's Court also issued the *Interpretation for Contract Law (I)* and the *Interpretation for Contract Law (II)*. These three civil single laws, together with the relevant judicial interpretations, narrowly support the judicial practices in relevant fields, and are about to go beyond the twenty-year expiration date.

(3) **Ten-Year Shelf Life Rice Dumplings: The *Real Rights Law* and the *Tort Liability Law***

After being deliberated for 8 times, the *Real Rights Law* was enacted in 2007. Thereafter, through the deliberation for 2 years, the *Tort Liability Law* was also enacted in 2009. These two laws reflect the legislative quality in the legislative mode based on cooperation between the Legislature and civil jurisprudential circle in the new century. Together with the relevant judicial interpretations, it is expected that most of the articles can be essentially compiled into the *Civil Code* during the more-than-ten-year shelf life.

(4) **Three-Year Fresh Rice Dumplings: The *General Provisions of the Civil Law***

The upsurge for the compilation of *Civil Code* which occurred ten years ago and led to the enactment of the *Real Rights Law* and the *Tort Liability Law* has gradually faded out after 2011 when WU Bangguo, the former chairman of NPC Standing Committee declared "the formation of socialist legal system with Chinese characteristics", and has not initiated any legislative process until 2014 when the "compilation of *Civil Code*" was formally determined by the *Decision of Rule by Law* adopted at the 4th Plenary Session of the 18th CPC Central Committee. According to the legislative procedure and legislative planning, through the process from drafting to adoption, the *General Provisions of the Civil Law* is treated as a basic civil law and is oriented as the general provisions of the *Civil Code* in the future. For the compilation of *Civil Code*, three years will be a relatively short processing period. At that time, maybe the *General Provisions of the Civil Law* is still fresh owing to the three-year limitation of action.[3]

3. Not to be or to Be: How the Rice Dumpling of *General Principles of the Civil Law* will Step Down from the Stage of History?

Different from most civil law scholars who are only concerned about how the *Civil Code* will step onto the stage of history, I'm also concerned about how *General Principles of the Civil Law* will step down. According to the *Legislation Law*, the legislative activities at the level of law only include "enactment", "amendment" and "abolishment", so that there are only two legislative modes for the compilation of *Civil Code*, namely "enactment-abolishment" and "amendment". In the "enactment-abolishment" mode, *General Principles of the Civil Law* will become invalid when the *Civil Code* comes into effect; in the "amendment" mode, *General Principles of the Civil Law* will be reborn after being amended into the *Civil Code*.

It is provided in Paragraph 3 of Article 62 of the *Constitution* that: "The National People's Congress shall exercise the following duties and powers: ... (3) To enact and amend ... basic civil laws." The essential difference in the above-mentioned two modes is that, for the "enactment-abolishment" mode, the right exercised is the right to enact basic laws as provided in the *Constitution*[4]; for the "amendment" mode, the right exercised is the right to amend basic laws as provided in the *Constitution*. It seems that only the enactment of a brand new civil code can meet the historical expectation, but achieving the continuity of validity of basic civil laws by means of amendment will better meet the needs of reality. In fact, in 1997, rather than enacting a new *Criminal Code* and simultaneously abolishing the old *Criminal Code*, the NPC comprehensively amended the old *1979 Criminal Code* into the new *Criminal Code*, so as to complete a legislative activity which should be called as the "Compilation of Criminal Code" in the terms used nowadays. In my opinion, maybe the "amendment" mode is the legislative choice which is more consistent with the original intention of decision of the "Compilation" of *Civil Code*, though it is not so splendid owing to the pragmatic choice.

---

[3]It is provided in Paragraph 1 of Article 188 of the *General Provisions of Civil Law* that: "The limitation of action of claim for the people's court to protect civil rights shall be three years. In case there are provisions in other laws, such provisions shall apply." It is provided in Article 206 that: "This Law shall come into effect as of October 1, 2017." If everything goes smoothly, it is expected that the *Civil Code* will come into effect as of October 1, 2020. As the basis for judgment, maybe the *General Provisions of Civil Law* is only applicable to the cases which occur after October 1, 2017 and are concluded before October 1, 2020. Owing to the three-year limitation of action, it is likely that the litigation for the cases occurring within this three-year period will be initiated after October 1, 2020, so as to make itself subject to the new *Civil Code*.

[4]The *Constitution* does not expressly provide the "abolishment right" for basic laws and even non-basic laws, and it should be concluded that the abolishment of laws is subject to the provisions of the *Legislation Law*.

4. **Wrapped or Not? The Foreseeable yet Uncertain Rice Dumpling of** *Rights to Personality Law*

The ability to foresee the future is highly appreciated. However, if someone foresees something but does not know it for sure, it is doubtful. Whether the *Rights to Personality Law* should be enacted as a separate volume is one of such complicated academic cases. Just as I had expected and was reluctant to see, taking the *General Provisions of Civil Law* as the first step of the compilation of *Civil Code* has detonated ahead of schedule the academic dispute about whether the *Rights to Personality Law* should be enacted separately. In the civil Jurisprudential circle, the common view on strengthening the protection on rights to personality has been formed, but there have been different opinions on whether the *Rights to Personality Law* should be enacted separately for long time. The scholars on the pro side believe that, in order to better protect the rights to personality, the *Rights to Personality Law* should be enacted separately; the scholars on the con side believe that, the separate enactment of the *Rights to Personality Law* will deviate from the traditional civil law theory and will make the system not so scientific. In addition to the above-mentioned scholars, some other scholars believe that, most of the disputes relating to rights to personality are disputes relating to tort liability. In the future, it is advised to separately set up the chapter "Tort Liability for Infringement upon Rights to Personality" in the *Tort Liability Volume*; with respect to the rules for utilization of rights to personality, the problem can be settled by expanding the application scope of the *Contract Volume* and the *Succession Volume* of the *Civil Code* in the future.

The "foreseeable yet unknown" mentioned by me mainly means the different interpretations given by the above-mentioned two groups of scholars for the expression "to protect the personal rights, property rights and rights to personality of people" in the *Report of 19th CPC National Congress*. I believe that, from the perspective of presumption of the reasonableness of the *Report of 19th CPC National Congress*, the "personal rights" in this report shall be considered as the personal rights in a narrow sense, namely substantial rights to personality. Accordingly, rights to personality means emotional rights to personality. Recognizing emotional "rights to personality", and listing them in parallel with the personal rights substantial rights to personality) and property rights are the recognition given by the *Report of 19th CPC National Congress* for the development of civil law theory in China. However, this can only be interpreted as further consolidating the common view on strengthening the protection on rights to personality, but still can't lead to the clear conclusion about whether the *Rights to Personality Law* should be separately enacted.

The first overall deliberation on the *Civil Code (draft)* by the Legislature of China occurred at the end of 2002, and at that time, the 4*th* volume of the *Civil Code (draft)* is the *Rights to Personality Law*, in parallel with the *Real Rights Law*, the *Contract Law*, the *Marriage Law*, the *Adoption Law*, the *Succession Law* and the *Tort Liability Law*. It is provided in Article 42 of the *Legislation Law* that: "For a bill which has been put on the agenda of the session of the Standing Committee, if deliberation on the bill has been postponed for two years due to major differences among the concerned constituents on major issues such as the necessity or feasibility of enacting such bill, or voting was postponed and the bill has not been put on the agenda of the session of the Standing Committee for two years, the Chairman's Committee shall make a report to the Standing Committee, whereupon deliberation on the bill shall terminate." With the initiation of the compilation of *Civil Code*, the *Rights to Personality Law* should be deliberated again if the deliberation for it has not been terminated through legal procedure. Since the deadline for the compilation of *Civil Code* is set as Year 2020, there is no sufficient legislative room left for the separate enactment of the *Rights to Personality Law*. The legislative activities are by no means the pure academic activities, but the political choice based on academic study. The existing academic opinions are sufficiently and clearly expressed, so in fact, whether the volume of *Rights to Personality Law* can be enacted separately has become an unsettled political choice for the design of macro-system for the compilation of *Civil Code*.

5. Acknowledgement

I would like to extend my sincere gratitude to Prof. Fei LIU, the Dean of China-EU Law School of China University of Political Science and Law, Prof. Björn Ahl of Cologne University, Dr. Ewan Smith of Oxford University, Dr. Rogier Creemers of Leiden University for their recognition of and recommendation for this Book, and extend my sincere gratitude to Mr. Jiang PENG, Editor of this book, and Dr. Tianshu ZHAO for their efforts made for the publication of this Book!

The Law School of Sichuan University has provided great support for the publication of this Book, the *LawSum Laboratory* has provided the data support for the writing of this Book, and Dr. Zhicheng WU of Oxford University as well as the students in Law School of Sichuan University including Jian GONG, Tao WU, Yawen LUO, Songyuan GU, Zhongxuan LIU, Chan LIU and Wei LIU have also spent much time and made great efforts for the publication of this Book. I would like to extend my gratitude to them!

Finally, I would like to extend my gratitude to the Project "Research on Reform of Tort Liability Law of China" (16JJD820015) of the Key Research Centre for Humanities and Social Sciences under the Ministry of Education and Law School of Sichuan University. It is their financial support that made publishing of this Book possible!

Prof. Dr. Zhu Wang

Director of Laboratory for Big Data in Law

Law School of Sichuan University

Director of Institute for Big Data in Rule of Law

Research Center for Civil and Commercial Jurisprudence
of Renmin University of China
wangzhu@scu.edu.cn
Drafted on Dragon Boat Festival in 2017 in Hengdian,
Yiwu Prov., P. R. China
Finalized on Kitchen God's Day of 2018 in Boao, Hainan Prov., P. R. China.

Reference

Wang Zhu, The Check List and Interpretation for the General Provisions of Civil Code of the People's Republic of China. Peking University Press, 2017